Library of
Davidson College

Hearing the Measures

Hearing the Measures
Shakespearean and Other Inflections

George T. Wright

THE UNIVERSITY OF WISCONSIN PRESS

The University of Wisconsin Press
1930 Monroe Street
Madison, Wisconsin 53711

3 Henrietta Street
London WC2E 8LU, England

Copyright © 2001
The Board of Regents of the University of Wisconsin System
All rights reserved

5   4   3   2   1

Printed in the United States of America

Library of Congress Cataloging-in-Publication Data

Wright, George Thaddeus.
　　Hearing the measures : Shakespearean and other inflections : selected essays / by George T. Wright.
　　　p. cm.
　　Includes bibliographical references and index.
　　ISBN 0-299-17190-6 (alk. paper)—ISBN 0-299-17194-9 (pbk.: alk. paper)
　　1. English literature—History and criticism.   2. Shakespeare, William, 1564–1616—Criticism and interpretation.   3. American poetry—20th century—History and criticism.
　　PR99.W8 2001
　　820.9—dc21

2001001948

Publication of this book has been made possible in part by the generous support of the Anonymous Fund of the University of Wisconsin–Madison

To poetry written in English
    and the poets who made it
    the readers who wanted to hear it and speak it
    scholars who have struggled to measure, explain, compare, and
                                            appraise it

and to friends and students who liked to listen to its words,
    its stanzas and speeches, long metrical stretches
    and lyrical patches
    and say, as they can, why they cared about it

Contents

List of Tables	ix
Preface	xi

Trope, Tense, Measure

1. Hendiadys and *Hamlet*	3
2. The Lyric Tense: Simple Present Verbs in English Poems	44
3. Supposing a Measure for *Measure for Measure*	73

Lines of the Poets

4. Wyatt's Decasyllabic Line	99
5. Donne's Sculptured Stanzas	123
6. Yeats's Expressive Style	134
7. Lowell's Pentameter Line	144
8. Hearing the Measures: A Review-Article	154
9. Pulse and Breath: An Exchange with X. J. Kennedy	203
10. Troubles of a Professional Meter Reader	214

Oral or Literate, Silent or Sounded

11. Blank Verse in the Jacobean Theater: Language That Vanishes, Language That Keeps — 235

12. An Almost Oral Art: Shakespeare's Language on Stage and Page — 250

13. The Silent Speech of Shakespeare's *Sonnets* — 262

Notes — 285

Index — 319

Tables

1a.	Hendiadys in *Hamlet*	31
1b.	Deviations from the usual noun-and-noun or adjective-and-adjective form	34
2.	Possible instances of hendiadys in *Hamlet*	35
3.	Hendiadys in Shakespeare's plays	37
4.	Frequency of progressive form verbs	66
5.	Symbols used by Derek Attridge to mark lines of verse	163

Preface

In thinking how to introduce these essays, how to explain in advance their belonging together in a book, I remember Josephine Miles and her story— was it about herself or a student?—of being asked to summarize what her dissertation was really getting at and realizing that she hadn't yet worked out the ways to say it. In another form it was Wordsworth's question to the leech-gatherer, framed for every writer who pretends to be doing useful work: "How is it that you live, and what is it you do?" In the spirit of Jo and William, then, let me try to say what I do in this book and what gives these disparate essays (and others not included here) a common theme or purpose. What aims, procedures, outcomes do they have in common?

The question I usually try to address in essays about poetry is: "Given the interest of the subject and the writer's attitude toward it, what is it in the language, in the English, that gives expressive force to this poem, this play, this line, this speech, this stanza?" In the best work, of course, it's likely to be many things, but I try to single out one or some and observe how pervasive or frequent or telling they are. Sometimes this involves a whole system of effects: the metrical system used by Shakespeare or Wyatt, the complex metrical and syntactical arrangements in Yeats's or Donne's stanzas or Lowell's sonnets. Sometimes such systems pit "mighty opposites" (*Hamlet,* 5.2.62) against each other: the play of the simple present tense against the present progressive in verse, of text against speech, of mistaken perspectives against true ones, of oral or literate, verse versus prose, silence and sound. What do we *hear,* what stands out as odd, as compelling, in a phrase, a stretch of verse, a verse play, in the language and dramaturgy of a play, a writer, or a period?

Over the years I have come to realize that, for better or worse, my way of taking in literary words is different from that of many perceptive readers. My particular vulnerability to writing has always depended on listening to its words, whether spoken aloud or half-heard in silence, so it has seemed natural to exploit that difference in essays and, here in this gathering of them, to signal that emphasis in my title. This seems especially appropriate when so many of the pieces concern Shakespeare and his contemporaries. The Elizabethans, after all, used to speak of going to *hear* a play. They *saw* it, too, of course, but their choice of verb suggests how much they were in the habit of experiencing theater through their ears. Readers like myself, even today, can hardly read anything—a poem, a novel, the newspaper—without hearing the words through that silent inner mechanism that plays them, syllable by syllable, to our minds. This makes it hard to skim, to speed-read, to scan for the gist only. But attention to the orders and euphonies of verse can offer satisfactions that seem not far short of those provided by the richest musical experiences; and they help us become aware of patterns in poetry that are aural or almost aural.

That is why a collection of essays about "hearing" includes not only essays that deal specifically with metrical analysis and theory but others that also suggest we take in by ear as well as by sense the kinds of present-tense verbs that poets use in their poems ("The Lyric Tense"), the rhetorical figures (like hendiadys) that point their phrases and grace their sentences, the silences that ring with alarm, anxiety, or apprehension through such lyric poems as Shakespeare's *Sonnets,* the peculiar oral-yet-literate condition of Jacobean drama, and even the language characters use in a play to frame their (mis)understandings of their situations ("Supposing a Measure for *Measure for Measure*"). For readers who listen to poetry spoken from the stage or hear it in the study "with eyes" (as Shakespeare speaks of it in Sonnet 23), verbs, figures, silences, texts, and "supposes" are *heard.*

Are they heard as measures? Certainly the effects of meter are heard as measures; among many other meanings the word *meter* had for Renaissance speakers, it designates a foot, one step through the line. The foot or line measures the rhythmic progress of English syllables from a beginning in speech to a pause or end in silence. The metrical foot is an obvious analogue to a musical bar or measure, and the repetitive beat that we hear in rhythmical lines, as metrists have often claimed, conveys or evokes or recalls parallel temporal systems that keep, vary, or disturb a palpable patterned order in our lives: the pulse or heartbeat, sexual excitement, the rise and fall of emotion and emphasis not only in speech but in every phase of human behavior.

The essays not specifically on meter invoke the term *measure* in a looser way. They mark repetitive elements of order, patterned components that reappear but not in any strict temporal scheme. Recurrent stylistic features like hendiadys or the simple present tense of action verbs, once we are alerted to them, remind us like bells that one measure of a poem's manner, and of its place among other poems of its moment and culture—*"Listen to it!"* say my italics—has made its appearance again. The verbal supposes that George Gascoigne's second edition of *Supposes* carefully marked for the reader's notice function in the same way, and more explicitly than in most texts, as audible reminders *("Did you hear that?")* of the very terms on which we attend and hear plays: supposing, as my title suggests, is one measure of Shakespeare's *Measure for Measure,* a means of registering, almost periodically, its action, its motifs, and its meanings. Finally, the silences of Shakespeare's *Sonnets* offer not so much a negative example of recurrent sound as, according to my argument, an insistence on the potentiality of silence, on the hopefulness shared by absence and solitude, and on the permanent accessibility, for silent poems, of beat, voice, emphasis, and measure.

For some readers, these concerns will categorize me, despite what seem to me strong differences, as a belated New Critic. On the other hand, my willingness to collect masses of evidence, to read tens of thousands of lines to clinch points about hendiadys or meter or the lyric tense, or to locate an important source of Wyatt's metric in fifteenth-century line-types and of Shakespeare's in the epic caesuras and broken-backed lines of older poets, may also be seen as connecting me (at a discreet distance, to be sure) with those indefatigable old-historical scholars who dominated literary (and especially metrical) criticism a century and more ago, Whatever the label, I do more readily plead guilty to the charge of trying always to answer W. H. Auden's central question about poems: "Here is a verbal contraption. How does it work?"[1] with the understanding that poetic contraptions are always fraught with human choices and intensities. The ethical behavior of characters and speakers is important to any analysis of how plays or poems work, but I do not scold bad cultures, only bad critics.

In writing these essays over more than twenty-five years, and in collecting them several years after my retirement from teaching, I must be conscious of having benefited greatly during my professional life, and even well before it began, from the examples, advice, and aid of mentors, colleagues, assistants, students, and friends. Some of them, to whom I owe very specific debts, are mentioned in the text or notes of essays. But I want to thank Rita Lagace George, Frieda Gardner, and Doug Manos for having helped assemble the evidence or put it in presentable form; Dorothy Conlan for valuable secretarial help over several years; and colleagues Arthur Greffen, the late Andrew MacLeish and the late Gordon O'Brien for advice on particular points. I am much in the debt of many colleagues and friends in the profession for encouragement in the kind of scholarly research I do and for just being here, there, or around (or far away) to talk with and learn from about poetry, especially Percy Adams, Jacob Adler, Chester Anderson, John F. Andrews, Kent Bales, Enikö Bollobás, Stephen Booth, T. V. F. Brogan, Kent Cartwright, Joel Conarroe, Heather Dubrow, Lonnie and Margery Durham, Norman Fruman, Philip Furia, Arthur Geffen, Edward Griffith, David Haley, Michael Hancher, Ian Higgins, Neil D. Isaacs, Russ McDonald, Peter Reed, Robert Sonkowsky, Ann Thompson, Helen Vendler, Herbert Weil Jr., and James I. Wimsatt. I am grateful too to scholars who have invited me to write essays for seminars, meetings, or books or who, in some cases, provided thoughtful and important advice in seeing the essays through to publication: the late Jonas Barish, David Kastan, Jill L. Levenson, Lynne Magnusson, C. E. McGee, James Mellard, Barbara Mowat, Alan Powers, Norma Procopiow, James Schiffer, and John Velz.

Among hundreds of students who have helped me read poetry more perceptively, I would single out especially my doctoral students who in writing dissertations on poetry became my teachers and my friends: Carolyn Allen, Alan Altimont, Michael Cavanagh, Frieda Gardner, Carol Gilbertson, Sandra Holstein, Miles Krogfus, Erle Patrick Moore, Paul Munn, Christine Roman, Robert Schuler, John Schwiebert, Ruth Thompson, and Donald Vanouse.

Generous help from institutions has also assisted this work. The University of Minnesota sometimes supported my research with sabbatical or single-quarter leaves or with research grants, and in the 1980s, fellowships from the John Simon Guggenheim Memorial Foundation and the National Endowment for the Humanities contributed meaningful financial and moral support. In recent years the University of Arizona, at the request of its Department of English has graciously extended library privileges to me.

I also owe a large debt, only deepened over the years, to my colleague Calvin Kendall for informed and thoughtful advice and sympathetic encouragement in this and other enterprises, and to earlier teachers who helped me learn just what my interests and talent might be good for: May Benning, whose high school Latin classes made me understand much about the linguistic structures of English; Lionel Trilling and Jacques Barzun, intellectual teachers and models at Columbia; and Josephine Miles, Willard Farnham, and Arthur Brodeur at the University of California, Berkeley, who helped me begin to fathom some of the relations between linguistic order, literary history, and verse.

TROPE, TENSE, MEASURE

And Mallarmé answered: "My dear Degas, one does not make poetry with ideas, but with *words.*"

—Paul Valéry

The three essays in this section grew out of undergraduate courses I was teaching and all took several years to research and write. "Hendiadys and *Hamlet*" (1981) speculated on Shakespeare's cunning use of a classical rhetorical figure, hendiadys, especially in *Hamlet,* where it appears most often and most tellingly, for it seems by its peculiar linguistic structure to underscore major themes in the play. "The Lyric Tense" (1974) grew out of my casual observation that the apparent stylistic simplicity critics have admired in lines such as Yeats's "I walk through the long schoolroom, questioning" is really not simple at all, that the verb used there is notably unspeechlike, but that it seems to borrow something of the flavor of genuinely speechlike uses of the English simple present tense. Both of these essays appeared first in *PMLA,* and both won the Modern Language Association's William Riley Parker Prize given to an essay published in *PMLA.*

The third essay in this section, previously unpublished, explores the mistaken suppositions that underlie *Measure for Measure*—or any play—and, incidentally, to suggest that the failure to understand how these "supposes" work can make critics seem as lost and baffled as any comic character.

Here, in effect, these essays say, are three things to listen for in plays and poems.

Hendiadys and *Hamlet*

> A horse and a man
> Is more than one,
> And yet not many.
> —*The Taming of the Shrew*

> What's his weapon?
> Rapier and dagger.
> That's two of his weapons.
> —*Hamlet*

Editors of Shakespeare have long been aware that the classical figure *hendiadys*—which, as a schoolboy, I learned to rhyme with *Hyades*—appears now and then in the plays, but no one has ever treated it as more than a technical curiosity. Scholars interested in Shakespeare's use of traditional rhetorical devices are content to mention it briefly as one among dozens of figurative patterns, drawn mainly from the practice of Latin poets and bearing formidable Greek names, that Elizabethan rhetoric books recommended to their readers as effective means of embellishing one's style.[1] But hendiadys deserves more thoughtful attention than it has ever been given, for Shakespeare uses it far more freely and frequently than his scholarly commentators have led us to believe—over three hundred times in all, mainly in the great plays of his middle career and most of all in *Hamlet*. Furthermore, the peculiar structure of hendiadys is native enough to Shakespeare's style, and so apt to his purposes, that any scholar or teacher of the plays may find it helpful to recognize this figure as one characteristic of the Shakespearean manner.

I

The basic pattern of hendiadys is simple enough. The Latin grammarian Servius, writing about A.D. 400, coined the term to describe a common figurative device in Virgil's *Aeneid:* the use of two substantives, joined by a conjunction (*et, atque,* or *que,* all signifying "and"), to express a single but complex idea. The most frequently cited example, however, is from the *Georgics* (2.192): *"pateris libamus et auro"* 'we drink from *cups and gold.*'[2] English translators normally suppress the oddity of this phrasing (the phrasing and oddity, we might say) by interpreting one of the nouns as dependent on the other: "we drink from golden cups." Similarly, *"membris et mole valens"* 'powerful in *limbs and weight*' (*Aeneid* 5.431) is usually rendered by some such phrase as "mighty in mass of limb" (J. W. Mackail).

Recent scholars of Virgil have questioned this traditional way of interpreting such phrases. It suits the name of the figure (*hendiadys* means, literally, "one through two"), but it does not account for the poet's deliberate stylistic choice of two parallel substantives instead of what we would call a noun phrase (noun and adjective [golden cups] or noun and dependent noun [cups of gold]). They wonder, indeed, whether there *is* such a thing as hendiadys. For when Virgil, they tell us, describes the ceremonial sacrifice at which the celebrants drink wine from *cups and gold,* he means us to grasp two ideas, not one: such an occasion requires the appropriate sacred vessel and an appropriately rich material. In the same way, to anyone observing the old hero Entellus in action, what is impressive is not simply his mightiness "in mass of limb" but, successively, his powerful limbs—his muscles—and, indeed, his whole massive figure. In both examples, and in many others, Virgil accurately conveys our dual perception of a dual phenomenon. The *et* in each phrase precisely registers the separateness and successiveness of the two distinct segments of the event. The perception may even be a triple one—of each idea in turn and then of their combination or fusion.[3]

When Shakespeare began to write, he had available to him no such subtle accounts of the phenomenology of Virgilian hendiadys. But we know how readily he adopted the rhetorical devices of classical poetry, which it appears he might have learned from three sources: the Latin authors, including Virgil, whom he read at school and later; Continental rhetoricians, from Cicero and Quintilian to Erasmus and Susenbrotus, whose rhetoric books included lists of tropes and schemes; and English rhetoricians especially interested in figures, such as Sherry, Peacham, Puttenham, and Day. In fact, we can be more precise about where Shakespeare learned hendiadys, for it has, among traditional figures, a unique history. It *never* appears in any ancient or medieval list of schemes or tropes or figures. The first Renaissance rhetorician to give a fairly clear account of it is Joannes Susenbrotus, whose *Epitome Troporum ac Schematum* was published in London in 1562 and became, according to T. W. Baldwin, "the new standard grammar school text on the tropes and schemes of *elocutio.*"[4] The earliest English rhetorician to mention hendiadys is Henry Peacham, but his first edition of *The Garden of Eloquence* (1577) gets it wrong; the second omits it. Puttenham's *The Arte of English Poesie* (1589) defines it correctly and gives several examples; so does the 1592 edition of Angel Day's *The English Secretorie,* though more briefly and less clearly. Although either or both of these works might have put Shakespeare in mind of hendiadys, it seems doubtful that his extensive use of the figure could have been based solely on the scanty treatment it is accorded by these two writers. It seems more likely either that he inquired about it and looked again into Virgil or, more probably, that he had studied the figure in school, from Susenbrotus or from a teacher of Virgil who knew Susenbrotus. Perhaps only if he had learned the figure as a schoolboy and practiced making up examples of his own, as the system then required pupils to do for the figures they did learn and as Baldwin shows Shakespeare must have done for other figures, could he have used it with such facility when he became a professional writer.

As we might expect with so *arriviste* a figure, Shakespeare's hendiadys does not follow exactly Virgil's usual pattern, in which, as Charles Gordon Cooper tells us, the second substantive explains or unfolds or augments the first (128–32). In Shakespeare's practice, the second may unfold the first ("ponderous and marble") or the first the second ("from cheer and from your former state"); or one may logically modify the other ("law and heraldry" for "heraldic law"); or, as is most usual, the parallel structure may mask some more complex and less easily describable dependent relation ("perfume and suppliance").[5] Shakespeare's examples are dazzlingly various; the developing playwright appears to have taken this odd figure to his bosom and to have made it entirely his own.

For, much as English poets have imitated Shakespeare, almost no one has followed him in this. Most later writers have wanted to be clear and precise, and hendiadys works to give a poetic passage that "perpetual slight alteration of language" that T. S. Eliot admired in Jacobean playwrights but that most writers of English prose and verse have avoided.[6] The same quest for clarity and precision has kept editors from recognizing hendiadys in all but a few of the passages in which it appears in Shakespeare's plays; hendiadys, far from explaining mysteries, establishes them. Whereas to point out the pattern of other figures is to contribute to a reader's understanding, to say that a phrase is hendiadys may only deepen its mystery. For, except in the simplest instances, hendiadys resists logical analysis: we all *know* that when Hamlet speaks of the soldiers of Fortinbras as going to their deaths "for a *fantasy and trick* of fame" (4.4.61) he means something like "for a deceptive dream of fame." But if we take the words one by one, it is hard to make them and their syntax add up to this meaning.

The central word in hendiadys is usually *and,* a word we take as signaling a coordinate structure, a parallelism of thought and meaning. Such coordinations are among our major instruments for ordering the world we live in; in turn, we rely on them for reassurance about the way the world is structured. Normally, when we meet *and* in a sentence, we can count on finding something in what follows it that parallels what led up to it. But in hendiadys, as in some related figures, this normal expectation is not met, or is even deliberately thwarted. In hysteron proteron, for example, the natural narrative order of events is reversed, as in Puttenham's illustration, "When we had climbde the clifs, and were ashore"[7] (and in Shakespeare's line describing how the ships of Antony and Cleopatra "fly and turn the rudder" [*Antony and Cleopatra* 3.10.3]). Zeugma and syllepsis frequently use *and* to join phrases that are not exactly balanced: in zeugma one verb, for example, may serve a whole list of nouns; in syllepsis the same arrangement may involve some trivial grammatical incongruity, as in "My Ladie laughs for joy, and I for wo" (Puttenham, 138), where, if the verb were repeated in the second clause, it would have to appear without the *s.*

All these figures derive their effect from their slight or ample deviation from normal patterns of coordination, patterns that exert great force on our linguistic lives. We expect small grammatical units joined by *and* to be parallel not only in grammar but also in bearing. They ought, we feel, to face in the same direction; otherwise, they strike us as bad English—or comic. We are amused when Lewis Carroll's Baker describes the correct procedure for hunting a snark: "You may seek it with thimbles—and seek it with care; / You may hunt it with *forks and hope.* . . ." Pope's witty zeugmas ("When *husbands, or* when *lapdogs* breathe their last" and "Dost sometimes *counsel* take—*and* sometimes *tea*") similarly exploit our shock at the violation of categories by using misleadingly coordinate nouns. Auden's poems of the 1930s use this technique frequently: "the student of *prose and conduct,*" "And *governments and men* are torn to pieces," "An afternoon of *nurses and rumours,*" "Abandoned by *his general and his lice,*" "And drugs to move *the bowels or the heart.*"[8] These poets are engaging in zeugma, not hendiadys, for each of these phrases binds in a syntactically parallel structure two disparate ideas, not two related ones. The technique is a witty way of recognizing that a linguistic structure can be filled in with blanks of very different sorts; more specifically, that in English, as in many other languages, we expect a conjunction like *and* to join together entities that are not only grammatically but conceptually assimilable. It may seem comic—even when the subject is ghastly, as in some of the examples from Auden—to be disoriented for a moment, but we are reassured by our certainty that the incongruity will not persist, that normally our language will range similar things together—concrete term with concrete term, abstract with abstract, things of one scale or category or context with comparable things. Indeed, our whole intellectual culture and all its achieved distinctions are engraved in our linguistic sense of parallelism, in our awareness of what, in our English speech, can decorously coordinate with what.

The Romans may have felt these structures differently. Even in Latin prose, as Cooper demonstrates, the conjunction is sometimes used to join substantives in the same peculiar way that we have observed is characteristic of hendiadys. The collocation of "a concrete and an abstract term," says E. Adelaide Hahn in the course of her persuasive disparagement of hendiadys in Virgil, "does not seem to have made upon the Roman mind the anomalous and even ludicrous impression which in English it frequently produces on us" (194). We are at a different stage of history, perhaps: we have more categories and we have grown more anxious about them. Whatever the explanation, hendiadys (if there is such a thing) has always struck English-speaking people as a disturbing and foreign device, and whenever it has turned up in the English language or in our literature, it has seemed an anomaly.

Some scholars claim that hendiadys occurs in English speech, but the claim is not entirely convincing. For one thing, the instances they cite usually join adjectives, or occasionally verbs, whereas hendiadys in Virgil and Shakespeare predominantly involves the linking of nouns. Fowler, in *Modern English Usage,* suggests that phrases like *nice and warm* are adjectival versions of hendiadys, that *try and do better* is a verbal example.[9] The familiar *go and see* is sometimes said to be another ("And they would *go and kiss* dead Caesar's wounds" [*Julius Caesar,* 3.3.137]); but this interpretation is doubtful unless the element of intention (go *to* see) is felt to be stronger than the element of temporal sequence (go first, then see); otherwise, any sequence of action verbs *(run and hide, approach and read)* would qualify. More scrupulously, Cooper suggests "Be a good fellow and close the door" (131). Here, as he argues, the second term explains or unfolds the first. We frequently join adjectives on the pattern of *nice and warm, good and loud, big and fat, sick and tired, long and leggy*. Each of these pairs represents a single concept in which the general idea contained in the first adjective is explained or specified or opened up by the second; and, insofar as such expressions may be continually invented, this pattern seems the closest thing to adjectival hendiadys in English. Formulaic phrases such as *nice and* and *good and* may be completed by virtually any adjective (or at least any pithy one) in the language. Being formulaic, however, they lack the element of surprise, of improvisation, and of eccentric coordination that we find in classical hendiadys. Other expressions of a similar kind include *hot and bothered, far and away,* and *still and all* (these last two adverbial in function) and the curious phrases *time and again* and *to hell and gone*.

To what extent such phrases become idiomatic in other languages I do not know, but in English at least they owe something to the gusto with which we collectively form what Logan Pearsall Smith calls "phrasal collocations or doublets, in which two words are habitually used together for the sake of emphasis."[10] He gives dozens of examples, including *fits and starts, high and mighty, rack and ruin*. Most of these are either parallel terms or synonyms, but in some pairs one term seems to modify, or lead to, the other: for example, *rough and tumble, fear and trembling, wear and tear*. Indeed, some Shakespearean expressions that are hendiadys (or almost hendiadys) have become familiar and even idiomatic staples of our speech: *sound and fury, slings and arrows, lean and hungry*. We know pretty well what they mean, and the doublet form has accustomed us to use, or listen to, similar phrases without asking how, given these words, we arrive at this meaning. How many of us, for example, understand the signification of both terms in *spick and span, part and parcel, null and void, hard and fast,* and *by hook or by crook*?

But the very familiarity of such phrases dissuades us from classifying them as hendiadys. That they have become idiomatic only emphasizes how unusual it is for us to link adjectives, nouns, or verbs *impromptu* in this pattern.[11] Nor is there any evidence that Roman speakers did so. Hendiadys is a literary device, a rhetorical figure that a few writers adopt and use for their individual purposes. Through it Virgil can make penetratingly accurate observations about events that are charged with meaning. Shakespeare's practice is, as we shall see, both different and various; his hendiadys usually elevates the discourse and blurs its logical lines, and this combination of grandeur and confusion is in keeping with the tragic or weighty action of the major plays.

We might expect a figure whose structure expresses the mystery of things to recommend itself especially to Romantic authors, but few of them seem to have been aware of hendiadys. The only examples I have noticed in the prose fiction of any period are Poe's "*ponderous and ebony* jaws" ("The Fall of the House of Usher," penultimate paragraph), which shamelessly copies the "*ponderous and marble* jaws" of Hamlet's father's sepulchre; and perhaps Hawthorne's "the *gnawing and poisonous* tooth of bodily pain" (*The Scarlet Letter,* chap. 12). As far as I know, the only poet since Milton to use it even occasionally is Dylan Thomas, whose language often aims at an archaic ceremoniousness and welcomes those dislocations of clear sense that hendiadys effectively provides. "In my *craft or sullen art*" is a possible example. We normally take *craft* here as a noun almost identical in meaning with *art,* but why should *sullen* modify one of these words and not the other? To place one adjective before *art* is to suggest that the first noun may have an adjectival force, that the phrase may mean something close to "in my crafty, sullen art." At the end of the poem the phrase is repeated without the adjective: "Who pay no praise or wages / Nor heed my craft or art." If this language seems more straightforward, it is nevertheless here that Thomas seems most closely to echo a Virgilian instance of hendiadys: *"res . . . laudis et artis"* 'a thing of praise and art' (*Georgics* 2.174)—that is, a thing that has received praise and was formed by art, a thing praised for its artistry, or, more probably, the theme of an art of praise.

In the same poem we are told:

> I labour by singing light
> Not for ambition or bread
> Or the *strut and trade* of charms
> On the ivory stages . . .

There is zeugma in "Not for ambition or bread"; but *"strut and trade"* surely means something like "parading for money." Thomas uses the device elsewhere, too, notably in "A Refusal to Mourn the Death, by Fire, of a Child in London": I shall not, he says, "mourn / The *majesty and burning* of the child's death." The linked nouns seem related to each other not as parallel objects of the verb but (1) as parallel elements in a phrase whose deep structure is two phrases: "the burning of the child" and "the majesty of the death," and (2) as elements in a further implicit phrase: "the majesty of the child's death by burning." Thomas has certainly achieved here something of the complexity of Virgilian hendiadys.[12]

As these examples suggest, hendiadys is often characterized by its elevation above the ordinary tone of conventional English and by a kind of syntactical complexity that seems fathomable only by an intuitional understanding of the way the words interweave their meanings, rather than by painstaking lexical analysis. These qualities perhaps make it easier to understand both why the device has been used so rarely by writers of the last few centuries and why it has been so little attended to by scholars. I have not looked closely at sixteenth- and seventeenth-century verse and prose, or at Jacobean drama, to see how extensively hendiadys is used in these precincts. But Sir Thomas Browne, whose affection for doublets amounts almost to passion, certainly falls into it occasionally: ". . . and therefore in this *Encyclopaedie and round* of knowledge, like the great and exemplary wheels of heaven, we must observe two Circles"; or "In that obscure *world and wombe* of our mother."[13] Prose after Dryden largely abandoned such flourishes, such baroque mannerisms (for so they must have seemed). In American literature, which preserved so many Elizabethan rhetorical habits, the ceremonious doubling of nouns (not hendiadys usually, but grandiloquent rewording—as it is, mainly, in Browne) continued through the eighteenth century and into the far from chaste prose of some American Romantics. If later poets ever gave a thought to hendiadys, they seem to have disdained it. Even the English Romantics, though they deliberately break up the measured antitheses that structure eighteenth-century verse, adhere, with certain exceptions that do not include hendiadys, to the sensible rules of discursive or descriptive prose. Milton uses hendiadys occasionally—some seventeen times in his three long poems[14]—but its grammatical oddity is not readily apparent in a style everywhere marked by syntactical transformations. Perhaps it is only in the earlier English Renaissance, when the style of prose and verse could tolerate and delight in overstated symmetries and congruities, that hendiadys could so casually take its place in a poetic style, and perhaps it could do so with great ironic effect only at the moment when confidence in those symmetries and congruities was being badly shaken. The wonder is that for all these years it has been so little noticed.

But Shakespeare's style—is it really possible to say it at this late date?—has never been adequately explored. In particular, the stylistic devices that make for elusiveness have not been amenable to study by most of the categorizing techniques with which scholars have approached the analysis of style. Hendiadys is too confusing, too disorderly; it is one strand of the verbal web that made Shakespeare's work seem to its early critics undisciplined and rough. Even in our own day, when the patterns of Shakespeare's imagery and dramatic structure are better understood, the kinds of discourse to be found in his plays still seem bewilderingly various, beyond the wisdom and reach of any single commentator. Critics who deeply analyze the action, structure, character, and imagery of the plays often take little interest in the figurative devices that seem merely decorative. But even those who study the playwright's style are likely to examine his tropes more closely than his figures.[15] We have lists of those figures, and we know how deeply Shakespeare had absorbed these classical patterns. But no one, to my knowledge, has found a way of showing us just how, in the plays from *Hamlet* on, when the school figures are loosened, transformed, adapted to his most complex purposes, the great Shakespearean style performs its work.

Hendiadys is, of course, only a single feature of that style, and only once, so far as I know, has any critic come close to discussing its effect. Granville-Barker, though he does not distinguish hendiadys from other doublets, accurately describes a style in which such word combinations play a prominent role:

> A very common English means of emphasis is what may be called "repetition by complement"; but, again, so common is this, its better-known locutions are so hackneyed, that their value is largely lost. "Flesh and blood," "safe and sound," "hue and cry," "kith and kin," "use and wont"—these are worn currency indeed. Shakespeare, in *Hamlet,* shows an extraordinary fondness for this device, and employs it, one would say, as carelessly as constantly. It may at times betoken the teeming mind—his own or his character's—finding two words as easily as one and too eager to be getting on to choose between them. The use of the conjunction makes smooth going for the verse, the familiar form and the bare addition to the meaning easy listening; and even when this last is negligible, as it is—to take four samples out of Hamlet's mouth alone in a single stretch of a single scene—in "book and volume," "grace and mercy," "strange or odd," "love and friending"—the actor's voice can itself color the second word to a richer implication. But the meaning is often definitely amplified or intensified; amplified in "grunt and sweat"; in "slings and arrows" a sense of piercing is added to a mere blow; and the suggestion in "pitch and moment" carries us upward first and then on. The sense is enlarged in "fit and seasoned" and "mortal and unsure"; its force is modified in "scourge and minister."

The concrete imagery of a noun turned adjective can add weight to the weightiest adjective, as with "ponderous and marble jaws"; or the simple image may be elaborated and made beautiful, as in "the morn and liquid dew of youth."[16]

Granville-Barker is probably right in thinking Shakespeare's doubling habit at times rather random and casual, even perfunctory (he gives some examples of "how tiresome the trick can be if it is overemployed" [170]). But he does not sufficiently recognize the elevating, dignifying, and even the estranging effect of the device in most of its appearances, nor does he see that in those examples that can properly be called hendiadys there is something more at work—not merely amplification or intensification but an interweaving, indeed sometimes a muddling, of meanings, a deliberate violation of clear sense that is in perfect keeping with Shakespeare's exploration, in this period, of "things supernatural and causeless" (*All's Well That Ends Well,* 2.3.3).

II

Phrases that look like hendiadys occur in all but three of Shakespeare's plays. Throughout his career he was fond of using nouns joined by *and* to give a feeling of elevation or complexity, and sometimes the nouns so joined seem unevenly matched in dimension or category. Thus, even as early as *Henry VI, Part II,* young Clifford is appalled that his father should die violently "in *thy reverence and thy chair days*" (5.2.48)—that is, in your reverend old age when you ought to be taking your ease in a chair. But only in 1599, in *Henry V,* does Shakespeare begin to use the device with some frequency. The eleven weighty plays he wrote between about 1599 and 1606 (i.e., from *Henry V* through *Macbeth,* but excluding *The Merry Wives of Windsor*) contain about 70 percent of all the hendiadys in the plays. Except for *The Merry Wives of Windsor,* in which there are no examples, the device appears at least eight times in every play Shakespeare wrote in these years, and in perhaps six or eight of these plays it is a fairly prominent stylistic feature.

He uses it most in *Hamlet,* sixty-six times, more than twice as often as in any other play. The other three great tragedies—*Macbeth* (18), *King Lear* (15), and especially *Othello* (28)—provide numerous examples of the figure. So do *Troilus and Cressida* (19), *Measure for Measure* (16), *Henry V* (15), and *Twelfth Night* (13); *As You Like It* (10) and *All's Well That Ends Well* (9) contain somewhat fewer instances, but each has more than any play earlier or later than this period. This list suggests that hendiadys is most congenial to Shakespeare's purposes in those plays that explore the problematical depths of thought and feeling, as opposed to those that survey, from a perspective less intensely or less personally involved, the spectacle of erring human behavior.

In general, it can be said that the device is appropriate to a "high style" and that it normally but not invariably occurs in passages of a certain elevation, dignity, or remoteness from ordinary experience. Goneril's rebuke to Albany, "This *milky gentleness and course* of yours" (*King Lear* 1.4.364), expresses her distant contempt for him; and when Northumberland says that Bolingbroke's company "hath very much beguiled / The *tediousness and process* of my travel" (*Richard II* 2.3.11–12), the fancy figure he uses underscores the unctuousness of his flattery. The occasion on which the Ghost of the elder Hamlet speaks hopefully of his sins being "*burnt and purged* away" (1.5.13) (i.e., purged by burning) is a supernatural one. Polonius instructing Reynaldo, Laertes advising Ophelia, Hamlet questioning the cosmos or defining poetry—all such ceremonies can evoke hendiadys, along with other formal locutions that estrange the diction from ordinary speech. In practice, hendiadys can often be distinguished only with difficulty from the normal use of the syntactical patterns it works through.

Adjectival hendiadys resembles the merely formal separation of adjectives that might easily be joined. In English we do not usually say, "The day was cold, clear," but we may say, "It was a cold, clear day." We make the sentence more deliberate if we separate the two adjectives: "It was a cold and clear day." We go still further toward elaborateness and formality if we say, "It was a cold and a clear day." Shakespeare uses this form often: "Why, 'tis a loving and a fair reply" (*Hamlet* 1.2.121), "It is a nipping and an eager air" (1.4.2), and "Where a malignant and a turbaned Turk" (*Othello* 5.2.353). Such phrasing, however, risks making it seem as if the speaker is talking about two different things, as indeed Claudius is doing when he says he is conducting his affairs "With an auspicious and a dropping eye" (1.2.11). But this merely ceremonious separation of double adjectives is distinct from adjectival hendiadys, in which the meanings of the adjectives interweave. When the Duke in *As You Like It* speaks of "This *wide and universal* theatre" (2.7.137), we understand him to mean something like "this theatre, wide as the universe" or "this wide theatre of the universe" (cf., in the prologue to act 4 of *Henry V,* "the wide vessel of the universe"). When Horatio says he would not believe in the Ghost "Without the *sensible and true* avouch / Of mine own eyes" (1.1.57–58), he must mean "the sensorily accurate testimony" of his eyes—that is, the first adjective must modify the second—or, if one prefers, "the accurate sensory testimony," with "sensory testimony" taken as a compound unit modified by "accurate." Either way the two elements of the hendiadys, though grammatically parallel, are not semantically parallel, and the most likely paraphrases would change the coordinate structure and make one of the two elements subordinate to the other or to a unit that includes the other. Similarly, when the Queen describes the about-to-be-drowned Ophelia as seeming for a moment to be "a creature *native and indued* / Unto that element" (4.7.180–81), most readers will hear in the phrase the undercurrent "natively indued"; the adjectives seem not parallel but part of a complex idea; a creature native to that element and hence endowed with the qualities necessary to live in it.[17]

When hendiadys involves nouns, as it does in Shakespeare 78 percent of the time (as compared with 19 percent for adjectives and 3 percent for verbs), it must be distinguished from the many commonplace expressions that have the grammatical form *noun a and noun b*, especially those of two types: first, ordinary collocations of related objects, groups, qualities, constituents, titles *(wind and rain, women and children, pen and ink, flesh and blood, time and place)*; second, mere rewordings of the same idea without any significant increment, usually for an effect of expansion or elevation (*lord and master, part and parcel,* from ordinary speech; *"help and vantage,"* from *Macbeth* [1.3.113]; *"chance and hazard,"* from *Antony and Cleopatra* [3.7.48]; and *"mute and dumb,"* from *Hamlet* [2.2.137]). Shakespeare, throughout his work, habitually indulges in this ceremonious parading of synonyms.[18]

These two familiar uses of the form (nouns joined by *and*) compose the norm, the background, against which we measure the oddness of hendiadys. Something like their pattern is what we expect from hendiadys and fail to get. Instead, we feel uneasily that the two words compose an idea more complex and less compound than their grammatical situation implies. Not *sound and sight,* but *"sound and fury"* (*Macbeth* 5.5.27); not *body and soul,* but *"body and beauty"* (*Othello* 4.1.217); not *intent and purpose,* but *"intent and coming"* (*Measure for Measure* 5.1.124). The effect of the figure, therefore, is usually of some meaning blurred, of a relationship inaccurately represented, and represented as more straightforward, more dignified, more grand than it actually is. "I have told you what I have seen and heard, but faintly," Edmund warns Edgar, "nothing like the *image and horror* of it" (*King Lear* 1.2.190–92). Certainly the horror of it is intensified by the hendiadys more than it would have been if Edmund had said, more conventionally, "the horrible image of it." It may be argued that Edmund's mind moves from the image to the horror, from the perception to its emotional quality; but this very movement, this procession of interior events, which deeply justifies the phrase, takes us by surprise and makes us feel, as the best examples of hendiadys tend to do, that some structural situation we had become ready for (our picturing something) has jumped and become a different structural situation (our being horrified at something). Edmund, of course, is lying, and so, it seems, is his syntax.

Like rhyme or slant rhyme in its near but not perfect repetition of an earlier event, hendiadys makes us do a double take, and many instances together may make us feel uneasy. Lady Macbeth challenges her husband "To be the same in thine own *act and valor*" (i.e., in this valorous act of yours) "As thou art in desire" (1.7.40–41). A moment later she is plotting to befuddle Duncan's officers "with *wine and wassail*" (1.7.64), which may mean "wine and ale," but because *wassail* often means "carousing, revelry," the phrase has some of the same imbalance as "beer and a party." A few lines later, having overwhelmed Macbeth's weak scruples (or, perhaps, weakness and scruples), she agrees that the grooms will be blamed for the murder:

> Who dares receive it other,
> As we shall make our *griefs and clamor* roar
> Upon his death?
>
> (1.7.77–79)

Some part of Lady Macbeth's specious persuasiveness may be due to, or reflected in, her use of hendiadys in all these passages: *"griefs and clamor"* means "clamorous griefs" or "wailing sounds," but the separation of the two ideas gives them an oddly empty, discordant, and disconnected feeling, not entirely unrelated to the feeling Macbeth has at the end of the play when he perceives life as "a tale / Told by an idiot, full of *sound and fury*" (5.5.27). As the griefs have been separated from the clamor, so the fury has been abstracted from the sound; nothing is compact, normal unions are disassembled.

In different characters, hendiadys may expose different qualities. In *Measure for Measure* the Duke's aloofness is perhaps partly conveyed by his using hendiadys eight times. In *Henry IV, Part II* the extravagance of Pistol's language is made vivid through the same figure:

> Thy Doll, and Helen of thy noble thoughts,
> Is in *base durance and contagious prison,*
> Haled thither
> By most *mechanical and dirty* hand.
>
> (5.5.35–38)

The first figure's *and* might well be *in,* and the last line means "by the very dirty hand of a workman." A low word like *dirty* in the grandiose setting of hendiadys, of course, produces bathos. But even in less antic characters, such as Polonius and Othello, the use of hendiadys may betray a tendency to orotundity. It may be mere rewording, not hendiadys, for Othello to claim, "I fetch my *life and being* / From men of royal siege" (1.2.21–22); to record his unwillingness, but for Desdemona's love, to put his "unhoused free condition / . . . into *circumscription and confine*" (1.2.26–27); and to exculpate his running off with her on the grounds that they have simply been married: "The very *head and front* of my offending / Hath this extent, no more" (1.3.80–81). But as we hear him speak of *"broil and battle"* (1.2.57), of "the *flinty and steel* couch of war" (1.3.231), of *"place and exhibition"* (1.3.238), of *"accommodation and besort,"* (1.3.239), of *"worldly matters and direction"* (1.3.300), we may find him excessively disposed to use the doublet theatrically. Certainly this construction contributes to the dramatic irony we feel in a passage like the following:.

> And Heaven defend your good souls, that you think
> I will your *serious and great* business scant
> For she is with me. No, when light-winged toys
> Of feathered Cupid seel with wanton dullness
> My *speculative and officed* instrument,
> That my disports *corrupt and taint* my business,
> Let housewives make a skillet of my helm,
> And all *indign and base* adversities
> Make head against my estimation!
> (1.3.267–75)

Not all the italicized phrases are hendiadys, but they all display Othello's carelessness about the precise relations between entities. He rewords for effect, though the second term is sometimes anticlimactic, and he occasionally falls into hendiadys, as when he rebukes his subordinates for quarreling "on the *court and guard* of safety" (2.3.216)—that is, on the very ground of the court whose function is to guard the safety of the people. Later, incorrigibly extravagant, he compares his constancy to that of "the Pontic Sea, / Whose *icy current and compulsive course* / Ne'er feels retiring ebb" (3.3.453–55). A duller but more logical phrasing might be "the Pontic Sea, the compulsive course of whose icy current. . . ." At the end of the play, with something of the Macbeths' ghastly disconnecting of related things, he advises Desdemona to pray to *"Heaven and grace"* (5.2.27).

III

But it is in *Hamlet,* above all, that Shakespeare uses hendiadys both to explore his characters and to probe his themes. The figure occurs here, by my count, sixty-six times, and the examples I list (see appendix 1, tables 1a–b, at the end of this chapter) seem to me only the fairly certain cases; there are many other phrases one might make a claim for, including one (Laertes' *"leave and favor* to return to France") that many editors routinely classify as hendiadys (see appendix 1, table 2, at the end of this chapter). The device is always somewhat mysterious and elusive, and its general appropriateness to the story and setting of *Hamlet* is obvious. All eight major characters speak hendiadys on some occasion, and so do some lesser figures. It appears in both verse and prose. Sometimes an instance occurs in isolation; sometimes we find several examples in a scene or even in a single speech. In the great enigma of *Hamlet,* this perplexing figure reminds us, in comic as in tragic moments, how uncertain and treacherous language and behavior can be.

Polonius's fondness for hendiadys appears most prominently in the scene where he shows Reynaldo how to elicit information about Laertes in Paris. The technique he recommends embraces *"encompassment and drift of question"* (2.1.10)—perhaps two techniques, but not really parallel. Reynaldo's "forgeries" about Laertes are to include only "such *wanton, wild, and usual* slips" (we should ordinarily expect *usual* to appear before the other two adjectives and to modify the compound substantive they compose with the noun—that is, such usual extravagances) "As are companions *noted and most known"*—that is, recognized *as* especially familiar—"To *youth and liberty"* (2.1.22–24)—that is, to youth when it is at liberty, or to youthful license. "And thus do we *of wisdom and of reach"* (2.1.64)—that is, "of far-reaching wisdom" (Harrison), or wise enough to see far, though *reach* and *wisdom* may be two distinct faculties—gain our devious ends. This advisory lecture Polonius calls *"lecture and advice"* (2.1.67), and when Ophelia tells him of Hamlet's strange conduct, he says, "I am sorry that with better *heed and judgment"*—that is, with the kind of close attention that would have permitted me to discern the truth—"I had not quoted him" (2.1.111–12).

Despite his "youth and liberty," Laertes is equally sententious, though he indulges more freely in rodomontade. Especially in his advice to Ophelia, his frequent hendiadys reveals his own uncertain and divided sensibility. It seems harmless enough when he warns his sister, "For *Hamlet, and the tri-*

fling of his favor [see n. 11], / Hold it *a fashion and a toy* in blood . . ." (1.3.5–6); that is, consider it capricious behavior of a kind we expect in men of spirit—a view consonant with that of Polonius, who three scenes later is plotting surveillance of such trifling in Laertes. Laertes also calls it "The *perfume and suppliance* of a minute" (1.3.9), a phrase that identifies the minute's nature (aromatic, hence insubstantial) and its evanescence (its being in short supply).

But in the long speech that follows, sometimes noted only for its sententiousness, Laertes goes on to develop a theory of division that reflects both his own furtive style and the dissociations that have often received attention in this play. In doing so he uses hendiadys lavishly, at least seven times in his forty-line sermon. He begins, strangely enough, by echoing Virgil's *"membris et mole,"* "For Nature crescent does not grow alone / In *thews and bulk*" and continues, "but as this temple waxes / The inward service of the mind and soul / Grows wide withal" (1.3.11–14). Now, as he proceeds, we begin to see that within his ponderous argument on the constraints and dangers of rank his syntax betrays his own baffled and unsteady equilibrium (and that of the play). Through all his graceful shifting from one sphere to another, what remains constant is his perception of doubleness in everything:

>Perhaps he loves you now,
>And now no *soil nor cautel* doth besmirch
>The virtue of his will. But you must fear,
>His greatness weighed, his will is not his own,
>For he himself is subject to his birth.
>He may not, as unvalued persons do,
>Carve for himself, for on his choice depends
>The safety and health of this whole state,
>And therefore must his choice be circumscribed
>Unto the *voice and yielding* of that body
>Whereof he is the head. Then if he says he loves you,
>It fits your wisdom so far to believe it
>As he in his particular *act and place*
>May give his saying deed, which is no further
>Than the main voice of Denmark goes withal.
>Then weigh what loss your honor may sustain
>If with too credent ear you list his songs,
>Or lose your heart, or your chaste treasure open
>To his unmastered importunity.

> Fear it, Ophelia, fear it, my dear sister,
> And keep you in the rear of your affection,
> Out of the *shot and danger* of desire.
> The chariest maid is prodigal enough
> If she unmask her beauty to the moon.
> Virtue itself scapes not calumnious strokes.
> The canker galls the infants of the spring
> Too oft before their buttons be disclosed,
> And in the *morn and liquid dew* of youth
> Contagious blastments are most imminent.
> Be wary, then, best safety lies in fear.
> Youth to itself rebels, though none else near.
> (1.3.14–44)

Body is one thing, the inner life another; the inner life is itself double ("mind and soul"); Hamlet's love may be pure now, but it is subject to corruption, free from neither *"soil nor cautel,"* neither "impurity nor deceit"— or are these qualities linked? Is deceit, falseness, a kind of soilure, or will the soilure of lust, when it appears, have to be covered up by deceit? Whatever that case, Hamlet's "will," even if virtuous, "is not his own." As minds (and souls) are subject to the size of bodies ("temples"), Hamlet is "subject to his birth"; as "head," he is subject to the "body" of Denmark, and his "choice . . . circumscribed / Unto the *voice and yielding* of that body"—unto its vote of approval. Hamlet is to the body politic what the mind or soul is to the body—inside it, restricted in movement and choices, unable to act without its acquiescence. Denmark's a prison. Paradoxically, the very grandeur of Hamlet's rank narrows his freedom and, to compound the paradox, makes his possible licentiousness, his "unmastered importunity" (his freedom in another sense), all the more dangerous to Ophelia. She, in her turn, is to become dual if she follows her brother's advice to "keep you in the rear of your affection"; Laertes even addresses her doubly: "Fear it, Ophelia, fear it, my dear sister"; and her double nature is to stay "Out of the *shot and danger* of desire"—that is, out of the range of danger, out of dangershot. Still masked, she may yet be unable to avoid calumny and disease ("canker" and "Contagious blastments") that attack "Virtue" and especially imperil anyone "in the *morn and liquid dew* of youth." Laertes' summary stresses the doubleness of youth that is both danger and guardian: "best safety lies in fear. / Youth to itself rebels, though none else near." The phrases, for all their elegance, betray his nervousness about the divided nature of selves.

That Ophelia has received the message becomes clear from her reply, in which she urges her brother:

> Do not, as some ungracious pastors do,
> Show me the steep and thorny way to Heaven
> Whilst, like a puffed and reckless libertine,
> Himself the primrose path of dalliance treads
> And recks not his own rede.
> (1.3.47–51)

His images of war, of masks, of disease are answered by her more lucid image of climbing; his hendiadys is echoed by her merely linked adjectives ("steep and thorny," "puffed and reckless"); but her phrases are drenched in the same erotic suggestiveness as his; and she, too, is apprehensive of conduct that is at odds with counsel. The little scene unfolds, in turn, a double Hamlet, a double Ophelia, a double Laertes, each threatened by internal "importunity," "affection," "dalliance," against which the strongest defense is "fear." The ironies accumulate, of course, until Laertes, after urging his sister so emphatically to "fear" (using the word four times), puts off her own advice with a shrug: "Oh, fear *me* not" (my italics), as, subsequently, he receives in silence, in boredom perhaps, as if not meant for him, his father's advice to be true to his own self, in order to avoid being false to any other man.

IV

This account of the doublenesses in part of one scene in *Hamlet* could, of course, be much expanded if we were to consider the whole play. Even in this scene the members of the family appear in pairs—Laertes and Ophelia, Polonius and Laertes (with Ophelia silent), Polonius and Ophelia—and the advice they give to each other contains many small ironies and reversals, which brilliantly expose the follies and hypocrisies of advice giving. The context of later developments, however, and even the solemnity and apprehensiveness about human nature that color the advisory speeches confirm the view that the doublenesses we perceive here are characteristic of the whole play and that hendiadys is a stylistic means of underlining the play's themes of anxiety, bafflement, disjunction, and the falsity of appearances.

The doublenesses in the play, the way the situations of the characters echo and recapitulate one another, the mirror imagery have all been treated at length by numerous critics. It may still be useful, however, to review the extraordinary degree to which *Hamlet* shows dualisms of one kind or another to be misleading, unions to be false or unsteady, and conjunctions of persons or events or objects to mask deeper disjunctions. For this kind of deceptive linking is exactly what hendiadys expresses. There are obvious pairs into whose presumed disjunctions we never inquire, but Rosencrantz and Guildenstern, Voltimand and Cornelius, and perhaps the English ambassadors are virtual parodies of human association, related characters into whose differences we need not look because they appear too distant from the center of our concern, almost identical twins, mirror images of each other, agents, double agents, about whom someone else might write a play but whose natures here require no close inspection. We do not know whether in the ceremonious exchange,

> *King.* Thanks, Rosencrantz and gentle Guildenstern.
> *Queen.* Thanks, Guildenstern and gentle Rosencrantz.
> (2.2.33–34)

the Queen, that "imperial jointress," is trying to show the joint monarchs' equal gratitude to the two men or is correcting the King ("Don't you remember? The gentle one is Rosencrantz"). But these pairs mainly serve, like ordinary conjunctions of nouns in sentences, as examples of undifferentiated unions against which other pairs in the play establish by contrast their patterns of eccentricity, of separateness and disjunction, and ultimately their incommensurability.

At the very beginning of the play, for example, when Bernardo and Francisco challenge each other ("Who's there?" "Nay, answer me"), who is on guard? Francisco presumably; yet it is Bernardo who gives the first challenge, though he must know that Francisco is there or thereabouts. We learn in a moment that, although Francisco is "sick at heart," it is not he but Bernardo who has seen a ghost; that another pair, Horatio and Marcellus, are "rivals" of Bernardo's watch; and that a different pair, Bernardo and Marcellus, have seen the Ghost on two previous occasions. In scene 2, Marcellus and Bernardo mainly answer Hamlet's questions in concert, and when Hamlet appears on the platform to confront the Ghost, Bernardo is absent; Marcellus and Horatio play virtually the same role in trying to restrain Hamlet; and after this scene Marcellus disappears altogether. Such a pattern of developing and dissolving pairs leaves this side of the stage, so to speak, entirely to Hamlet and Horatio, who are united by their initials, their common experience of the university, their friendship, their sympathy, their confidence, by the incorporation, as it were, of one into the other (who "wear[s] him / In my heart's core—aye, in my heart of heart" [3.2.77-78]), and by their commitment to Hamlet's cause and story. If there exists in the play any image of a true conjunction of spirits, it is surely that of Hamlet and Horatio, though it is not Hamlet *solus* but his anima who chooses his friend ("Since my dear soul was mistress of her choice / And could of men distinguish, her election / Hath sealed thee for herself" [3.2.68-70]).

But all the other relationships in the play, all the other parallels, are misleading, suspect, corrupt. Mirror relationships are frequent, but they offer no true images. Hamlet and Laertes, sons of murdered advice-giving fathers, destroy each other; Fortinbras, their foreign shadow, acts in his own sphere, waits in theirs; Hamlet's father Hamlet is the ghost of himself, the ghost of his son; Gertrude wavers between two brothers, two portraits; the Polonius family echoes the Hamlet family: two men, one woman, two generations, one parent dead. But in every apparent identity some features are different: Laertes misses the point of everything, Hamlet must experience each event in its profoundest terms; the Ghost is a ghost, not Hamlet's father exactly, and since others see him he is not simply a part of Hamlet; Claudius and the elder Hamlet are utterly different in character, as are their marriages to the same woman; and Polonius and his family are partly victims, partly agents, of the Hamlet family. The doubling in every mirror falsifies. The mirrors of other persons, of the clouds, of ghosts; the glass of fashion; the glass of guilt ("You go not till I set you up a glass / Where you may see the inmost part of you" [3.4.19-20]); even the mirror of art, the play with its Italian murder mirror—all these, though they expose the truth, fail to give us true reflections.

The unions themselves are extremely tenuous. Polonius and his affectionate family are easily undone, for beneath their intimacy lie contempt, theatricality, and deviousness. Polonius shows no warmth to Ophelia; he offers his son sententious counsel and spies on him. Laertes finds his father tedious and resists even his sister's friendly advice; and the revenge he takes for both, ill-considered and futile, succeeds in completing the destruction of his family, a result that, even in his dying moments, he seems not to notice. The marriage of Gertrude and the elder Hamlet, for all its apparent affection ("Why, she would hang on him . . ."), is easily relinquished; that of Gertrude and Claudius, though neither ever quite repudiates it, is corrupt, resting on murder, adultery, and bad taste. At the heart of the play are Hamlet's uncertain relationships with mother, father, and uncle, the oedipal conflicts and evasions that are clearly a source of his problem. Throughout, Hamlet is tormented by the joinings he sees about him: "I say we will have no more marriages. Those that are married already, all but one, shall live; the rest shall keep as they are" (3.1.154–57). Claudius, similarly, is tormented by his own false relationships: false brother, false king, false husband, false father to Hamlet, false even in contrition, his words false to his thoughts.

In effect, the play calls into question—and hendiadys helps it to do so—all relationships, familial, political, cosmic, and even artistic. As a tragic hero of unprecedented intelligence and awareness, Hamlet doubts not only his own personal relationships and the relations of powers in a state but also the relation of human beings to the whole cosmos in which they live, the unity of one's own identity, and even the relations of individuals to one another in conversation, in the dialogue of plays, in aesthetic roles. Almost every conjunction he finds false:

> God hath given you one face and you make yourselves another.
> (3.2.149–50)

> Look here upon this picture, and on this,
> The counterfeit presentment of two brothers.
> (3.4.53–54)

> The body is with the King, but the King is not with the body.
> (4.2.29–30)

> Was't Hamlet wronged Laertes? Never Hamlet.
> If Hamlet from himself be ta'en away,
> And when he's not himself does wrong Laertes,
> Then Hamlet does it not, Hamlet denies it.
> Who does it, then? His madness. If't be so,
> Hamlet is of the faction that is wronged,
> His madness is poor Hamlet's enemy.
> (5.2.244–50)

This last speech, however, is spoken by the same young man who earlier rebuked his mother for thinking him mad:

> Mother, for love of grace,
> Lay not that flattering unction to your soul
> That not your trespass but my madness speaks.
> (3.4.144–46)

Hamlet is full, as we know, of references to mirrors, to paintings, to plays, all of which contribute to the same complex presentation of false parallels and unreliable conjunctions. What has been noted less often is the extent to which characters act *through* others. When at any given moment on the stage two persons appear to be in conference, we are likely to understand them better as one character working through the other—as indeed it is through all the characters together that we see their world, their stage, the age and body of their time pressing its form. Again, this situation is exactly that of hendiadys. The play is full of agents, and the characters use them lavishly, but most of the time, as it turns out, the agents never really succeed in accomplishing what they set out to accomplish. Claudius works through Laertes, uses him almost as his mask, just as he has earlier used Laertes' father. This father and son are killed as they front for him; to kill Hamlet the father and Hamlet the son, he pours equivalent "leperous distillment[s]" into their ears—poison in one's, Laertes' challenge in the other's. Claudius uses others as well—Gertrude, Rosencrantz and Guildenstern, his ambassadors, England, Osric, and "your better wisdoms" of the court he has won. Polonius works through Ophelia, Reynaldo, the players, and—fatally for him—the Queen. Laertes pleads through Polonius for permission to go to France; he works through the King to avenge his family. The Ghost uses Bernardo, Marcellus, and Horatio to get to Hamlet, who then becomes the Ghost's agent in securing revenge. Bernardo and Marcellus work through Horatio to get to Hamlet. Hamlet himself uses players, pirates, guards, England, his mother, and Horatio to serve all sorts of purposes, from exposing the King to disposing of Rosencrantz and Guildenstern, to reporting his cause aright. In almost all these examples, the chief instigator gives his agents careful instructions about how to proceed; a remarkable proportion of the play consists of just such instructions: do this, don't do that. In the service of one plot or another, these employers of agents use various props—poison, a play, an antic disposition, letters and seals, arras, masks, and rhetoric of many kinds. The problem for everyone who employs agents or props is to know which ones to choose and how to manipulate them, but every tool becomes, sooner or later, another image of oneself, one's mask, one's mirror, one's hands, and all these images may come to seem insubstantial. "These hands are not more like," Horatio says, to verify the Ghost (1.2.212)—more like each other, he means, than the Ghost is to his memory of Hamlet's father. No one's plot entirely succeeds. The great employers of agents—Claudius, Hamlet, Polonius, Laertes—all see their plans go awry and come to grief.

    Such frustration is clearly in the nature of things. However much mirrors, paintings, or plays can show us, the shadows they reflect elude our grasp. Hamlet calls into question every dimension of reality, but all his techniques for probing, for questioning the causes of the world, the cause-effect nature of its processes, end by casting doubt on causality itself and even on motive. Motive and cause, much speculated on in the play, turn out to be deeper than anyone can fathom. (Why do Hamlet and Gertrude especially act as they do? We never know.)

In a sense, madness carries the enigmas only one step further. It is not only Hamlet and Ophelia who bear watching; all the members of the two families behave unaccountably and exhibit signs of disturbance. Claudius's guilt paralyzes him:

> And like a man to double business bound,
> I stand in pause where I shall first begin,
> And both neglect.[19]
>
> (3.3.41–43)

Gertrude's situation is equally appalling:

> Thou turn'st mine eyes into my very soul,
> And there I see such black and grained spots
> As will not leave their tinct.
>
> O Hamlet, thou hast cleft my heart in twain.
>
> (3.4.89–91,156)

We see Ophelia pathetically "Divided from herself and her fair judgment" (4.5.85)—a phrase that, if we do not take it as hendiadys, shows Ophelia now in three segments. Laertes may be, as Claudius suggests, "A face without a heart" (4.7.110). Polonius invites the King to "Take this from this, if this be otherwise" (2.2.156), which it is; in an unexpected fashion, the offer is redeemed. These are all violent or shocking images, and they suggest the extent to which these six main characters are, like the syntax in hendiadys, disjoined, stricken, divided within.

Causality, purpose, persons all askew. But the distinction basic to all these is that between heaven and earth, opposite entities that need to be in harmony if any other conjunctions are to be trusted. Again and again Hamlet invokes both of them:

> Heaven and earth!
> Must I remember?
>
> (1.2.142–43)
>
> O all you host of Heaven! O earth!
>
> (1.5.92)

> There are more things in Heaven and earth, Horatio,
> Than are dreamt of in your philosophy.
> (1.5.166–67)

In both the first act and the last, the king's cannon announce his drinking to the heavens, which echo back to earth. Hamlet knows well enough, however, how false such noises are. At one moment he considers the earth "a sterile promontory" and the heavens "a foul and pestilent congregation of vapors" (2.2.310–15). While Ophelia calls on heaven to restore him (3.1.138,147), Hamlet cries in self-disgust, "What should such fellows as I do crawling between heaven and earth?" (3.1.129–30). Horatio, early in the play, sees "Heaven and earth" as having "together demonstrated" in Denmark graphic signs of events to come (1.1.124). Laertes also complains that the odd circumstances of his father's death and burial "Cry to be heard, as 'twere from Heaven to earth" (4.5.216), and so enraged is he at first "That both the worlds I give to negligence" (4.5.134). If the two worlds he refers to are this one and the next, they represent a conjunction like that between heaven and earth. Heaven and hell are often linked in the play; Ophelia at her death is suspended for a while between air and water; the Ghost inhabits at least two realms. The play and the players move between Denmark and England, the land and the sea, the terrifying heights of the castle and its courtly depths, between formal and personal occasions, between impotence and action, between verse and prose, between "natural" and "unnatural" behavior, between reasoning and rashness, and so on.

What the play suggests, and what hendiadys helps convey, is that the conjunctions on which life depends, on which this world's customs and institutions are founded, cannot be trusted. The ultimate disjunction that hendiadys and the play express is that between man and the world (family, nation, or cosmos), apparently in union with each other but actually in deep opposition, disequilibrium. Like the "union" that Claudius throws into the cup, "Richer than that which four successive kings / In Denmark's crown have worn" (5.2.284–85), this one is deadly poison. As madness is a loosening of connections (that mimics murder, fratricide, regicide, or monkeys jumping from roof-tops [3.4.192–96]), so is hendiadys; as mirrors and paintings mock the reality they pretend to reproduce, so hendiadys mocks normal unions of entities. A miniature stylistic play within the play, hendiadys holds its mirror up to *Hamlet* and—like the court scenes, the duel, the arranged performance of the players, and other stage devices and significant turns of language—enforces our awareness of the drama's central action. For in hendiadys, as in the play, we experience an encounter between two mismatched and incommensurable forces, in open and yet obscure relation to each other, joined yet disparate, one pair in the sentence and one in life (or in this representation of life). And as in each the halves cannot fit easily together, so between the two realms, between the linguistic emblem of hendiadys and the situation of Hamlet in the world, there is no simple concord, no clear and easy passage from one to the other. In hendiadys the words are as isolated as the characters, as aloof as Hamlet, and the device itself as ill at ease in the language as Hamlet is in Denmark.

V

Whatever the role of hendiadys as a stylistic emblem of the major meanings of *Hamlet,* our awareness of its extensive use in the play can at least throw light on some important passages. Because phrases involving hendiadys are not often understood as such, their meanings are jumbled, reduced to a stricter logic than the verbal situation can justify, or even entirely misread. *Hamlet* and most of Shakespeare's other plays of this period contain far too many examples of hendiadys to permit discussion of all of them, but it may be helpful to inspect a few famous instances—or, rather, famous phrases not often recognized as instances. Scholarly readers at least ought to understand that such familiar phrases as "sound and fury," "slings and arrows," "whips and scorns," or "scourge and minister" are not ordinary unions of nouns but instances or cousins of this peculiar Latinate figure.

Some phrases are simple enough. When Hamlet promises the Ghost to erase from memory everything "That *youth and observation* copied there" (1.5.101), we understand immediately that these terms are not separate but compound, that he must mean "youthful observation," the habit of observation that he has engaged in up to this moment, which is to say, in his youth.[20] Ophelia's description of Hamlet as "The *expectancy and rose* of the fair state" (3.1.160) is easily translatable as "the rosy expectancy," the man whom everyone has been expecting to become, as king, the fairest flower of our country. The Ghost supposes it likely that, when he tells his tale to his son, Hamlet's "*knotted and combined* locks" will part (1.5.18)—that is, not two different kinds of locks but locks that are combined by being knotted, by growing together. Soon the Ghost must return to "*sulphurous and tormenting* flames" (1.5.3)—that is, to flames that torment *because* they are sulphurous. Hamlet, on seeing the Ghost, wonders why his father's sepulcher "Hath oped his *ponderous and marble* jaws" (1.4.50)—that is, heavy *be-*

cause marble. (The phrasing here, in a question that seeks a cause, obscures a cause.) Gertrude asks Rosencrantz and Guildenstern "To show us so much *gentry and goodwill*"—courtesy and goodwill, but also the goodwill we expect of gentlemen like yourselves—"As to expend your time with us a while / For the *supply and profit* of our hope" (2.2.22–24)—to supply, to our advantage, the thing we are hoping for. The King suspects that *"the hatch and the disclose"* of whatever Hamlet is brooding over "Will be some danger" (3.1.174–75): the brood, when we know what it is. (*Disclose,* for Shakespeare's audience, would be a pun; the verb meant both "hatch" and "reveal.")

Once we realize that Shakespeare is using hendiadys freely, some passages become clearer, or at least their obscurity grows brighter. The *"slings and arrows* of outrageous fortune" (3.1.58) are not parallel terms; one is an instrument for slinging, the other is the thing slung, but slings do not sling arrows; in speech we might expect "bows and arrows" or "slings and bows" or "slings and stones" or "stones and arrows." If the phrase Hamlet uses is not exactly hendiadys, it is at least more comprehensible in a setting where hendiadys is a prominent figure. The *"whips and scorns* of time" (3.1.70), which Hamlet, in the same soliloquy, doubts we would want to bear if we did not fear death, also come from different categories; one is concrete and metaphorical, the other abstract and immediate, and together they might seem out of focus if we were not so accustomed to the pattern of hendiadys. Time or a satirist's scorn may make us feel whipped, or the two words may express two ways time has of punishing us (wrinkles and disappointment), but the terms seem to interweave their meanings as simple conjoined nouns do not usually do.

Hamlet's remarks on "playing" yield up more of their meaning when we notice their use of hendiadys. The purpose of playing, he tells us,

> was and is to hold as 'twere the mirror up to Nature—to show Virtue her own feature, scorn her own image, and the very *age and body of the time* his *form and pressure.* (3.2.23–27)

The last phrase surely means "the imprint, or stamp, of his form," though we may also be justified in hearing a more complex meaning: "his form and the stamp of his form."[21] But whose form? The previous phrase is more puzzling, but I take the two terms it joins to be not *age* and *body* but *age* and *body of the time.* For one thing, "age . . . of the time" is meaningless, as Dr. Johnson noted. On the other hand, *age* and *body of the time* are clearly not parallel, but what happens here is what frequently happens in hendiadys:

the second term unfolds the first. The very age—that is to say, the period of time, conceived as a body—will find the imprint of its figure in the mirror of stage representations.

While readings based on hendiadys are sometimes not much at variance with traditional ones, an awareness of this device and its peculiar structure can help us appraise more clearly the meanings of many phrases cast in this pattern that elude our exact understanding. The usual assumption of editors, when confronted with a phrase in the *a* + *b* form, is that the linked words are either synonymous or complementary. It might help their readers—*us*—if they realized that Shakespeare frequently uses a third pattern, which, though it works differently in different examples, constitutes a distinct alternative way of organizing compound phrases. The function of this third pattern is evidently not to resolve ambiguities but to assert them, to acknowledge and dramatize the elusiveness of even the simplest relations, and at once to deny and to extend the adequacy of linguistic forms to convey our experience.[22] Instead of retreating in dismay before such phrases, we might, with whatever misgivings, surprise them in their mimetic shadows with Francisco's scholarly cry: "Stand, and unfold yourself."

Appendix 1

Table 1 lists the instances of hendiadys I have found in *Hamlet*. In all these the two conjoined terms are not quite parallel, as I hope readers will see. Almost half of them are discussed in the text; for the rest I have proposed brief paraphrases (admittedly too prosaic sometimes) or additional notes and comments. I have listed also, in table 2, another twenty-three phrases that are probably not hendiadys but that come close. In the last analysis, they seem to me not convincing examples, but they give some idea of the curious ways in which Shakespeare, during this period and especially in this play, doubled his nouns and adjectives. There are dozens of other doublets *(climatures and countrymen, rogue and peasant slave, baked and impasted, dull and muddy-mettled, pitch and moment, shreds and patches, thoughts and whispers, bugs and goblins, woe or wonder)* in which the terms are parallel but suggestive.

It is often difficult to be sure which category a phrase belongs to: clearly parallel (but unusual), almost hendiadys, or hendiadys. Editors differ with one another and sometimes with the *OED;* my readings are sometimes at variance with all others. Similarly, the table showing the incidence of hendiadys in all Shakespeare's plays (appendix 2) should be regarded as tentative; careful as I have tried to be, I may have missed or misread some phrases. In deciding whether phrases are true instances of hendiadys, I have been most skeptical about those in *Hamlet,* to avoid buttressing with weak examples a case that seems strong without them.

Hendiadys and *Hamlet*

Table 1a. Hendiadys in Hamlet

Line	Speaker
1. Without the *sensible and true* avouch (1.1.57)	Horatio
2. But in the *gross and scope* of my opinion (1.1.68) = full breadth	Horatio
3. Well ratified by *law and heraldry* (1.1.87) = heraldic law	Horatio
4. In the *dead vast and middle* of the night (1.2.198) = desolation of midnight, or the dead and desolate midnight	Horatio
5. For *Hamlet, and the trifling of his favor* (1.3.5) (see n.11)	Laertes
6. Hold it *a fashion and a toy* in blood (1.3.6)	Laertes
7. The *perfume and suppliance* of a minute (1.3.9)	Laertes
8. In *thews and bulk* (1.3.12) = physical size	Laertes
9. And now no *soil nor cautel* doth besmirch (1.3.15)	Laertes
10. Unto the *voice and yielding* of that body (1.3.23)	Laertes
11. Out of the *shot and danger* of desire (1.3.35)	Laertes
12. And in the *morn and liquid dew* of youth (1.3.41) = the fresh morning, or morning freshness	Laertes
13. *Angels and ministers of grace* defend us (1.4.39) = angels who minister grace	Hamlet
14. Hath oped his *ponderous and marble* jaws (1.4.50)	Hamlet
15. When I to *sulphurous and tormenting* flames (1.5.3)	Ghost
16. Are *burnt and purged* away (1 5.13)	Ghost
17. Thy *knotted and combined* locks to part (1.5.18) (Folios read *"knotty."*)	Ghost
18. The *thin and wholesome* blood (1.5.70) = thin because wholesome (or vice versa?)	Ghost
19. That *youth and observation* copied there (1.5.101)	Hamlet
20. Within the *book and volume* of my brain (1.5.103) Two competing senses of *volume* are felt here: (1) tome, (2) "Size, bulk, or dimensions (of a book)" (*OED*). At first glance, the two words seem nearly synonymous, but the phrase also seems to mean "within the book and largeness of my brain," i.e., "within the spacious book of my brain."	Hamlet
21. These are but *wild and whirling* words, my lord (1.5.133) = wildly whirling	Horatio

Table 1a. *continued*

Line	Speaker
22. But, sir, such *wanton, wild, and usual* slips (2.1.22)	Polonius
23. As are companions *noted and most known* (2.1.23)	Polonius
24. To *youth and liberty* (2.1.24)	Polonius
25. According to *the phrase or the addition* (2.1.47) = form of address (Folios read "the phrase and the addition.")	Polonius
26. Of *man and country* (2.1.48) = the man's country	Polonius
27. So, by my former *lecture and advice* (2.1.67)	Polonius
28. I am sorry that with better *heed and judgment* (2.1.111)	Polonius
29. And sith so neighbored to his *youth and havior* (2.2.12) (Folios read "*youth and humour*")	King
30. To show us so much *gentry and goodwill* (2.2.22)	Queen
31. For the *supply and profit* of our hope (2.2.24)	Queen
32. On such regards of *safety and allowance* (2.2.79) = "on such conditions with regard to the public safety [or your own safe-conduct] as are (in this document) submitted for your approval" (Kittredge)	Voltimand
33. In *form and moving* (2.2.316–17)	Hamlet
34. how *express and admirable* (2.2.317)	Hamlet
35. The appurtenance of welcome is *fashion and ceremony* (2.2.388–89) = "formal ceremony" (Harrison), conventional formal greeting	Hamlet
36. That lend a *tyrannous and damned* light (2.2.482) = damnably pitiless, or the kind of pitiless light that shines on the damned	Hamlet
37. But with the *whiff and wind* of his fell sword (2.2.495) = whiffing wind, whiff as of wind, the whiff *of* wind that his sword makes in striking through the aIr	First Player
38. they are the *abstracts and brief chronicles*[23] of the time (2.2.549–50)	Hamlet
39. The *expectancy and rose* of the fair state (3.1.160)	Ophelia
40. And I do doubt *the hatch and the disclose* (3.1.174)	King
41. and the very *age and body of the time* (3.2.26)	Hamlet
42. his *form and pressure* (3.2.26–27)	Hamlet

Hendiadys and *Hamlet*

Table 1a. *continued*

Line	Speaker
43. So far *from cheer and from your former state* (3.2.174) = from your former cheerfulness	Player Queen
44. That *live and feed* upon your majesty (3.3.10) = live by feeding	Guildenster
45. But in our *circumstance and course of thought* (3.3.83) = as far as we mere mortals can judge	Hamlet
46. That blurs the *grace and blush* of modesty (3.4.41) = the innocent (blushing) grace of a modest young woman	Hamlet
47. Yea, this *solidity and compound mass* (3.4.49) = solid compound mass (the earth)	Hamlet
48. *A combination and a form* indeed (3.4.60) = a form made up by combining the qualities of various gods	Hamlet
49. Upon the *heat and flame* of thy distemper (3.4.123) = hot flame	Queen
50. That I must be their *scourge and minister* (3.4.175) = scourging minister	Hamlet
51. No, in despite of *sense and secrecy* (3.4.192) = good sense, which calls for secrecy	Hamlet
52. We must, with all our *majesty and skill* (4.1.31) = royal skill	King
53. If his chief *good and market* of his time (4.4.34) = "the best use he makes of his time" (Onions)	Hamlet
54. That *capability and godlike reason* (4.4.38) = godlike capacity of reason	Hamlet
55. That for a *fantasy and trick* of fame (4.4.61)	Hamlet
56. Which is not *tomb enough and continent* (4.4.64) = a large enough tract of land to provide a tomb	Hamlet
57. Divided from *herself and her fair judgment*[24] (4.5.85)	King
58. Burn out the *sense and virtue* of mine eye (4.5.155) = sensory virtue, capacity to see	Laertes
59. *So crimeful and so capital* in nature (4.7.7) = so capitally criminal, so criminal as to deserve to be punished by death	Laertes
60. That I, in forgery of *shapes and tricks* (4.7.90) = imaginary tricks	King

Table 1a. *continued*

Line	Speaker
61. For *art and exercise* in your defense (4.7.98) (see appendix 3, No. 8)	King
62. Or like a creature *native and indued* (4.7.180)	Queen
63. Of *bell and burial* (5.1.257) = religious burial	First Priest
64. Between the *pass and fell incensed points* (5.2.61) = between the thrusting points	Hamlet
65. That might your *nature, honor, and exception* (5.2.242) (see appendix 3, No. 9)	Hamlet
66. I have a *voice and precedent* of peace (5.2.260) = an opinion that will serve as a precedent	Laertes

Note: By speaker the above 66 instances of hendiadys break down as follows: Hamlet, 23; Laertes, 11; Polonius, 7; King, 6; Horatio, 5; Queen, 4; Ghost, 4; and 1 instance each by Ophelia, Guildenstern, Voltimand, First Player, Player Queen, and First Priest. There are 60 verse instances and 6 prose instances, the latter all spoken by Hamlet.

Table 1b. Deviations from the usual noun-and-noun or adjective-and-adjective form

Deviation	Instances and examples
noun-*and*-adjective-noun	4 (12, 38, 47, 54)
a-noun-*and*-*a*-noun	2 (6, 48)
the-noun-*and*-*the*-noun	2 (25, 40)
noun-*and*-noun phrase	4 (5, 13, 41, 45)
noun-noun-*and*-noun	1 (65)
adjective-adjective-*and*-adjective	1 (22)
adjective-*and*-adverb-adjective	1 (23)
verb-*and*-verb	1 (44)
noun-(other word)-*and*-noun	1 (56)
so-adjective-*and*-*so*-adjective	1 (59)
noun-*and*-adjective-adjective-noun	1 (64)
from-noun-*and*-*from*-noun phrase	1 (43)

Table 2. Possible instances of hendiadys in *Hamlet*

Line and comment	Speaker
1. Why this same *strict and most observant* watch (1.1.71) = rigorously observant?	Marcellus
2. Of unimproved mettle *hot and full* (1.1.96) = full of heat?	Horatio
3. For *food and diet,* to some enterprise (1.1.99) If diet = regular provision, maintenance, it *includes* food.	Horatio
4. Of this *posthaste and romage* in the land (1.1.107) = hurried activity?	Horatio
5. Who, *impotent and bedrid,* scarcely hears (1.2.29) = feeble to the point of being confined to bed	King

6. Your *leave and favor* to return to France (1.2.51)
   Both words mean permission. The same phrase occurs in
   Henry VI, Part III (3.3.60).
	Laertes

7. My *thoughts and wishes* bend again toward France (1.2.55) = wishful thoughts?	Laertes

8. And bow them to your gracious *leave and pardon* (1.2.56)
   Synonyms. But the implied pun (leave to leave) has led some
   editors to gloss "permission to depart."
	Laertes

9. As he in his particular *act and place* (1.3.26)
   = in the context of his saying such a thing?
   (Folios read "peculiar *sect and force.*")
	Laertes

10. Oft breaking down the *pales and forts* of reason (1.4.28) = the fence stakes that fortify reason?	Hamlet
11. By this *encompassment and drift of question* (2.1.10)	Polonius

12. And thus do we *of wisdom and of reach* (2.1.64)
   = two faculties, but with a hint of "far-reaching wisdom"
   (Harrison)
	Polonius

13. Roasted in *wrath and fire* (2.2.483) = the fire's wrath? But Pyrrhus is roasted in both.	Hamlet
14. Out of *my weakness and my melancholy* (2.2.630) = my weakness *of* melancholy?	Hamlet
15. The *slings and arrows* of outrageous fortune (3.1.58) Not parallel, but not interrelated.	Hamlet
16. For who would bear the *whips and scorns* of time (3.1.70) = the scorns that whip? But whips = satirical lashings.	Hamlet

Table 2. *continued*

Line and comment	Speaker
17. Even to the *teeth and forehead* of our faults (3.3.63) = forward parts, but distinct	King
18. That it be *proof and bulwark* against sense (3.4.38) Shakespeare normally uses *proof* as an adjective meaning tested, strong, impenetrable, but it is often used of armor and can even mean "armor of proof," as it probably does here.	Hamlet
19. His *form and cause,* conjoined, preaching to stones (3.4.126) = his person and his cause	Hamlet
20. The *ratifers and props* of every word (4.5.105) Synonyms, but the meaning of *word* is obscure.	Gentleman
21. As had he been *incorpsed and deminatured* (4.7.88) = incorporated and made one nature with	King
22. That, on the *view and knowing* of these contents (5.2.44) = intelligent perusal, but probably in two stages, i.e., as soon as you have glanced at this letter and realized what it asks for	Hamlet
23. As deaths put on by *cunning and forced cause* (5.2.394) The last phrase refers to Hamlet, who has acted under compulsion; Claudius has practiced cunning.	Horatio

Appendix 2

Table 3. Hendiadys in Shakespeare's plays

Plays	Lines	Hendiadys	Nouns	Adjs	Verbs	Advbs	Every—lines
Henry VI, Part I	2,677	1	1				2,677
Henry VI, Part II	3,162	1	1				3,162
Henry VI, Part III	2,904	0					—
The Comedy of Errors	1,778	2	2				889
Richard III	3,619	3	2	1			1,206
Titus Andronicus	2,523	3	3				841
The Taming of the Shrew	2,649	0					—
The Two Gentlemen of Verona	2,294	1	1				2,294
Love's Labour's Lost	2,789	1		1			2,789
Romeo and Juliet	3,052	5	4	1			610
Richard II	2,756	6	6				459
A Midsummer Night's Dream	2,174	2		2			1,072
King John	2,570	7	5	1		1	367
The Merchant of Venice	2,660	5	5				532
Henry IV, Part I	3,176	7	5	2			457
Henry IV, Part II	3,466	7	3	7			492
Much Ado about Nothing	2,826	3	2	1			942
Henry V	3,380	15	9	5	1		225
Julius Caesar	2,478	8	7	1			310
As You Like It	2,867	10	5	4	1		286
Twelfth Night	2,690	13	9	3	1		207
Hamlet	3,931	66	53	12	1		60
The Merry Wives of Windsor	3,018	0					—
Troilus and Cressida	3,496	19	18	1			184
All's Well That Ends Well	2,966	9	8	1			330
Othello	3,316	28	25	3			118
Measure for Measure	2,821	16	13	3			176
King Lear	3,334	15	11	4			222
Macbeth	2,108	18	10	7	1		117
Antony and Cleopatra	3,063	8	7		1		383
Coriolanus	3,410	7	7				487

Table 3. *continued*

Plays	Lines	*Hendiadys*	Nouns	Adjs	Verbs	Advbs	Every—lines
Timon of Athens	2,373	3	2		1		791
Pericles	2,389	4	2	1	1		597
Cymbeline	3,339	4	3	1			835
The Winter's Tale	3,075	2	2				1,538
The Tempest	2,064	2	2				1,032
Henry VIII	2,822	6	6				470
The Two Noble Kinsmen	2,817	4	4				704
Shakespearean Addition to *Sir Thomas More*	165	2	1	1			83
Total	108,967	313	244	60	8	1	348

Note: For the line counts of all but the last two works I have relied on Bevington; for that of *The Two Noble Kinsmen* on the Signet edition. I counted the lines of the last item from the text in Harrison.

Appendix 3: Some Doubtful Readings of the *OED*

The *OED* is an invaluable aid in interpreting phrases in Shakespeare, but it sometimes misleads editors by inventing meanings for words in particular contexts. When it encounters phrases of the *a* + *b* form, it often assumes that *b* is either a synonym for *a* or a logically complementary word. But if the phrase is hendiadys, we may be able to interpret it without going beyond the normal meanings of *a* and *b*. Here are ten examples, some of which have puzzled editors for centuries.

1. In *King Lear,* Kent discusses the "division . . . 'twixt Albany and Cornwall"—a natural subject, as we have seen, for hendiadys—and observes that they

> have—as who have not that their great stars
> *Throned and set high?*—servants, who seem no less,
> Which are to France the *spies and speculations*
> Intelligent of our state—what hath been seen,
> Either in *snuffs and packings* of the Dukes . . .
> (3.1.22–26)

The first italicized phrase is a marginal case of hendiadys (set high on a throne?), and the third probably lists two different but parallel things (quarrels and intrigues). But the second phrase, along with the first four words of line 25, regularly baffles editors. Dr. Johnson conjectured that *speculators* was intended, and most modern editors have followed the *OED,* which gives "An observer or watcher; a spy" as one meaning of *speculation.* But only in this line has the *OED* found the word used in this sense, and it offers no instances of the word's meaning a person in any other sense. If we see that Shakespeare is using hendiadys, we should have no trouble with the phrase. It means "spies and observations" (i.e., the spies who are watching us closely to give information about our condition). When Othello, using a similar phrase, speaks of his "*speculative and officed instrument*" (1.3.271), he is referring to the faculty of watchfulness that is required by his position.

2. The *OED* similarly invents a special meaning for *descent* (which some editors follow) on the basis of Edgar's charge that Edmund is

> from the extremest upward of thy head
> To the *descent and dust* below thy foot
> A most toad-spotted traitor.
> (5.3.136–38)

"Descent," says the *OED*, appears here and nowhere else in English with the meaning "That to which one descends; the lowest part." When one has become accustomed to Shakespeare's hendiadys, it is easy to interpret the first noun as adverbial in feeling: all the way down to the dust below thy foot. If this construction seems loose, it is loose in a very Shakespearean way.

3. The *OED* is probably also wrong about Othello's use of *accommodation*. Prepared even on the night of his marriage to "undertake / These present wars against the Ottomites," he says,

> I crave fit disposition for my wife,
> Due reference of place and exhibition,
> With such *accommodation and besort*
> As levels with her breeding.
> (1.3.237–40)

"Besort" means "suitable company," according to the *OED*—i.e., attendants. The word apparently does not occur outside Shakespeare, and he uses it only once elsewhere, as a verb. But the *OED* definition seems based on reasonable inferences from the meanings of *assort* and *consort*. It would be logical, then, to expect *accommodation* to have the modern suggestion of *lodging*, and the *OED* encourages this interpretation by citing the line to illustrate the sense "Room and suitable provision for the reception of people; entertainment; lodgings." But this is the earliest use cited for this meaning; the next is in 1650, and the earliest for the verb *accommodate* with a similar meaning is 1715. It is much more likely that Shakespeare is here using *accommodation* in that more general sense in which the *OED* quotes him and Ben Jonson as using *accommodate* in 1597 and 1598: "To furnish (a person with . . . something requisite or convenient); to equip, supply, provide." In this reading the two words *accommodation* and *besort* are not parallel but an ordinary instance of hendiadys: "with such provision of attendants" for my wife "As levels with her breeding."

4. To illustrate its definition of *sufferance* as "Damage, injury," the *OED* cites the phrase *wrack and sufferance* from *Othello* (2.1.23) and gives no other source for this meaning before 1823. Once we recognize the presence of hendiadys, the phrase can be more plausibly understood to mean "the wrack suffered by the most part of their fleet."

5. Another example is *paragons* in the lines "He hath achieved a maid / That paragons *description and wild fame*" (*Othello* 2.1.62). The *OED* reads *paragons* as meaning "To excel, surpass"; as far as it knows, the word is

Hendiadys and *Hamlet* 41

never again used in this sense by anyone. But the normal meaning of *paragon* as a verb is "To place side by side; to parallel, compare" or "To match, to mate." These meanings make perfectly good sense if we see that the phrase that follows is hendiadys: a maid who matches *the* (extravagant) *descriptions given by wild rumor.*

6. The *OED* tells us that only in Shakespeare does *motive* mean "A moving limb or organ" and cites two references. In the first, from *Richard II,* the context makes clear that *motive* does, in fact, refer to the speaker's tongue: "my teeth shall tear / The slavish motive of recanting fear" (1.1.192–93). But the term can still be taken here in the more general sense given by the OED as "A moving or inciting cause." The second reference is to *Troilus and Cressida.* Ulysses, speaking of Cressida, says, "her wanton spirits look out / At every *joint and motive* of her body" (4.5.57). This phrase seems to be hendiadys: at every joint and moving cause or element of her body. The sense suggests that Cressida is very sexy when she moves, and the joints and moving are essentially one operation. (Cf. Hamlet's "In *form and moving* how express and admirable," and the discussion of the line in n. 20.)

7. To support one obsolete definition of *vail* as "The going down or setting of the sun," the *OED* cites only the eloquent lines with which Achilles introduces his murderous attack on Hector in *Troilus and Cressida:*

> Look, Hector, how the sun begins to set.
> How ugly night comes breathing at his heels.
> Even with the *vail and darking* of the sun
> To close the day up, Hector's life is done
> (5.8.5–8)

But the use of the word here—which though powerful, is not, I think, an instance of hendiadys—is obviously connected with some meanings of the archaic verb *vail,* especially "To lower (a weapon, banner, etc.); to cause to allow to descend or sink." The phrase must mean "Even with the lowering and darkening of the sun." The sun is darker *because* lower, but it does not violate our idioms or our ordinary sense of things to speak of the two actions in succession. In both this example and the previous one, the *OED* has attributed a much too specific meaning ("tongue," "of the sun") to a general term ("motive," "vail"), as, in one way or another, it probably does for all the other words for which I cite *OED* definitions in this appendix.

8. The OED cites only Claudius's lines "And gave you such a masterly report / For *art and exercise* in your defence" (4.7.97–98) to illustrate mean-

ing *6b* of *exercise:* "Acquired skill. *Obs.*" This definition was apparently invented to make *exercise* parallel to (and virtually synonymous with) *art.* But Hardin Craig implies that the phrase is hendiadys when he glosses it "skillful exercise." Meaning 3 will cover the ground: "The practice (of virtues and vices); the habitual carrying out (of any particular kind of conduct); . . . the execution of (functions)." To exercise is to use, and Claudius is praising Laertes for exercising the art of self-defense, for being so skillful *(art)* a practitioner *(exercise)* of it. Troilus uses the words similarly in his fearful survey of the charms of "Grecian youths," who are "flowing o'er with *arts and exercise*" (*Troilus and Cressida* 4.4.80). It is not that they excel in theory and practice as some editors haplessly suggest, but that they perform with skill. (The Folio reading is "Flawing and swelling o'er with arts and exercise." To substitute "theory and practice" for the last three words makes the line sound foolish.)

9. The passage the *OED* cites as its only illustration of meaning *6b* of *exception*—"Dislike, dissatisfaction. *Obs. rare*"—is Hamlet's conciliatory speech to Laertes before their duel:

> What I have done
> That might your *nature, honor, and exception*
> Roughly awake, I here proclaim was madness
> (5.2.241–43)

Editors variously gloss *exception* as "disapproval" (Craig, Signet), "resentment" (Harrison), "distaste" (Rylands), and "objection, resentment" (Kittredge). Their difficulty is understandable; but that *exception* is clearly not a third term parallel to *nature* and *honor* even Laertes acknowledges in his response. He declares himself "satisfied in nature" but not "in my terms of honor"; he does not mention exception but treats it implicitly as a general term relating to the other two. Hamlet evidently means that Laertes' nature and honor (two distinct things) might take exception, might object, might become aroused and resentful.

10. In a scene from *Henry VIII* that is usually attributed to Shakespeare, the Lord Chamberlain, speaking of Wolsey's devious activities, says, "The King in this perceives him how he *coasts / And hedges* his own way" (3.2.38–39). The italicized phrase is probably not hendiadys, for the two words describe different but comparable modes of movement, the cautious sailing close to a coastline (*OED* meaning 4, of which this would be a figurative instance) and the running along behind a hedge, in the *OED* sense of "To go aside from the straight way" (cf. Ulysses' "Or hedge aside from the direct

forthright" [*Troilus and Cressida* 3.3.158]), "to shift, shuffle, dodge. . . ." Quite unnecessarily, the *OED* offers a special meaning of *coast* to accommodate this one passage: "To move in a roundabout course, proceed circuitously." The editors evidently wanted to give *coasts* a definition that includes the deviousness implicit in *hedges*.

The Lyric Tense
Simple Present Verbs in English Poems

Distinctions between the English simple present and progressive forms have long intrigued and perplexed students of language.[1] The relations between these speech forms are complex, inconstant, peculiar to English, and difficult to formulate. No wonder, then, that linguists have almost entirely limited their interest in these forms to their occurrence in speech. When they cite poems or prose writing, they do so with a certain discomfort, because no one has any precise idea of the relation, in any remote age, between the language of poems and the language of ordinary talk. We may sense here and there in speakers a reluctance to use certain forms in polite discourse, or in the elevated regions of verse, but we can only guess at the degrees or kinds of pressure writers have felt to use or not to use one form or another.

It is understandable, then, that almost no one has written about the incidence of progressive and simple present forms in English verse. In modest numbers these forms have sometimes been counted, either as part of a study of the language of a certain writer or of an era, or as offering evidence for the unquestioned historical increase in the use of the periphrastic verb forms in English speech from medieval to modern times.[2] But hardly any interest has been taken, by linguists or critics, in the distinctive ways in which poets use progressive and simple English verbs. Yet the practice of poets on this point is extremely curious and revealing.

I

"I walk through the long schoolroom questioning." Reading that first line of Yeats's "Among School Children," we admire it as simple, ordinary, natural English. It reports an event that has happened—is happening—happens. Such a confusion in our own verbs may show us that Yeats's, after all, is not so speechlike as it first seems. We accept "I walk" as a normal poetic locution not because it is normal speech but because other poets have used such verbs as Yeats does. In fact, they are a familiar staple of poetic practice, appearing in Blake's "I *wander* thro' each charter'd street," in Shelley's "I *fall* upon the thorns of life! I *bleed!*" or "I *die!* I f*aint!* I *fail!*" as in Keats's "Darkling I *listen*" and in Auden's "I *sit* in one of the dives / On Fifty-second Street." But widely as the form occurs in poetry, it is nevertheless notably unspeechlike.

For in spoken English, although we still often use the form *I walk,* we use it infrequently as an independent verb and almost never without some temporal or conditional or even metaphysical qualifier, explicit or understood, which provides the action verb with some dimensional context. (Not *I walk in the park,* but *Every morning I walk in the park.*) Oddly enough, the time of simple present action verbs is almost never simply present. The action described may be habitual *(I walk nights),* future *(I walk there tomorrow),* conditional *(If I walk six miles in two hours),* true in general *(I walk on my hind legs),* or ceremonial *(I walk about this town where I was born),* yet in all such examples the action described need not be taking place at this moment. Mental, factual, or abstract verbs *(see, know, contain, consist of, appear, possess)* are different: they normally define or frame a reality whose design includes but is not exhausted by the present moment, and they take progressive forms only when there is some suggestion of a physical (or kinesthetic, or sometimes just intensely personal) ingredient in their meaning *(I am seeing whether I can fix this leak).* Even then the form they take may seem faintly contorted: *I am loving this concert; This issue is mattering to me more than I expected.* Verbs denoting unrepeated physical or partly physical actions taking place now—*walk, fall; listen, watch*—normally take the progressive form in the present tense: *I am walking, I am falling, I am listening.*

As a rule, then, physical events take the form of process, mental events or facts the form of definition. Knowing how fragile and changeable our consciousnesses are, how comparatively solid and definite a physical action is, we might expect exactly the opposite pattern. Yet our speech emphasizes the authority of our senses, feelings, and thoughts; for everything else that we do, it tends to deny accountability beyond the passing moment. For implicit in the progressive form, at least when it is used as exclusively as we use it to report ongoing actions, is a doubt or a carelessness as to the significance of all but the present time period. What is transpiring now—that is what matters. Historically, then, the sense of action as permanent or true, a sense traditionally implicit in the English simple present form, has yielded ground to the sense of present action as immediate but momentary. In the last analysis, the extensive displacement in speech of the simple present by the progressive present—of truth by data, of authority by experience—reflects the history of Western sensibility.

II

In poetry, however, the situation is less clear-cut. If in speech the progressive form has for many centuries gradually displaced the simple present from uses still reserved for it in many European languages (where *je vais, je marche, ich gehe, vô, vado, cammino* may describe an event of the moment), in verse something different has happened. In the first place, progressive forms have not increased gradually in English poetry; they have, indeed, increased, but only by fits and starts and with occasional surprising backings-up. A survey of 326,000 lines by some fifty-nine British and American poets shows that the ratio of progressive verbs to lines of verse increases from Chaucer to the Renaissance (whose poets vary remarkably in their willingness to use progressives), then diminishes consistently through the seventeenth and early eighteenth centuries, revives somewhat in Cowper, more in Blake, increases substantially in the Romantics, remains at a steady high figure through the nineteenth century, wavers oddly in the first, the great, generation of modern poets, then rises to an unprecedented high among contemporary poets. A table showing the results of this survey, with a discussion of their significance, is appended to this essay. For our immediate argument, what the survey suggests most strongly is that, in choosing their locutions for use in poems, poets are guided only partly by what is available in contemporary speech but more powerfully by what in that speech serves their expressive purposes.

The Lyric Tense 47

Furthermore, despite the extensive incursions of the progressive in poetic as in ordinary speech, the simple present form has continued to be used widely, not merely on all those occasions when neither the progressive nor any other locution provides a plausible alternative, but on many occasions when the progressive might reasonably have been preferred. Vague as it is, poets evidently feel this unlocated "tense" to be significantly expressive. They use it not merely for economy, nor from the desire to avoid a cacophonous sequence of progressive forms. Progressive forms, after all, may be dramatically powerful, as in Swinburne's evocation of the hushed evening, "The light *is listening*" ("A Vision of Spring in Winter") or in Iago's lines intended to place vividly before Brabantio's eyes the present plight of his daughter:

> Even now, now, very now, an old black ram
> *Is tupping* your white ewe.
> (*Othello*, 1.1.87–88)

Modern poets especially have found many effective uses for progressive verbs, but the simple present has remained central in poems, apparently because it carries meanings and overtones that have come to be important to poets. The rest of this essay will try to describe these meanings and overtones and to suggest that from one period to another of poetry in English they may have altered somewhat in character and function.

III

In studying the continued dominance of the simple present in poetic language, we should keep in mind the limits of the discussion. In the first place, a great many poems in English are fixed in other times, past or future, or in other moods, imperative or conditional. Even when the present is in evidence, if a simple present form is used in poetry just as it would be used in speech, its poetic occurrence is, for our purposes, irrelevant. Many simple form verbs in poems are mental verbs—*I think, I see, I consider*—and naturally take, in poems as in speech, the simple present form. Many simple present verbs *are* located temporally, conditionally, or otherwise ("Whenas in silks my Julia *goes*") and would sound perfectly normal even in contemporary speech. Many poetic verbs describe actions that are recurrent, typical, characteristic ("Brightness *falls* from the air"). But the center of our discussion must be those simple present verbs that apparently describe a physical action perhaps repeatable but taking place only once as far as we can judge from the evidence before us: *I sit* in one of the dives, Darkling *I listen, I walk* through the long schoolroom questioning.

To account for the use of such verbs by poets who would not have found it natural to use them so in speech, it may be suggested that in such lines the ostensibly present activity (of walking, listening, or sitting) borrows meaning (directly or by contrast) from all the contexts, all the familiar occasions, on which we use the simple present in speech, or on which earlier poets have used it in poems. It borrows, no doubt, from the historical present, from our experience of present verbs used to describe a past action; we catch, therefore, in Yeats's or Keats's lines a sense *as of* past action—not that the poet ever tells us that the event is a past one, but that in some obscure way we feel it as *pastlike,* though not exactly past. Similarly, the present verb in such contexts borrows from the context of repeated action: we feel in an introductory *I walk* or *I sit* or *I stand* a solidity, a portentousness, a freedom from singleness. If, in the absence of those markers that would signal habitual action—*sometimes, often, every morning*—we do not feel the action as one that is regularly performed, neither does it seem an action performed just once. It is too definitely there, not only in the sense that it can be returned to again and again but in the sense that it remains, it abides.

But in such verbs the habitual context normal in speech works on us primarily by its absence. Those lines that most clearly define the practice I am describing appear to withhold deliberately any definite information about the time level of the action. Such signals as *yesterday, three years ago,* or *this morning* do not occur in these poems—naturally enough, for they would seem to make obligatory the use of the past tense rather than the present. But neither does the poet usually say *now,* and even when he does ("*Now* on this spot *I stand* with my robust soul") we have no precise idea of when "now" is. We know of "now" only that it is the space of time (anything from a moment to an eternity) during which "I stand." What appears to be true in many poems is that the simple present verb at the beginning of a poem or a passage, instead of being located by a time word or phrase, itself serves, along with descriptive imagery, to locate the action. But not in time!

By using the simple present without specifying the time of the action, the poet locates it in a realm outside our normal conscious time world, where every event must be assigned a more precise temporality. In speech such vagueness is hardly possible, for even when we are far from clocks, our eyes (or other senses) give us some awareness of the time of day and the season of the year; and, except during periods when our speech patterns are likely to be as distorted as our sense of time (in trances, under drugs, half asleep, or drunk), we always know that time, measured or unmeasured, is passing. Present events, therefore, are always located for us, at least by implication, and our speech reflects our knowledge of when we are. Even when in speech we use the historical present, we use it only when the level of past time has already been established clearly by past tense verbs or adverbial constructions. But in poetry, as even more in film, we often do not know at all when the events are supposed to have taken or to be taking place. The actions described seem suspended, removed from the successiveness of our ordinary time levels, neither past, present, nor future, neither single nor repeated, but of a different dimension entirely.

Thus, such cries as Shelley's "I *fall* upon the thorns of life! I *bleed!*" or even Marvell's much earlier "Ensnared with flowers, I *fall* on grass" function basically as imitations of ordinary speech that stop short of exact reproduction. If either poet had added the word *often* to his line, the situations would have been strikingly different: I *often fall* upon the thorns of life; Ensnared with flowers, I *often fall* on grass. Once the note of habitual action is struck, the peculiar quality I am trying to account for is lost. The action is no longer temporally anomalous, no longer in a dimension of its own but in one of the familiar dimensions of everyday life and speech. To put it in linguistic terms, it has often been noted that the simple present is an unmarked tense, as opposed to past tenses (marked with *-ed* most often). In the poetic phrases I speak of here, not only is the present verb itself unmarked by morphological markers as in speech; it is unmarked by syntactical or contextual signals as well, which can hardly ever happen with action verbs in speech. In effect, therefore, what we find in such verbs is a new aspect or tense, neither past nor present but timeless—in its feeling a lyric tense.

If we do not know when the action is taking place, however, we still feel that it takes time. In speech the simple present, in time clauses introduced by *when, as, while, after,* often describes an activity somewhat prolonged *(As I walk down the street, I think of you)*. Meeting *I walk* apart from such conjunctions, we fill in where we can, which is to say that we catch a hint of this prolongation. Because what goes on in the poem is characteristically a meditation of the poet, it is fitting that the verbs denoting the poet's physical activity should be prolonged, for the physical action frames the mental action just as the subordinate verb in sentences like *As long as I walk, I feel calm* frames the main verb. The poet's presentation, his pageant, profits from the sense we have of prolongation; he makes us feel that the interlude taking place is not only timeless but somehow enduring; it is outside of time but it has duration—a very special state but common to all art. The statements made in the lyric tense may not occur more than once, but they keep occurring. Yeats in his schoolroom does not walk *again* when we reread the poem; rather, when we return to the poem we find him *still* walking, Whitman *still* standing, Keats *still* listening in the dark.

Similarly, this lyric tense often has a hint in it of futurity, a rudimentary memory perhaps of the futurity suggested in ordinary sentences like *Tomorrow I go home*. The hint is at best slight and fragile; in many lyric tense verbs it is not present, but it gives to some verbs in some poems a feeling of being on the verge of something to come. This sense seems present, vaguely, in Yeats's line, "*I walk* through the long schoolroom questioning," in Hopkins's "*I wake* and feel the fell of dark, not day," and in Blake's "*I wander* thro' each charter'd street." True, these are opening lines, and we inevitably expect more. But lyric tense is often used to open poems, the progressive rarely. For the lyric tense conveys a portentousness that is absent from the progressive. If Yeats had written, "*I am walking* through the schoolroom questioning," we would not, as we do on hearing the line he *did* write, lean forward mentally in anticipation of the coming action.

Even when lyric tense occurs later in the poem, it often conveys a quality ordinarily absent from the progressive, a sense of longing, of yearning, of straining, as it were, for the next moment. This is especially to be felt in first-person examples, such as this passage of Swinburne:

> I *reach* my heart out toward the springtime lands,
>   I *stretch* my spirit forth to the fair hours,
>   The purplest of the prime;
>   I *lean* my soul down over them, with hands
>   Made wide to take the ghostly growths of flowers;
>   I *send* my love back to the lovely time.
>   ("A Vision of Spring in Winter")

The poet here may look back, but the verbs press forward. Again the feeling achieved is highly lyrical, far more so than if progressive forms had been used.

Another context from which the lyric tense borrows is the conditional context defined by the subordinating conjunction *if*. The action described in a lyric poem is tentative, provisional. We do not usually call it fictional, but we still feel it to be the product of design, of conscious contrivance. The lyrical mode, like that of drama or fiction, is hypothetical and experimental: like the scientist, the lyric poet offers us a situation *(I sit in one of the dives, I walk through the long schoolroom, The curfew tolls the knell of part-*

ing day) and then proceeds to place in this frame his formulation of events. Like the scientific experiment, the poem is repeatable;[3] it is also nonhistorical, in the sense that the scientific experiment is nonhistorical. This is why we use the present tense to describe events in literary works: they go on again and again. Response to the poem varies, taste in poems changes, interpretations multiply; but the experience of tenses, of word meanings, of the general sequence of events, of what in the broadest sense *happens,* changes no more than a scientific experiment that, when looked at in the light of later theory, may seem to have meanings very different from when it was first performed.

Why then does the scientist typically use the past tense to describe his experiment while the poet frequently uses the present? Because the scientist must be cautious, discreet, careful not to claim more than the events warrant. Therefore, he says something like: "On this occasion the substance turned brown." Poets, too, often describe their occasions in past tenses. But their lavish use of present tenses as well suggests a willingness to generalize from the beginning. Where the scientist permits himself to frame general propositions only at the conclusion of his descriptions of events, the poet's discipline permits him to use the language of generalization throughout. Both poet and scientist mean to make their proposals persuasive, but the procedures governing their presentations are different—the poet's figurative, the scientist's logical. They both make claims, both aim at conviction; the poem, like the scientific paper, stirs in the reader the same mixture of tentative assent and skepticism with which we normally greet such claims and resist conviction.

If lyric tense echoes the hypothetical suppositions of scientific language, it echoes also the general statements of science and other branches of knowledge. We do say of *objects,* of *entities,* that they *stand, sit, lie:* the river *runs* south; the land *falls* away to the left; the cliff *drops* straight down. When there is a hint of this third-person usage in the lyric first-person verb, it contributes to a feeling of detachment and impersonality. To some degree the poet seems to be looking at his own "I," to be observing its actions as he would observe the reticulations of a landscape, from a point of view at once dispassionate and involved. Again this feeling is strongest in lines that open poems—in Yeats's "I walk through the long schoolroom," for example—perhaps because the verb is there employed to fix the setting and so conveys some of the same feeling as a landscape description.

A much more striking echo of this kind of generalization is to be heard sometimes when poets use lyric tense to describe persons other than the "I."

On such occasions the persons described may acquire a strangely monumental character, as if, like landscape, they were there forever, conditions of life:

> The pure contralto *sings* in the organ loft . . .
> (Whitman, "Song of Myself")

> She *turns* and *looks* a moment in the glass,
> Hardly aware of her departed lover.
> (Eliot, *The Waste Land*, ll. 249–50)

Indeed, this usage is an aspect of the generalizing function of action verbs. We say that a proposition *holds:* the earth *revolves* around the sun. Struck by this usage, grammarians usually contend that the distinction between the simple present and the progressive present "is not a time-distinction" at all. "The basic meaning of the simple present tense is the constitution of things, logical, physical, psychological, essential, etc.; of the present progressive, mere occurrence" (Calver, 317). In effect, the simple present is the tense of "the truth." Nashe tells us: *Strength stoops unto the grave.* It is true: strength may not be stooping at this moment, but it customarily, regularly does so. A temporal pattern is implied, or perhaps the *if* that lurks behind generalizations: *If* strength (exists), then it stoops. When Yeats says, "*I walk* through the long schoolroom questioning," do we not catch some hint of the flavor of the general proposition? In addition to all its other shades of meaning, *I walk* proposes itself to us not merely as a personal report but as a broad truth; there is at least a shadow of an eternal condition: the schoolroom is the world, and Yeats walks through it forever. We find the same shadow in Keats's majestic ending of "To Autumn," where the time word *then* introduces, as we expect, simple present verbs that imply habitual action *(mourn, bleat, sing);* but when the verbs that follow *now* keep to the simple present *(whistles, twitter)* in resistance to our expectation of a present progressive to describe what is going on at the moment, we feel that these actions, and the present moment itself, have been drawn into the realm of permanence and eternity:

> *Then* in a wailful choir the small gnats *mourn*
>   Among the river sallows, borne aloft
>   Or sinking as the light wind lives or dies;
> And full-grown lambs loud *bleat* from hilly bourn;
>   Hedge-crickets *sing;* and *now* with treble soft
>   The red-breast *whistles* from a garden croft;
>   And gathering swallows *twitter* in the sky.

The Lyric Tense 53

In such lines as these the difference between the progressive and the simple present seems most crucial—perhaps because it is so delicate. The distinction of meaning between these two forms is, after all, often very slight; for just this reason one of them could come to displace the other. Both forms, for example, may express futurity: *I go there tomorrow; I am going there tomorrow.* Both may imply regular, habitual activity: *Every day he comes* (or *is coming* or *has been coming*) to see me. Both may be used in conditional contexts: *If I walk* (or *am walking*) *in the right direction.* And both may describe prolonged activities: *As long as I walk* (or *am walking*), I feel calm.

But the emphasis is always faintly different, according to whether the progressive or the simple present is used. A poet who makes a choice between two such phrases as "The years *are rolling on*" and "The years *roll on*" probably makes it mainly on the basis of emphasis. The progressive describes an action of which the most immediately significant characteristic is that it is happening "now," and usually the context does not suggest, as does that of the simple present, that the action is frequently performed or is eternally true. The assumed adverb for the simple present is *generally, typically, regularly,* or *always:* The years roll on *always;* Brightness falls from the air *regularly.* The progressive's adverb is *now* or *nowadays* or *lately.*

The simple present thus *may* describe an action that is happening now, but the emphasis rests on some larger temporal pattern; the progressive, exactly contrary, *may* describe an action that is part of some larger temporal pattern, but the emphasis rests on its taking place *now.* This may account for our retaining the simple present for mental verbs, for they seem to describe *potentialities that are constant* rather than mental *events: I remember, I believe, I understand.* Even *I think now* or *Now I remember* presumably describes conditions that will endure from "now" on. In the same way, reports of sensory experience usually imply the possession of permanent capabilities. *I hear the bell* implies that we expect to go on hearing it, as long as it is ringing; we expect to because we *can* hear. *I am listening to the bell,* on the other hand, emphasizes the immediate activity and suggests nothing about continuing capacity; it assumes, presupposes capacity, but makes no prediction about its continuance. Frequently, in fact, one is obliged to say: *I am listening but hear nothing; I am looking but see nothing.* The following columns perhaps make clearer the difference between the way our speech treats ongoing sensory or intellectual activities (A) and the way it treats capabilities that are being exercised at the moment (B):

A	B
I am watching the road	I see the road
I am listening to the bell	I hear the bell
I am touching the wall	I feel the wall
I am sniffing the air	I smell a rat
I am tasting the wine	This wine tastes sour
I am thinking about your beauty	I think you are beautiful

It may be suggested that the sentences in column A are particulars that move in the direction of the general; those in column B are generalities that include particulars. In any case, the simple present gives a feeling of permanence, of general validity, so that when it occurs in verbs of physical action *(I walk, I fall)*, there is often a kind of elevation that we feel in its use, again a lyrical quality. The physical action seems to have been transfigured into a permanent process; ceasing to be action, it becomes sensation, vision. And it is true that in a great many poems of the last two centuries the poet's announcing an action of his own at the beginning of his poem is a signal by which we understand that he is about to show us his vision. By using the simple present form of the physical action verb, the poet anticipates the visionary substance of his poem; the visionary feeling casts its shadow back, as it were, on the physical action that introduces the vision. Or else the action itself touches off, activates, the vision. Thus Blake's "I *wander* thro' each charter'd street," Shelley's "I *arise* from dreams of thee," Auden's "Now from my window-sill I *watch* the night," and a host of other first lines. Third-person examples, often equally visionary, also abound, from Pound's "See, they *return*" to Plath's "The Sunday lamb *cracks* in its fat."

Whether lyric tense verbs come early or late in poems, they characteristically convey a sense of elevation and, often, of solemnity that seems appropriate to visionary experience. Because vision and ritual are closely connected, lyric tense borrows, too, from the ceremonious present. Whitman's announcement,

> Here, coffin that slowly passes,
> I *give* you my sprig of lilac,
> ("When Lilacs Last in the Dooryard Bloom'd")

has its counterpart in ordinary elegiac utterance and in other sorts of ritual descriptions, from the sportscaster present ("Smith *takes* the ball, *rolls* to his right . . .") to the self-descriptions of the laboratory professor ("I *pour* the liquid . . . I *turn up* the flame") or the magician ("I *shuffle* the cards"). In all such cases, we feel that the action announced constitutes an occasion, and the speaker's verb declares the public character of the action described. When *poets* use the tense, therefore, to describe what they or others are doing, these actions acquire a faintly or strongly ceremonial character. This is especially true in first-person examples, where the poet, in announcing his ceremonial actions, seems at times to be playing a priestlike role, as in fact he is often very close to doing in elegiac poems, early and late:

> I *come* to pluck your berries, harsh and crude
> (Milton, "Lycidas")

> I *sing* of brooks, of blossoms, birds, and bowers
> (Herrick, "The Argument of His Book")

> I *sound* my barbaric yawp over the roofs of the world.
> (Whitman, "Song of Myself")

> I *renounce* the blindness of the magazines.
> (James Wright, "A Prayer to Escape from the Market Place")

> I *offers* you this handkerchief
> (John Berryman, Dream Song 76: "Henry's Confession")

In "I *walk* through the long schoolroom," too, there is something of this priestlike manner, Yeats projecting an image of the self into the role of symbolic hero, actor, celebrant.

This ceremonious feeling is reinforced by our sense that the modern or Romantic poet's typical use of the simple present to describe ongoing actions is, again in part, an unconscious archaism. It recalls earlier times when speakers could use the tense regularly to describe immediate action, when Horatio and Marcellus could say of the ghost of Hamlet's father, in a tense that must then have been normal in speech, as now it is not: "Look, my lord, it *comes*. . . . It *beckons* you to go away with it. . . . It *waves* you to a more removèd ground." But even more sharply than ancient speakers, whose practice we can only infer, the use of lyric tense recalls older poets (and foreign poets, too) who commonly used the simple present to report ongoing events. When Stephen Dedalus writes, "I *go* to encounter for the millionth time the reality of experience," the verb form he chooses has a theatrical ring and shows that, whatever his capacities at this point in his career, he is still viewing his life in the light of literary or epic models, as well as still watching himself as one watches a landscape, projecting himself as a ceremonial hero and proposing his departure as an action of rather monumental significance.

Later poets unquestionably have used lyric tense partly in echo of earlier ones. Even the most primitive of contemporary poets, if they follow the tradition of poetry in English at all, must have ringing in their ears, however distantly, the rhythms, tones, and constructions of earlier poets. If the development of their own gifts modifies what they inherit, they must nevertheless retain many traditional poetic practices. In the last century or so, the attention of poets and their innovative impulses have been directed toward many matters of diction, imagery, rhythm, symbolic technique, and point of view, and it is understandable that in what seems so relatively minor a matter as that of the choice between two present verb forms they should follow without much anguish the practice of their predecessors. In fact, contemporary poets have found lyric tense so congenial that, if anything, they use it more intensively than any generation before them. They probably do so in part because the simple present has acquired an augmented expressiveness in verse, an air of archaism, from the very fact of the progressive's being more and more widely used in speech.

Lyric action, then, insofar as it is defined by these unspeechlike present tense verbs, is timeless yet permanent, pastlike yet edging toward the future, repeatable yet provisional, urgent yet distant, ceremonious and archaic. Deliberately bypassing all the modifiers that normal speech requires, the lyric present appears to offer as actual, conditions that we normally accept only as possible, special, figurative, provisional. Furthermore, because only mental or abstract present events are ordinarily described in this tense without the usual qualifiers, the use of action verbs in the same tense without qualifiers gives a mental (or abstract) feeling to these verbs, too. The actions described seem filtered through imagination or memory, or performed under a spell; each scene takes on a visionary quality. No matter how directly the poet speaks, how ordinary his diction, his use of lyric tense declares his poem a poetic occasion, the kind of occasion on which the poet stands, as it were, between two worlds, between the actual and the provisional (the possible, the imagined, the miraculous, the transcendent), looking back into the literal reality we inhabit together, but seeing its literal features joined together in a new pattern that is full of import and does not occur in actual life.

IV

It frequently happens that simple present verbs occur in sequences and may at first seem to have hardly more lyrical quality than the stage directions of a play, which usually take the same verb form. When Cowper writes,

> I *twirl* my thumbs, *fall* back into my chair,
> *Fix* on the wainscot a distressful stare,
> And, when I hope his blunders are all out,
> *Reply* discreetly
>   ("Conversation," ll. 115–18)

we feel that he is simply marking off successive segments of a whole action.[4] Yeats's "I *walk* ... A ... nun ... *replies*," similarly sets the stage for the ambulatory meditation that follows. Can we not, therefore, read it more matter-of-factly, as a simple variation on "Enter Yeats"?

Probably not. Once in the poem, the description or direction can never recover its status as a simple signal. As it happens, even stage directions are characteristically cast in the simple present for reasons not unrelated to those that account for the use of lyric tense. Elizabethan stage directions, for example, take a variety of verb forms, and it was only after a considerable competition with hortative, anomalous, participial, and specially past and imperative forms[5] that the simple present, no doubt because of its suggestion of permanent availability, became the standard tense for the stage direction. Indeed, some early stage directions exhibit a certain expressiveness in the simple present: "Here he *kisseth* Diccon's breach" *(Gammer Gurton's Needle)* or "Then he *breaks* Michael's head" *(Arden of Feversham)*—an expressiveness that in *The Spanish Tragedy* achieves a sinister lyricism: "He *whispereth* in her ear," "He *diggeth* with his dagger."

In short, the stage direction may be augmented into expressiveness, but the simple verb of a poem can hardly be diminished to a mere signal. Action verbs cast in the simple present will almost always have some of the suggestive powers I have been describing. These powers seem especially present when a first-person speaker describes his physical actions, and they seem, both in first- and third-person uses, to have acquired unprecedented strength in the last two hundred years. In that period, as I have been suggesting, the simple present action verb in poems, far from describing a present action, more typically denotes an action envisioned, frozen, enchanted, recaptured, and its use, in even the most ironic, the least sentimental poem, confers on the poem a touch of the sublime.

This sublimity, this sense of enchantment, seems to me essentially a quality of the lyric poem, or of passages we call lyric when they occur in other kinds of writing, and for this reason the term "lyric tense" seems to fit this poetic use of the simple present. Most authorities define lyric by reference to its subject (the poet's feelings) or its forms (sonnets, odes, songs), but whatever restrictions these modes of definition place on the lyric, we should remember what is at least equally important about the lyric poem—that it turns on our experience a perspective that is different from that of ordinary life. It is more than a mere commentary on the poet's subject through the medium of a particular conventional form; it is a new light on the experience of human beings in a world full of feelings and troubles. And the only way to ensure that the light will be new is by removing it from ordinary reality, estranging the poem in just the right way from the world it refers to. In this process, in establishing the lyric stance (still, to be sure, no guarantee of the poem's value), the lyric present tense frequently plays a significant role.

It must be recognized that other verb forms used in lyric poems share this disembodied air, this feeling of enchantment or estrangement. The past of poems is almost as shifty a time level as the present, and past tense poems typically neglect, as speech cannot, to fix the time of the action with reasonable precision. "St. Agnes' Eve! Ah, bitter chill it was!" St. Agnes' Eve, yes, but what year, what century? We have the appearance of that precision with which we fix dates in ordinary life, but here the precision is illusory, a precision as to the time of year but not as to the year's position among other years. The effect is gothic perhaps: we are furnished with the inner details, as of a house, a castle, or a soul, but where in the world it is remains obscure.

In many simple lyrics the past is similarly unlocated, and we consequently feel something of the same disjunction that we meet in the lyric simple present. There is a different tone but a similar feeling of elevation that derives from temporal anomalousness in Blake's "I *wander* thro' each charter'd street" and Wordsworth's "I *wandered* lonely as a cloud." In ordinary speech and writing, after all, we expect to be told when every event in the simple past has taken place; as with the simple present, we require some temporal qualifier like "yesterday" or "last year." Once the time has been established, of course, our sentences can carry on without additional adverbial markers: "Yesterday I *wandered* (or, more likely, *was wandering*) . . . when I *saw* . . . daffodils . . . The waves *danced,* but they *outdid* . . . I *gazed* and *gazed.*" But we need that first adverb, and Wordsworth, like other lyric poets, declines to give it to us. Not that he *chooses* to withhold it; it is simply traditional lyric practice to omit it.[6]

Other verb forms, too, are used in poems as we do not use them in speech—notably, imperative forms, whose poetic functions deserve extended analysis. Why, then, does it seem appropriate to speak of the present tense only, and only of that tense's simple form, as lyric? In describing that form as lyric, am I not just describing what is poetic about poetry? In part, this is true, and this essay might go on to discuss dozens of other unspeech-like devices—of structure, imagery, and tone—that lyric poems use to capture that quality of estrangement that is part of the lyrical feeling. Just which devices do most to establish the lyric as lyric will vary from poem to poem. But, in general, the crucial lyric *verb* is the simple present because, although pasts and imperatives may be unlocated, the reverberations set up by their nonlocation are less extensive and profound than those set up by the nonlocation of simple present verbs.

This is true, I think, for several reasons. First, the simple present serves many more and more subtle and varied purposes in speech than imperatives, pasts, and even progressives serve, and the possible overtones set up by its unqualified use in lyrics are far richer and more complex. Furthermore, present and past verbs of action relate in entirely different ways to our ordinary life. Past action (or future), because it is not physically before us, needs to be *put* there; past verbs describe, recount, inform; they tell what happened, who was there, what it looked like. Present verbs of action are more mysterious, for in speech there is no point in such description; anyone present can see for himself. If some Horatio says to us,

> But look, the morn, in russet mantle clad,
> *Walks* o'er the dew of yon high eastward hill,
> (*Hamlet* 1.1.166–67)

we reply impatiently, "I see it, I see it!" The exception occurs when what is going on is not clear to the eye, when not mere information but *explanation* is needed. Past and future verbs give information; present verbs give meaning. And we feel this meaningful dimension as part of the ordinary signification of present tense verbs.

Another related consideration is that the present unlocated physical action proposed by "lyric tense" is a virtual contradiction in terms: how can action be physical and yet unlocated? *Past* unlocated physical action is unusual, but, after all, memory—the normal channel of all past events—is also phantasmal, not physically before us. Hence the poetic past and the actual past are carved out of the same psychic material, as the poetic present and the actual present are not. The joining together of these two presents, familiar as it is to all of us from long practice in reading poems, is an extraordinarily paradoxical event and one that lies at the root of consciousness, intelligence, sympathy, and art. Of all these processes the simple present verb is a paradigm.

V

The kind of feeling that seems to me resident in the present tense of poems has occasionally been glanced at in the work of poets and critics but hardly ever looked at closely. The only extended discussion I know is Susanne K. Langer's chapter on literature in *Feeling and Form*.[7] Seeing literature as "virtual memory," Langer is concerned to explain why it uses the *present* tense so often to create a "virtual past." The answer is that the present is "the tense of timelessness" (267), especially appropriate to lyric poetry:

> The whole creation in a lyric is an awareness of a subjective experience, and *the tense of subjectivity is the "timeless" present*. This kind of poetry has the "closed" character of the mnemonic mode, without the historical fixity that outward events bestow on real memories. . . . Lyric writing is a specialized technique that constructs an impression or an idea as something experienced, in a sort of eternal present . . . the lyric poet creates a sense of concrete reality from which the time element has been canceled out, leaving a platonic sense of "eternity." (268; Langer's italics)

Although my account of lyric tense is fuller and more involved—helpfully, I hope—than Langer's, her insight into the function of the present in lyric and perhaps in all poetry seems to me very accurate. The device of lyric tense ushers us into a world of fiction, a world of "virtual experience," whose values and relations are largely set before us by truth-telling simple present verbs. Like other poetic devices that make poems different from speech—elaborate images and figures, complex metrical or stanzaic structures, descriptions of immediate scenes, intricate conventions of address or sequence, all those devices that contribute to a poem's achieving a much higher degree of form than we ever find in the language or events of ordinary life—lyric tense helps to elevate, to make not merely permanent but monumental and mythical that virtual experience we find at the center of the poem.

It does so differently at different times. Although something of that eternal tense is to be felt in the verbs of Shakespeare, Pope, Shelley, Yeats, and Louis Simpson, each era handles the device in its own way and uses it for its own hardly explicit purposes. If the simple present is, after all, the tense of "the truth," then whatever a poet speaks of in that tense will be his key to truth, to reality. The Elizabethan poet uses it to describe general forces or conditions ("Brightness *falls* from the air"), the eighteenth-century poet to present typical events ("The curfew *tolls* the knell of parting day"), and the modern Romantic poet either to frame his perceptions ("Darkling I *lis-*

ten"), to fix or memorialize his own actions ("Flower in the crannied wall, I *pluck* you . . . I *hold* you") or to register the unintelligible life around him ("A Negro *sprouts* from the pavement like an asparagus").[8]

There is no space here adequately to develop and qualify these suggestions. Changes in the poetic use of the simple present, as of other speech forms, have been gradual and subtle; to describe them justly would require many pages. Because modern poets use lyric tense so much, however, it seems proper to conclude this essay by speculating briefly on the contemporary force of the simple present verb in poems. If earlier poets can be said to use the tense to define and characterize (as in the Renaissance), to generalize (eighteenth century), and to envision (Romantic), the chief use of the form by contemporary poets is to mythify. Again and again the simple present tense helps to fix images or scenes sharply in mind, to etch small tableaux in which action and gesture, shrewdly selected for their capacity to sum up a complex total situation, are suspended, frozen. Yeats's wild swans "*drift* on the still water." Pound's Bertrans de Born

> *bends* at a table
> Scribbling, swearing between his teeth; by his left hand
> *Lie* little strips of parchment covered over.
> ("Near Perigord")

Similarly:

> He *moves* in darkness as it seems to me,
> Not of woods only and the shade of trees.
> (Frost, "Mending Wall")

> The paratroopers *fall* and as they fall
> They *mow* the lawn.
> (Stevens, "Esthétique du mal")

It is only a step from such uses to the conveying of the whole modern predicament through such portentous verbs:

> The glacier *knocks* in the cupboard,
>   The desert *sighs* in the bed,
> And the crack in the tea-cup *opens*
>   A lane to the land of the dead.
> (Auden, "As I Walked Out One Evening")

It is true that the progressive is sometimes used by modern poets, with some of the same effect of strangeness, to describe those dreamlike sequences of events that film seems especially well suited to present and has probably made us more alert to.[9] Robert Bly, for example, uses many progressives, even to introduce poems: "I *am driving;* it is dusk; Minnesota. . . . The soybeans *are breathing* on all sides" ("Driving toward the Lac Qui Parle River"). Like other Bly poems, this one uses a good deal of lyric tense, too: "The small world of the car / *Plunges* through the deep fields of the night / . . . / This solitude . . . / *Moves* . . ." And he ends:

> The lamplight *falls* on all fours in the grass.
> When I reach the river, the full moon *covers* it;
> A few people *are talking* low in a boat.

In such a poem both present forms work, though in slightly different ways, to secure the effect of wonder that Bly is after. Yet even when the two present forms work in concert, the progressive form is mostly used as accessory. Especially for recent poets wary of the entanglements of myth and symbol, it provides the vivid activity of the moment as relief from the large predications of the simple verb. Yet the progressive action is likely to be drawn into the circle of wonder that the simple verb has for a long time been used to evoke. For most poets, even when it appears in company with the progressive, it is still usually the simple form that decisively captures that disoriented feeling, to the point sometimes of vertigo. Yeats, in "The Second Coming," for example:

> . . . somewhere in sands of the desert
> A shape with lion body and the head of a man,
> A gaze blank and pitiless as the sun,
> *Is moving* its slow thighs, while all about it
> *Reel* shadows of the indignant desert birds.
> The darkness *drops* again . . .
> . . . .
> And what rough beast, its hour come round again,
> *Slouches* towards Bethlehem to be born?

Such verbs as *Reel* and *Slouches,* describing actions going on at the poem's present moment, have a strong mythic force. Modern poets have used them extensively not merely to define, to describe, or to envision but to mythify reality, to suggest in the frozen stance of the speaker (Shapiro's "My soul *stands* at the window of my room"; Hughes's "I *sit* in the top of the wood, my eyes closed") or in the selected detail of the motion around us (Ginsberg's "A black horse *bends* its head to the stubble"; Simpson's "The fowler *packs* tobacco in his pipe") something that deserves to be held, fixed, memorialized.[10] These verbs are all about us in modern poetry, and although they are used to achieve a great variety of poetic effects, the quality that seems most distinctive about their contemporary use is exactly this mythical quality, strong even in antisymbolist poets (Larkin's "Church Going" uses "I *step* inside . . . / . . . I *take off* / My cycle-clips in awkward reverence"; Gunn's "On the Move" is largely in lyric tense: "They *scare* a flight of birds across the field / . . . / They *burst* away").

As progressive forms, then, have become more freely used by poets to describe continuing actions, the simple present has come increasingly to describe actions that we apprehend as virtual, dreamlike, the material of myth. Samuel Beckett's Molloy tells us: "When I try and think riding I lose my balance and fall. I speak in the present tense, it is so easy to speak in the present tense, when speaking of the past. It is the mythological present, don't mind it."[11] In modern poems our classical tense of truth has indeed become the tense of myth, the device by which we pass all outer activity into the realm of the mythical imagination. The lyric tense detail is almost always felt as symbolic, and as with Yeats's swans that drift or his birds that reel, the tense often appears at the most climactic moment, the moment at which some symbolic transformation, some metamorphosis, takes place—in William Carlos Williams's "The Yachts," for example, where the churned waves turn into human arms thrashing: "Arms with hands grasping *seek to clutch* at the prows" (instead of *are clutching* or *are seeking to clutch*). On such occasions the device of lyric tense seems not merely to frame but almost to *be* the metaphor: it is metaphorical even to pretend that the images of poems are either present or true.

For what is truth, anyway, but myth, but experience caught and fixed? If our poets keep repeating, "I stand, I sit, I walk," if they seem almost obsessed by the need to report their own actions and the quivers of the world about them, it is probably because these data are what they feel they must hold on to. It seems entirely possible that every age celebrates in the truthful simple present not so much the truth it is sure of as the truth it feels slipping away—for the Renaissance, its forms of order; for the eighteenth century, its sense of relations; for the Romantics, the power of vision; for us, the coherence of action. In some degree poetry is, like all art, and like life, a resource for resisting the various modes of dissolution, a technique that becomes at moments triumphant and exuberant as it asserts and celebrates the powers of life, its brightness, even as that brightness falls from the air.

For the reality that underlies our myths and metaphors may be our skepticisms rather than our beliefs, our despair rather than our faith. "Not the fruit of experience, but experience itself, is the end," wrote Walter Pater a century ago. Not experience but experience set down may be all that we can trust in our time. As even the symbols withdraw from our ears their comforting reverberations of meaning, our poets grow content simply to record the data: *I go there, birds fly.* Maybe it will mean something, maybe something will justify its having been recorded. We become more adept at fleshing out the record, at fishing for patterns the final meaning of which is as obscure as ever. A world that is at once lucid and impenetrable—Kafka's world, and ours—permits to its poets only the protracted exploration, sometimes anguished, sometimes delightful, of ultimately meaningless procedures.[12]

We explore, too, all possible new dimensions of reality—those we enter through dreams, film, drugs, myth, or that occupy the borders between life and art, between symbolic and literal action—as if we sensed that somewhere in the catacombs of possible life we would discover that "truth" of which lyric tense can only afford us glimpses. From Unamuno and Kafka to Robbe-Grillet, Borges, Nabokov, Barthelme, Fellini, Antonioni, one has difficulty deciding whether any event is actual present or memory or fantasy or belongs to some other dimension of time or reality. Some novelists even use the present as the basic tense for extended narratives (Cary, Updike, Lessing, Robbe-Grillet). Yet, is the effect really to intensify the actualness of the events, or is it to qualify and compromise that actualness, to throw a house of fiction around the actual? By now, after all, we know that the devices we have developed for increasing the vividness and intensity of our writing, for achieving the illusion of actuality, never quite achieve it. What they achieve is the illusion of illusion: we *think* it is ourselves in the mirror, but we *know* it is nothing.

Appendix: Frequency of Progressive Forms in Poetry in English

Table 4 (pp. 66–67) shows the frequency with which each of fifty-nine poets and two period anthologies use progressive form verbs. Although the number of lines surveyed varies from one poet to another, the sample is an enormous one by any standard (326,000 lines of verse).[13] Several poets are represented in the sample by *all* their original nondramatic verse. Drama and translations were systematically excluded as perhaps distorting the picture. After obtaining large samples of major poets, and of some minor ones, and smaller, confirmatory samples of numerous, mainly lesser poets, I surveyed two period anthologies—*Englands Helicon* (1600) and *Naked Poetry* (1969). For Chaucer I accepted the progressives listed by J. Kerkhof in his *Studies in the Language of Geoffrey Chaucer* as probably exhaustive, though I did not accept all of them as authentic progressives.

Frequently it was difficult to decide just when a participial form was merely a predicate adjective and when it seemed to be part of a genuine progressive verb. In Sidney's lines, for example,

> Seely shepheards *are* not *witting*
> What in art of Love *is fitting*

I took the first verb as a marginal progressive but rejected the second. Generally cautious, I ruled out all cases where the participle was one of a series (but not the first) of what seemed adjectival modifiers, as in Chaucer's "That heven is swift and round and eek *brenning.*" But in Sylvia Plath's "Is she dead, *is* she *sleeping?*" I hesitantly read a progressive. Such a phrase exhibits the grammatical ambiguity that the progressive has always had in English. I tried to make consistent decisions for all the poets, and the size of the sample, far larger than any comparable study of progressives, must have preserved a reasonable validity.

One surprising, if relatively minor, result of the survey is that the poets we think of as colloquial and therefore likely to use the progressive with something like its frequency in speech do not necessarily do so at all. Donne, the most lively and speechlike of Renaissance poets, uses only one progressive in all his work, while Browning, the most animated Victorian poet, uses progressives less frequently by far than most of his contemporaries. On the other hand, Herrick, Frost, and Cummings, also poets whom we think of as relatively informal in their language, use many more progressives than most of their contemporaries. Apparently, all kinds of energy do not equally make use of progressive forms.

Table 4. Frequency of progressive form verbs

Birth date	Poet	No. of progressives	No. of lines	Ratio
1340?	Chaucer	29	41,956	1:1,447
1503	Wyatt	0	4,599	0:4,599
1536	Sackville	1	553	1:553
1554	Spenser	10	10,191	1:1,019
1554	Sidney	10	7,036	1:704
1562	Daniel	2	3,110	1:1,555
1563	Drayton	14	4,104	1:293
1564	Shakespeare	11	5,203	1:473
	Englands Helicon, 1600[a]	24	4,721	1:197
1574	Donne	1	8,817	1:8,817
1574	Jonson	8	8,500	1:1,063
1591	Herrick	13	10,000	1:769
1593	Herbert	10	5,543	1:554
1594	Carew	0	2,245	0:2,245
1608	Milton	11	13,197	1:1,200
1612	Butler	4	2,098	1:525
1613	Crashaw	0	1,010	0:1,010
1621	Marvell	1	2,090	1:2,090
1622	Vaughan	1	2,305	1:2,305
1631	Dryden	7	11,617	1:1,660
1647	Rochester	0	1,008	0:1,008
1688	Pope	3	10,000	1:3,333
1700	Thomson	1	11,487	1:11,487
1716	Gray	3	1,835	1:612
1721	Collins	0	1,562	0:1,562
1731	Cowper	10	18,922	1:1,892
1757	Blake	9	5,014	1:557
1759	Burns	43	5,085	1:118
1770	Wordsworth	42	6,315	1:150
1771	Coleridge	23	3,549	1:154
1788	Byron	15	3,029	1:202
1792	Shelley	112	10,000	1:89
1795	Keats	76	8,765	1:115

The Lyric Tense 67

Table 4. *continued*

Birth date	Poet	No. of progressives	No. of lines	Ratio
1809	Tennyson	82	10,000	1:122
1812	Browning	40	10,000	1:250
1819	Whitman	72	7,305	1:101
1822	Arnold	5	1,800	1:360
1828	Rossetti	8	1,000	1:125
1828	Meredith	9	1,000	1:111
1837	Swinburne	4	6,142	1:1,535
1844	Hopkins	10	1,000	1:100
1865	Housman	26	3,219	1:124
1865	Yeats	83	9,007	1:109
1874	Frost	20	1,002	1:50
1879	Stevens	19	3,000	1:158
1883	Williams	24	1,850	1:77
1885	Pound	35	6,111	1:175
1887	Marianne Moore	11	1,000	1:91
1888	Eliot	30	3,460	1:115
1894	Cummings	19	1,000	1:52
1899	Crane	8	2,000	1:250
1907	Auden	56	4,000	1:71
1908	Roethke	17	1,000	1:60
1914	Dylan Thomas	22	2,695	1:123
1914	Stafford	30	1,000	1:33
1917	Lowell	22	953	1:43
1923	Simpson	130	3,050	1:23
1923	Dickey	28	1,000	1:35
1926	Snodgrass	13	1,000	1:77
1969	*Naked Poetry,* 1969[b]	124	6,640	1:54

[a]Excluding poems by Shakespeare, Sidney, Drayton, and Spenser.
[b]*Naked Poetry: Recent American Poetry in Open Forms,* ed. Stephen Berg and Robert Mezey (Indianapolis: Bobbs-Merrill, 1969). Counted, in order of increasing use of progressives, were poems by Kinnell (1:250), Creeley (1:228), Snyder (1:125), Patchen and Levine (1:100), Levertov (1:82), Kees (1:72), Ginsberg (1:71), Berryman (1:55), Rexroth (1:45), James Wright, Merwin, Mezey, and Plath (1:36–38), Berg (1:25), and Bly (1:19). The poems of Lowell, Roethke, and Stafford were counted from other volumes.

The table confirms our expectations that progressives have come to be used more frequently as the centuries have proceeded. What is surprising is the irregularity of the increase. Chaucer uses progressives though not abundantly, but Elizabethan practice is remarkably varied. Some poets use none at all (Wyatt) or next to none (Daniel, Donne), while others use them frequently (Sidney, Drayton, Shakespeare, and the poets of *Englands Helicon*). It is clear, at least, that many Elizabethan writers felt no hesitation in using progressive forms, sometimes very forcefully, as in the third quatrain of Drayton's famous sonnet, "Since Ther's No Helpe":

> Now at the last gaspe, of Loves latest Breath,
> When his Pulse fayling, Passion speechlesse lies,
> When Faith *is kneeling* by his bed of Death,
> And Innocence *is closing* up his Eyes . . .

Such lines make clear that even this early the progressive form, although it may not have served all the functions it now serves and probably occurred less frequently in speech than it does now, was fully available to the poet who wanted to describe an action taking place now.

Thus, of the eleven Renaissance poets surveyed who were born in 1593 or earlier, more than half (and those of *Englands Helicon* taken as a group) use a progressive verb more often than once in 770 lines. The ratio for all the poets of this era is 1:696—one progressive in every 696 lines. Then a strange restraint begins to take hold: of those surveyed, only one poet born in the next 120 years (Butler, in his highly eccentric *Hudibras*) uses as many progressives as one in a thousand lines.[14] Furthermore, every major poet from Jonson to Milton to Dryden to Pope to Thomson uses proportionally fewer progressives than his predecessor. In all his verse Thomson uses only one progressive verb, Collins in his smaller work none at all. From Crashaw (b. 1613) to Collins (b. 1721) the ratio of progressives to lines of verse is 1:2,682.

As the eighteenth century wanes, however, progressives begin to reappear, timidly in Cowper, more strongly in Blake. And then, as if the neoclassical poets had only been holding back the floodwaters, the progressives wash in on the crest of the Romantic tide. Burns uses proportionally more of them than any English poet before him. From Burns to Housman, Romantic and Victorian poets, various in other respects, are quite consistent in using a progressive form about once in every 100 or 150 lines. (The ratio for the group as a whole is 1:128.) If Shelley exceeds this norm, it is because he likes to play with a progressive form only recently reclaimed for poetry:

> The waters are flashing,
> The white hail is dashing,
> The lightnings are glancing,
> The hoar-spray is dancing—
>   Away!
>
> The whirlwind is rolling,
> The thunder is tolling,
> The forest is swinging,
> The minster bells ringing—
>   Come away!
>   ("The Fugitives")

Arnold (1:360) and Browning (1:250), on the other hand, appear as laggards in the general swing to the progressive. But Swinburne (1:1,535) alone retains a classical severity in his verbs, using progressives more sparingly than Chaucer, Spenser, Shakespeare, Jonson, or Milton.

The first generation of modern poets is sharply divided into two groups: the stately formalists (late Yeats, Stevens, Pound, and Crane), whose average ratio is 1:200, a distinct reversion toward older practice; and the more informal talkers (Frost, Williams, Moore, and Cummings), whose average ratio is 1:66. Eliot (1:115) falls almost squarely between the two groups, leaning perhaps, and perhaps surprisingly, toward the informalists. The disparity in this generation of poets is the most striking for any period since the Renaissance.

The next generation, however—poets born during the twentieth century—shows a marked increase in the use of progressives and a far greater uniformity in its usage: if we except a few poets of *Naked Poetry,* who are represented in the survey by five hundred lines or less, only Dylan Thomas among poets born in this century retains a ratio (1:123) common among Romantic and Victorian poets. From Auden through Snodgrass and the poets of *Naked Poetry,* the collective ratio for the poets of our time is 1:48, lower than that of even the most colloquial poet of any previous generation.

To sum up these changes: although English speech has used progressive forms widely since the Renaissance (they are recognized as a standard if peculiar feature of English in grammars of the seventeenth and eighteenth centuries), and although such forms have presumably (it is hard to be sure) been increasing *steadily* in the extent of their use in speech, the increase in their use in poetry has been remarkably unsteady, and when it has come it has come in great waves. Particularly striking are the virtual nonuse of progressives for more than a century of neoclassic poetry and the great jumps in use first by Romantic poets and then by our own contemporaries—jumps so great that in both eras the *average* ratio of progressives to lines is lower than the ratio of even the most eccentric earlier poet. The inescapable conclusion is that the choice between simple and progressive forms is made by poets (or by eras of poetry) on the basis of rather complex psychological and philosophical considerations.

For example, it seems clear that after the acceptance of progressives by the Renaissance as (among other things) an attractive means of registering foreground activity ("A Gentle Knight *was pricking* on the plaine"; "Now day is doen, and night *is nighing* fast"—Spenser) or of working out, in tableau depth, a design of contrasting actions ("Justice *is feasting* while the widow weeps"—*The Rape of Lucrece*), the seventeenth-century movement toward generality found progressive forms not much to its purpose. When Thomson, in whom this movement reaches its furthest point, describes a scene, it is a typical scene; his seasonal descriptions are of events and actions that take place repeatedly and so require the simple present form. Here, for example, is his description of the lover in "Spring":

> Sudden he *starts,*
> Shook from his tender trance, and restless *runs*
> To glimmering shades, and sympathetic glooms,
> Where the dun umbrage o'er the falling stream,
> Romantic, *hangs;* there through the pensive dusk
> *Strays,* in heart-thrilling meditation lost,
> Indulging all to love: or on the bank
> Thrown, amid drooping lilies, *swells* the breeze
> With sighs unceasing, and the brook with tears.
> Thus in soft anguish he *consumes* the day,
> Nor *quits* his deep retirement, till the Moon
> *Peeps* through the chambers of the fleecy east,
> Enlighten'd by degrees, and in her train
> *Leads* on the gentle hours: then forth he *walks*
> Beneath the trembling languish of her beam,
> With soften'd soul, and *woos* the bird of eve
> To mingle woes with his: or while the world
> And all the sons of Care *lie* hush'd in sleep,
> *Associates* with the midnight shadows drear;
> And, sighing to the lonely taper, *pours*

> His idly-tortur'd heart into the page,
> Meant for the moving messenger of love;
> Where rapture *burns* on rapture, every line
> With rising frenzy fired. But if on bed
> Delirious flung, sleep from his pillow *flies,*
> All night he *tosses,* nor the balmy pow'r
> In any posture *finds;* till the grey morn
> *Lifts* her pale lustre on the paler wretch,
> Exanimate by love; and then perhaps
> Exhausted Nature *sinks* a while to rest,
> Still interrupted by distracted dreams,
> That o'er the sick imagination *rise,*
> And in black colours *paint* the mimic scene.
> (ll. 1024–56)

Later poets, more interested in the action that occurs only once and struck by its occurring *now,* might use progressive forms to describe some of these actions, might say that the umbrage *is hanging,* the Moon *is peeping,* the lover *is tossing* in his sleep, might highlight at least *one* of these actions by using a progressive form against a background of simple present forms.[15] But Thomson cares only for the general instance, for a single time level, and for a spatial arrangement uniformly lighted; the simple present is therefore entirely, and exclusively, to his purpose.

Note that, for all his wariness of progressive forms, Thomson by no means avoids the present participle. On the contrary, even in this passage adjectival forms in *-ing* appear eight times and a full-fledged present participle twice. Eighteenth-century poetry, in fact, is full of expressions like "He stood waving," "He sits piping," a form that no doubt seemed more proper and Latin than the progressive (*stat clamans* is acceptable Latin, *est clamans* grotesque, degenerate) and one that, unlike the progressive, emphasizes the enduring nature of the frame action *(stood, sits)* within which the more immediate gesture *(waving, piping)* takes place. Vivid but subordinate—that is the place of the participial adjective in the eighteenth-century verse tableau, where activity is contained by context.

The nineteenth-century increase in progressives reflects not merely the wider use of the progressive in colloquial English but the increased willingness of poets to employ it in the sublime art of poetry. They are more willing to do so for two reasons, which are finally the same: they want to use the real language of men, a language that by now decidedly includes the progressive, and they are becoming more and more interested in particular events in all their immediacy, events as sources of knowledge and not merely as particularizations of truths. The progressive is therefore useful for rendering vividly the data of actual experience, as in Wordsworth's lines: "The broad sun / *Is sinking* down in its tranquillity." "And all that mighty heart *is lying* still."

When early-twentieth-century poets, or at least some of them, despite their professed affection for natural English, show somewhat less readiness to use the progressive than their nineteenth-century predecessors, it is, I think, because the simple form is better suited to the symbolic and mythical modes that attract poets like Yeats, Pound, Stevens, Crane, and Thomas. Yeats's practice is especially instructive: his use of the progressive sharply declines in the course of his career, even while his language and diction, as everyone says, become more plain and ordinary. In his early poems (through *In the Seven Woods,* 1903) he uses progressive verbs frequently, about once in every 45 lines. From *The Green Helmet and Other Poems* (1910) through *Michael Robartes and the Dancer* (1921) he uses one in every 111 lines. In later volumes the ratio is cut to one in every 286 lines. Progressives frequently occur in his early ballads, hardly at all in his later ones.

The sharp increase in the contemporary use of progressives in poems is probably related to the widespread retreat from symbolism. The disposition of recent poets to be content with modest observations instead of universal syntheses permits the progressive to appear prominently in a poetry whose representations may often be of "something I was just noticing the other day" rather than of Leda and her swan. As we have seen, however, because of its special powers the simple present more than holds its own in the language of contemporary poetry.

Supposing a Measure for *Measure for Measure*

PISH-TUSH. I am afraid that, unless you can obtain a substitute—
KO-KO. A substitute? Oh, certainly—nothing easier. (To POOH-BAH.) I appoint you Lord High Substitute.
POOH-BAH. I should be delighted. Such an appointment would realize my fondest dreams. But no, at any sacrifice, I must set bounds to my insatiable ambition.

—W. S. Gilbert, *The Mikado*

> Or in the night, imagining some fear,
> How easy is a bush suppos'd a bear!
> —*A Midsummer Night's Dream*

Gascoigne's *Supposes*

No Elizabethan dramatic work plays so doggedly on a single word as George Gascoigne's *Supposes,* his somewhat amplified translation of Ariosto's comedy *I Suppositi.*[1] Obsessed with the word *suppose* and its variant forms, Gascoigne repeats them twenty times in the 222-word "Prologue or argument" and five times more in the play's final 62-word speech; in the play itself he provides marginal tips for twenty-four supposes, often characterizing them: "a shamelesse suppose," "a crafty suppose," "a knauishe suppose"; others are "stoute," "doltish," "shrewde," and "needlesse." He is clearly intrigued by the ambiguities of "supposes" and its Italian original "suppositi," which means substitutions more than suppositions and has sexual overtones, too. But Gascoigne's "Prologue" shifts Ariosto's emphasis from substitutions to supposes, and from sexual superimpositions to misidentifications; "our Suppose," he writes, "is nothing else but a mystaking or imagination of one thing for an other," and he cites the main examples from the play: "the master supposed for the seruant, the seruant for the master: the freeman for a slaue, and the bondslaue for a freeman: the stranger for a well known friend, and the familiar for a stranger" ([12]).

For Gascoigne, it is not just that one person pretends to be someone else but that others are deceived by this pretense. His emphasis is entirely on how the substitution is taken in and results in a misunderstanding of the true relations of people, an imagining of a situation as other than it actually is.

For the Elizabethans frequently, and for Shakespeare typically, *suppose* denoted an unsubstantiated guess or a mistaken belief ("Holding a weak *supposal* of our worth" [*Hamlet* 1.2.18]; "So shall I live, *supposing* thou art true, / Like a deceivèd husband" [Sonnet 93.1–2].[2] Sometimes, as Gascoigne shows, the suppositions are "true" or "right" by accident, by mistake, a character having fallen into a turn of phrase that just happens to describe a situation accurately, though he doesn't realize he has done so.[3] But usually the supposes that count are impersonations that deceive other characters. Supposes in the sense of substitutions provide the ground for supposes in the sense of false inferences, which characters engage in as they try to read the world before them.

The situation of deceived characters, then, is like that of an audience in the theater, where actors' impersonations provide the basis for an accepted train of supposed relationships and events. But in the theater the audience participates knowingly in the deception. Gascoigne's phrase, "mystaking or imagination," implies or conceals similarities but also differences in the mental operations of character, actor, and audience (one character mistakes, another deceives, the actor pretends, and the audience acquiesces in the illusion), and it suggests that Gascoigne was partly aware that supposes are the basis of all drama, not just of this play or this kind of play.

Most critics, in discussing theatrical illusion, tend to speak as if there were only one, as if when the curtain rises we there and then assent to the theatrical fiction as a whole. But what happens as the play proceeds is that we are continually asked to suppose things about the characters and the action. To attend a play is normally to participate in a rapid series of supposals, which come on fast as the play develops, one event after another feeding and filling our understanding of the fictional universe being constructed before us and within us. That is the point of Gascoigne's constantly directing our attention to supposes that appear in his text. It is his way of showing how frequently we go through this mental operation of supposing (guessing, hypothesizing, theorizing) in the theater but also, by implication, in the ordinary life from which drama takes its cues.

Shakespeare Supposing

Shakespeare goes much further than Gascoigne or Ariosto in treating the theater situation as a complex structure of supposes. If his most direct debt to *Supposes* is his borrowing of its plot for the subplot of *The Taming of the Shrew,* Roman drama and history provided him with similar plot devices for other plays built on mistakes or deceptions. Compared with earlier Elizabethan playwrights, Shakespeare complicates and multiplies the false supposes under which his gullible characters labor; like theatrical audiences—like *us*—they seem hungry for supposes. Throughout his work characters adopt disguises, change costumes, are misidentified, misread visual or political clues, make verbal mistakes, play-act, pretend to beliefs or affections they do not hold, or are miraculously transformed into other creatures or into people they never supposed they could become. Lies, deceptions, mistakes, and impersonations make his characters' dramatic lives treacherous for them and appealing or appalling to his audience. Indeed, from this point of view the art of Shakespeare's plots can largely be described as the tangling (almost incessant) and disentangling (frequently deferred) that grow out of the characters' misreading of their situations. Mistakes by the deceived and maskings by their deceivers mirror their counterparts in life and in the theater and are followed at some point in most of the plays by unmaskings, by moments in which the masking personages resume their original identities, disclose or discover their true ones, undeceive their victims, or adopt new masks. These undisguisings are especially dramatic in some plays, where they dismantle earlier confusions, mistakes, and misapprehensions, resolve tensions, and clarify where the characters and their world are to be left. They restore not only the identities of the misread characters but the normal conditions of life. Often involved in this kind of restoration is a further level of recovery: the actual reclaiming of lost members of a family, who may reappear, through this unmasking, after a few weeks (as with Edgar in *Lear,* or Sebastian in *Twelfth Night*) or after many years (as in *The Comedy of Errors* and all four romances).

The discovery of lost relatives emphasizes the spirit of restoration and recovery with which Shakespeare's plays, especially his comedies, frequently end. The device signals not only that we are back, more or less, to normal but also that events from now on may reap the additional benefits that the unfolding plot has provided, with all the wonder and sense of miracle that such a recovery can confer. Finding, as Gonzalo assures us, is what everyone does at the end: Ferdinand finds a wife, Prospero a dukedom, "and all of us, ourselves, / When no man was his own" (*The Tempest* 5.1.212–13). That such a blessed moment should come at the end is fitting because it is then that the actors themselves are restored to their own identities. "Now," as the actor playing Prospero tells us, "my charms are all o'erthrown, / And what strength I have's mine own, / Which is most faint . . ." (Epilogue, 1–3). The audience is in the same boat, as it will all too soon recognize. The actors are not dukes or Romans, but countrymen, and the stage is only a metaphorical island; all the supposes have not changed the day or the weather or anyone's identity. Nothing at all has happened, except that actors and audience have once again gone through this delicious, if unsettling, practice of supposing. If supposing is grand, to be released from its "bands" is also splendid.

Especially if the suppositions have been troubling or absurd. In *A Midsummer Night's Dream,* for example, the lovers and the mechanicals provide instances of different kinds. Puck's mistake, together with the mischievous games he plays, confuses the male lovers' allegiances and results in further misreadings by Helena and Hermia and exhausting shows of combat by the men, and the release they experience when the mistake is corrected feels to them all like waking from a dream. Whether anything really transpired in the supposed wood near Athens is an issue they cannot clearly resolve, and in this uncertainty they resemble audiences leaving a theater (or their own later selves after viewing the mechanicals' performance) without knowing exactly how to answer the perennial riddle: does anything happen in the theater? *Their* audience—Hippolyta and Theseus—take different views, Theseus arguing that the lovers' account is mere imagination, Hippolyta that they couldn't have dreamed it all:

> But all the story of the night told over,
> And all their minds transfigur'd so together,
> More witnesseth than fancy's images,
> And grows to something of great constancy;
> But howsoever, strange and admirable.
> (5.1.23–27)

Similarly with the mechanicals. Whenever Shakespeare presents a play within a play, the audience is invited to notice how the inner play mirrors the outer one, and how the roles of actor, audience, and playwright are doubled and italicized. In *A Midsummer Night's Dream* we are most entertained by the mechanicals' inability to understand the system of supposes on which a theatrical enterprise rests (a failure that echoes the lovers' inability to understand the supposed reasons why people love). They cannot see what it means to play a part, to pretend to be someone else—and, as the other side of the supposition, how readily an audience accepts this pretense. Bottom at first supposes he can take several roles, not grasping that the characters must appear on the stage together; and in thinking the audience must be told that he is not Pyramus but Bottom the weaver, and that the lion is Snug the joiner, he feels obliged, in effect, even as the theatrical illusion is constructed, to puncture it. Ironically, at this moment, as part of Shakespeare's stage-illusion, Bottom is "chang'd," "translated" (3.1.114, 119), not into a legend or a lion, but into a freak of nature, part man, part ass—in one sense what he has been all along, but also, unlike his fellows, privileged to live at once in two mutually mirroring but uncommunicating worlds—like the audience, who also can see and hear the fairies but may not speak with them, as Bottom can do. Although the artisans' play is trumped by this mythological master-move, they are not entirely wrong about what kind of transaction between company and audience a play is; they are only very unsophisticated. After all, if the audience thought Bottom was "really" transformed, they too would clear out of these woods. But we know, as Bottom's friends do not, that his translation is another suppose of the play; we know it partly because we are experienced playgoers accustomed to such surprises, but also partly because Puck has already told us, possibly with a wink but without overstressing the point, that he is planning some diversion. So when the mechanicals judge that the audience must be warned to read appalling stage events as only pretenses, they are right, but they are too naive to understand that such a warning is implicit in the supposing of a play.[4]

Supposing a Play

Supposing is so central for Shakespeare, not only as a given of his theater but also in the design and detail of his plots, that a play like *Measure for Measure* can be built on substitutions and supposals (the Duke's plots, Angelo's plans, Isabella's hopes, Claudio's fears). The audience itself somehow understands that a substitution is a sort of narrative or dramatic hypothesis *(what if Angelo were in charge instead of the Duke?)*, and that plays are largely built upon characters' expectations—realized, disappointed, or constantly revised—about what other characters will do *(suppose that Isabella will sleep with me, suppose that Claudio will approve my decision not to).*[5] Everyone watching the play has learned how to make such supposals; we use them outside the theater to construct our understanding of the world, and of our own place in it, and to cope with small and large spatial, social, and psychological encounters every day and almost every minute of our waking lives *(what if it snows tomorrow? will that car cross into my lane?).* Now as the play proceeds we watch the characters doing the same.

As it works through its series of supposes, a play suggests even more—that when our ordinary strategies for gauging our world become confused or are deeply subverted by deceptions, we may suffer tragic distress or comic anxiety. Characters in every Shakespearean play experience this kind of trauma when they misread their situations and suppose that Iago is honest, Hero unfaithful, or Kent disloyal. Tragedy results when the mistakes of major and usually powerful characters lead to fateful actions based on radically erroneous readings of the world. In comedies such mistaken suppositions become the basis of further amusing errors and are corrected in time to prevent permanent damage to the characters we most care about. But whether the genre is history, comedy, tragedy, or romance, the Shakespearean pattern typically traces the trouble that arises when ambitious or deceived characters—overreachers or undersuspecters—make false suppositions and come to at least temporary grief. In some of the subtlest cases, even characters whose suppositions about intended actions turn out to be largely true may be blind to their more distant consequences (e.g., Hamlet, Buckingham, Iago, the Macbeths).

In this situation, replete with dramatic ironies, the sharpest irony is that the very vehicle that shows us all this—the play itself—practices, as its stock-in-trade, the same mistaken supposing that it is telling us causes such serious and even deadly consequences in actual life. On the stage, however, the terms that govern our framework of supposes are clear, and the invitation to the audience to participate in the imagining of the stage events is followed by no material consequences. In the theater we are immune, we cannot get into trouble. We go through the [e]motions of imagining, of supposing, without suffering the penalties that typically await comic and tragic protagonists. (Or we suffer them only as states of readiness to suffer, as virtual suffering.) We experience the play's projected terrors and torments, but we do so without risk, without cost, without jeopardy.

We can't live without making guesses—it is part of our animal endowment. But plays scare us, in effect, with bad guesses, by imitating the experience we all have of misjudging our predicament, and they show us either how funny such mistakes are *(I thought my next step was safe, but I didn't see the banana peel; he thought he was reading Olivia's letter in private, but he didn't know they were listening and that the letter wasn't really from Olivia)* or how fatal *(I thought Iago was honest)*. As we watch characters making and paying for such mistakes (by falling on their faces, looking foolish, or self-destructing), we feel a complex tension and satisfaction. Having made such errors ourselves, we identify with the character before us who is making them now, or we relish his discomfiture; but we also see that this time we ourselves are suffering no consequences, not even when we are fooled by unexpected turns in the plot. Just as we wake from a difficult dream to find that we don't, after all, have to face the anxieties or disasters it had harried us with, so in the theater we know, as often as we need to remind ourselves, that despite our sympathy with the tormented figures onstage we are not actually suffering these torments—and neither are they, for they are "only acting" and this is "only a play." We are watching the sort of action that gives pain in real life, but we have found a way of doing so without having it hurt.

If the general situation that obtains in the theater is constructed out of supposes, playwrights in plotting build further structures of suppositions. Only by grasping what the characters suppose about their situations can we figure out what is going on in the play. Much of what they suppose we, too, must suppose if we are to follow the plot at all: when two gentlemen claim they are friends, we suppose it is so, but new information may alter that supposition. We accept the explicit identities of characters (Isabella is Claudio's sister, Pompey a bawd, Angelo the Duke's deputy) and their professions of loyalty or sympathy until we have reason to doubt such claims (Lear's elder daughters don't *sound* as if they love their father). As contrary evidence accumulates, we find a growing disparity between some characters' supposals and our own. We know, for example, that Duncan and his court are wrong to trust the Macbeths, but we also suspect the Macbeths are wrong in supposing the murder of Duncan will bring them joy.[6]

Supposing the Duke

Hardly any scholars have connected Gascoigne's *Supposes* to Shakespeare plays other than those that directly borrow from its plot: *The Taming of the Shrew* and some other early comedies.[7] But as with other plays of Shakespeare, the plot of *Measure for Measure* is rippled with substitutions, deceptions, mistaken identities, and argumentative errors—with supposes that generate much of its structure and meaning.[8] At the outset, the Duke turns over his authority to a substitute, Angelo; Angelo leaves the hard courtroom work to his "secondary," Escalus, who sees to it that an incompetent constable like Elbow will no longer serve as perpetual substitute for abler men in his ward. The Duke arranges for Mariana to keep Isabella's assignation with Angelo—the famous bed trick—and conspires with the Provost to substitute another head for Claudio's: Barnardine is the preferred substitute, but when, like Pooh-Bah (whose motives are different, though both are "absolute for life"), he declines to serve, a substitute substitute is found in Ragozine, whose already dead head can easily be mistaken for Claudio's. In the final scene, the Duke switches roles twice, appearing first as himself, then as Friar Lodowick, then again as himself when the slanderer Lucio unmasks him, as the Duke will soon unmask Lucio. Mistakes and misapprehensions abound; at every point someone is misreading someone else because of the multiple lies and deceptions, the "fantastic tricks," that the major characters—notably, the Duke and Angelo—play before us. But some of them—from Angelo to Froth—are confused or self-deceived, misreading their own situations and acting on mistaken assumptions and inferences about where they stand or what the issues are or what kind of a world they are living in. The audience's part is to read these misreadings.

Among all the confusing devices, however, one stands out as virtually governing all the rest, and it deserves special attention because it constitutes a major point on which Shakespeare departed from earlier versions of his story.[9] All other versions he might have read or seen introduce the imperial figure only as an authority to which the already outraged heroine appeals for justice. Shakespeare alone keeps the Duke on the scene and makes him aware, *before it happens,* of Angelo's plan to seduce Isabella. This change not only gives the Duke's relation to these events a wholly different cast; it also alters radically the terms on which the other characters experience the play's major action. For the Duke, far from being ignorant of local events, as everyone supposes he is, and as the comparable authorities are in all the pre-Shakespeare versions, learns more than anyone else of what is really going on. The Duke's presence in Vienna means that although other characters take the events that transpire there at face value, and suppose, for example, that Claudio will be executed, or that Angelo's vice will go unpunished, we suspect these suppositions are false. We watch these troubled people acting in dead earnest as they wholly misconceive the nature of the situation they are in.

In this world protected by the continued but invisible presence of the Duke, the characters, never dreaming that this dimension of their problem even exists, repeatedly make supposes that are valid in the framework of their own assumptions but not for the Duke and the audience. Claudio, awaiting execution, looks to his sister for help, but the audience knows that his only hope for life rests with Brother Lodowick, who has advised him to prepare for death. Isabella believes her failed appeal to Angelo has condemned her brother and isolated her; we suspect that the Duke will save them both. We see more than Lucio, Escalus, Angelo, the Provost. We know that there is an unrecognized power on the scene in Vienna—the Duke in disguise—and we see him permitting all the characters except Friar Thomas to make the crucially false supposition that he is absent, unaware, indifferent, "travell'd to Poland" (1.3.14); like the Christian God, that *deus absconditus,* he is closer than they think. We see him trying to resolve the play's problems by inducing its characters to make further mistaken supposals, or to join in deceptions that mislead others. They do not catch on to what is really happening because they do not know he is the Duke.[10]

As critics have often observed, Duke Vincentio resembles Prospero in *The Tempest* in managing a complex series of events as if they were playwrights, and, along with such other play-directing characters as Richard III, Hamlet, Iago, the Macbeths, and Paulina, their speeches reflect the difficulties of timing, preparation, management, and coping with surprises. Prospero's magic is matched by Vincentio's insight, alertness, and opportunism, and in both plays other characters are amazed at what seems the "pow'r divine" (5.1.369) of these dukes. The implication here is a familiar Shakespearean one, that directing or authoring a play, or a play within a play, is analogous to commanding a kingdom or God's universe: in all these endeavors a directing intelligence manipulates the supposes of the people over whom it holds sway; in theory at least, it does so for their own good, and sometimes without their becoming aware of it. In *Measure for Measure* it is tempting to read the unrecognized presence of a powerful duke as a figurative means both of alluding to the remote but effective (and presumably benevolent) presence of King James I and of adumbrating the common Christian view that God is present everywhere, an observer and sometimes an actor in all the scenes of our lives.

From this point of view, any deep psychological analysis of this godlike, kinglike, play-directing personage is a little beside the mark. The play of *Measure for Measure* is not a freestanding study of how the egoistic desires and "anxiety of self-representation" of an autocrat interfere with his official responsibilities.[11] In any coherent production, what draws us into the action, at least from 3.1.152 on, is the Duke's complex struggle to put things right, to block the execution of Claudio, to keep Angelo's treacherous conduct from victimizing Isabella, to take advantage of this opportunity to redress Angelo's mistreatment of Mariana, to curb the slanderous tongue of Lucio, and to bind up the city's moral wounds by whatever makeshift means he can. The playwright who frames this plot knows what it is to make headway against all the nagging, trivial, irrelevant, pesky distractions and obstacles that keep his play from realizing (as, of course, it never can do) some previsioned form, and this is the course, the action, the matter that is dramatized in this play. Things disobedient and people unpredictable keep getting in the producer's way—in *Measure for Measure* as in *The Tempest*—and the two absentee dukes, Viennese friar and Milanese sorcerer, are always on the verge of having their plans go awry. In effect, even while Vincentio's power depends on keeping the other characters secure in their mistaken supposes, his own presumptions are repeatedly flouted, shown to be mistaken—that Angelo will live up to his bargain with Isabella, that Pompey will reform, that Barnardine will submit to execution, that Claudio will be content to die, that the Duke's subjects, such as Lucio, will acknowledge the Duke's virtues and good intentions and will give a veridical account of him. Any spectator at a relatively straightforward production of the play is likely not to be indignant at the Duke's intrusions into the lives of his subjects but to be amused at all the human perversities that keep this sometimes testy authority (like Prospero also in this) from tidying up the Viennese stew as he'd like. Only in the final scene, which, like any theatrical production, is a triumph of plan (script) and improvisation, does the Duke manage to put all the recalcitrant pieces of his puzzle in place and secure the rough justice that answers to Isabella's earlier description of a proper human authority (2.2).[12]

But a duke's power is never complete; he must always wrestle with frail and intransigent human material, must deal with people as they are. The playwright must put up with the limitations of actors and the physical theater, as passages in *Hamlet* and *Henry V* famously show; perhaps also, like God, he must put up with the failings of the characters he has created—Prospero with humans who resist fitting in with his plans, Vincentio with various deadly sins and with vicious and ignorant people who handle and mishandle supposes of their own in ways that mock and shadow his.

Deposing Elbow; Pompey Supposed

Elbow and Pompey, for example, show how ignorance and vice can derange the language needed to administer a state's judicial system. As logical thought is built on assumptions from which consequences may be deduced or inferred ("If our virtues / Did not go forth of us, 'twere all alike / As if we had them not"—1.1.34–36), so the law's language is built on supposes, on *if*-clauses that suppose certain conditions or premises and are completed by statements about consequences: "If a person breaks a law, he will suffer an appropriate penalty." In this play's Vienna, however, much doubt exists as to whether certain laws and punishments are appropriate, whether bad laws ought to be enforced, whether those who violate the laws will be caught or charged or punished, and just who is guilty of what. Vienna's problems are closely related to the uncertainty about these matters, which is another way of saying that different people suppose different things about them. For all its reliance on logic, the law, like the hangman's art, is a mystery; it needs to be studied; it needs to be explained; laws apply differently to the city and the suburbs, to ordinary fornicators and those who are betrothed, and even to different couples betrothed in somewhat different ways. The law of the convent operates differently from the law of the state, and earthly laws from those of heaven.

Such distinctions, and the confusion they generate, contribute to the disorder we find in this play. It is the Duke's responsibility to clarify some of these confusions, to resolve the runaway supposes into a manageable order, and he has his hands full. So does Escalus, in trying to sort out the case Elbow puts before him and Angelo. Angelo gives up on it, but Escalus sees it through. What makes it especially troublesome is that the language Elbow and Pompey use, one out of ignorance, the other out of mischief, mocks the logical supposes of the law. In Elbow's frequent *if*-clauses, a favorite construction of his, the conclusions rarely depend upon, or even connect with, his premises:

If these be good people in a commonweal . . . I know no law (2.1.41–43)

If it please your Honor, I am the poor Duke's constable, and my name is Elbow (47–48)

. . . *if it be not a bawd's house,* it is pity of her life (75)

If ever I was respected with her, or she with me, let not your Worship think me the poor Duke's officer (176–77)

One hardly overstates the case to suggest that Elbow's failure to master the language of supposes is a source of his incompetence.

In contrast, Pompey, who offers to be "supposed upon a book" (154), uses the form only for quibbles and prophecies, which aim at destroying its coherence. Asked by Escalus, "What do you think of the trade, Pompey? is it a lawful trade?" Pompey replies: "If the law would allow it, sir" (225–27), avoiding "the Lie Direct . . . with an If," as Touchstone recommends (*As You Like It,* 5.4.97–98). But Pompey's main tactic is to predict that the laws regulating prostitution will be economically disastrous:

> *If you head and hang all that offend that way but for ten year together,* you'll be glad to give out a commission for more heads. (238–40)

> *If this law hold in Vienna ten year,* I'll rent the fairest house in it after threepence a bay. (240–42)

> *If you live to see this come to pass,* say Pompey told you so. (242–43)

In response to all this bibble babble, Escalus has to avoid being taken in by two specious varieties of suppose, by Elbow's inanities and Pompey's prognostications. Good officer of the court that he is, he reasserts its coherence by using a form of suppose that is a model for the law: ". . . let me not find you before me again upon any complaint whatsoever . . . *If I do . . .* I shall have you whipt" (245–50), a threat, however, that on Pompey's later arrest does not appear to be carried out. In this city, it seems, even the best of officials can let things slide.

What Would You Do?

Crucial in the debates between Angelo and Isabella is the difficulty each has in fencing with the other's supposes, which include suppositions, substitutes, and ethical alternatives. In opposition to Angelo's view that the law simply is what it is, Isabella suggests, early in Act 2, Scene 2, that Claudio's sentence might be different. Her *ifs* are *what-ifs.* The law may be the law, but Angelo's statement of its self-identity leaves the loophole that the law does not act mechanically but requires the agency of a judge—here, Angelo himself—who *might,* she argues, take a different view. To support her argument she does what a good casuist does: she supposes cases, and to present them with polemical force she skillfully uses conditional and anomalous verbs: *would, might, were, may.* When Angelo's indicative verbs insist, "I *will* not do't," and "Look what I *will* not, that I *can*not do" (2.4.51, 52), she returns:

"But can you if you *would?*" and "But *might* you do't . . ." (51, 53), and she soon begins a series of supposals that shift the identities of judge, defendant, sister, and even God:

> If he *had been* as you, and you as he,
> You *would have* slipp'd like him, but he, like you,
> *Would not have* been so stern.
> (64–66; emphasis mine, here and later)

> I *would* to heaven I *had* your potency,
> And you *were* Isabel! *Should* it then *be* thus?
> No; I *would tell* what *'twere* to be a judge,
> And what a prisoner.
> (67–70)

When Angelo persists in stating that the law just *is*—"Your brother *is* a forfeit of the law" (71–72)—she widens the argument: human judges should follow God's example and temper justice with mercy. After all:

> How *would* you *be*
> If He, which is the top of judgment, *should*
> But *judge* you as you are?
> (75–77)

Angelo responds: "It *is* the law, not I condemn your brother" (80). He only administers it and, by being just, saves other sinners from falling (100–104). But Isabella counters that mercy better becomes a human judge than severity, especially if the judge shares–as Angelo may–the "natural guiltiness" of Claudio. This imagining at last touches Angelo, who acknowledges to himself that "She speaks, and 'tis / Such sense that my sense breeds with it" (141–42).

In sum, Isabella's series of supposes expands Angelo's imagination of the law and of his position as its human scourge and minister, though it turns out that his improved ability to suppose, to recognize that he, too, might give way to the same temptations as Claudio, takes a different course from the one she intends. She supposes that seeing his likeness to Claudio will make him pity her brother, but it does nothing of the sort. Angelo, from this point on, is wholly intent on seducing Isabella. If her argument about mercy has touched him at all, it may have given him reason to suppose, as Claudio later guesses (3.1.109–14), that the sin he longs to commit is a pardonable one.

Their second scene (2.4) proceeds very differently: it is Angelo now who, eager to dispute, takes the lead in imagining hypothetical cases. Suppose, he says, I pardoned a murderer (as the Duke does later); that would be no worse than pardoning a man like Claudio (as the Duke also does) who, breaking God's law, fathers a child out of wedlock (42–49). When Isabella unwarily responds that in human law at least fornication is not so serious an offense as murder, Angelo's sup-pose is ready:

> Then I shall *pose* you quickly.
> Which had you rather, that the most just law
> Now took your brother's life, or, to redeem him,
> Give up your body to such sweet uncleanness
> As she that he hath stain'd?
> (51–55)

Not to save your brother, he suggests, would be to contribute to his murder; wouldn't you prefer to commit what you argued was the lesser sin? In Act 2, Scene 2, Isabella had also said: What if Claudio, or I, were the judge? Now Angelo offers her a different role: What if you were the victim? The terms of the question have found a new form: not, what if he were in your position, or if I were, or if you were in his, or if God judged you as you judge Claudio, but what if you were in this imagined, this supposedly fictitious, position—which you are? If you were, if the suppose were not merely a suppose,

> *Might* there not *be* a charity in sin
> To save this brother's life?
> (63–64)

She misunderstands:

> Please *you* to do't,
> I'*ll* take it as a peril to my soul
> (64–65)

Angelo insists:

> Pleas'd *you* to do't at peril of your soul,
> *Were* equal poise of sin and charity.
> (67–68)

Angelo's verbs by now are largely subjunctive, his propositions hypothetical, conditional, casuistical, and Isabella has trouble knowing how to take them. The difference between "Please" and "Pleas'd" is characteristic. "Please" (64) = if you *will* do it, I *will* take it on my head. "Pleas'd" (67) = if you *were* to do it, that *would be* a good act. Impatient, finally, at finding her responses perverse or obtuse, he puts his proposal plainly, but still in the form of a suppose, and his subtle speech negotiates the line between supposing there *is* and supposing there *were:*

> Admit no other way to save his life,
> (As I subscribe not that, nor any other,
> But in the loss of question) that you, his sister,
> Finding yourself desir'd of such a person,
> Whose credit with the judge, or own great place,
> *Could* fetch your brother from the manacles
> Of the all-binding law; and that there *were*
> No earthly mean to save him, but that either
> You *must* lay down the treasures of your body
> To *this supposed,* or else to let him suffer—
> What *would* you *do?*
> (88–98)

In response to her supposes of the earlier scene, he has found a way to confuse two speech acts—the supposition and the proposition[13]—to steer deftly between describing the actual situation and imagining a hypothetical one. Admit, he says (that is, acknowledge that there is, or suppose that there were) no alternative way to save his life—I don't mean to suggest that there is, or that any other hope exists, but just for the sake of argument—than that you, your brother's sister, being desired by someone with influence over your brother's judge, or by the judge himself—in either case, by someone who could free your brother from those chains of law that wholly bind him—... But the grammar has broken down: "that you, his sister" has not been completed by any verb, unless it figures strangely as, along with "credit ... or ... place," a kind of distributed subject of "Could fetch." No wonder Isabella is bewildered. Suppose further, Angelo goes on, that the only means *on earth* to save your brother were for you to surrender your chastity to this imagined person, or to let him (your brother—or is it this supposed high-placed fetcher?) endure what he must endure, what would you do?

But here this devil's argument, masterly as it is, has left a devilish loophole. Angelo unwittingly concedes that there is "No earthly mean to save him," and the form in which he pursues this thought offers an unintended alternative to the course he is recommending. "Either" and "earthly" are the key words here: "either" Isabella must "lay down the treasures of [her] body" to Angelo, or she can "let him suffer." If "him" refers to Angelo, letting him suffer is indeed the proper way to proceed; insofar as it refers to Claudio, that, too, is appropriate: like all men, Claudio must suffer for his sins and be redeemed, perhaps, by his Maker's mercy, not by his sister's sin. Letting him suffer is the other way, the Christian way, the *heavenly* "mean," to save him.

If Angelo's speech has pretended to a balance between proposing and supposing, her conditional verbs (*"were* I . . . I*'ld wear* . . . I*'ld yield"*—100–103) make clear that it is she now who keeps his proposition at bay by treating it as a supposal. "Then *must* your brother *die*" (104), Angelo concludes. His *must* is especially telling, as it is the form for both the indicative and subjunctive moods. It means at once (1) If you *were* to take this line, your brother *would have* to die; and (2) As you *do* take it, he *will* have to die. Although Isabella must see by now what he is driving at, her language keeps the discussion hypothetical and fictional:

> And *'twere* the cheaper way:
> Better it *were* a brother died at once,
> Than that a sister, by redeeming him,
> *Should die* for ever.
>   (105–8)

The flashing discussion that follows shows both parties making quick responses to gain the advantage. When Isabella admits that she has spoken too permissively of Claudio's vice, Angelo purrs, "We are all frail" (121), preparatory to proposing that she acknowledge the frailty she shares with all women. Isabella seizes on the phrase to renew her plea for her frail brother's life—frail he is, but so were many others who have not been condemned (121–23). It does her no good. Angelo insists on the frailty of *women,* which marks them for their "destin'd livery" (138). He speaks "more gross" (82) at last, but the suppose he offers is a promise or a bribe: Claudio will not die "if you give me love" (144). We learn later that this is a false suppose, that he will not pardon Claudio on any account, and Isabel's threat to denounce him is an empty one. Empty, too, as we soon make out, is her supposal that Claudio's honor will not permit him to hope his sister will give up hers in exchange for his life.

The debate between Angelo and Isabella has followed a pattern of shifting supposes, as each struggles to make the other imagine the situation before them as different from the straightforward criminal case that Angelo at the beginning has insisted that it is. She wants him to imagine a justice tempered by mercy; he wants her to condone a justice corruptible by bribes.

Each, in effect, has devised a suppose that the other cannot possibly accept, and the bargain they enter into is one that neither will honor.

Supposing Isabel

The Duke's continued presence in Vienna constitutes one major change that Shakespeare made from all earlier versions of his story; another is found in Isabella's refusal to accede to Angelo's offer. Shakespeare must have seen that the young woman of earlier versions, though much more sympathetic than her oppressor, is hardly a model of resolute Christian virtue. Her motive in sleeping with the Angelo character is to save her brother (and perhaps marry her seducer), but once the King (or Emperor) has compelled the marriage, her aim is to preserve her criminal husband's life. Earlier versions emphasize her eloquence, the difficulty of her position, and her cleverness, persistence, and prudence in getting what she wants, but they do not stress her virtue, if virtue includes an unmarried young woman's chastity, as it nearly always does in Shakespeare. Shakespeare presumably wanted to make a different point or pattern—to contrast her authentic virtue with a puritan's surface rectitude.[14] Accordingly, he doubles her character, shearing off her practical, what's-to-be-done side onto Mariana, and leaving Isabella, for all her brilliance in argument, attentive only to ethical imperatives. Shakespeare alone gives her a religious vocation, emphasizes her interest in the virtues of silence and obedience, and shows her incapable of even considering Angelo's offer and distressed that her brother is not equally repelled by it. Through this doubling procedure, Shakespeare further contrives to give Isabella the chance to plead (or not) for Angelo's life while she still supposes he has had Claudio killed and without the additional motive (as in the earlier versions) of preserving her own marriage to her seducer.

This change has the effect of making Isabella's moral struggle both more dramatic and more consistent. It accounts for her inflexible refusal to agree to Angelo's terms; for a nun (or almost-nun) to do so would be genuinely shocking, whether or not the act was forced. It also permits Shakespeare to present her experience as a series of tests or trials similar to those that Angelo and others undergo, and directly contrasting with Angelo's. Her first test, clearly, is to resist seduction by Angelo. The second is to resist Claudio's appeal for his life. This is a harder test than the first, for her refusal makes her seem a party to his condemnation, and it leads her into anger and an unjust severity toward Claudio's all-too-human appetite for life.[15]

Because Isabella does not know that the Duke is still in Vienna and still, in his hidden way, in command of events, she undergoes these first two tests under the misapprehension that Angelo's power to execute her brother is not itself subject to arrest. This ignorance allows her to see her situation and Claudio's as potentially tragic and makes her ethical choices authentic, unclouded by false hopes (e.g., of Angelo's sudden reformation). The third test depends on her not being aware that the Duke has prevented Claudio's execution, and it clarifies why he subjects her to such pain and grief in act 5: if the first two tests have shown how courageously she resists evil, even under the strongest pressure, the third shows how a good woman can also forgive her enemy. With nothing to gain from Angelo's continued life, and in the face of the Duke's lurid assurance that if she pleads for him "Her brother's ghost his paved bed would break / And take her hence in horror" (5.1.435–36), she kneels and speaks for Angelo. Because the Duke knows Claudio is alive, his disingenuous suppose can only be testing the extent of Isabella's charity.[16]

Her plea for Angelo takes the form of Gascoigne's "true" or "right" suppose: "Look, if it please you, on this man condemn'd / *As if my brother liv'd*" (5.1.444–45). And so he does. Her virtue, one might argue, has touched on the truth of her own and her brother's situation, and, though she doesn't quite realize it, her later words about Angelo, "His act did not o'ertake his bad intent" (451), apply to her brother's execution as well as to her own averted rape. At this tense moment the challenge to Isabella, and through her to the audience, is especially crucial: faced with tyrannical injustice, tempted to save the life of someone you love by committing what to you is a deadly sin, forced to tell that loved one that you cannot do it, required to plead your cause in a public street before skeptical authorities, then urged to beg on your knees for the life of the man who has caused you all this grief, WHAT WOULD YOU DO? As we noted earlier, the question that drama (sup)poses is a question without risk, and, unlike Isabella, the audience is not obliged to answer it, but one measure of the play's success is whether it induces readers or viewers to reflect on it, to suppose it might refer to them. This is a deeper response, I venture to suppose, and more in keeping with the historical play's evident intention, than easy indignation at a seventeenth-century autocrat's eccentric style of government.

Supposing the Difficult

Audiences, and members of audiences, come to the theater with different sets of expectations, and some supposes will be more difficult for them to make than others. A playwright as shrewd as Shakespeare, though intent on making his series of supposes entertaining, also wants to stretch the expectations of his audience—indeed, like the Duke, to test their capacity for supposing. In *Measure for Measure* the hardest character for a modern audience to suppose is the Duke himself, a puzzling figure who acts many different roles: Renaissance prince, medieval monk-confessor, discriminating justicer, eligible bachelor, and active instigator of the other characters. Recent productions, suspicious of authority, have frequently made him a figure of fun, something of a fool, "a genial bumbler."[17] His arbitrary and inconsistent judgments at the end of the play have also troubled audiences and readers. On the other hand, if we concede that much in his character or behavior might have recalled to a contemporary audience the habits or outlook of King James himself, before whose court we know that the play was performed late in 1604, it is hard to suppose that Shakespeare and his company could have regarded the Duke and his way of resolving the play's moral problems with anything like the hostility and contempt that many modern critics and directors show toward him.[18]

If we keep before us this historical context, it is tempting to suppose that the Duke, as author of the play's major supposes, contriver of its final unmaskings, and judge of its crimes and misdemeanors, is revealed at last to the other characters as the imaginative and moderate judge whom Isabella's argument to Angelo earlier supposed: one who, though he has "a giant's strength," refrains from using it "like a giant" (2.2.109–10) for the self-display that is signaled by "thunder." His judgments all serve to restore, correct, and restrain, or offer new terms of life even to the wayward or brutal. But they should not be taken as a model for earthly justice. Rather, like the good-natured dances that complete a comedy, they mark an occasion of special celebration: Claudio's death and Angelo's worst offenses have been seen to be almost miraculously negated, well- and ill-sorted couples are pairing off, the clever and benevolent ruler has been restored to his grateful people, and an almost indiscriminate amnesty rather than strict justice is, appropriately, the order of the moment.[19] His proposal of marriage to Isabel, far from constituting the monstrous violation of her feminine integrity that some contemporary critics find in it, may be supposed a confirmation, or a softer version, of her original vow of silence and obedience. Early in the play she is eager to embrace these virtues; later, Angelo, enchanted as he is with her disobedient intellect and her formidable powers of speech, arrests her words and commands her to silence. The speechless sexual encounter that he thinks he has imposed on her constitutes a devilish travesty of the nun's entering into her new life as a bride of Christ. The Duke's proposal offers her a more appealing, less confining version of what she was seeking in the first place—"What's mine is yours," he tells her, "and what is yours is mine" (5.1.537)—and if we are not ourselves unjust to the rough justice achieved by the Duke, this strange and much misread personage at the center of the play, we may suppose that for her to accept his offer is, by the logic of the play, perfectly appropriate. Indeed, the silences in the final scene that have encouraged critics and actors to speculate on the possibly dissident or indignant attitudes of other characters[20] might be more persuasively interpreted as evidence of their relief, satisfaction, and amazed acquiescence in what the Duke has accomplished. (See Hayne, esp. 25–29.) Is it really plausible to suppose, as some directors and actresses suggest we should, that Isabella can forgive Angelo for his plot to seduce her and for killing her brother (as she thinks when she pleads for his life), but cannot forgive the Duke, who has saved her brother's life, for not telling her the good news promptly? Would such a forgiving woman be indignant at his proposal of marriage?

For modern democratic readers to suppose the legitimacy of an authoritarian system of justice may be "hard, almost impossible" (to quote Regan on how difficult it is to put up, and put up with, King Lear—2.4.242), especially if, like me, they no longer subscribe to the religious beliefs that underlie this play and the political culture in which it was produced, beliefs still expressed in the autocratic imagery of lord, master, servant, and commandments. We may wish that *Measure for Measure* were putting its cases somewhat differently, and it is tempting to suppose the Duke a fool if we dislike his role as a wielder of arbitrary power in a strongly patriarchal world. A similar antiauthoritarian wish may lie behind the effort to suppose that plays like those of Shakespeare are not written by authors but are largely the result of collaborations in which the author disappears as a recognizable or important contributor. But the playwright, however much he may be aided by his sources, his company of players, his compositors, and his culture, still largely controls the supposes of his play and of his characters, and his power, if not absolute, is, like that of the Duke, often wide and, in its sphere, commanding.

It may also be the focus of the playwright's own play. If *Measure for Measure* measures the tension between the assumptions of secular justice and those of Christian mercy, like other plays it offers as well a paradigm of drama itself, but one that is unusually rich in paradigmatic instances. The substitutions in the play figure those that are needed to perform it: an actor plays the Duke, who plays a monk (Bottom was right: you *can* play more than one part); he says in effect to the actor who plays Angelo, "You be the Duke"; a boy acts Isabella, who urges another boy-woman to take her part in a scarcely supposable offstage sexual encounter. These substitutions and others (of character, action, or rhetoric) are known to the audience, which infers from them a chain of complex story developments, some unshown, and a series of complex ethical judgments, often blurred, that follow from all these supposes—until in the final scene, a triumph of planning and improvisation by the Duke, the masks are removed. When Lucio "Pulls off the friar's hood, and discovers the Duke," most of the mistaken supposes under which the characters have been laboring are instantly corrected: Lucio's, that he can go on lying about how he heard the friar slander the Duke;[21] Angelo's, that his high position is proof against the charges Isabella has made; Mariana's and Isabella's, that the powers of the state are hopelessly ranged against their petition for justice. But all of them still think Claudio dead, a belief whose continuance is essential to the Duke's testing of Isabella's charity. After she pleads for Angelo, and Angelo confirms his penitence, the discovery of Claudio allows all the characters to join the Duke and the audience in that shared lucid understanding with which comedies typically end. All the mistaken supposes on which the play has depended are here dissolved, and it is not necessary for every character to speak in order to bring the comedy to a close. No one but Lucio protests; the others presumably enjoy the byplay and accept, without reservation, the Duke's final disposition of blessings and advice.[22]

The play is a comedy still. Although it has often been, to this point, a dark and troubled one, with the revelations brought about by the final scene's double unmasking the world is shown to be, after all, what the characters, with their limited vision, had feared it was not—still, despite its volatile human evil, under the watch and guidance of a benevolent intelligence. We do not need to overread the Duke allegorically as a shadowy stand-in for a deity to recognize that the city he presides over does indeed bear a resemblance to the protected world of Christian doctrine or Stuart monarchy, with its obscure but sympathetic god or king endeavoring still to keep his unruly people in touch with justice, mercy, virtue, and love. But the play itself, with its "mystaking or imagination of one thing for an other," mirrors the common, often comic, often agonizing, supposes of ordinary life, and the theatrical situation itself.

Appendix: On Slander and Self-Regard

Lucio's slander, for all its comedy, is a heavy fault and deserves severe punishment in a play devoted to sorting out supposes. As Thomas Wilson puts it in a passage familiar to us from Iago's paraphrase, "Who steals my purse steals trash": "slaunder is thefte, and . . . every slaunderer a thief. . . . a slaunderer is worse than anye thiefe, because a good name is better than all the goodes in the worlde. . . . a thefe may restore that agayne whiche he hath taken awaye, but a slaunderer can not geve his good name againe, which he hath taken from him" (*The Arte of Rhetorique,* ed. Thomas J. Derrick [New York, 1982], 255–56). Shakespeare's Sonnet 121 is equally hard on what sounds exactly like Lucio's offense, which maligns the "straight" by charges of which the slanderer himself is guilty ("bevel"). The Duke himself might have written this sonnet, especially lines 5–6: "For why should others' false adulterate eyes / Give salutation to my sportive blood?" This sonnet's speaker, like the Duke, does not find the slanderer amusing (as of course the audience of *Measure for Measure* does and should), and, as far as I know, no commentator on the poem has pronounced its speaker guilty of "self-exculpation."

Unlike many modern critics, who find Lucio's behavior merely comic, "playfully fractious," and even sensible and "sane," medieval and Renaissance writers and artists took a much more serious view of slander, regarding it as "the speech of envy, one of the Deadly Sins, and associated . . . primarily with Satan's malevolence." (Joyce H. Sexton, *The Slandered Woman in Shakespeare* [Victoria, B. C.: University of Victoria, 1978, ELS Monograph Series No. 12]). That Shakespeare took the same view seems clear from his wholly unsympathetic portrayals of the chief slanderers in his plays: Don John, Iago, Edmund, and Iachimo. For slander is a kind of obverse of the usual form of supposing; it asks the listener not only to suppose that the slanderer is speaking the truth, but also to suppose that a perfectly innocent person (Hero, Desdemona, Edgar, Imogen) is false. In slandering the Duke, Lucio is conforming almost exactly to the behavior of these other slanderers; the difference is only that the effect is comic and the audience is amused by knowing that he will surely get his comeuppance. By inventing stories about the Duke's psychic life—his "campaign" (Berger, 394) to "scapegoat" Angelo, his lascivious secondhand pleasure in the bed trick, his perverse desire to manipulate everyone else and "exculpate" himself from all responsibility, some modern critics seem to be conniving in Lucio's slander (or are fictional characters fair game?).

As for the charge that "Lucio's slanders are much less damaging than the Duke's exhibition of indignant, obsessive self-regard" (Bradshaw, 191), note that almost all Shakespeare's rulers and tragic personages, as well as many comic characters, are self-regarders, deeply interested in the picture they present to others. The Duke is not exceptional in this, but his critics condemn in him what in others is sometimes an amusing and even forgivable comic trait and in kings and dukes understandable: they are always on display, and their fortunes often depend on how they appear to others. One might write a book on the varieties of self-regard, richly revelatory of character but by no means always a sign of wickedness, to be found in Beatrice and Benedick, the Prince of Morocco, Berowne, Richards III and II, Othello, Malvolio, Proteus, Falstaff, Prince Hal, Wolsey, Posthumus, Leontes, Cleopatra, Coriolanus, Caesar, Juliet, Lear, and Hamlet, among many others. In some characters it is not an attractive quality, but it plays differently in different contexts, which there is not space to sort out here. Contemporary critics' contempt for the Duke's occasional speeches of self-regard may owe something to D. H. Lawrence's condemnation of this vice (which was echoed in the 1930s by W. H. Auden and others).

LINES OF THE POETS

> . . . the way a leaf
> Above the table spins its constant spin,
> So that we look at it with pleasure, look
>
> At it spinning its eccentric measure . . .
> —Wallace Stevens

In the 1980s I began to write in earnest about English metrics. The essays in "Lines of the Poets" show this interest variously, as they study Wyatt's strangely metered poems in the light both of earlier and of later English poetry (1985); the powerful stanzas mixing pentameter and shorter and longer iambic lines that Donne contrived for his *Songs and Sonets* (1988); Yeats's short poem, "Crazy Jane on God," and its elegant use of meter, rhyme, phrasing, and imagery to design stanzas of great subtlety and strength (1982); and Robert Lowell's pentameter line as it figures in the shifting back and forth between formal and free verse that marked Lowell's whole career (1981).

The polemical review-essay "Hearing the Measures" (1997) considers in detail four contemporary contributions to metrical theory and criticism, ranging from the intelligent (but, I argue, sometimes flawed) work of Derek Attridge and his disciple Brennan O'Donnell to two much less impressive (and, in my view, less responsible) practitioners of the critical craft. This long review discusses, among other things, the kinds of notation critics can usefully choose to represent what we hear in a line of verse, and it insists as always on our need to *listen* to the rhythmical patterns of poetry.

"Lines of the Poets" concludes with two more personal essays. "Pulse and Breath" (1971), along with the friendly exchange of views that it led to with X. J.

Kennedy (1993), debates the different kinds of appeal represented by free verse and formal verse. "Troubles of a Professional Meter Reader" (1994) offers a brief account of my involvement in metrical study and surveys the different incapacities for coping with metrical problems that afflict specialists of different kinds—linguists, "timers," actors, theorists, editors, and even literary meter readers like myself.

Wyatt's Decasyllabic Line

I

Sir Thomas Wyatt's irregular decasyllabic line has never been clearly understood. Even those readers who have liked his "rougher" sonnets and such other metrically difficult poems as "They fle from me" have not been sure how the lines are to be read. The twentieth-century reader of poetry has learned to value expressive departures from metrical norms, to enjoy the irregular harmonies of Donne, the sprung rhythms of Hopkins, and even a free verse built on looser verse principles. Indeed, smoothness in verse has come to be regarded as dull and monotonous, and the long critical preference for Surrey's correct over Wyatt's ambiguous rhythms has turned, during this century, entirely to Wyatt's advantage. Despite the renewed interest in his poetry, however, Wyatt's strange meters seem almost as baffling as ever. "This is a vexed question," one of his most prominent critics and editors wrote in 1974, "which will never, I think, be settled to everyone's satisfaction."[1]

Yet the materials for understanding the metrical system Wyatt used in his rhythmically puzzling poems have long been available to scholars, and recent studies of his manuscripts, of his courtly career, and of the nature of the court in which he served can only help us to see his art more clearly. In the last few decades, despite enormous difficulties, editors of Wyatt have been working to achieve reliable texts of his poems,[2] and other scholars have made it far easier to understand the conditions under which Wyatt and other "courtly makers" of the period composed their lyric poems.[3] As text and milieu become more intelligible, so should Wyatt's metrics, and we need not rest content with the incomplete or mistaken "solutions" that have periodically proceeded from critical bewilderment. On the contrary, if we know where to look for guidance, we can even now see Wyatt's metric in relation to the prosodic system he inherited, to some features of the Italian one that influenced him, and to the one that became dominant after his death.

That Wyatt's meters must be approached in the context of all these systems has not been widely recognized, and recent study of Wyatt's meter has been clouded by scholars' apparent ignorance of the complex metrical situation that obtained in England between Chaucer and Surrey. The understandable prejudice against pedantic (Germanic) techniques of prosodic classification and genealogy ("*Classificatum est,*" rails Saintsbury, "and apparently nothing more is thought necessary"[4]) has so disinclined modern scholars to read old-fashioned prosodists that most of those who write on Wyatt's metrics, even when they acknowledge his debt to an older tradition, seem impatient with its details. Still, we cannot possibly appraise Wyatt's metrical technique without establishing, by informed analysis, what in his lines is new and what is inherited.

Saintsbury, like many earlier prosodists, thought Wyatt didn't quite know what he was doing: "We seem to be looking from afar at a man running or walking over a course beset with all sorts of visible stumbling-blocks and invisible snares, into which and over which he is perpetually stumbling and tumbling, yet picking himself up and pressing on towards the goal."[5] It was thought for a long time, in fact, that while Wyatt was thrashing about in a syllabic swamp, Surrey mastered the trick of writing a proper ten-syllable line. Until scholars got the dates straight and realized how much older Wyatt was (born fourteen years before Surrey), it was even for a while the prevailing view that Surrey had generously shared the secrets of his art with Wyatt the backward pupil.[6] But even now the myth of Wyatt's metrical incompetence has not been set wholly to rest, for many of his poems are hard to assimilate to any pattern we are used to hearing as iambic pentameter. For example:

> Like to these unmesurable montayns
> Is my painfull lyff the burden of Ire,
> For of great height be they, and high is my desire,
> And I of teres, and they be full of fontayns.
> (XXXIII)

Only the fourth line seems regular, by the standards of later verse, and the others have seemed to skillful later readers to provide evidence that Wyatt "is, like some of his predecessors, floundering about for a foothold on stresses that may happen anywhere in the bog."[7]

The chief difficulty with such a view is that many of Wyatt's decasyllabic lines are perfectly sound, some whole sonnets are metrically regular, and many shorter-line poems are not only regular but seem expert in their handling of rhythms. How then can we believe that so assured a master would, in effect, go to pieces metrically when confronted with the decasyllabic line, and then only in *some* poems?

Since Saintsbury's day, however, Wyatt's critics have felt more indulgent toward his breaking of metrical pattern. Most contemporary readers prefer his enigmatic rhythms to the "improved" lines that appeared over his name in Tottel's *Miscellany* in 1557, and the usual critical view sees Wyatt's verse not as a stumbling effort to master iambic pentameter but as obscurely obedient to principles of its own, which Wyatt uses with skill to achieve important, original, and profound effects. It has even been proposed that all of Elizabethan poetry is, after Wyatt, a frightful falling off and that in the interests of smoothness even Shakespeare, at a high moment of *Macbeth*, "behaves [prosodically] like one of Pavlov's dogs."[8] An extreme position, but Wyatt's verse makes a strong appeal to many modern readers, and it is easy to feel, after immersion in its "hesitant, pausing rhythms,"[9] that the smooth metrical finish of later iambic verse is tripping and trivial by comparison.

One theory that has commanded attention in recent decades is that Wyatt's aim in his difficult sonnets, and in all his apparently decasyllabic verse—at least in the lines that do not scan—was not to write iambic pentameter but to compose in rhythmic phrases. This theory undoubtedly derived support, and perhaps inspiration, from C. S. Lewis's earlier suggestion that the fifteenth-century heroic line, with its strong caesura, is really a fusion of two-stress and three-stress phrases like those that often appear in popular shorter-line lyrics of the period.[10] The full phrasal view, however, is the work of D. W. Harding, who believes that Wyatt employs a "pausing rhythm" in much of his verse, following "the general plan of two balancing rhythmical units in a line, with a pause dividing them."[11] The units so divided may or may not compose a metrical line—apparently, Wyatt didn't care and saw no problem in mixing flowing lines and pausing lines. Raymond Southall carries this kind of analysis further by showing how Wyatt's lines use this pausing rhythm to achieve dramatic poises, balances, and "see-sawing" rhythms.[12]

These studies, especially Southall's, have made us more alert to Wyatt's skill in manipulating phrases. But the effort to see Wyatt's verse as somehow related to the decasyllabic line is not entirely wrongheaded. If the Chaucer that Wyatt inherited was misprinted and misread, a tradition of iambic verse still beats strongly in all but his most inept imitators; no one can doubt for a moment that in his four-stress lyrics Wyatt used it almost all the time; and the problem that remains, and that Wyatt prosodists of the rhythmic school have really not even touched upon, is that although all poets compose in phrases as well as lines, there is no evidence whatever in the metrical history of Wyatt's time to suggest that anyone, in that period so remote from free verse, ever dreamed of equating the phrase with the line or half-line, or thought of an unmetered phrase as a metrical unit, which is essentially what the rhythmic theory claims. That is to say, the rhythmic theory doesn't solve the problem of Wyatt's metrics because it doesn't address it; it merely asks us to look at something else.[13]

Those who offer a phrasal analysis of Wyatt's verse are the more disposed to do so because the contrary view—that Wyatt's poems follow an essentially iambic pattern, but with wider-than-usual variations from the metrical norm—was long ago proposed in a notably unconvincing form by Wyatt's early twentieth-century editor, A. K. Foxwell.[14] Her argument, later supplemented by Frederick Morgan Padelford,[15] contends that Wyatt uses monosyllabic, anapestic, and trochaic feet, slurs many liquids and nasals, sometimes compresses such endings as *-eth, -en, -on, -er,* and *-ing,* sometimes treats long vowels or diphthongs as dissyllabic, accents some syllables oddly, and occasionally substitutes alexandrines or four-stress lines for the usual pentameter. In effect, these scholars, by jumbling together Wyatt's metrical paradigms, metrical variations, syllabic procedures, and accentual conventions, make his principles sound bewilderingly chaotic. As critics have understandably complained, an iambic pentameter that departs so often and so promiscuously from the norm is no longer iambic pentameter. To be sure, many of these variations are encountered in what later became traditional decasyllabic poetry, or in Chaucer, but some of them go beyond the bounds of normal variation and, especially in prolific combination, produce a line that at least seems to require special description.

In my view, the truth about Wyatt's metric is to be found by steering deftly between this Scylla and Charybdis, but nearer, in this case, to Charybdis. There is something to be said for those who emphasize Wyatt's skill in maneuvering his phrases, but much more for those who insist that, strange as they sometimes sound, the lines Wyatt was writing are decasyllabic. Indeed, he appears to have been the first English poet to grasp—but in a different form from his distant successors—the dual basis of English iambic verse: that the metrical line and the natural rhythm of the language engage each other in a continuing struggle and, in order to abide harmoniously in each other's presence, submit to certain standard modifications. In this process, the decasyllabic line may accept variations and rearrangements, and the rhythm of English speech may be gently distorted by syllabic extensions or compressions, by grammatical inversions, and by direction of stress to some normally unstressed syllables. Wherever the language forces the meter a little, the result is likely to be expressive; where the meter forces the language, the result will seem formal. These two powers, of expressiveness and formality, largely organize Wyatt's meter, and we may see them as standing, respectively, for the rival authorities that compete constantly in the world his poems present: the baffling, contradictory, obsessive, and insistent inner feelings, and the laws of court, king, and savior.

II

Contrary to what some critics have thought or feared, Wyatt knew how to write a regular decasyllabic line. His poems include hundreds that give us no difficulty at all. In fact, by far the greater number of decasyllabic lines in his sonnets and psalms are highly regular. At least nine of his thirty decasyllabic sonnets are regular throughout. He typically ends his sonnets with regular lines and frequently begins them so—which implies that the variant line was an instrument for suggesting complication, for expressing the agitated states of mind that the interior lines of his sonnets are appropriately designed to present.

Wyatt's metrical departures are essentially of two kinds: casual and structural. By the first term I mean the variations that became standard in later iambic verse—spondees, pyrrhics, and trochees—along with some other metrical patterns that did *not* become standard later on, and that make his verse seem odd: for example, a pyrrhic followed by a trochee, or a monosyllabic foot (itself odd-sounding to our ears) followed by a trochee, or an iamb followed by a monosyllabic foot. Because Wyatt was working at the beginning of the iambic tradition, he had no way of knowing which variations would become acceptable features of that tradition, and his invention of others should be taken as evidence of a fine ear, not a poor one.

But Wyatt did not invent the decasyllabic line, and part of his difficulty is found in the structure of that line as it came down to him from Chaucer. It came down in more than one form, and Wyatt, like later Tudor poets, was engaged in an effort to recompose it. That the final -*e*, which might or might not be pronounced in Chaucer's verse, had disappeared from English speech was only a small part of the problem; after all, the poems of Wyatt and his contemporaries still pronounce -*es* frequently and -*e* sometimes if they need it to fill out a line. But the available editions of Chaucer were corrupt and implied either that Chaucer had a faulty ear or that he had used a peculiar metric. Such Scottish writers as Henryson and Dunbar retained Chaucer's metrical regularity, but his chief English successor, John Lydgate, developed some deviant lines, which became standard for English poets composing in "iambic pentameter." These deviations were classified long ago by the German scholar Schick:[16]

   a. Regular iambic pentameter (ˇ′ˇ′ˇ′ˇ′ˇ′).
   b. Regular, except that there is an extra unstressed syllable before the caesura (ˇ′ˇ′ˇ | ˇ′ˇ′ˇ′).
   c. Regular, except that the line lacks an unstressed syllable after the caesura (ˇ′ˇ′ | ′ˇ′ˇ′).
   d. Regular, except that the line lacks an unstressed syllable at the beginning (′ˇ′ˇ′ˇ′ˇ′).
   e. Regular, except that there is an extra unstressed syllable at the beginning (ˇˇ′ˇ′ˇ′ˇ′ˇ′).

These types seem simple enough, and poets of the fifteenth and early sixteenth centuries used them freely. One result was to make the verse of the period sound, to a modern ear, unmetrical. After all, the "headless" line *(d)*, though often used by Chaucer, appears infrequently in English poetry between Wyatt and James Merrill, so to begin a line with a stressed syllable that is not part of an initial trochee may surprise and disconcert us. But its oddity is mild compared with that of the so-called broken-backed line *(c)*, which gives us an apparent monosyllabic foot in the middle ("Ăfóre hĭs brést, | fráwtўd wíth dĭsése" [CVIII, 68]);[17] and the extra syllables of *b* and *e* provide what sound like anapests to a later ear—not for us a serious blemish but, except for some later dramatic blank verse (including Shakespeare's), unusual in English iambic pentameter from Surrey to Cowper. Metrical scholars have also not realized how often these types are combined, especially in the verse of Wyatt.

The variations at the beginning of the line are relatively easy to get used to; it is the variations at the caesura that make Lydgate's line sound aberrant. We should remember that the decasyllabic verse most familiar to us requires no caesura at all; that in later centuries a pause, if it occurs, may occur anywhere within the line, not necessarily after or near the fourth syllable, although throughout the history of iambic pentameter the fourth syllable has seemed to most poets a likely place to pause. Heptameter lines tend to break after the eighth syllable and to divide into segments of four stresses and three stresses. But iambic pentameter does not work that way. In contrast to all other widely used verse forms in English that are longer than trimeter, the decasyllabic cannot, like the octosyllabic, divide into two equal parts—and does not, like the heptameter, divide into, successively, a longer and a shorter segment. If the decasyllabic divides into two phrases, three stresses appear on one side of the break and two on the other. But in iambic verse of this period that breaks somewhere, the most common arrangement is 2–3; the 3–2 division is less common, and pauses may occur elsewhere as well, though with less frequency.

But there is a substantial difference between a line like Wyatt's "I fynde no peace | and all my warr is done" (XXVI), in which the break comes cleanly after the fourth syllable, and either of these two lines:

> Whŏm móre thĕn gód / ór hy̆msélllff hĕ mýndy̆th
> (CVIII, 26)
>
> Thĕ sówle wĭth mércy̆, / thăt mércy̆ só dĭd Crýe
> (CVIII, 298)

In the first of these two lines, our sense of a missing syllable requires us to stress *or* and thereby to call attention to the whole phrase *or hymsellff,* the importance of which we might otherwise miss. In the second line, the third foot is not an anapest; what looks like its first unstressed syllable belongs metrically to the first half-line. That is, the pause in such a line is obligatory, structural; it is an authentic caesura, and this kind has often been called an epic (or feminine) caesura. Lines like these seem different in character from regular lines that offer what seems rather a discretionary break at the fourth syllable ("They fle from me that sometyme did me seke"); but both these kinds are different in nature from decasyllabic lines that break not at all ("The multitudinous seas incarnadine" or "What though the radiance which was once so bright"). The Lydgatian line especially, with its distinctive pause, seems stitched out of two half-lines, and the caesura is a crucial structural fact.[18] It is probable that the powerful tradition of four-stress alliterative verse encouraged English poets to think of the strong caesura as a necessary feature even of the five-stress line and to treat this line not as a disguised version of four-stress verse (as some scholars have argued) but as like it in being made up of two component halves, which find their places on either side of a decisive midline break.

Poetry composed this way involves the fitting together of two half-lines, the first consisting of 3–6 syllables (but usually 4–5), the second of 5–7 (but usually 5–6). At the end or at the beginning of each half-line there may be an extra unstressed syllable; at the beginning of each, one may be omitted. But the key to the line's structure is the joining, and every competent poet from Lydgate to Wyatt who composed in this pattern must have known it, as the frequent, or even regular, manuscript inclusion of a virgule (/) at the caesura proves. He must have known, specifically, that he had at his disposal at least eight metrical line-patterns (not Schick's five), depending on how many syllables the two half-lines contained, and even assuming no further deviations. That is, he could use any of four patterns in the first half-line:

a. ⌣ˊ⌣ˊ		c. ˊ⌣ˊ	
b. ⌣ˊ⌣ˊ⌣		d. ˊ⌣ˊ⌣	

And he could use any of four patterns in the second half-line:

e. ⌣ˊ⌣ˊ⌣ˊ		g. ˊ⌣ˊ⌣ˊ	
f. ⌣ˊ⌣ˊ⌣ˊ⌣		h. ˊ⌣ˊ⌣ˊ⌣	

From these half-line patterns (a–h) he could make up eight basic line-forms, each of which could be varied by a feminine ending.[19]

1.	⌣ˊ⌣ˊ ⌣ˊ⌣ˊ⌣ˊ		5.	ˊ⌣ˊ ⌣ˊ⌣ˊ⌣ˊ
1f.	⌣ˊ⌣ˊ ⌣ˊ⌣ˊ⌣ˊ⌣		5f.	ˊ⌣ˊ ⌣ˊ⌣ˊ⌣ˊ⌣
2.	⌣ˊ⌣ˊ ˊ⌣ˊ⌣ˊ		6.	ˊ⌣ˊ ˊ⌣ˊ⌣ˊ
2f.	⌣ˊ⌣ˊ ˊ⌣ˊ⌣ˊ⌣		6f.	ˊ⌣ˊ ˊ⌣ˊ⌣ˊ⌣
3.	⌣ˊ⌣ˊ⌣ ⌣ˊ⌣ˊ⌣ˊ		7.	ˊ⌣ˊ⌣ ⌣ˊ⌣ˊ⌣ˊ
3f.	⌣ˊ⌣ˊ⌣ ⌣ˊ⌣ˊ⌣ˊ⌣		7f.	ˊ⌣ˊ⌣ ⌣ˊ⌣ˊ⌣ˊ⌣
4.	⌣ˊ⌣ˊ⌣ ˊ⌣ˊ⌣ˊ		8.	ˊ⌣ˊ⌣ ˊ⌣ˊ⌣ˊ
4f.	⌣ˊ⌣ˊ⌣ ˊ⌣ˊ⌣ˊ⌣		8f.	ˊ⌣ˊ⌣ ˊ⌣ˊ⌣ˊ⌣

Lines based on all these line-types appear in poetry written between Chaucer and Wyatt. For the sake of clarity and succinctness, the list below omits lines with feminine endings:

1. Ănd wáke ăll níght, / ănd sléep tĭll ít bĕ nóon
   (Skelton, "The Bouge of Court," st. 55)

2. Fŏre wél thŏu wóst / íf Ĭ sháll nŏt féine.
   (Lydgate, *The Temple of Glas*, II, 911)

3. Tŏ máke thĕe mérrў, / ăs óthĕr féllŏws dóne.
   (Skelton, "The Bouge of Court," st. 55)

4. Bў tástĕd swétenĕs / máke mĕ nót tŏ réw.
   (Wyatt, LXXIX, 3)

5. Whát ărt thóu? / Ĭ sáw thĕe nów bŭt láte.
   (Skelton, "The Bouge of Court," st. 54)

6. 'Áy,' quŏd hé, / 'ín thĕ dévĭl's dáte,'
   (Skelton, "The Bouge of Court," st. 54)

7. Sól ănd Lúnă / wĕre clýpsўd óf thĕr líht.
   (Lydgate, "Letter to Gloucester," 29; virgule in text)

8. Wás I névĕr, / yét, ŏf yóur lŏve gréevĕd
   (Wyatt, IX, 1)

Occasionally, poets writing in this mode place the caesura after the line's third main stress, which means after the fifth, sixth, or seventh syllable. When such lines follow the eight variant patterns above, they form eight subtypes, which occur less frequently than the eight basic types, probably because the later caesura is felt to weaken the end of the line and perhaps to invite enjambment.

1a. Tŏ wálke ўn tó thĕ brígge / & táke ă bóot.
   (Hoccleve, "Mâle Règle," 190; virgule in text)

2a. Yĭt máist thŏu stónde ĭn gráce / íf thŏu wílt.
   (Hoccleve, "Dialogue with a Friend," 686; virgule in text)

3a. Nŏwe lást ŏr nót fĕr fróm ĭt / ĭt ís nŏ fáile.
   (Hoccleve, "Dialogue with a Friend," 529; virgule in text)

4a. Nŏr háue hĕ táke ă púrpŏs / þt mŏot néede.
   (Hoccleve, "Mâle Règle," 75; virgule in text)

> 5a. Hére mў práyer ŏ lórd, / hĕre mý rĕqúest.
> (Wyatt, CVIII, 727)
>
> 6a. Yíf sŏ wére thĕes lándes / wére ălle óon.
> (Lydgate, "Epithalamium for Gloucester," 166; virgule in text)
>
> 7a. Cáll hĭm Álĕssaúndrĕ, / ănd sáy thăt Pán
> (Wyatt, CV, 48)
>
> 8a. Bý thăt líttlĕ cónnĭng / thát Ĭ háve.
> (Skelton, "The Bouge of Court," st. 55)

These patterns are essentially displacements of the fourth-syllable caesuras; the phrase in the first half-line is simply two syllables longer, the phrase in the second half-line two syllables shorter.

Much more rare is the line that includes a strong break at other points—after the first or fourth stresses; when this happens, the line still almost always breaks again near the fourth or sixth syllable:

> Hap / or fortune / in Conclusioun
> (Lydgate, "Prologue to the Siege of Thebes," 69; virgules in text)
>
> Eerthely god / piler of life / thow helthe
> (Hoccleve, "Mâle Règle," 8; virgules in text)

The first four basic line-types may be further varied by an extra unstressed syllable at the beginning of the line:

> 1b. Whŏsŏ líst tŏ hóunte, / Ĭ knów whĕre ís ăn hýnde
> (Wyatt, VII, 1)
>
> 2b. Thŏrrŏugh rócký sées, / ovĕr hílles ănd pláynes
> (Wyatt, VIII, 46)
>
> 3b. Fŏr ŏf gréat hĕight bé thĕy, / ănd hígh ĭs mý dĕsíre
> (Wyatt, XXXIII, 3)
>
> 4b. Ŏf mў mástĕr Lýdgăte, / with dŭe éxĕrcíse
> (Hawes, "The Pastime of Pleasure," Dedication, 48)

I have found no lines, in Wyatt or other poets, that combine the *a* and *b* types; the extra syllable at the beginning must have seemed incompatible with a late caesura, perhaps because it would make the line's opening phrase too long.

These eight basic line-types, with variants (*a, b,* and *f*) that can generate as many as forty different line-patterns, essentially derive from the normal line (1), the broken-backed line (2), the line with an epic caesura (3), and the headless line (5), and their combinations (3 and 2 produce 4; 5 and 2 produce 6; 5 and 1 produce 7; 5, 3, and 2 produce 8). Oddly enough, when the epic caesura turns up in a broken-backed line (4 or 4*a*) the result may sound like normal iambic pentameter; it may not have sounded that way to the poet.

To later ears, most of these lines were unmetrical. They have too many syllables (3, 3*a,* 1*b,* 3*b,* 4*b*) or too few (2, 5, 6, 8, 2*a,* 5*a,* 6*a,* 8*a*), or they contain monosyllabic feet in midline (2, 2a, 2b, 6, 6a). We can tolerate the headless lines (5, 5*a,* 8, 8*a*) and perhaps the ones that appear to have a medial anapest (7, 7*a,* 3, 3*a*), but the only ones we understand as "regular" iambic pentameter are lines 1 and 4 (and 1*a* and 4*a*). Insofar as these lines can be regarded as ancestors of later iambic pentameter, they suggest that traditional regular lines are of two types, depending on whether they pause after the fourth (or sixth) or after the fifth (or seventh) syllable—or, in other words, on whether their rhythm is essentially iambic and runs *with* the meter, or trochaic and runs *against* it. The difference is that between "When I do count the clock that tells the time" and "And pity, like a naked new-born babe," although many later lines fall between these rhythmic extremes.

This eight-line system was Wyatt's keyboard. He could find any of these lines in earlier poets (several of them in Chaucer), who used them almost exclusively for variety and convenience. That is to say, a verse that included only one or two line-types would have seemed monotonous and dull. Variety was needed to make the verse musically flexible, to keep the reader's ear occupied with attractive sound. And this metrical system, before Wyatt, basically used a multiplicity of line-types, rather than numerous metrical substitutions, to achieve variety. Then, too, so various a system made it much easier to accommodate the phrases that might occur to the poet. Indeed, the prosy character of much fifteenth-century poetry suggests how little some poets revised the phrases that came into their heads. For the first half-line at least, almost any phrase of three, four, or five syllables, or even six, could, with a little pruning, fit one or another of the possible half-line types; the second half-line, though stricter in meter, could be further varied by an occasional trochaic departure.

Wyatt, too, uses the keyboard for variety and convenience, as every good poet must. His unique contribution to it is that he uses it also for expressive purposes. He had already learned how metrical variations from a steady iambic base could be used for expressive purposes in a four-beat meter. In "My lute, awake," for example, the brief four-syllable phrases are repeatedly accented by expressive trochaic variations:

> Perchaunce the lye *wethered* and old,
> The wynter nyghtes that are so cold,
> *Playning* in vain vnto the mone;
> Thy wisshes then *dare not* be told;
> Care then who lyst, for I have done.
>
> And then may chaunce *the to* repent.
> (LXVI)

The variant phrases intensify the sarcasm that drenches this speaker's utterance and convey the injured feeling with the needed bite.

To move from four beats to five does not normally entail a radical stylistic upheaval, but Wyatt, in his early sonnets, those "unmesurable montayns" whose meter is so enigmatic, evidently found an opportunity to use for expressive purposes not only those metrical variations in which he was already well schooled but also the multiple paradigmatic lines of the decasyllabic tradition he found in Lydgate and Skelton. Most of the time he was translating from the Italian, usually Petrarch, and he must have realized that in the Italian sonnet form he had touched a deeper current of poetry. Whereas the rime-royal stanzas common among Chaucer and his successors were an admirable form for continuous stately narrative or for the expression of public sentiments, the Italian sonnet, with its interweaving rhymes and flowing, yet segmented, sentences, its multiple elisions (which hurry the line) and its lingering feminine endings, seems fitted for a much more private utterance, especially for the tracing of half-hidden, debating, contradictory, and ironic feelings that course within the troubled breast of a lover.

Southall argues convincingly that Wyatt's best verse is "a psychological drama of inner perturbation and distress" (67); it "expresses the doubts, anxieties, trials and tribulations of an unusually sensitive mind confronting a perplexing and dangerously insecure world" (69). The poems in octosyllabic meters, with their sharp rhythms, portray this perilous realm through formal pairings and confrontations, half-line matching half-line, rhymed line matching rhymed line. The effect perhaps is of a brightly decorated jousting or dancing, the oppositions well-lit and precisely set up, even though we know that beneath them lurk questions about love and court that are deliberately left unresolved. But the sonnets are darker altogether, the balances (between two-foot and three-foot segments) less precise, less predictable. The longer line lends itself to many different internal arrangements; its ambiguous oppositions must be posed more problematically within or between half-lines, between line and line, quatrain and quatrain, though even here, in the management of the sonnet's segments, Wyatt the master of balanced phrases rarely lets his periods correspond to his quatrains. The long but faintly out-of-step procession of self-judging, self-condemning utterances conveys the troubled turning of a mind in anguish or uncertainty. The mystery of love's insecurity, its incessant bewilderments, can be intimated through the obscurity of the rhythms, the obsessive hesitations, quickenings, and tightenings of the jointed line.

It seems likely, therefore, that as he wrote out his versions of Petrarch's poems, with the Italian texts constantly before him, Wyatt was trying to provide in English a poetic texture similar to Petrarch's. One way to do this was to make frequent use of elisions, of lengthenings and shortenings of syllables within the line, in order to render in an English equivalent the Italian manner of racing over some syllables and pausing importantly on others. The Lydgatian decasyllabic was an obvious model, and he used it for these translations. It is possible that until this time he had not much written either this version or the regular Scottish decasyllabic; that almost all of his earlier poems were in shorter meters. But for a sensitive metrist the eight-line system provided opportunities to imitate the Italian system of alternately speeding and slowing syllable-groups. The extra unstressed syllable at the beginning of the line, at the caesura, or at the line-ending might recall the tumbling trochaic rhythms of the Italian hendecasyllable, even at the risk of occasionally losing the iambic feeling. Furthermore, the shortening of syllables that we call elision, synaloepha, synaeresis, or syncope may indicate only a metrical value, not a real amalgamation of distinct syllables; after all, words like *frossen* and *stondeth* (see below, 113) can only with difficulty be made to sound like monosyllables even when we agree to think of them that way for the meter's sake.[20] If Wyatt was, indeed, trying to find an English equivalent for the Italian of Petrarch, the syllabic ambiguity of English *-e, -es, -ed, -eth,* and *-en,* especially in the metrical setting of the Lydgatian line, afforded him the most promising opportunities.

In translating a sonnet like Petrarch's "Orso; al vostro destrier si po ben porre," for example, Wyatt (in XXVII) could hardly have failed to notice certain lines that seemed in Italian to be sounded with an epic caesura:

> So brama onor*e* / e'l suo contrario aborre?
> Non sospirat*e:* / a lui no si po tôrre.
> (4–5)
>
> Co'l signor mi*o,* / che non po seguitarme.
> (13)

The elision or synaloepha required at the first two junctures (marked here with a virgule) does not entirely suppress either italicized vowel; rather, the vowels are fused, but the effect to an English ear would have been much like that of the epic caesura. As we might expect, the type-3 line turns up at least twice in Wyatt's poem (7, 8).

Wyatt's use of the traditional line, then, is far more purposeful and intelligent than that of his post-Chaucerian predecessors, who for the most part adopt it automatically, without any thought about its inherent capacities, as a narrative or celebratory instrument—the poet's fife and drum. Even if their lines, too, can be seen, with the aid of the eight-line system, as more often regular than we have been used to finding them, they seem to drift from one line-type to another for no *expressive* purposes. In the same spirit, they rarely introduce pyrrhic, spondaic, or trochaic variations in order to reflect meaning in sound. They understand meter purely as a frame, not as an expressive instrument.[21] But Wyatt, no doubt because of his wider acquaintance with Continental models, especially with Petrarch, is utterly different from all his predecessors, including Chaucer, in regarding meter as an expressive material whose departures from exact metronomic repetition can reflect the changing emotions of a troubled speaker and incorporate some of the syllabic texture of Italian verse. This is not to say that earlier poets never write an expressive line, but that they fall into it only occasionally at best—instinctively, not consciously and as a matter of consistent artistic principle. But Wyatt means to do it, and his difficult sonnets do it in almost every line. In composing this way, he may be asking that variable line he inherited to attempt something it was not developed to do, and that the later, stricter pentameter line would be better fitted for. He even appears to have realized this, and to have made his later sonnets, and his satires, cling more closely to an iambic norm. But what we can discern in his extraordinary sonnets is an extremely able and inventive metrist struggling to invest a brisk and racy metrical system with a flexible expressiveness that is at this point literally foreign to it.

III

To appraise both Wyatt's resources and his problems, we can look at one of his metrically puzzling sonnets (XXIX) and see how all the lines conform to the system of line-types described above. Some of the lines are susceptible of alternative readings, but still without going beyond the system I have outlined. In the scansion that follows, I have ignored possible pyrrhics and spondees in order to show unambiguously where the metrical stresses come. But trochaic inversions are shown in lines 2, 3, and 11. Note, too, that in an actual reading of such lines it is possible that stress was sometimes more evenly distributed between competing syllables than a scansion indicates—for example, *moisteth, streght from, fruytles.*[22] (It may help the reader to be reminded that among the line-types an *a* appearing with a number signifies a late caesura, *b* an extra initial unstressed syllable, and *f* a feminine ending.)

		Line-type
	Ăuýsĭng thé brĭ́ght bémes / ŏf thése făyer Iýes,	1*a*
	Whĕre hĕ is thăt mýn / óft móistĕth ănd wásshĕth,	2*f*
	Thĕ wĕrĭd mýnde / stréght frŏm thĕ hért dĕpártĕth	1*f*
	Fór tŏ rést / in his woroldlỹ párădíse,	5
5	Ănd fýnde thĕ swéte / bítter vndĕr thĭs gýse.	2
	Whát wĕbbes hé hăth wróught / wĕll hé pĕrcévĕth	5*af*
	Whérebỹ wíth hĭmsélf / ŏn lóve hĕ pláynĕth	5*af*
	Thăt spurreth wĭth fyér / ănd brĭdĭlléth wĭth Íse.	1
	Thús ĭs ít / ĭn súche ĕxtremĭtĭe bróught:	5
10	Ĭn fróssen thŏught nówe / ănd nówe ĭt stondeth ĭn fláme;	1
	Twỹst mísery and wélth, / twíst érnĕst ănd gáme;	2
	Bút fĕw glád / ănd mány a dỹvĕrs thóught	5
	Wĭth sóre rĕpéntaŭnce / óf hĭs hárdĭnés:	4
	Ŏf súche ă róte / cómĕth ffrúyte frŭytlés.	2

Metrically, we find here eight different line-types (four basic ones): a different scansion might produce others.[23] Some caesuras are not very strong (lines 7, 9, 13), but in several other lines our sense of the caesura helps to give the needed weight to certain syllables or to separate the strong syllable just before it from the one just after (lines 2, 6, 14). Wyatt evidently wants a slow-moving meter that hesitates at the line's center and then lurches forward again, sometimes it seems reluctantly, sometimes almost in pain. We need not claim that all Wyatt's effects are successful, or even that this is one of Wyatt's finest poems; but it exhibits his metrical art clearly, shows the variety of lines he deployed and his typical use of elision, synaloepha, syncope, and trochaic variation.

It also shows how his meter modifies the natural speech-rhythm of English phrases. To meet the requirements of the meter, Wyatt apparently does not need in this sonnet to pronounce the silent *-e* in "bemes," "mynde," "webbes," "swete," and "rote," but he contracts some disyllables ("spurreth," "frossen," "stondeth") and fuses some contiguous vowels ("he is," "many a," "misery and"). The four broken-backed lines (2, 5, 11, 14) throw extra stress on "myn" or "oft" and on "bit-," "twist," and "com-." For the meter's sake Wyatt inverts natural word order ("from the hert departeth," "with himself on love he playneth," and lines 9–10), and places stress on what would normally have to be an unstressed syllable ("the" [1], "but" [12]). All these devices are common in Wyatt's verse. He does not have recourse to this last speech distortion as often as other poets in this tradition, but it certainly occurs.

But while the meter is influencing our pronunciation and hence our phrasing, the phrases Wyatt has chosen are modifying the meter. If in line 1 the meter tells us to stress "the" and "these," natural English rhythm claims more attention for "bright" and "fayer." The accommodation that results gives more than the usual speech-stress to the minor words and more than the usual metrical emphasis to the major words in unstressed position. As we have learned to say, "-ing the" is a pyrrhic, "bright bemes" a spondee; the pattern recurs in the last four words of the same line. Fourth-foot trochees in lines 2 and 11, and probably in line 5, seem also to be required by Wyatt's choice of phrases; all three occur after the monosyllabic third foot of a broken-backed line and result in a pattern that later would be felt as inadmissible in iambic pentameter: three successive metrically (not just semantically) stressed syllables.

Throughout the sonnet the phrasing constantly directs our attention (and tension) to different parts of lines: in line 3, to the trochee that begins the second half-line; in line 5, to the juxtaposition of "swete" and "bitter"; in line 8, to the contrast between the hurried "spurreth" and the restrained "brídïlléth" (along with the opposition between the two other key words, *fyer* and *Ise;* in line 9, to "extremitie," whatever metrical reading we give it (no ordinary one is possible); in line 10, to the repeated "nowe"s that guard the caesura and to the two contracted disyllables they separate; in line 11, to the parallel noun-groups, either of which we may see as occupying most of the line; in line 12, to the few words of the first half-line and the relative many of the second; in line 14, to the internal rhyme "rote-ffruyte" and the disheartened reversal of accent in the last foot that withdraws emphasis from the very syllable we have just heard internally rhymed.

This directing of attention to different parts of different lines means that every line has a different interest-structure, if we can call it that. The antitheses of mynde-hert, swete-bitter, fyer-Ise, nowe-nowe, misery-welth, ernest-game, few-many, and rote-ffruyte are all given different metrical treatment, and the other lines, even when they lack contrasting words or phrases, all exhibit unique methods of accommodating the phrase to the meter. The mellifluous harmonies later developed preeminently by Spenser, Shakespeare, and Milton are not yet evident here, but that should not keep us from seeing the considerable art that Wyatt is engaged in, an art of phrase-placement and metrical manipulation far more resourceful than that of any poet since Chaucer, and inferior to Chaucer only in fluency, not in psychological expressiveness.

Even if other readers may prefer different metrical readings for some of the lines of XXIX (see n. 23), two conclusions emerge from this kind of analysis (which can be used to elucidate all of Wyatt's difficult sonnets): first, Wyatt is really using a metrical system; he is not just composing poetry in phrases, though phrases are important to him. He has a keyboard, which produces coherent lines of basically iambic verse; and although some of his lines, like some of Donne's, may puzzle us, we need not feel baffled. Second, Wyatt uses expressive metrical variations far more often, and to much better effect, than any earlier English poet. Far from being an incompetent metrist stumbling in the dark toward Surrey's smoothness, Wyatt was mastering a highly complex and varied metrical art.

But we can put the whole case in more comprehensive form: Wyatt's metrical system, used in almost all his verse, is a four-part system, the parts of which should not be confused. It consists of:

1. *Metrical forms.* For the decasyllabic line, an array of Lydgatian line-types with strong midline breaks, which sometimes appear elsewhere than after the fourth or fifth syllable.
2. *Metrical variations,* like those used later on: trochees, some spondees and pyrrhics, a very occasional anapest; and some combinations that never became standard for iambic pentameter (e.g., a monosyllabic third foot; a pyrrhic foot followed by a trochee).
3. *Syllabic procedures:* elision, synaloepha, syncope, expansion of monosyllables into disyllables, and so forth. Some of these techniques remained available to poets for centuries.
4. *Accentual conventions:* especially, near-spondaic pronunciation of some disyllabic words or phrases; shifting of level stress in many words, notably Romance words, for which a definitive pronunciation had evidently not yet become established *(fortune, vertue);* and occasional use of "thwarted stress"—that is, unspeechlike stress on minor syllables instead of those it would be more natural to stress.

The phrasing arrangements Wyatt uses are at a further level of organization. They work with and through the others to secure effects of balance, opposition, intensification, crispness—sometimes of speechlike authenticity. Phrase joined to phrase composes Wyatt's typical line. The phrases, normally two to a line, are themselves usually different in character and feeling (i.e., composed of different kinds of grammatical units, though often with sharply contrasting features). The skill required to write such a line appears to consist in deploying phrases that combine this difference with this capacity for contrast. As we read these sonnets, we have a strong sense of the phrase and of the line, a much weaker sense both of the sentence and of the quatrain (or tercet). The struggle of the agonizing lover seems reflected in the difficulty with which the distinctive phrases combine to form a patterned line, and perhaps also in the clumsiness with which the lines combine to form larger prosodic units. But to what extent this clumsiness is intentional is hard to say. Wyatt *appears,* here as in other sonnets and generally in his pentameter verse ("They fle from me" is one happy exception to the rule[24]), to be absorbed much more deeply in the problems of assembling phrases into lines than in the problems of arranging those lines into groups that flow melodiously and please the ear with the larger patterns of quatrain or stanza.

This preoccupation with the line, to the injury of the line-flow, would be more than compensated for by perhaps two generations of sixteenth-century poets, who, abandoning Wyatt's complex decasyllabic system described above, would find easier terms on which to make single lines and would interest themselves in the problems of composing harmonious stanzas or sonnets that course more fluently from quatrain to quatrain than these difficult poems of Wyatt ever do. But he may have come round himself to this position—or at least part way. The sonnets that were evidently composed later take two crucial steps toward smoothness: they drop the problematical rhymes and they stick very largely to the 1*(a)* or 4*(a)* line-types. The surer rhymes and more regular meter help us to feel as well a greater quatrain- (and tercet-) integrity.

IV

The knack of *hearing* Wyatt's rhythms vanished soon after his death. Surrey and his successors—and probably even Wyatt himself—abandoned the jointed or Lydgatian line for a smoother one. In this new line, we find at first, and for several decades, an almost invariable habit of arranging the syllables with a pause, required or at least possible, after the fourth syllable. That is, of the eight basic line-types available to practitioners of the Lydgate line, only the first (the pure *a* line) is regarded as perfectly metrical. To readers who have developed a feeling for Wyatt's richer, if problematical, harmonies, this reduction of possibilities may seem an impoverishment, and that it should have occurred in so musical a period as the early to middle Tudor (say, from 1540 to 1570) is surprising but not unaccountable. For the meter Wyatt used in his sonnets was even then too difficult for his readers. It takes considerable metrical sophistication to hear what is happening around a Wyatt caesura. Even Lydgate, in candid moments, admitted to being an uncertain metrist,[25] and fifteenth-century poets from Hoccleve to Hawes wrote lines that at best are "syllable-filled and rhythm-empty."[26] Despite his metrical facility, Skelton, after "The Bouge of Court," gave up on iambic pentameter. If poets have such a hard time with meter, if Lydgate himself can't always manage to write a Lydgatian line, what can be expected of mere readers?

For the trouble with Wyatt's system is that even someone who understands it may not see how individual lines are meant to be read. Certainly, readers may disagree over the scansion of later iambic pentameter lines, but not normally to the same extent. In the most intriguing of Wyatt's sonnets, several or most or sometimes almost all the lines present perplexing problems of metrical interpretation. It happens repeatedly in these sonnets that we don't know which reading to prefer. Should we take this line, "Though othre be present thou art not all behinde" (XXVII, 8), as one of those hexameters that apparently turn up from time to time in the sonnets? Or this way:

Thŏugh ŏthre bĕ présĕnt / thou art not all behinde

—that is, as a type-3 line? Should we read a phrase like "Thorrough sharpe sees" (XXVIII, 2) as "Thŏrroŭgh shárpĕ sées" *(e)* or as "Thŏrróugh shărpĕ sées" *(a)* or as "Thŏrroŭgh shárpĕ sées" *(a)*? Here, probably, it doesn't much matter how we read the phrase, but what about "retorning to lepe into the fire" in Poem LXXIX? This is the most dramatic line in the sonnet, but it seems to break either the meter or natural English rhythm. Should we read it this way:

rétŏrníng tŏ lépe ĭntó thĕ fire (type 5 or 5*a*)

on the theory that the stress-pattern of the Romance word *retorning* was still unfixed? Or as a type-2 line, forcing emphatic stress on *lepe*?

rĕtórnĭng tó / lépe ĭntó thĕ fire

This pleases my ear, but could any sixteenth-century poet have imagined a caesura splitting an infinitive? Or as a line invented for the occasion,

rĕtórnĭng ˌ / tŏ lépe ĭntó thĕ fíre,

in which the missing stressed syllable expressively, but very unconventionally, conveys the heart-in-mouth excitement of the leap?

Lines that raise such problems appear abundantly in these sonnets, and Wyatt's apparent freedom in expanding or compressing syllables, in shifting or displacing accents, and above all in moving from one metrical paradigm to another frequently makes it hard if not impossible to prefer one reading to another. It may be that this continual metrical uncertainty is an appropriate feature of a poetry whose main theme is uncertainty. But for many readers this will seem cold comfort: as the history of Wyatt's reception shows, it is hard for a reader even to get to the point of seeing more or less clearly what, in a given line, the metrical alternatives must be. And without such sophistication, one's experience of Wyatt's metric is necessarily blurred, incomplete, and unsatisfying.[27]

Despite the changes in literary taste that have enabled modern critics to prefer Wyatt's verse to Surrey's, it has continued to be the prevailing view that Surrey and his Elizabethan successors, in writing a smooth and regular iambic line, were escaping from the highly irregular decasyllabic art of their predecessors. But this misstates the nature of the change. Poets after Chaucer—from Hoccleve and Lydgate to Barclay, Hawes, and Skelton—were, like Chaucer himself, often obsessively regular, perhaps as much so as Surrey and the early Elizabethans. The difference between the two groups is only partly a difference in efficient adherence to a metrical norm, which, admittedly, some of these earlier poets find difficult to maintain. It is also that Surrey and his successors are using a reformed version of the decasyllabic line—a version that has only one basic paradigm, not several. Poets of neither group use many trochees, spondees, or pyrrhics to vary the metrical paradigm (though some use more than others); but Surrey and company *sound* more smooth than the post-Chaucerians because their paradigm is the same in every line. Lydgate, Hoccleve, and others, for all their undeserved reputations as incompetent or careless metrists, write lines that just as regularly pound out the required stresses, but the lines whose requirements they are meeting with considerable correctness have a number of alternative metrical architectures.

Thus, in the following lines (admittedly more various than most), Lydgate meets exactly the requirements of the meter. The phrasing conforms exactly to the meter and never exerts against it any pressure worth mentioning. The seven lines belong to six different line-types, but whatever the line-type the phrasing sits down neatly within it:

	Line-type
Ănd ón thĕ wállў̆s / ŏf Thébĕs láy hĕr fón	3
Rĕióysĭng hém / ŏf thís ŭnháppў̆ eúre	1
wénў̆ng thérbў̆ / grétlў̆ tó rĕcúre.	8
Ănd ón hĕr tóurĕs / ás thĕy lókĕn oúte,	4
Théy ŏn Grékў̆s / énviŏuslý gă̆n shóute	8
Ănd, óf dĕspít / ánd grĕt énmў̆té	2
Bád hĕm fóolў̆s / gŏn hóm tŏ hér cŏntré.[28]	7

Gascoigne never wrote anything more regular. And, except for the really incompetent poets of the Chaucerian tradition, these lines by Lydgate are representative of the decasyllabic art of English poets between Chaucer and Wyatt.

It may sound odd to speak of deviant lines as alternative paradigms rather than as variations, but there is a fundamental and unrecognized difference between multiple-paradigm metrical systems and single-paradigm systems—between, for example, the four-stress alliterative verse of Old English, with its fixed types, and the four-stress accentual verse of, say, some nursery rhymes or W. H. Auden's *The Age of Anxiety*. In the multiple-paradigm system, the variant patterns are usually themselves invariable (or very nearly so); in the single-paradigm system, as we know from the subsequent history of iambic pentameter, the variant features—in this case, increased or diminished stress on any syllable in the line, but with limits on their combinations—may result in an infinite number of rhythmic contours. This is not possible for the decasyllabic verse written by poets from Chaucer to Skelton, but Wyatt in his later poems is moving toward it.

One further point about Lydgate and his successors: to say that poets during this period were writing within a multiparadigm system is not to suggest that all of the possible line-types were equally congenial or were used with equal frequency. Lydgate certainly appears to write the type-1 line whenever he conveniently can, and it is because his verse sometimes gives the impression of backing into other line-types inadvertently, of using them only when he can't quite fashion a "regular" line, that critics have come to regard the other line-types as inherently bad, as blemishes. Derek Pearsall, whose perspective on this and other matters is always balanced and perceptive, acknowledges that Lydgate's variant lines, which he found in Chaucer "perhaps more often than we know of in carelessly written copies, and elevated into types," are "perfectly acceptable variants in themselves when supported by the rhetorical context."[29] But in a period when the conventions of verse apparently require strict adherence to regularity in meter (that is, sparing use of metrical variations), there is some virtue in using a variety of line-types either to avoid monotony or as an alternative pattern that may, here and there at least, be rhetorically apt.[30]

Once we understand the structure of Wyatt's decasyllabic lines and their relation to earlier and later practice, we are in a position also to make reasonable inferences about the development of his own decasyllabic art. Wyatt's early and most irregular sonnets use a relatively large number of line-types, which in conjunction with much syllabic manipulation (audible elision and contraction) convey the troubled state of mind of the Petrarchan lover. The later sonnets use line-types 1, 1*a*, 4, and 4*a* almost exclusively; five sonnets (XLVII, CCXI, CCXVII, CCXXIII, and CCXXVI) and the double sonnet (CCXXXVIII) use nothing but type-1 (or, rarely, 1*a*) lines. The need for syllabic adjustment also sharply declines. The result is regular iambic pentameter, with consistent (and somewhat monotonous) slight breaks after every fourth syllable:

> But as for me though that by chaunse indede
> Change hath outworne the favour that I had,
> I will not wayle, lament, nor yet be sad,
> Nor call her fals that falsley ded me fede,
> But let it passe and think it is of kinde
> That often chaunge doth plese a womans minde.
> (CCXVII)

It appears from their metrical styles alone that the Satires and Penitential Psalms also belong to this later period. The great majority of lines fall into the 1 or 4 classes, the frequency of the latter suggesting a development toward a more flowing verse. Occasionally, we find a passage in which the line-types vary a great deal, and then these changes are clearly used along with trochees, pyrrhics, and spondees as expressive resources.

		Line-type
	I am not he suche eloquence to boste,	1
	To make the crow singing as the swanne,	2
45	Nor call the lyon of cowarde bestes the moste—	3
	That cannot take a mows as the cat can:	1*a*
	And he that diethe for hunger of the golld	1 or 3
	Cáll hĭm Álĕssaúndrĕ, ănd sáy thăt Pán	7*a*
	Pássĭth Apollo in musike manyfolld;	3 or 4*a*
50	Praysse Syr Thopas for a noble tale,	5
	And skorne the story that the knýght tolld.	4
	(CV, 43–51: Satire I)	

Wyatt's Decasyllabic Line 121

The variety of line-types here (perhaps eight in nine lines) does much to enforce Wyatt's irony. Wherever there is an extra or an omitted syllable, the tone is sharpened: we feel the sarcasm in "the crow / singing as the swanne" because of the two successive stressed syllables, and the extra little catch at the center of lines 45 and 49, perhaps also of 47, makes the argument sound more headlong. The unusual 7*a*-pattern in line 48 seems likewise energetic, for it appears to begin the line with three successive trochees; the line ends iambically, but the next one has several features that revive the trochaic feeling. The headless line 50 *sounds* clipped and caustic. These striking effects, which Wyatt uses skillfully here and can call up at will when he needs them, work in conjunction with metrical substitutions to give the passage its strength of movement: the pyrrhic-spondee combination at the end of line 46 (unusual before Sidney), and the trochee that begins line 49. Finally, the disyllabic pronunciation of *knyght* in line 51 (which lets it rhyme with Wyatt) gives a special intensity to the poet's scorn for these scorners.

Wyatt is moving here toward a distinctive decasyllabic style comparable to those of later masters. Set beside these poems, the early sonnets *are* the stumbling experiments critics have often felt them to be. But when Wyatt presents David's self-blame in the first Penitential Psalm, he largely abandons the French polysyllabic words of aureate verse and develops a monosyllabic style that joins a steadier iambic meter to emphatic and expressive phrasing. In this style, repeated words and phrases, internal rhymes, expressive trochees and spondees, an epic caesura (type 3), alliteration, assonance, and consonance, and similar devices intensify the feeling in a way that is characteristic of poems of the later sixteenth and of the seventeenth century and utterly beyond the reach of such earlier poets as Lydgate, Hoccleve, and the rest:

		Line-type
	I lord ame strayd: *I*, sek withowt recure,	1
	Fele al my *lym*s, that have rebe*lld for fere*	1
	*Sha*ke in di*spa*yre, onle*s* thou me a*s*sure	1
100	*Mye fle*sshe is *trou*bl*ed, my* ha*rt* doth *feare* the *speare;*—	3
	That dread of death, of death that ever lastes,	1
	Threateth of *right* and draw*eth neare* and *neare*	1
	*M*oche *more my sowle* is *tr*ow*b*l*ed by* the *b*la*st*e*s*	1
	Of *theis*e a*s*s*awltes, th*a*t c*ome *as th*ick *as* h*a*yle,	1
105	Of wor*ld*l*y*e v*an*y*ti*e, th*at t*empt*ac*ion *c*ast*es*	4
	A*gay*n*st* the *weyk*e bu*l*warke of the *fle*sshe *frayle:*³¹	1*a*
	(CVIII, 97–106)	

After Wyatt, poets went further toward standardizing the iambic line, but they did not much advance the development of its expressive resources, which remained latent for more than a generation while poets learned to write the measured line. The development of a simpler metric than the multitype jointed line had several important results. It assured a wider audience, and it encouraged a larger number of writers to try their hand at an art that seems to promise success on easier terms. It made possible, too, the development of smoother melodic currents throughout a quatrain, tercet, or couplet. In retrospect we can also see that the simpler metrical base offered exactly the opportunities for expressive variation that would later form the peculiar wealth of a great metrical tradition. For it was only after the Tudor poets had simplified the poetic line that Sidney, Shakespeare, and Milton could make those spondaic, pyrrhic, and trochaic departures from it that give it its force and character. Their line is not so multiform as Lydgate's, but it is much more economical; it permits fewer variations from the norm (and the norm is more definite), but those few make it possible to bring into play an immense range of quickly recognizable speech-patterns.

In the last analysis, the jointed line, brilliant as it is in the hands of a master, is inherently too subservient to the spoken phrase, too deficient in predictable musical pattern. Because the basic pattern is variable, we may not be sure what the variations vary from, so our sense of them as variations is diminished and confused. The advantage of iambic pentameter, as later poets used it, lies in its formal simplicity, absolute in itself, which can yet be shaken and invaded and all but overwhelmed by natural English phrasing. The jointed line, by its very structure, gives away too much to the spoken phrase; we feel, as we read it, that the formal side of the struggle between the line and phrase, between life-conditions and the immediate life that they test, is underrepresented. We don't feel this, of course, in the strong meters of the octosyllabic poems of Wyatt nor, I think, in the Satires and Penitential Psalms; but in the early sonnets it is as if the power that constrains human action and struggle is too shapeless to offer a convincing antagonist to the dark inner turmoil of the speaker. In these poems Wyatt sometimes makes this situation, this existential incoherence, wonderfully moving, but its force rests on a precarious metric. The metric of Shakespeare—thanks largely to Wyatt himself—will be more solidly constructed.

Donne's Sculptured Stanzas

Although modern critics have discussed John Donne's *Songs and Sonets* from almost every conceivable point of view, few of them have even mentioned what may be the most important structural fact about them—that many of them interweave pentameter lines with iambic lines of other lengths to form stanzas of complex design.[1] Few such stanzas were written in English before Donne; earlier lyric strophes of mixed line-lengths usually avoid the pentameter as perhaps in character hostile to the melodic flow: too ponderous, too grave, too stichic. In all of Shakespeare's songs, to go no further, not a single pentameter appears. Except for Sidney in a few poems, Donne is the first English poet to see the expressive possibilities of combining iambic pentameter with shorter and longer iambic lines to form strophic units notable at once for their lyric flow and intellectual density. It looks as if poets realized instinctively what has taken literary critics almost four hundred years to see, that pentameter is different from other line-lengths[2] and that whenever it dominates a stanza or a poem or a whole play, its strength and heft make for a significantly different kind of verse from that which marks forms written in other line-lengths. The previous essay shows how much it evidently disconcerted Wyatt to move from the relatively simple, middle-dividing octosyllabic line to the dangerous decasyllabic. He and his successors almost never mixed the five-foot line with others—either with accentual four-stress verse or with iambic forms in trimeter, tetrameter, or hexameter. When longer or shorter lines appear in Shakespeare's plays, they are clearly temporary excursions; in verse passages the pentameter always dominates.

Donne used the stanza of mixed line-lengths to combine feelings of very different sorts into poems of remarkably complex, often mercurial, tone. These different feelings proceed from the lines' different structures and the different relations between phrase and line that those structures entail. Usually, the line of two or three feet will consist of a single phrase; the tetrameter is variable, but if it contains two phrases, it will often divide in the middle. The pentameter must be made up of at least two phrases, or its single phrase must be developed with greater complexity, and it cannot divide in the middle. The shorter lines are also less open to metrical variation; hence, both metrically and syntactically, the pentameter line makes for complexity, and it offers room for the more subtle development of an idea or an image. The constant movement that we sense in most of Donne's lyrics proceeds not only from his lively syntax and vigorously prosecuted images and arguments, but also from the mixture of lines that in their very lengths convey feelings, and even attitudes toward experience, of very different sorts. These feelings and attitudes are not easily characterized, but, in general, the shorter lines tend to emphasize the quick, light, fast-moving, and relatively uncomplicated, even comic, exploration of a subject; the long ones tend to deepen, intensify, and complicate it, to slow it down and make it more serious, more problematical. So brief a summary seems much too formulaic. Obviously, Donne's lyrics do not change their tone abruptly from line to line. Nevertheless, again and again they broach in short lines a subject that at first seems frivolous or playful but is gradually given amplitude through a series of more expansive pentameter lines, which as it were raise the subject to a higher level of serious meditation.

In "The triple Foole," for example:

> I am two fooles, I know,
> For loving, and for saying so
> In whining Poetry;
> But where's that wiseman, that would not be I,
> If she would not deny? 5
> Then as th'earths inward narrow crooked lanes
> Do purge sea waters fretfull salt away,

> I thought, if I could draw my paines,
> Through Rimes vexation, I should them allay,
> Griefe brought to numbers cannot be so fierce,   10
> For, he tames it, that fetters it in verse.[3]

The first five lines begin lightly enough; even the fourth, though pentameter, is caught up in the quick movement of thought; still, its two phrases begin the broaching of a subtle question. Lines 6–7 suddenly deepen the tone with their evocative imagery; the tendency of the shorter line 8 is to simplify again, but the completion of its thought in the pentameter line 9 turns out not to be so simple, after all; such is "Rimes vexation." And the concluding pentameter couplet maintains the achieved level of probing thought. The next stanza follows a similar pattern.

"The Sunne Rising" proceeds in much the same way:

> Busie old foole, unruly Sunne,
> Why dost thou thus,
> Through windowes, and through curtaines call on us?
> Must to thy motions lovers seasons run?
> Sawcy pedantique wretch, goe chide   5
> Late schoole boyes, and sowre prentices,
> Goe tell Court-huntsmen, that the King will ride,
> Call countrey ants to harvest offices;
> Love, all alike, no season knowes, nor clyme,
> Nor houres, dayes, moneths, which are the rags of time.   10

At first the light short lines seem to draw the longer ones into their own field of force, but the pentameter lines, even when used in the service of apparent mischief, have a way of giving it greater range (see, for other examples, "The Flea" or "The Curse"). Lines 3–4 have space to detail and extend the inquiry only begun in lines 1–2; if lines 5–6 (longer than 1–2) have enough room to provide concise pictures of sun, schoolboys, and prentices, the gesture of line 7 and the metaphorical suggestiveness of line 8 are more ample; lines 9–10 clearly raise the whole discussion to a new level of significance. We have come a long way from the first two lines, and it is largely the pentameter lines that have carried us there, not just because they are longer and can contain more syllables and substance, but because the longer line has a nature different from the others, and its almost inevitably greater metrical and syntactical complexity enables it to introduce into any poem a kind of high seriousness that, even when the subject is comic, lends it range and resonance.

Another poem proceeds in eleven–line stanzas of tetrameter and pentameter to explore "Loves infiniteness":

> If yet I have not all thy love,
> Deare, I shall never have it all,
> I cannot breath one other sigh, to move;
> Nor can intreat one other teare to fall.
> And all my treasure, which should purchase thee,   5
> Sighs, teares, and oathes, and letters I have spent,
> Yet no more can be due to mee,
> Then at the bargaine made was ment,
> If then thy gift of love were partiall,
> That some to mee, some should to others fall,   10
>   Deare, I shall never have Thee All.
>
> Or if then thou gavest mee all,
> All was but All, which thou hadst then,
> But if in thy heart, since, there be or shall,
> New love created bee, by other men,   15
> Which have their stocks intire, and can in teares,
> In sighs, in oathes, and letters outbid mee,
> This new love may beget new feares,
> For, this love was not vowed by thee.
> And yet it was, thy gift being generall,   20
> The ground, thy heart is mine, what ever shall
>   Grow there, deare, I should have it all.
>
> Yet I would not have all yet,
> Hee that hath all can have no more,
> And since my love doth every day admit   25
> New growth, thou shouldst have new rewards in store;
> Thou canst not every day give me thy heart,
> If thou canst give it, then thou never gavest it:
> Loves riddles are, that though thy heart depart,
> It stayes at home, and thou with losing savest it: 30
> But wee will have a way more liberall,
> Then changing hearts, to joyne them, so wee shall
>   Be one, and one anothers All.

Each stanza begins with two relatively simple ideas, which are then expanded in a series of four pentameter amplifications. Then, in the first two stanzas, a return to tetrameter (7–8, 18–19) keeps the tone light before two lines of pentameter and a final one of tetrameter. But in stanza 3 the pentameter development of the theme has grown too serious for a return to tetrameter in line 29; pentameters continue until the final line, which, though shorter, confers ease and finality on the closing stanza without returning the poem to its earlier level of the merely amusing.

This kind of transaction between pentameter lines and lines of other lengths can be found in virtually all of Donne's lyric poems that combine these different lengths. On the whole, the least successful poems are those that do not allow the pentameters to play pointedly off the shorter lines—for example, "Breake of Day," "A Valediction of my name, in the window," "Loves exchange," and "Witchcraft by a Picture." "Valediction of the booke" seems top-heavy; its stanzas' opening pentameter lines achieve a certain seriousness, which the succeeding short lines tend to trivialize; and the penultimate pentameter is inadequate to restore the tone. The final hexameter, here as elsewhere, does not function as a stately line; it divides too easily in half, whereas one key to the pentameter's impressiveness is precisely that it doesn't.

These shaped, these sculptured, stanzas make it possible for Donne to manage several kinds of stylistic and conceptual contrasts. On the one hand, we detect in these poems a sensibility that is strong, direct, and decisive—like a short line; but this sensibility is also capable of worrying an image or a situation, of probing its own insecurities, of questioning its old assurances. The speakers of poems may phrase some ideas quickly, boldly, clearly:

> Only our love hath no decay
> ("The Anniversarie," 7)

> Now thou hast lov'd me one whole day,
> To morrow when thou leav'st, what wilt thou say?
> ("Womans constancy," 1–2)

But other ideas may receive a much more knotty and enigmatic, or at least segmented, exposition:

> O perverse sexe, where none is true but shee,
> Who's therefore true, because her truth kills mee.
> ("Twicknam garden," 26–27)

> If, as in water stir'd more circles bee
> Produc'd by one, love such additions take,

> Those like so many spheares, but one heaven make,
> For, they are all concentrique unto thee
> ("Loves growth," 21–24)

> Till then, Love, let my body raigne, and let
> Mee travell, sojourne, snatch, plot, have, forget,
> Resume my last yeares relict: think that yet
>   We'had never met.
>   ("Loves Usury," 5–8)

In effect, while Shakespeare, in the *Sonnets,* was exploring a largely different set of poetic devices for registering subtle mixtures and advances of feeling from quatrain to quatrain[4] Donne was devising the sculptured stanza. What both solutions to the problem of rendering complex emotions have in common is the iambic pentameter line. Shakespeare, in the *Sonnets,* uses it almost exclusively, developing its ability to intimate and undermine a great range of expressive tones. Donne, in his songs, combines it with other lines to suggest the volatile motions of human feeling. The constantly altering line provides a fitting emblem for the harried or troubled lover, probing his prison, his passions, his powers, his mutability, his mixed condition.

In some respects, the verse style of such stanzas has to be different from that of the rhymed pentameter couplets Donne was writing in much of his other poetry. The couplets are often enjambed; the thought runs headlong over line-endings, breaks frequently in midline; and the stichic (line-by-line) arrangement of the verse encourages a verse art of continuous development and complication. The satires, elegies, Anniversaries, epicedes, and "Letters to Severall Personages" written in this form are usually composed in single blocks, some of them several hundred lines in length; the arguments and instances are successive and cumulative, and we rarely have any sense of a finely formed and partitioned oration, only of an arguer arguing on and on. When he comes at last to an end of his arguing points, he stops. Such a summary does less than justice to some of these couplet-poems in which the points are skillfully made and compose an impressively precise and logical discourse; but it is true to the *feeling* conveyed in these poems. For most modern readers, the relative unattractiveness of these poems comes about largely because the poet goes so doggedly at his objects of concern or attack (and partly because those objects, unlike the vagaries of love, are of little interest to modern audiences). In comparison, the *Songs and Sonets* show a capacity for ambivalence and change of pace, for both self-assertion and self-review, that is remarkably fresh and lively. Above all, the sculptured stanzas are *stanzas,* and they show Donne's willingness, suspended in most of his longer-line poems, to mark off his subjects into significant constituent parts, which can be developed in strophes that share a shape but are often sharply distinctive in tone and feeling.

The combination of clarity and weightiness, of liveliness and profundity, that Donne achieves in his lyric poems is rare in English poetry, and it is largely a consequence of the sculptured stanza (in the hands of a poet who knows how to use it). For someone writing this stanza, one of the basic problems is that of flow, but flow is of several kinds. The single line, long or short, must often make an impression as a single, uninhibited measure of rhythmical thought; but it must also combine with others to compose both multiline sentences and stanzas. The rhymes must mark line-endings and hence, for the listening reader, the line-lengths, but they must not delay unduly the movement of the thought and the sentence. In this movement, the short and the long lines both play their collaborative roles, simply or tensely advancing the formal patterns and the tough ideas.

In the following stanza, for example, the amplitude and dignity of the three-phrased first line slip into the looser robes of the shorter lines that follow, only to have the stanza much more ponderously step off its last four lines of pentameter as the poet turns from the youthful lovers to his dead wife (?) and his own deep gloom:

> You lovers, for whose sake, the lesser Sunne
>   At this time to the Goat is runne
>   To fetch new lust, and give it you,   40
>   Enjoy your summer all;
> Since shee enjoyes her long nights festivall,
> Let mee prepare towards her, and let mee call
> This houre her Vigill, and her Eve, since this
> Both the yeares, and the dayes deep midnight is. 45
>   ("A nocturnall upon S. Lucies day," 38–45)

"The Anniversarie," too, the tetrameter lines tend to present one segment of the thought in relatively simple terms; it is left to the pentameter lines and the final hexameter to develop the subtler or weightier ideas through several series of phrases that divide the lines into phrasal segments, yet sometimes spill over the line-endings. For the reader the pleasurable effects of combining such contraries as simplicity and complexity, formal neatness and advancing depth, are a direct consequence of the mixture of tetrameter and pentameter lines, along with one hexameter that here affirms the grandness of the lover's claims. (It is probably able to do this effectively because, unlike many hexameters, this one—l. 30— does not divide neatly in the middle.)

> And then wee shall be throughly blest,
> But wee no more, then all the rest;
> Here upon earth, we'are Kings, and none but wee
> Can be such Kings, nor of such subjects bee;
> Who is so safe as wee? where none can doe 25
> Treason to us, except one of us two.
> True and false feares let us refraine,
> Let us love nobly,'and live, and adde againe
> Yeares and yeares unto yeares, till we attaine
> To write threescore, this is the second of our raigne. 30
> ("The Anniversarie," 21–30)

The same principle—shorter lines for relative simplicity of expression, longer ones for more complex syntactical development of deeper levels of feeling, often through brief phrases that segment the line—can be seen in the following stanza:

> First, we lov'd well and faithfully,
> Yet knew not what wee lov'd, nor why,
> Difference of sex no more wee knew, 25
> Then our Guardian Angells doe;
> Comming and going, wee
> Perchance might kisse, but not between those meales;
> Our hands ne'r toucht the seales,
> Which nature, injur'd by late law, sets free; 30
> These miracles wee did; but now alas,
> All measure, and all language, I should passe,
> Should I tell what a miracle shee was.
> ("The Relique," 23–33)

Although there are limits to how simple a long line may be, or how knotty a short line, each kind appears occasionally to abet the interest of the other. The long line can have a marked simplicity about it:

> And now good morrow to our waking soules,
> Which watch not one another out of feare
> ("The good-morrow," 8–9)

> I can love her, and her, and you and you,
> I can love any, so she be not true.
> ("The Indifferent," 8–9)

> Something did say, and something did bestow
> ("The Legacie," 6)

> Love's not so pure, and abstract, as they use
> To say, which have no Mistresse but their Muse
> ("Loves growth," 11–12)

Note that some of these lines would seem to flow even faster without the commas; that we do not know whether the commas are Donne's or an editor's; and that commas do not necessarily imply pauses in Donne's poetry. He frequently elides over them.[5]

Or the short line conveys, through ellipsis, conciseness, or metrical tension, far more than we expect it to do:

> She'is all States, and all Princes, I
> ("The Sunne Rising," 21)

> The Phoenix ridle hath more wit
> By us, we two being one, are it.
> ("The Canonization", 23–24)

> Ends love in this, that my man,
> Can be as happy'as I can; If he can
> Endure the short scorne of a Bridegroomes play?
> ("Loves Alchymie," 15–17)

The first line in this last passage has only seven syllables, but its metrical complexity and its succinctness encourage us to pronounce the words much more slowly than we do in the swift-moving five-beat line that follows. "Farewell to love" has several passages in which, paradoxically, it seems to be the short lines that cover a lot of ground while the long ones race more quickly to their ends, though ultimately, of course, it must be the long ones that confer amplitude, seriousness, and depth on the developing discourse, as the last lines of the second quotation show:

> Since so, my minde
> Shall not desire what no man else can finde
> (31–32)

> But, from late faire
> His highnesse sitting in a golden Chaire,
> Is not lesse cared for after three dayes
> By children, then the thing which lovers so
> Blindly admire, and with such worship wooe
> (11–15)

The short lines may not only carry a considerable burden of meaning, but they may be segmented, too, like the longer ones; and yet the longer ones end up carrying still heavier burdens:

> Were I a man, that I were one,
> I needs must know; I should preferre,
> If I were any beast,
> Some ends, some means; Yea plants, yea stones detest,
> And love; all, all some properties invest
> ("A nocturnall upon S. Lucies day," 30–34)

And both kinds, the short as well as the long, may be broken up by internal pauses and enjambments, into phrases that the line-lengths hardly measure:

> I, by loves limbecke, am the grave
> Of all, that's nothing. Oft a flood
> Have wee two wept, and so
> Drownd the whole world, us two; oft did we grow
> To be two Chaosses, when we did show
> Care to ought else; and often absences
> Withdrew our soules, and made us carcasses.
> ("A nocturnall upon S. Lucies day," 21–27)

That is, there is no formula. Although, in general, the pentameter line may be associated with complexity and depth, and the shorter line with clarity and speed, each may, on occasion, take on the properties of the other.

If it is true that the liveliness and deep interest of Donne's songs owe much to their use of iambic pentameter in combination with other lines, what explains the success of the four excellent poems Donne wrote without using iambic pentameter at all? Eleven of his poems avoid iambic pentameter; seven of these seem to me among his less successful lyric poems ("The undertaking," "A Feaver," "Communitie," "The Message," "The Baite," "Negative Love," and "Selfe Love"), partly because they lack the agile shifts in tone that we find in the sculptured poems. Of the other four, two are written in stanzas of varying, but always short, line-lengths; two are in rhymed octosyllabic quatrains. "Goe, and catche a falling star" achieves its unique position among English lyrics through metrical shifts and tensions not unrelated to those we find in the sculptured stanzas.[6] "Sweetest love, I do not goe" is much smoother, but it also realizes its special character in part by sudden metrical shifts: the unexpectedly short fifth line; the change to trochaic meter in lines 6–7, and back to iambic in line 8.

The quatrain poems—"A Valediction forbidding mourning" and "The Extasie"—are a special group. In form they resemble "A Feaver" and "The Baite," but their tone is *sui generis,* even among Donne's works. The effect he is aiming at here in both poems is a steadiness of concentration, a firmness of relation, for which a sculptured stanza, with its volatile, changeable line, would serve poorly. These are poems of quiet tone, almost trancelike, and they rightly occupy an honored position among Donne's poems. It is also worth noting that descriptions of Donne as a "metaphysical" poet are often largely based on these two far-from-typical poems, whose mood and feeling are quite exceptional. The usual song or sonnet of Donne is of the kind I have been describing: a poem that requires quick shifts in tone and feeling, a lively and changeable speaking voice, and, even in poems of deep gloom, such as "A nocturnall upon S. Lucies day," a playful, even mercurial, treatment of love, life, meter, mood, and feeling.

Yeats's Expressive Style

I

"The chief characteristic of poets," said I. A. Richards once, "is their amazing command of language." The statement is so true as to seem comically obvious, yet one can read through volumes of contemporary literary criticism without finding a single reference to this "chief characteristic." Much of our critical writing might just as well be about works translated into English, for it concerns only such translatable stuff as imagery, symbols, myths, metaphors, allegory, irony, and other structuring tropes. But why the poet wrote these words and not others, how he fashioned his phrases, his sentences, his lines and his periods—such questions are apparently, for many critics, an impertinence. Some of the leading journals in our profession devote themselves entirely to questions of literary theory, to international questions of philosophy and aesthetics, and one can frequently hunt through their elegant pages by the hundreds and never encounter more than a lonely handful of lines of verse. It is not simply that criticism of this sort has subordinated poetry to philosophy; it has ceased to be connected to poetry at all, or at least with that chief characteristic of poets, their amazing command of language.

Yet, surely for most readers of poems what distinguishes a first-rate poet from others is the brilliant phrasing, the power not merely to parade ideas and images in impressive structures but to find exactly the right words, rhythms, and phrases to do so memorably. To be sure, "Spirits are not finely touched but to fine issues," and we want to be able to gauge as perfectly as we can the issues that are at stake in the finest poems. But unless we keep close to the words in which the issues are broached, and touched, we may find our attention wandering from the poem to our paraphrases of it, from the words set in their form to those mere notions, mere ideas, mere fancies that people who hate poetry find it easy to attack. The oddest thing about good poetry is that most of it is satisfactory as wisdom only as long as it remains embedded in its words. To explain what it means is justifiable only if what we say in explanation goes back, as it were, into the original words—that is, helps us to catch the life in those words.

One difficulty in talking about the art of William Butler Yeats (or anyone's) results partly from the ease with which we are distracted from it. We cannot, after all, see what Yeats is doing as a poet unless we come to know a great deal about his ideas and about his life, which are intriguing in themselves. But we also lack a method for discussing matters of artistic skill. We are repelled, on the one hand, by the vagueness of old-fashioned effusiveness—for me always best represented by the story I heard, when young, of the Harvard professor who would read a great lyric to his classes, then gaze at them intently and say, "Gentlemen, a gem! A gem!" Still, one knows how he felt. On the other hand, the exhaustive categorical descriptions of the parts of speech used in a poem—the kind familiar to us in some of the studies by Roman Jakobson, for example—achieve at best a pyrrhic victory over vagueness. They guard us against the perils of normative criticism, they keep our attention on verifiable evidence; but the danger of such studies—their relentless cataloguing, what we feel to be their inhuman hardness in the presence of poems that have moved us, along with certain methodological reservations we may have about the centrality or significance of the categories they use—all make some scrupulous critics feel that, much as we would like to talk precisely about a poem's art, we certainly don't want to sound like *that*.

Any scholar of Yeats, for example, knows how many critical studies about him are devoted to explaining his ideas; how few, even in an age reportedly dominated by New Criticism, to analyzing his art. There is one very useful book on his rhyme;[1] two less satisfying ones on his prosody; Ellmann's treatment of his ideas is notable for its tact, its respect for the poems, and its unfailing commitment to its essential purpose of illuminating the words and structures of Yeats's career; Parkinson too is unusually interested in the details of Yeats's word-art; and Curtis Bradford's studies in *Yeats at Work* offer useful evidence about the way Yeats composed his poems.[2] There are other critics, too, whose analysis of meanings never violates our sense of the poems as structures of well-positioned words, phrases, lines, and line-groups. But considering how much has been written about Yeats, it is astonishing how little attention has been given to the chief thing about his poems that makes so many people love to read them—not his visionary messages and his theory of history but his arresting phrases, his modeled lines, the movement of thought and feeling through stanza or section, the way his poems are made to seem to express simply and intensely some whole deep region of feeling: in short, his verbal art.

What one wants is a way of pointing to features of poems that might escape notice but, once observed, do seem to account, at least in part, for the poem's strength. If it is the linguistic features one wants to point to, the words and the way they are put together to enchant us, as opposed to the philosophic, mystical, historical, biographical assumptions that lie behind the poem and its words, then one has to use a technical vocabulary—grammatical and metrical terms like verb, clause, iambic feet, and so on. But the way one writes about such matters need not be dry-as-dust.

All this is by way of introduction to the essay that follows, which offers a detailed analysis of what seems at first view a simple poem by Yeats. For many years I have admired this little piece (a gem! a gem!) and have only gradually come to recognize the complex system of grammatical, syntactic, prosodic, and imagistic contrasts and parallels that account for its expressiveness. At the risk of tediousness I try to explain how these patterns are set up, repeated, varied, combined, and resolved in the words and phrases of the poem, and to show by this analysis something of what we mean when we speak of the elegance and resourcefulness of Yeats's style.

II

The little poem in question, "Crazy Jane on God," is a brilliant example of the powerful work Yeats wrote in his later years. The texture and syntax are "simple"; that is, the clauses are short and relatively unencumbered by complicating substructures; the diction seems plain and unsophisticated; the verse structure is easy to hear or see; the refrain provides an obvious unifying device; each stanza develops a different image, and the fourth returns, with proper symmetry, to the situation of Crazy Jane with which the poem began. Within this apparent simplicity, however, the poem enfolds a highly structured system of contrasting and counterpointed syntactical, prosodic, and symbolic features. The patterning of these features, of asymmetries within symmetries, of complex balances of the predictable and the surprising, gives pleasure by the way (to anyone who has developed a taste for this kind of patterning), and finally yields meanings much more suggestive than we would normally expect to find in a poem whose surface seems so simple.

The poem essentially turns on several kinds of stylistic variables: the meter, varied in each stanza, varies within each from two to three feet per line; the rhyme scheme, regularly *abaccb,* diverges into slant rhyme and has some inherent oddities—instead of three sets of *ab*-lines, the fourth line in *c* breaks the expected pattern, the fifth is an unexpectedly quick echo of the fourth, and the last, invariable line, though it completes, but always with a slant rhyme, the second line, is so separate and so final that it seems at once both involved and uninvolved in the rhyme pattern. It performs, thus, in the rhyme scheme the same function it performs in each stanza's pattern of meaning: it recalls, but vaguely, the particular image or rhyme to a general pattern ("*All things,*" or *b*). Along with such metrical motions, and the movement from stanza to stanza, each controlled by a different image, we can also trace a strategy in the development of nouns, verbs, adjectives, and prepositional phrases, each of which figures in a contrast with other elements of the same or different kinds. To see how this works, we need to go through the poem.*

Crazy Jane on God

That lover of a night
Came when he would,
Went in the dawning light
Whether I would or no;
Men come, men go:
All things remain in God.

Banners choke the sky;
Men-at-arms tread;

---

*Permission granted by A. P. Watt Ltd. on behalf of Michael B. Yeats and Anne Yeats. Reprinted with permission of Scribner, a division of Simon & Schuster, Inc., from *The Collected Poems of W. B. Yeats,* Revised Second Edition, edited by Richard J. Finneran. Copyright 1933 by Macmillan Company. Copyright renewed © 1961 by Bertha Georgie Yeats.

> Armoured horses neigh
> Where the great battle was
> In the narrow pass:
> *All things remain in God.*
>
> Before their eyes a house
> That from childhood stood
> Uninhabited, ruinous,
> Suddenly lit up
> From door to top:
> *All things remain in God.*
>
> I had wild Jack for a lover;
> Though like a road
> That men pass over
> My body makes no moan
> But sings on:
> *All things remain in God.*[3]

In the first stanza repetitive structures constantly frame contrasts:

1. Came / Went
2. he would / I would
3. lover Came / Men come
4. Men come / men go
5. Came . . . Went . . . come . . . go / *remain*
6. Men . . . men / *All things*

These central antitheses, which enliven the argument at every point, are reinforced by other syntactical parallelisms that hide (reveal) contrasts:

7. Came when he would / Went . . . Whether I would
8. he would / I would or no

As in this last example, there are structurally parallel elements that are syntactically nonparallel:

9. of a night / in the dawning light

Here the preposition is different, the second element has an extra word, an adjective, and, although the rhyming words directly contrast, the first is a noun phrase, the second an adverbial phrase. The first phrase, too, has an ambiguity absent in the second: "of a night" probably means "at night," perhaps implies "nightly," but can mean "one night" or even "of night"—

like Romeo, this lover loves the night more than the light. The stanza's third prepositional phrase omits the article:

10. of a night / in the . . . light / *in God*

An ambiguity also splits "Came" in line 2, so that to its external contrasts (noted above in 1, 3, 4, and 5) are added internal ones: "Came" clearly means both "Arrived" and "Had orgasm," though this second meaning is controlled and limited by the immediately following contrast in "Went." (The same thing happens later in the line that is in part a ribald joke: "Men come, men go.") The ambiguities in "of a night" and "Came," however, encourage us to hear a subdued ambiguity in the second "would": "Went . . . Whether I" wanted him to, or "Went . . . Whether I" went with him? Even the earlier "Would" shadows a second meaning and a third: "Came when he" wanted, "Came when he" was in the habit of coming, or "Came when he" was bound to, and this last meaning, at least in the (dawning) light of the whole poem, is reinforced by its tone of cosmic fatalism. Even in the first stanza this tone begins to be heard in the movement from the specific to the general:

11. That lover . . . I . . . Men . . . men . . . *All things*

Altogether, these contrasts are so persuasive and suggestive that they shape our reading of the stanza, direct us first this way, then that. Every syntactical element, every word, functions to establish the design or to vary it, and the effect is of a simple and definite statement simply, but sharply and constantly, altered, of meaning continuously turning in its verbal form into other meaning as time turns "That lover" into "men" who come and go. But the refrain, general as it is, peers back at the specific: the individual thing remains despite all this coming and going. In what sense it remains *"in God"* is not yet clear.

The second stanza changes the scene; the key words are different, and the stanza introduces different contrasts, framed in the three main clauses (the structure here is consistently triple where that of the first was dual):

1. Banners . . . Men-at-arms . . . Armoured horses.

The three subjects are of different syllable-lengths (2, 3, and 4 syllables) and are differently constituted noun-groups (single noun, hyphenated noun, adjective-plus-noun).

2. choke . . . tread . . . neigh.

The three verbs are alike in being five-letter monosyllables, different in being differently accompanied:

3. choke the sky (verb-object)
   tread (simple verb)
   neigh Where . . . (verb plus adverbial clause)

The above patterns (1, 2, and 3) differ further in that the first moves from small to large, flimsy to powerful, simple to expanded, the second is constant, while the third moves from relative complication to simplicity to greater complication. The substantives of stanza 2 are generally more complex in form than those of stanza 1; the pattern of "Armoured horses" is echoed in "great battle" and "narrow pass" and even in *"All things,"* but these compound substantives appear between the simple "Banners" and "sky" at the beginning and *"God"* at the end, so that we sense through the stanza a motion from simplicity through complication to simplicity. This impression is reinforced by the way in which the syntactical simplicity of the first two lines gives way to the syntactical elaboration of lines 3–5, which in turn gives way to simplicity again in line 6. This observation reminds us how differently structured the first two stanzas are: stanza 1 has a kind of 2-2-1-1 syntactical structure; the arrangement of stanza 2 is 1-1-3-1. Apart from the refrain, verbs move in stanza 1 from past to present; in stanza 2, from present (historical present, or so it seems at first) to past; stanza 1 used two subordinate clauses (in lines 2 and 4); stanza 2 uses only one, also in line 4 but it continues into line 5. Stanza 2 also reduces the number of prepositional phrases from two to one (apart from the refrain), but greatly increases the number of complex noun phrases from one to four. Only one key word is repeated: "men." But in stanza 2 they are "Men-at-arms." Aside from the refrain, the first stanza moves from singular substantives to plural, the second from plural to singular. All of these contrasts, both within stanza 2 and between the two stanzas, enforce our sense of the variety and strength of the phrasing, especially the strength of the refrain in that it is made to apply equally to verbal complexes of such different construction and feeling.

The third stanza diverges from its predecessors even more sharply than they differ from one another. If the second stanza's subject is puzzling until "narrow pass" identifies the Battle of Thermopylae, the third stanza's "their" remains enigmatic throughout. In the stanza proper (before the refrain, that is) only one finite verb appears, and only in a subordinate clause; prepositional phrases are here more prominent than ever; and there is only one subject, "house," which therefore receives special prominence; finally, we meet here for the first time an adverb ("Suddenly") and a participle ("lit up"—though "Armoured" anticipates it). The meter of the two earlier stanzas has been fairly regular. In the first stanza, lines 2 and 5 are short (two feet), and lines 2, 3, and 4 begin with stressed syllables and therefore move speedily before the expressive spondees of line 5. In stanza 2 the headless lines 1, 2, and 3 impart a clipped, quick quality to the treatment of the great battle; the short fifth line (short a syllable, short a strong initial stress) seems descriptive of the narrow pass. Stanza 3, however, alters the norms of the meter even more substantially. Line 1 is regular iambic, line 2 has the headless form familiar from stanza 2, but lines 3 and 4 are thoroughly anomalous. Line 3,

$$\text{Ŭnĭnhábĭtĕd, rúĭnŏus}$$

resists assimilation to an iambic pattern, and rather seems to be composed, more or less, of a trochee and two dactyls, even though its final syllable, which slant-rhymes with "house," is thus left without stress. Read this way, the line seems as stark, as anomalous, as the weird house it is describing, and the next line supports this impression:

$$\text{Súddĕnlў lít ŭp}$$

One can read "up" with more force to be sure (/⌣⌣/ or /⌣\⌣/ or /⌣//) but in no case will a natural reading seem a normal variation from iambic meter. The last two lines restore the iambic norm, but we know that to get there we have gone through a profoundly disorienting two lines, as if for the moment of our vision of the house, the natural order of things had been swept aside.

This is indeed the case, and other features of the stanza encourage us to feel it: the unlocated "their," when pronouns, after all, ought to have antecedents; the strange procession of prepositional phrases that begin as initial ("Before their eyes"), become unidiomatically medial ("That from childhood stood"), and end as terminal and decisive (lines 5 and 6); the internal rhyme just before the strange line 3 ("-hood stood": listen to "-hood stood / Unin-"); and what seems the deliberate separation of substantives from any adjectives that describe them "... house ... childhood ... door ... top." "House," especially, is separated by a full line or more from "Uninhabited, ruinous" and "lit up." The resulting effect is very mysterious: what house? whose childhood? whose eyes? How can such a house be lit up? Why not from bottom to top? The absence of verbs reinforces our sense of ellipsis. We read these words as enigmatic clues, as fragments of experience whose significance, however, remains unclear. It is clear, of course, if we know Yeats's *Purgatory* and realize that in his view a moment of passion is eternal and can, under proper conditions, light up its former setting no matter how that setting may have changed; all things remain in being. But even if we know, the feeling is one of strangeness, and the prosodic and syntactical oddities contribute to it. Here, as in stanza 1, we move from singular to plural but also from an inclusive substantive ("house") to the *"All things"* of the refrain. The lines group here 1-2-2-1, and the stanza's relative clause seems its largest single unit.

The same thing is true of the principal subordinate clause in stanza 4, but it here empowers the subdued triumph with which the poem concludes. Again the structure is 1-2-2-1, but the feeling is very different because the nouns and verbs have returned to full value as subjects and predicates. Line 1 gives us a full clause, so that the subordinate material of lines 2–3 has a different function from the corresponding lines of stanza 3: this qualifies, whereas that defined; besides, the governing subordinate verbs come not in lines 2–3 but in 4–5, which reverses the pattern of stanza 3, where the verb came in line 2 and then modifiers piled up. In stanza 4 we might well read the structure as 1-4-1, with the first and last lines fully independent and comparable: the specific and the general truth, between them the crucial simile and statement.

The verbs here follow the pattern we have noticed before of increased dimension followed by diminution: "had . . . pass over . . . makes no moan . . . sings on . . . *remain*"—that is, a pattern of 1-2-3-2-1 (in number of words). The prepositional phrases here have a different quality, too: "for a lover . . . like a road . . . *in God.*" Although reminiscent of the phrase-pattern of stanza 1, these do not place in time or space as the earlier ones did, but define (Jack) and compare (body and road); and this comparison, as we shall presently see, embodies the whole burden of the poem. We may note also that the *w*-sound, so prominent in stanza 1, returns here only in *"w*ild," the stanza's single adjective (except for the refrain's *"All"*); and the consonance pattern of ". . . men . . . *remain*" that was suggested in stanza 1 is here elaborately developed into the alliteration-assonance-consonance pattern of "men . . . My . . . makes . . . moan . . . *remain*" (to say nothing of the other *n*'s and *o*'s in the stanza).

This sense of return is appropriate, not only because we have come back from Thermopylae and Purgatory to Crazy Jane's own memories, but also because the meter, rhyme scheme, and sound patterns have all been engaged, for the poem's life (which is continuing), in reconciling what changes with what endures. Stanza 4 returns us to the poem's key ideas and words: to "I," to love as the central subject, to the words "lover" and "men." Here that "lover" becomes "Jack" (general to specific) and we have moved back to the personal after the cosmic excursions of stanzas 2 and 3. The "pass" of stanza 2 has turned into a verb; in a different sense, it has turned into "road," and implicit in these transformations are the sexual meanings familiar from stanza 1: to "pass" over a body is a sexual gesture; "over" reminds us of the usual physical position of a man during sexual intercourse. To pass in this sense is thus to act (despite the connection with *passive*); and this series of associations recalls the "Men-at-arms" who were *treading* a road; *tread,* of course, is often used (by Yeats, among others) as a sexual term, though mostly for nonhuman animals. It is possible, too, that the Passover is faintly suggested here: the body survives the death that seemed certain, the involvement in generation that seemed sure to eventuate in death.

Two major images of the poem are "house" and "road." Implicitly or by association, the body is compared to both. It is not merely the house in stanza 3 that seems transfigured, but, as stanza 4 assures us, Crazy Jane's body, and the association of body and house is a traditional one. In effect, since time is, in stanza 2, implicitly compared to a "pass"—Thermopylae is history; events struggle to survive—the suggestion seems clear that the body itself *is* time, a permanent register of all that happens successively. Indeed, the body is very close to being thought of here in the same terms as Yeats uses elsewhere to admire a work of art. It remains, and it sings, like the golden bird of "Sailing to Byzantium." Body and soul are here, as so often in Yeats, not merely complementary elements of reality, but different sides of the same reality, encompassing all of the most comprehensive polarities that define the vast and changing cosmos. It is not merely God that remains, but "things" that remain in him. Nothing that ever is wholly can ever wholly not be. All things, or at least all things that qualify by virtue of their participation in passion, remain in being. And it is, in large part, Yeats's control of linguistic patterns that permits the poem to convey, through its symmetries and variations, the continuity of life and art, the correspondence between Crazy Jane's body and her passion, and the transforming power that turns her passion—and his—into this carefully structured poem about it.

Lowell's Pentameter Line

From the point of view of measure, Robert Lowell's career, like an iambic foot, shifts back and forth—through the early period of regular (and rhymed) iambic pentameter, the freer experiments of *Life Studies* and *For the Union Dead*, the strict octosyllabic couplets of *Near the Ocean*, the unrhymed sonnets of *Notebook, History, For Lizzie and Harriet, The Dolphin*, and the final free verse of *Day by Day*. This is a sometimes confusing but not incoherent progress. "I can't understand," he once wrote, "how any poet, who has written both metered and unmetered poems, would be willing to settle for one and give up the other."[1] His own mind, seizing, barnaclelike, on everything it could use in the way of rhythms (as well as images, structures, forebears), would leave no mode unexplored, unexhausted.

When we survey his lifework of poems, however, it is not hard to see as the norm for his verse the iambic pentameter line—like Boston, like marriage, a norm from which he was always departing. The rhythmic chain of connected feet or connected beats symbolizes for Lowell other kinds of connections. As his poetry matures, its discourse grows less argumentative or moves from an argument of assertions to one of impressions and associations; its syntax becomes less consecutive;[2] it habitually seeks coherence in metonymic or metaphoric connections: tracing the historical origins of personal, family, or national disaster, or recognizing their analogues in historical figures and the behavior of animals or objects. But to connect is not to explain, and the line itself endures challenges and subversions.

Lowell's early verse is strong and regular. His iambic pentameter makes use of the standard variations but includes some idiosyncratic differences. His work is unusually full of monosyllabic nouns, verbs, and adjectives, of the kind that Hopkins and Dylan Thomas loved: *blast, roil, lash, rock, drags, guts, hacks, whacks,* to name a few. These often combine with articles, prepositions, and pronouns to form iambs, or with other important monosyllables to form spondees; pyrrhics and spondees frequently appear together, to such an extent that in some lines they crowd out the normal iambs:

> *Snow warred* on the *El's world* in the *blank snow.*
> (*Mills,* 51)[3]
>
> *Cry out* on the *long night* for the *hurt beast*
> (*LWC,* 9)

Lowell makes clever use of initial and medial trochees; his midline breaks are variously placed. Wordplay is common, and what is probably Lowell's most distinctive stylistic feature, the repetition of words and phrases: "seaward and seaward" (*LWC,* 11), "splatters and splatters" (*LWC,* 14), "Now south and south and south" (*LWC,* 33), "How can we stop it, stop it, stop it?" (*LWC,* 37), "God wills it, wills it, wills it" (*LWC,* 39), "the flies, the flies, the flies" (*LWC,* 47), "yuck-a, yuck-a, yuck-a, yuck-a" (*Mills,* 25), and, most tellingly, "If God himself had not been on our side, / If God himself had not been on our side" (*LWC,* 10), and "Cut your own throat. Cut your own throat. Now! Now!" (*LWC,* 61). This almost obsessive Tennysonian repetition persists through Lowell's career. Even in his early poems, too, he varies the pentameter norm by throwing in an occasional short or long line; and he is fond of writing lines in which a trochaic inner rhythm runs counter to the iambic pulse:

> And candles gutter by an empty altar
> (*LWC,* 28)
>
> Sea-monsters, upward angel, downward fish
> (*LWC,* 14)
>
> What's happened to that porpoise-bellied priest
> (*Mills,* 37)

My husband's Packard crunches up the drive.
(*Mills,* 31)

Probably the most notable metrical feature of Lowell's early iambic pentameter is his enjambment—not just the traditional practice of letting the sense run over the line without the hindrance of commas or stronger punctuation, but an enjambment, reminiscent of Hopkins, which lets the line-ending constitute a sharp break in phrasing: "her four / Room kingdom" (*LWC,* 25), "the sea / Gull" (*LWC,* 39). The line-ending frequently separates a verb from its immediately following object ("earned / It" [*LWC,* 52]; "give / You" [*LWC,* 69]) or an adjective from its noun, even when the two are felt to form a compound noun or a compound adjective, as in "rice / Fields" (*LWC,* 48), "eye- / Teeth" (*Mills,* 10), and "the life / Insurance calendar" (*Mills,* 5). These enjambments sometimes make it difficult to give the following line a natural reading, and the verse may appear to offer conflicting messages. The smooth meter implies, on the one hand, that everything is under control, that reality is being set in order, that the sentences through which we are receiving Lowell's account of it, though full of the life that his trochees, spondees, and pyrrhics are expressing on its behalf, are being contained within the verse's metrical system. But the enjambments show a disparity between the sense and the line. The line stops, but the sense runs a little bit over. Or it runs a little bit short, and Lowell begins a new sentence on the line's tenth syllable. When the new sentence begins with a word like "It" (*LWC,* 41) or "May" (*LWC,* 23) or, more frequently, "Here" (*LWC,* 34, 53, 55, 57), we have no real clue to what is coming and the word looks like a nervous fulfillment of the rhyme rather than a natural way of continuing the train of thought. It may be intended to look that way. But whether the sentence runs over or under the line, the effect is of a temporary failure of congruence—a failure that, in the early poems at least, tends to be countered by Lowell's notoriously strong last lines, in which sentence, line, and poem conclusively end together:

The Lord survives the rainbow of his will.
(*LWC,* 14)

The Child is born in blood, O child of blood.
(*LWC,* 7)

The small-mouth bass breaks water, gorged with spawn.
(*LWC,* 61)

Even in the early, formal, often rhetorical and high-sounding verse, Lowell frequently wrote lines that sound perfectly natural and colloquial:

> I run about in circles till I drop.
> (*LWC*, 44)

> I want to leave my mother and my wife,
> You wouldn't have me tied to them for life.
> (*LWC*, 45)

> Little by little; but it does no good.
> (*Mills*, 38)

Later, when he gave up the prophetic formality of his early poetry, it was in favor of a new style that was to be "more colloquial" and proselike. To break "through the shell of his old manner," he started to use "short line stanzas" and "drifting description."[4] He may have felt that the long sentences of the early volumes, which are sometimes strung through more lines and subordinate clauses than they seem able to sustain, provided an inauthentic structure for the poems' discourse, and he began to break down his units of syntax, make them briefer and less hypotactic, and locate them in a more confused and rambling mind, usually his own.

With these purposes, Lowell turned to free verse, except that it wasn't quite free. Critics have differed on whether, for example, "Skunk Hour" is free verse or iambic. However we hear individual lines, we can probably say that Lowell began in the poems of *Life Studies* to find a principle of metrical uncertainty that perfectly suits his poetic themes. The free verse of many other poets is entirely intelligible without any knowledge of an earlier iambic tradition. We know in general, but we don't keep hearing in the verse, what it is free from. But Lowell's free verse of this period is constantly hinting at its "lost connections" (*LS,* 100) with iambic meter. Iambic lines, often pentameter, keep turning up in what are ostensibly free-verse poems:

> which Grandpa made by blending half and half
> (*LS,* 74)

> nineteen, the youngest ensign in his class
> (*LS,* 86)

> to check the parking meter violations
> (*FTUD,* 37)

Such vestigial traces of an officially extinct meter are peculiarly appropriate for a volume devoted to remembering the often distant past. In fact, we find two sorts of poems in *Life Studies* and *For the Union Dead:* free verse poems with hints of regular iambic, and mainly iambic poems in which the meter goes free now and then. From line to line of either sort of poem we hardly know what to expect of the meter, and the same is true of the rhyme, which often appears in these volumes unpredictably and irregularly. Form seems accidental, something that merely occurs in experience here and there or is, on occasion, violently exposed, as in the perversely lined ending to the poem on Delmore Schwartz:

> The Charles
> River was turning silver. In the ebb-
> light of morning, we struck
> the duck
> -'s web
> foot, like a candle, in a quart of gin we'd killed.
> (*LS,* 67)

When Lowell returned to "regular" meter in earnest—in the hundreds of "blank verse" sonnets he wrote and rewrote for the volumes *Notebook, History, For Lizzie and Harriet,* and *The Dolphin,* from 1967 to 1973[5]—he found what seems to me his mature and most perfectly expressive metrical style. Lowell himself notes of these poems: "My meter, fourteen line unrhymed blank verse sections, is fairly strict at first and elsewhere, but often corrupts in single lines to the freedom of prose."[6] It would be difficult, though, to say which of his lines Lowell thought of as exhibiting "the freedom of prose,"[7] because the lines show every degree of irregularity imaginable in a blank verse meter. But *can* prose enter verse in the way his description suggests? Can "single" prose lines appear without being measured by and inducted into the metrical patterns around them? Lowell's, in any event, is a blank verse that tolerates tetrameter or hexameter lines with some frequency and that also includes lines with very unorthodox metrical contours. Some examples, with suggested stresses:

> dróps stríke with the tóck of the tówn clóck
> (62)
>
> but hé eásily héard vóices on the ríver
> (91)

Jóhn Crowe Ránsom at Kényon College, Gámbier, Ohío
(52)

púlse, stóp the blóodstream as íf it hit róck
(53)

unaccústomed to súch drínk, they thoúght it góod
(58)

rétribútion, as I líe awáke básking
(45)

A repéating flý, blúeblack thúmbthick—só gross
(21)

down the Húdson, twíce as wíde as it is, wíde as the Mississíppi
(35)

At the énd of the long wálk, your óld dog díes of jóy
(40)

pássed mány varíeties of úntried béing
(34)

    Enough lines are regularly iambic to establish that as the basic norm and to justify Lowell's claim that he is writing blank verse, but such lines as these are really written in a kind of five-stress accentual meter, a meter toward which much of the best blank verse written in our time often tends—Stevens's, for example—as a natural consequence of the nineteenth century's increasing preference for accentual over accentual-syllabic meters. As we come to each line in these later poems of Lowell, we presumably try to find somewhere (anywhere) the five syllables whose stressing will permit us to read it in the most natural way. That, at least, is likely to be the procedure for anyone who has at all developed an iambic sensibility. The phrasing is colloquial, very easy and loose; we suspect, probably incorrectly, that the poet has done little or nothing to adjust the phrases to fit the metrical requirements, has instead allowed the metrical paradigm to expand or multiply to accommodate scores of different-sounding line-patterns. We may even feel a kind of wonder, as we read, that so many conversational phrases, so various in their rhythms, should make it into blank verse, but this is what many of the great poets have made readers feel as they have domesticated one wild variety of common speech after another "to the dense and five-times wounded" blank verse line. (*Notebook,* 97)

It is not, of course, merely the meter that is elusive. The poems are now mottled with many ellipses, which signal shifts of image, time-level, point of view, context. "My mind can't hold the focus for a minute," writes the poet in "Harvard" (79), and it is part of his craft to show, in many of these poems, the precariousness of his train of thought. The sentences, too, often have a more meager structure than they did in the earlier era of rolling periods and complex syntactical constructions. Now a poem may begin with a list of names—"Hitler, Mussolini, Daladier, Chamberlain"—continue with what seems like a murmured summation of their mutual enterprise, Munich—"that historic confrontation of the great—" then break as the poet makes his ironic and at first verbless observation: "firm on one thing, they were against the war" (52). Punctuation is pushed to the limit of its resources to mark the various sorts of digression, divagation, and stop; the first six lines of this poem end, respectively, in a colon, a dash, a semicolon, a period, a comma, and a question mark followed by three periods.

At the same time, the thought is often, as here, not hard to follow. We pick it up quickly, if we know anything at all about the subject. Even if we can't quite make out what's going on because we are ignorant about Lowell's personal life or his historical topic, we can see plainly enough the kind of shifts his mind is making; we understand, more or less, its species of disturbance. The sentences grow more inward, less formally complete; they begin with gerunds, repositional phrases, fragments of conversation, names, remarks, aphorisms; and though the blank verse line, subject as always to midline breaks, encourages lavish enjambment, the peculiar phrase- or even word-breaking enjambments so common in Lowell's early poetry are less usual here. They turn up in "turn- / ing up" (21), "lobster- / shell-red" (24–25), "half / an hour" (174), but they seem no longer an inevitable feature of every poem. On the contrary, as the continuity of thought grows more elusive, the lines gain in integrity. Most of the poems seem written line by line, perhaps revised line by line, each line a distinct unit in a fourteen-line set. (In this respect, as in their metrical irregularity, they might have been written by Wyatt.) That is, frequently Lowell's thought or image is complete in a single line, or in two lines taken together, and hundreds of lines are quotable as more or less complete and intelligible by themselves.

The art of these sonnets is thus a mosaic art, the art of fitting together elusive images, impressions, mutterings, connective phrases into fourteen metrically elusive yet elusively coherent lines. The lines evade strict definitions of iambic or pentameter; the phrasing evades explicit formulation of its ironic purposes; but out of this nettle evasion we pluck this flower precision.

The most successful sonnets (though the poems, of course, also evade being sonnets) seem to me the ones in which we (and Lowell) appear most to be lost, where the imagery is puzzling, the syntax sometimes broken, the connections not wholly clear, the meter problematical. In such poems the struggle for form seems most convincingly embodied, and that, after all, is largely the point of these pieces, as it is in much of Lowell's work. What we see in the poems of every period is a voracious sensibility turning its manifold experience into fragments of lyric, testifying, with what is left of a disintegrating poetic tradition, to the achievements of disconnection and the experience of foraging for form. The trouble with the early poems was that form seemed to come too easily: the virtuoso poet could rhyme and meter at will, enclose any subject in his perfectly tinkling or thundering folds. Lowell's later art required him to break up the meter, the sentence, the tableau in the interests of reconstituting them, or something more satisfyingly like them, in a more inclusive yet inconclusive whole. To put it in archaeological terms, from the fragments of his own sensibility, drenched as they are in history, the poet makes new ruins.

This is a strategy, we know, that other writers have also found, and that has been almost inevitable for the generation of poets that followed the Modernists. After Dylan Thomas, whose verse epitomized and embarrassed the modernist style, even poets older than he felt compelled to abandon Romantic speech and to clear their poems of prophecy, windy rhetoric, poetic razzle-dazzle, and unearned iambic pentameter. For meter—in particular, the relation of the metrical paradigm to speech, as that relation is embodied in the verse—always carries symbolic force, different in every era and somewhat different for every poet. In the Renaissance, for example, divergences between meter and natural English convey—especially in the plays and poems of Shakespeare—a powerful continuing struggle between authority and aspiration, between law and impulse, between universal order and particular evasions of it. By the eighteenth century, the opposition seems narrower in focus—between human waywardness and social order. In the nineteenth century these relations grow blurred and confused: as meter becomes more accentual, its beat seems to stand for natural forces, rhythms, powers. The shift to looser, free verse forms in the twentieth century may mean that many poets are renouncing these deep rhythmic connections to divine, social, and natural systems of order in favor of an art of speech that is merely human. But for the poet who still writes in iambic pentameter, the relation between the metrical norm and the natural English rhythms that must always resist and challenge the norm seems most often, in my view, to reflect a continuing and profound struggle between what the poet recognizes as deep and durable design—whatever empowers coherence, equilibrium, civility, sanity in human or cosmic affairs—and the richly troubled moments of personal distress and dissonance, or of doubt that any such design exists or is accessible to us.

Some such elemental schema seems to me to underlie Lowell's use of blank verse in the poems of *Notebook* and *History* and to give them a strength that his earlier iambic verse, for all its crooked enjambments and powerful currents of feeling, never achieved with comparable authenticity. Or it may be that what one senses as the guiding power in the early verse—the Old Testament God of law and vengeance—is not, for us (or for me—or even for Lowell), so plausible a power as the less autocratic one that can be felt as resident in the later poems. It may be rash to try to characterize so implicit a force too precisely, but for Lowell it seems to be something like the great pageantlike system we inhabit, that system of seasonal renewals and remorseless aging by virtue of which our sense of what has been—history: personal, family, national, cultural—makes dense and impressive the momentary experiences that engage and damage us line by line and day by day.

Lowell's last verse—that of *Day by Day*—which appears to represent a return to the freer form of *Life Studies* and *For the Union Dead*, can be characterized rather as a free-verse version of the mosaic art he had developed in *Notebook* and *History*. For in most of these poems, too, each line presents a separate syntactic phrase, different in structure, different in the shape of its speaking, from lines before it and after it. The line's obligations to meter, rhyme, and stanza have vanished entirely; unlike the earlier experiments, this is genuine free verse. But free verse comes in several varieties—one major type relies on repetitive rhetorical structures (frequently anaphora) to supply the sense of regularity and order that has been relinquished with meter, rhyme,and stanza; another arranges lines that look casually similar on the page but are subtly different in structure and bearing. This second art, which is Lowell's, depends on a looser framework of order than we are used to, brief and tentative parallelisms, balances of subjects and predicates, of substantives and modifiers, of phrases turned with a formidable subtlety and resourcefulness, within which to build its fragile variations of tone:

> Southbound—
> a couple in passage,

> two Tennessee cardinals
> in green December outside the window
> dart and tag and mate—
> young as they want to be.
> We're not.[8]

All these lines arrange bits of English in very different syntactical and rhythmic combinations. What is constant is the line, our sense of it as the frame for each line-making phrase, but the frame is no longer pentameter—or iambic. The poetry seems to say, like other free verse written in this mode—by Adrienne Rich, for example—that a line of free verse can be any phrase, with any metrical contour, which combines with other phrases different in form and linked in meaning to compose an intriguing series of shapes and tones. But this is just what Lowell was doing with pentameter lines in the penultimate phase of his career: varying the form of each line, complicating the sequence of lines. To my perception, it looks as if these modes of verse, to which he remained alternately constant throughout his writing life, are not so different as we have made them out to be, or as Lowell himself apparently once thought. The art of versification is always an art of mosaic; it always consists of joining together orders of similarity with orders of difference in ways that seem compelling and significant. Perhaps in our time, in Lowell and others, we can see the poetic line undergoing a formal distress that becomes the basis for its successful rehabilitation: the measured line breaking down, the free verse line helplessly assuming form, turn out to be equally expressive modes for a poet who was, in Auden's phrase for Henry James, a "Master of nuance and scruple."[9]

Hearing the Measures
A Review Article

> The poets and the audiences of 1590 and 1600 were in love with the unrhymed pentameters. To us familiar; to them a Newfoundland. They ran riot with the discovery, as an age does when a new creative medium falls to its portion. They heard the beat with rapture. Even when the poets and players subtilised the beat, it must have been still a more powerful presence and a greater source of positive, conscious enjoyment than we in our sophistication will usually let it be.
>
> —Herbert Howarth

Derek Attridge. *Poetic Rhythm: An Introduction.* Cambridge: Cambridge University Press, 1995.
Brennan O'Donnell. *The Passion of Meter: A Study of Wordsworth's Metrical Art.* Kent, Ohio: Kent State University Press, 1995.
Alan Holder. *Rethinking Meter: A New Approach to the Verse Line.* Lewisburg, Pa.: Bucknell University Press, 1995.
Burton Raffel. *From Stress to Stress: An Autobiography of English Prosody.* Hamden, Conn.: Archon Books, 1992.

I

Prosody, as Alan Holder suggests in his effort at *Rethinking Meter,* is a hotbed of confusion, double-talk, inaccurate analysis, and extravagant claims. The nature of rhythm, and the kind of life it assumes in poetry, are explained or perceived differently by different readers, and as everything else has multiplied in our time, so have theories that try to account for the movement of sound in poems. Stressers and timers, as George Saintsbury called them, have perhaps always been with us, and new perspectives on language and literature—Russian formalism, structural linguistics, Chomskyan generative theory, New Criticism, free verse, and New Historicism, to mention a few—have spawned approaches to prosody so specialized that their adherents find it increasingly difficult to learn from one another, a condition exacerbated by the habit of dogmatic belief in the rightness of their own views and the inadequacy or absurdity of others'. That seems particularly natural to experts in this field. When I first ventured into this kind of study, coming to it as a teacher of literature, I remember being surprised to find that the books on meter were shelved in the library under Language, not Literature, and my surprise was a sign of my readiness to understand meter as an instrument of aesthetic effect rather than as a feature of language (though now I think of it as both). But the question arises constantly as to whether prosody is "essentially" or primarily a matter of linguistics or aesthetics, of rhythmic sound or of syntax, of dramatic speech in performance, or of the allocation of major and minor words to strong or weak positions in metrical lines. Without agreement on such topics, and starting from different sets of assumptions, the different schools have developed remarkably different methodologies and, for the most part, regard their rivals with varying mixtures of indifference, hostility, and contempt. A critic like Alan Holder, whose book (reviewed below) should probably be entitled *Rejecting Meter,* has little difficulty in making the internecine wars between and within these schools (especially within the "classical," "foot-bound" approach to meter) an object of ridicule.

Holder's position, nevertheless, is hardly a serious one, because his amusement at the antics of prosodists in distress is apparently based on the view that they really have nothing to study, that the very notion of meter as a recurrent rhythmic pattern is a delusion, and that the hundreds of scholars and critics who have, over several centuries, made it their study have been occupied with nothing more substantial than the crazy scientists of Laputa whom Swift so effectively satirized in *Gulliver's Travels.* Much nonsense, though, and equally unbecoming disputes have scarred the history of law, religion, politics, philosophy, and literary criticism, to go no further, but they do not often lead to the conclusion that the objects of these inquiries do not exist. That informed and intelligent debaters may sometimes express foolish views on a subject does not vaporize the subject.

For readers of poetry (students, scholars, critics, actors), but not necessarily for linguists, whose interest is likely to be more theoretical, the main point of metrical study is to provide coherent and consistent guidelines for following, by ear or voice or eye, the rhythmic patterns that poets have composed in their poems. Traditional English prosody has usually described these patterns in terms borrowed from ancient poetry written in quantitative meters, which are very different from the accentual or strong-stress meters common in English verse. This has resulted in the widespread perception that this system of prosodic analysis fails to fit the body of verse it is supposed to describe and analyze, and virtually all the newer linguistic and some of the literary approaches to English prosody attempt to modify, recast, and reframe the questions, especially to recognize that an accentual language in which the prominence of syllables is based on stresses is utterly different from ancient languages like Greek or Latin in which the prominence of syllables was largely based on length or duration or pitch (though sharpness of accent could also play a role). Even if sixteenth-century English "iambic" verse evidently developed as a kind of accentual equivalent of the Latin iambic pattern, the equivalency is not perfect. After all, if, in theory at least, a long syllable in Latin was equal in duration to two short syllables, that arithmetical equivalence had no counterpart in an English syllabic system, unless in triple-rhythm verse. But the English duple verse we find in Chaucer, and again in Tudor poets of the mid-sixteenth century, was different and was based on an alternation of less stressed and more stressed syllables, sometimes perhaps confirmed by the longer duration of the stressed ones but much more often not. The stressed syllable might simply be said more sharply or louder, but it might last no longer than the unstressed one, and, in fact, as iambic verse came more and more to be written in the mid-sixteenth century, the tune it generated was typically a tripping one in which it was easy to hear a succession of lesser and greater points of stress. The key was the alternation—of sharpness, perhaps of loudness, but not of alternately long-held and quick-spoken syllables. This kind of thing:

> Thou Cupide God of love, whom Venus thralles do serve,
> I yield thee thanks upon my knees, as thou dost well deserve.
> By thee my wishèd joyes have shaken of[f] despaire,
> And all my storming dayes be past, and weather waxeth faire.[1]

Verse as regular as this, fixing its stresses firmly in the even-numbered syllables of the line, raised no immediate practical or theoretical problems. Very occasional variations in stress—major monosyllabic words in unstressed positions or reversals of the lesser-greater pattern especially in the first two syllables of the line—did not substantially disrupt a listener's sense of alternation as the basic rhythmic feature of the line. But when, in the next generation, poets began to employ these and other variations more frequently and to make them a familiar part of the metrical design, the theoretical difficulties began. The alternation still persists as an easily heard phenomenon, but it is subject to modification by an array of deviations from the pattern that have led most poets and metrists in the centuries that followed to view the resulting line as most helpfully described as being composed of "feet," that is, of segments consisting of a normally lightly stressed syllable followed by a more strongly stressed one (⌣ ′ in the usual graphic representation). This may seem at first like just another way of defining alternation, but in practice it allows the scanner of a line to treat each pair of syllables independently, so that both syllables of one pair may be lightly stressed and both syllables of the next strongly stressed. If, then, the third of this series of four syllables is more strongly pronounced than the second (say, ⌣ ` ^ ′, in the Trager-Smith four-level system), the principle of alternation will seem to be violated, unless we maintain that what matters is the relative strength *within each pair*. The problem here, however, for many critics of this system is that we do not normally hear lines in two-syllable segments. But, after all, the "foot" theory does not claim that we do, only that it is because of the structural design (too quick in passing to be consciously picked out but graphically analyzable if we wish to write it out and slow it down) that we accept this slight modification of the alternation principle. Some prosodists maintain, quite reasonably, that when the stricter alternating verse changes into a verse that tolerates and even enjoys the variations made possible by the analysis of the line into feet—notably, the trochaic "inversion" (′ ⌣ for ⌣ ′) and the pyrrhic-spondaic combination (⌣ ⌣ ′ ′), we are really talking about a different meter.[2] But it seems just as reasonable to maintain that when this happens, as it appears to have done quite palpably with the verse of Sidney and Shakespeare, the alternating meter has simply evolved into a looser form, a form about which it may be said that it tends to function somewhat less as a continuing musical mode of presentation that is pleasing in itself and for its own sake and somewhat more as a base from which expressive variations may occasionally mime the action or feeling conveyed by the words.[3]

Although the theoretical misgivings took a long time to find their way into writing about meter, some evidence of the period's uncertainty about the iambic decasyllabic line's structure is to be found in the great variety of metrical styles that poets devised. Spenser's usually regular and mellifluous metric (derived from Chaucer) is vastly different from Jonson's more spare but still regular lyric verse, but Donne's apparently deviant verse style is extraordinarily different from either. Shakespeare's dramatic verse undergoes extreme changes from his early plays to the late. Milton's epic blank verse is in a class by itself—radically enjambed, and following some deviational patterns hardly known earlier, unless in late Shakespeare. The more "correct" iambic verse that developed through the seventeenth century and remained dominant through much of the eighteenth was seen by its practitioners and their critics as a needed corrective to the licenses practiced by their older and wilder precursors—in effect, as a means of saving iambic verse and its permissible range of variations in the alternating decasyllabic pattern from tendencies that would undermine its structure and, by implication, the culture's inherent commitment to order.

By the nineteenth century the foot found deeper trouble. Poets began to write more poems in triple and dipodic meters and to sprinkle extra syllables in the duple feet of iambic poems. The effect was to make decasyllabic verse more accentual and to call into question the syllabic ingredient in its structure. Now, instead of the ear's hearing the intervals between the beats of the line as occupied—and indeed *measured*—usually by a single syllable, the measurement was increasingly achieved by a stricter keeping of time, regardless of whether one or two syllables intervened between the stressed ones. One result was that critics and readers began to hear "iambic" verse more and more as a stricter accentual system than it had probably been from the mid-sixteenth century to the mid-nineteenth century, a tendency that, as we shall see, has reached a significant critical climax in the metrical theory of Derek Attridge. On the other hand, the subordination of all metrical poetry to an ever-more-popular "free verse" has caused many readers to lose their ability to hear metrical verse as such (or at least to pay much attention to its pattern), a tendency that, as we shall see, has attained a kind of critical climax in the antimetrical polemics of Alan Holder. Both of these critics, in effect, show what happens as centuries pass and a people loses the tune of an older style of verse, as, even in the Renaissance, most readers had already lost their ability to hear the tunes of Latin verse, a phenomenon which, ironically, has been most masterfully chronicled by Derek Attridge in his splendid account, *Well-Weighed Syllables.*[4]

II

Attridge's current book, *Poetic Rhythm: An Introduction* (1995, henceforth *PR*), is derived from a longer and more detailed study published in 1984, *The Rhythms of English Poetry* (London: Longman) (henceforth *REP*). This earlier work is an elegant effort to put literary prosody on a sound linguistic basis and yet to explain how the management of metrical forms by English poets enabled them to enhance the expressiveness of their poetry, a subject of primary concern to literary critics. *PR* has grown out of *REP,* but it is meant for students and it presents essentially the same view of meter, but more genially, less as a rule-driven system and more as a descriptive account of English meters. To appraise this account, however, we need first to review how *REP* approached this subject.

In many ways *REP* was an admirable and successful undertaking, a landmark in practical prosodic analysis. Attridge is a first-rate explainer, and he uses this talent to summarize various approaches to prosody that have been used in our time: "classical" (stressers), temporal (timers), and linguistic (structuralists and generativists). He finds all of these wanting, but he also learns and borrows from all of them. After a fine section on "Rhythm" and the way it operates in English speech and hence in English poetry, *REP* analyzes how metrical rules operate in English verse and how different contexts and "conditions" work to complicate the elementary structures of English versification.

The formulation of rules would appear to have two purposes: (1) to theorize meter for linguists—that is, to account systematically for the structured ways in which metrical patterns and linguistic forms intersect in verse; and (2) to help expert readers explain to beginners how metrical poems work. Neither of these is easy, partly because few experts have the credentials needed to throw light on both, and a persuasive account of either depends on some accurate understanding of the other. Even linguists who care for poetry are often not notably sensitive to its aural patterns, and literary metrists are usually limited to what O. B. Hardison Jr. called "applied prosody"[5]—that is, the detailed study of line patterns or of particular lines of verse, usually through scansions that run the risk of being impressionistic rather than, in some sense, objective. On the other hand, the formulation of rules that govern the rhythmical structure of metrical lines is likely to become a project without end, forever seeking an elusive precision. From my point of view—that of an unreconstructed literary metrist and applied prosodist—it is not rules that will help most readers to get the hang of, say, iambic pentameter, not rules that prescribe and forbid, but orderly and accurate description that tells us what happens rhythmically in poems that use this meter.

Happily, that is what Attridge largely gives his readers in *PR.* Although the rules he has formulated in *REP* remain implicit throughout *PR,* in the later book, because it is intended for students, he does not burden the reader with their neo-Euclidean formulation. Instead, he explains—and does this brilliantly—what rhythmic patterns we are likely to encounter consistently in the metrical lines of English verse, how beats can be heard, and offbeats, and how frequently the beats are arranged in sequences of four, and the four-beat lines in groups of four. The basic terms are made available to readers in an unfailingly intelligent and fluent commentary, about which one's only complaint might be that the author asks a student in his opening pages to master too much abstract material too soon, with too few friendly examples. Of course, a wise teacher can help students through this initial difficulty, and for any teacher of the subject it is a pleasure to read a well-informed guide who is so expert and so sensitive to the movements of rhythmic verse.

He is particularly helpful in showing how the natural "peaks" of spoken language can be converted, in verse, to metrical beats. For "We are all experts in rhythm and meter" (43) and respond from our earliest years to the beats we can hear and reproduce in nursery rhymes and other wholly accessible popular forms of verse, all of which we understand to be intimately connected to the rhythms of the language we are learning to speak. Attridge shows charmingly how easy it is to turn almost any stretch of spoken English into verse (49–52), especially into the 4 × 4 pattern that he argues persuasively is almost anyone's standard notion of what verse is. He makes the important point (overlooked, as he justly remarks, in "many scansions and discussions of verse") *"that STRESSES are different from BEATS; they often coincide, but they are not the same thing"* (64, his emphasis). So, though his scansion system provides a / for stresses, it provides a different mark, _, to signal a beat; a stress that is also a beat receives both marks: L. To his great credit, he keeps emphasizing the difference between stresses and beats, insisting that we do not have to say a syllable strongly to recognize it as a beat. "All that is necessary is a *distinct* pronunciation, allowing each syllable its own rhythmic space" (109). Alas, I shall use this sensible formulation against several of his claims.

What is striking about Attridge's approach to English meter is that, in company with the "timers," he regards accentual or "strong-stress" verse as central and develops a method of scansion based on the beats and offbeats that are clearly audible in this kind of verse. He contends, quite plausibly, that virtually all English verse, except iambic pentameter and other kinds of syllable-stress verse, is essentially four-beat accentual. Lines of hymns and ballads that appear to have only three beats make up the deficit with a fourth, silent one, and almost all other kinds of lines—fourteeners, poulter's measure, most hexameters, limericks, and much verse whose lineation is deceptive—turn out to be written not only in four-beat lines but in four-line stanzas. The 4 × 4 pattern is the basic form for English poetry, the kind of rhythm that every child can recognize and respond to, from "Nursery rhymes, street games, popular ballads, advertising jingles, sports chants, rap lyrics, and . . . other kinds of widely familiar verse" (63). For this verse Attridge develops a notation based on symbols for beats (B) and offbeats (o). Both the analysis and the notation are explained clearly and work well. The perception that this kind of poetry often, even usually, and perhaps almost always, implies measured pauses at the end of shorter lines, and that these lines, so augmented, take their place in a 4 × 4 metrical design, ought to command the assent of most readers, critics, and linguists.

But to give an adequate account of poetic rhythm in English requires an equally convincing analysis of the two main systems of verse that are not subsumed in the 4 × 4 pattern but have produced an extraordinary proportion of the most impressive poetry in the language: iambic pentameter and free verse. For free verse Attridge has to find other terms and methods to study its very different way of moving (more on that later); for iambic pentameter (and a few of its metrical cousins), he adapts the system that has worked so well for accentual verse. But when this beat-driven system is extended to the syllable-stress verse that Attridge acknowledges is less strongly determined by beats (*PR,* 97–100)—traditional iambic pentameter, or, more broadly, accentual-syllabic verse—it seems inadequate to measure, explain, and illustrate what is going on in iambic pentameter, and it inevitably implies that iambic pentameter is a much more accentual meter than it is.

Attridge, of course, is quite convinced of the contrary—that "classical" metrics cannot explain traditional poetry as well as his new system can (*REP,* 10–18 and passim). Traditional prosody "presents a dizzying array" of technical terms (*PR,* xix), and its foot-scansion "works only for those who already know what is going on" (*PR,* xix) He regards its notation and terminology as not only elitist (xix) but as insufficiently flexible and nuanced, resting as it does on intuitions of performance rather than on rules derived from linguistic evidence about English phonology—that is, about where to place stress when one reads verse lines aloud or scans them in writing. For Attridge, as for the generative metrists, a meter is based on rules. In *PR* he mentions generative theory only in his Glossary and describes it there as seeking to define what is metrical and what is not: "the limits of metricality" (219). *REP,* though it treats generative metrics critically, is more respectful and considers it promising (34–55, 149–51). It may be that his respect for this kind of theory has declined with the years, but in neither book does he question the key idea of generative theory, that rules can be formulated that generate "all the acceptable lines in this or that variety of English metre," except to object that their rules "do not, however, generate *only* such lines" (50). He rightly criticizes the generativists for their relatively crude instruments (sensitive, but to the wrong matters) for analyzing iambic pentameter. He even admits: "There comes a point where rhythmic distinctions are too fine to be captured in manageable rules, and one has to say with Saintsbury, 'The ear must decide'."(152). But his method of analysis in *REP* is to set out carefully formulated "rules of metre." Although most of these seem valid for accentual verse, with its strong beats and its minor, "offbeat" syllables that are unambiguously minor, for a meter as subtle as iambic pentameter the rules may start out simple enough, but the complexity of this meter's variations leads to increasingly complex explanatory procedures. Attridge runs into the same problem that helped to discredit the generativists: once you start formulating rules, marginal or tricky cases lure you into elaborating subrules and rule expansions to cover every possible condition, and the supposedly simple and economical language of rules begins to sound like this:

> *An implied offbeat may occur only (i) when it is immediately preceded or followed by a non-final double offbeat,*[6] *or (ii) in observance of an initial inversion condition.* (194)

The notation, too, that Attridge has developed for his system, though it is meant as an improvement on the unattractive Greek terminology of classical English metrics, has grown astonishingly complicated. Toward the end of *PR* (213–14), he lists the symbols used to mark lines of verse for what he calls single- and double-line scansion (see table 5). And this is the simplified version, reduced in *PR* so as to be printable on computers from the somewhat more cumbersome notation of *REP,* which includes ô, ŏ, ò and $\bar{\text{B}}$ (for implied offbeats, double offbeats, and demoted and promoted syllables respectively).

But even when the rules have been intelligibly formulated (and the new nomenclature and notation learned), it must be shown how they apply to lines that seem to disobey or evade them, and much of Attridge's earlier book, *REP,* is spent, in effect, justifying the rules—that is, showing how they generate iambic lines that seem to Attridge on "the borders of metricality" (233) . They raise problems for his system largely because, despite his

Table 5. Symbols used to mark lines of verse

Single-line scansion	Double-line scansion
/	Above the line
\	+s
⌊	-s
⌉	s
x	(s)
x̱	^s
-	
[⌊]	Below the line
[x]	B
⌊	b
a/	~B
|	o
R	"
F	*
M	[B]
ANT	[o]
ARR	^
STA	
EXT	
>	

insistence that "We are all experts in rhythm and meter" (*PR*, 43), a truth that I have no quarrel with, it is not easily demonstrable that everyone is an expert in hearing the rhythms of iambic pentameter. To make good his claims that we can all hear this meter easily, too, he subscribes to dogmas (again, as the generative metrists and other prosodists do) about which kinds of words or syllables in metrical lines *must* receive stress.

This is treacherous ground. Drama coaches usually want to say, "Read the line naturally," with an awareness both of the beat and of the sense, noting in particular, as the English director John Barton urges his actors, the antitheses that are often the key to the intelligible and forceful speaking of Shakespeare's lines.[7] Traditional metrists like myself would nowadays usually add that where the line seems to violate the meter it will often be sufficient to "tilt" the pronunciation of the words just slightly (it will need no more than that) in order to keep the line audibly in touch with the metrical pattern. (The word "tilt" is W. K. Wimsatt's,[8] and the idea has made excellent sense to most traditional readers of verse. See, for example, Cable's approving words about it, 123–27.) Such tilting strikes Attridge as a violation of normal stress pattern, which for him derives from the linguistic ability to distinguish two classes of English words, content words and function words. Content words (nouns, verbs, adjectives, and adverbs) convey "a full meaning by themselves"; function words (such as prepositions, articles, conjunctions) "depend on other words for their meaning" (*PR,* 27) Attridge is no doubt aware how inadequate these definitions are—as if, for example, the noun "priority" conveyed more meaning than the preposition (or conjunction) "before." He accepts them, presumably, because he wants to train students to see major words as the likeliest candidates for stress, and minor ones as long shots. But this procedure then compels him, as it has other metrists, to take a lot of it back, for it turns out that, more often than anyone might expect, "content words" are *not* stressed. In certain circumstances their claims to stress are less pressing than those of other syllables, or they come where the metrical beats cannot conveniently fall, where the language does not need them for beat-words—they may get some degree of stress, but their stresses do not count as beats in, say, the five-beat line; whereas function words may get to occupy a beat, even without being strongly stressed. Here are two examples from Browning's *The Ring and the Book,* as Attridge scans them in *PR* (252). (Beats are underlined, whether they appear on strongly or weakly stressed syllables.)

    <u>/</u> x   /   <u>/</u> x   <u>/</u>   x <u>/</u>   x <u>/</u>
1. Dip a broad melon-leaf that holds the wet

    <u>/</u> x   x   <u>x</u>   x <u>/</u>   /   <u>/</u> x <u>x</u>
2. Presently, though my path grew perilous

These lines seem to me impeccably scanned and their delivery can be made metrically coherent by only a little tilting, but Attridge, whose theory does not permit him to resort to a notion of tilting, has to explain why, in a normal delivery of these lines, what seem like stronger words *(broad, grew)* don't attract a beat and what look like weaker syllables *(though, -ous)* do. To explain this, Attridge uses, as metrists of other schools have done, the terms *demotion* and *promotion,* terms that seem to me particularly unfortunate (like *substitution* and *inversion*), because they imply that someone (but who? the poet? the reader? Attridge?) has, at some definite moment, downgraded or upgraded a syllable in a line (or substituted or inverted an already written foot). But lines of verse get written as they are written; poets do not write their lines as perfectly regular icons and then promote or demote certain syllables. They may fiddle with the words till they sound right, but they do not demote or promote syllables. What do the terms mean, anyway? Not, apparently, that the words are spoken more softly or loudly than we would normally speak them—Attridge specifically denies that (*REP,* 168; *PR,* 71, 75)—but that we see with our eyes and note with our sense of English grammar that a major (or a minor) syllable is sitting in the line where it may not belong. The sense of grammar is apparently what counts. What has happened here is that Attridge, like many of his peers, has first "promoted" *all* the stressed syllables in the language's content words (i.e., declared them eligible, by class or nature, to carry a beat) and "demoted" all the syllables in the language's so-called function words (declared them, by the same standard, ineligible to carry a beat); and then he has found it necessary to demote some of the first (promoted) group when they actually appear in verse lines, and to promote some of the second (demoted) group. But the whole idea of promotion and demotion is cumbersome, abstract, and unnecessary. Why not take the language as it comes, recognizing (1) that much of the time major words do get stress but that frequently they do not because other words they keep company with sometimes seem to have a better right to it, and (2) that poets, observing this, have placed the stress-attracting words, whether minor or major ones, in the positions that normally take stress? Especially in the packed lines we meet in much poetry the expectations we have for the language generally may not hold; the poets themselves may find it interesting and expressive, or interesting and rhythmically attractive, to violate our expectations and to let words we have categorized as major or minor resist or attract stress in response to what the meter and the language, working in concert, ask them to do. "The ear must decide."

For many lines of English accentual-syllabic verse, Attridge's system of scansion works well enough, given his procedures for promoting and demoting, and his pages are rich with perceptive observations on language and poetry. But there are two kinds of line especially on which he differs from traditional metrists in his scansion. One of them is the line that many readers and critics (e.g., Jespersen, Winters, W. K. Wimsatt Jr., and Cable) have testified to hearing as a series of ascending stresses, sometimes numbered 4-3-2-1.[9] Because 4 is weaker than 3, and 2 than 1, many metrists have thought the set of four syllables intelligible as, in effect, two iambic feet, though iambic in different ways or on different scales. But for Attridge, though he admits that there may be "a slight blurring of the rhythm between the adjacent nonstress and stress" (182), the four syllables are to be heard as an "introductory double upbeat and concluding pair of beats" (183). T. V. F. Brogan has questioned Attridge on this "metrical figure,"[10] giving as examples such lines as Pope's:

    4 3 2   1
3. *On her white breast,* a sparkling Cross she wore

and Sidney's:

    4 3 2 1
4. *That in one speech* two Negatives affirm

    4   3   2 1
5. *With how sad steps,* O Moon, thou climb'st the skies

As Brogan points out—very sensibly, in my view—these syllables may be read, in an iambic pentameter context, as pyrrhic and spondee, in which the two syllables of both feet, though close to each other in strength, fit the iambic pattern of less stress—more stress. What matters is the *relative* degree of stress (lesser followed by greater) within each pair. Attridge in reply shows how strongly accentual his reading of this meter is: "I hear a line with a certain number of rhythmic peaks," not one "with five syllable pairs" (12). Whereas Brogan argues for paying attention to meter and meaning in deciding just how stresses should fall, Attridge replies, "My evidence is English phonology" (12)—and, in effect, that settles the matter: major words deserve more stress than minor ones. With his students, he prefers, he says, "to create an awareness of fundamental rhythms based on beats and offbeats, before moving to the syllabic tradition of analysis which divides lines up into pairs" of syllables (18). But Brogan hears beats and offbeats, and so do I; we just do not require the beats always to fall on so-called major or content words. We do not require it because the language does not require it; our evidence, too, is English phonology, but an English phonology unencumbered by (elitist?) dogmas about compulsory stressing of privileged syllables.

    What Attridge says here in 1987 is much more absolute than his words in *REP* about "metrical subordination": "the specific conditions of a particular line . . . can induce *any* monosyllable or disyllable to lose all or some of its stress" (235). By that standard, if one can show a likelihood that lines of the type Attridge refers to here were not read his way but tended to keep the initial beat on one of the first two syllables of the four, then one may read these lines differently from Attridge, and many metrists and readers have done so through the centuries. Indeed, in the face of strong evidence to the contrary—in the published scansions of metrists and literary critics, in recordings by actors and poets, and in other kinds of evidence that attest to the way earlier poets and critics read this metrical figure—the burden of proof is still on Attridge to show convincingly why the phonological patterns of prose should overweigh the metrical pattern when all the metrical pattern needs to be realized is a slight, very slight, hardly detectable augmentation of emphasis on one syllable and diminution of force on another, just enough to make sure that even without strong stress the beat will be felt on the second syllable, not on the third.

In taking this stand, Attridge appears to be legitimizing a reading of lines like these that will skip lightly over the first two syllables and come down sharply on the third: On her *white breast;* That in *one speech;* With how *sad steps* (the audible steps, of course, disappear with this reading). And the same lurch is to be heard in thousands of other lines that English poets have written—I suspect, without ever imagining that readers, much less professional metrists, would countenance such a lurch. He scans, for example, Keats's line from the "Ode on a Grecian Urn" like this (*PR,* 120):

    x *L* x   *L* x *L*x   x   *L*   *L*
6. Thou foster-child of si*lence and slow time*

a reading that lurches where it ought to slow down over the last four syllables. Then there is the often debated line from Shakespeare's Sonnet 30 (with Attridge's scansion [*REP,* 261]):

7. When to the se*ssions of sweet si*lent thought
   B   ŏ   B   ŏ   B ô B

And there are lines like these from Arnold's "The Scholar-Gypsy," which Attridge sets for students in *PR* and then scans himself in the "Suggested responses to the exercises" (248):

                  x   x *L* [x]*L*
8. Screen'd is this nook *o'er the high half*-reap'd field[11]

    x   x *L*   *L*
9. *Through the thick corn* the scarlet poppies peep

   x   x   *L*   *L*
10. *And round green roots* and yellowing stalks I see

         x   x *L*   *L*
11. Of bloom *on the bent grass* where I am laid

    x   x *L* *L*
12. *And the eye tra*vels down to Oxford's towers

Each of these lines includes the kind of four-syllable combination that traditionally has been called a pyrrhic-spondee: x x \ /. The first two syllables lack one of Attridge's major words, whereas the last two syllables are both major. Not even *round* is major enough to entitle it to a beat; we may have trouble suppressing it, but it is only a lowly preposition, and that settles it. In Attridge's speech-world, the major syllables must receive stress (and the beat) because they are used to receiving stress in the speech of native speakers. Discussing a similar line from Crabbe's *The Village* (1.112) in *REP,* which he gives a double-line scansion,

  -s   -s +s +s
13. *And a bold, art*ful, surly, savage race
    ŏ   B ôB

Attridge says that "there can be no question about the scansion" because the first two syllables "are clearly to be regarded as -s," that is, unstressed (216).

But of course there can be a question; the first two syllables may normally go unstressed, but in lines like these a beat (and perhaps a stress) may still be heard on one of them. We can also establish the questionableness of his ruling by finding phrases in poems that do not distribute stresses as Attridge says they must. To begin with, it seems almost self-evident that the exercise lines quoted above (8–12) are susceptible of another reading. Three of the phrases have almost exactly the same syntax: they begin with a preposition followed by *the,* a monosyllabic adjective, and a noun (or the first syllable of another adjectival phrase). Many readers would therefore have no difficulty placing a little more emphasis on the preposition (especially when the preposition is a location marker: *o'er, through, on*) and a little less on the adjective, with the result that the first *beat* of the phrase falls on the first-syllable preposition and the second on the fourth syllable:

    /   ˘ \ /
Through the thick corn, etc.

The whole series thus constitutes a milder version of the familiar trochee-spondee pattern, though this, as we shall see, is a major reason why Attridge will have nothing to do with it. But Attridge's own Promotion Rule allows it: "an unstressed syllable may realise a beat when it is not adjacent to a stress in the same line" (*REP,* 168). That rule would allow beats on

Hearing the Measures 169

"Through" (in 9) and on "And" in (12) and (13) and would justify those readers and actors who have heard or read a slight stress on the "And" in lines like these from Tennyson's "Morte d'Arthur":

14. *And the long rip*ple washing in the reeds (117)
15. *And the third time* may prosper, get thee hence (130)
16. *And the long glo*ries of the winter moon (192)

And if on those line-initial syllables, why not when the metrical figure occurs in an echoing phrase later in the line? Otherwise, the echo will not be heard:

   ◢   ⌣   \   *L*   ◢   \   *L*
17. *On the waste sand by the waste sea* they closed. (Tennyson, "The Passing of Arthur")

Attridge, however, scans it like this (*PR,* 120):

   x   x   *L*   *L*   x   x   *L*   *L*   x   *L*
   On the waste sand by the waste sea they closed.

Did Tennyson's voice really lurch its way through such lines? Though I remain doubtful, it seems to me not entirely impossible, but I do not believe for a moment that Pope made a habit of doing the same lurching when he began lines in his *Essay on Man* with such phrases as: "From the green myriads," "To the first good," "In the same temple," "In the small circle," "As the small pebble." Pope was a stickler for correct technique, and most poets at least from Dryden to Johnson would have been scandalized by anapests leading to monosyllabic feet. But if we are supposed to hear the lurching pattern in these lines, why not in these: "When his lewd father," "When the loose mountain," "Lo, the poor Indian," and many others? The notion that such traditional poets would tolerate an anapest followed by a monosyllabic foot seems remarkably anachronistic.[12]

Consider another line of Tennyson (from "In Memoriam," 7, 12):

18. *On the bald street breaks the blank day*

It looks, on the face of it, as if the second half-line echoes the first, but this can only be heard if one recognizes that for Tennyson's ear (the best in English poetry, according to Auden), "On" was heard to be stressed almost as strongly as "breaks":

     L   \   *L*   *L*   \   *L*
     On the bald street breaks the blank day

If phrases like these can be scanned as I suggest, at least as a permissible option, why should they not when they occur in midline or at line's end? Here, with some suggestions for scansion, are some early examples, written at a time when, as almost everyone agrees, the sixteenth-century line was still very regular:

                              ⊥   x \ L
19. That cannot take a mouse *as the cat can* (Wyatt)

                             ⊥   x \ L
20. With sodein noise thondred *on the left hand* (Surrey)

                          ⊥   x   \   L
21. They his bare neck beheld, *and his hoar hairs* (Grimald)

Or these from "Dulce Bellum Inexpertis" by Gascoigne, our best authority for the view that he and his contemporary Tudor poets would not suffer gladly the lurching movement that displaces the beat from an even-numbered syllable:

22. But who they be now her*ken and take heede*
23. Oh Epitaphe of ho*nor and high happe*
24. And he that keepes his Maj*esties great seale*

Later, the poets do this kind of thing often. Here are two, among many, from Herbert:

25. As the day less*ens, and his life with it*
26. Finds his crackt name at length *in the church-glasse*

Sidney has plenty of such lines; Jonson uses them to speak of Shakespeare:

27. And though thou hadst small Lat*in and less Greek*
28. He was not of an age, *but for all time*

Shakespeare's own work is full of them. These are from the *Sonnets:*

29. But as the marigold *at the sun's eye* (25:6)
30. All days are nights to see *till I see thee* (43:13)
31. So long as youth and thou *are of one date* (22:2)

In all of these the first or second syllable of each italicized pair might imaginably be given a little more stress—just a little more!—and the anapest disappears. Many readers of 29–31 would find it easy to give some slight additional stress to *at, till,* and *are;* some would find it more satisfying to stress *I* or *of* a little more prominently.

Other lines from the *Sonnets* that can easily be made to avoid the lurch by giving just a shade more stress to the second of the four syllables in question, or, even without more stress, speaking the second syllable without hurrying:

32. Whence hast thou this becom*ing of **things ill*** (150:5)
33. Thy bosom is endear*ed with **all hearts*** (31:1)
34. The world will be thy wi*dow and **still weep*** (9:5)

Contemporary poets, or even some earlier twentieth-century ones, might hear these italicized words as lurches, but to attribute them to much earlier poets is hardly credible, and, in my view, Attridge does no service to students in making them believe that earlier poets really heard the lines that way. Even if he himself does not adopt the lurch in reading all these lines, it is hard to see how he can discourage his students from doing so when the second syllable of such a group is a preposition or a pronoun (or the last syllable of a polysyllabic word)—that is, when even though it belongs to an unfavored grammatical category it can in speech sometimes compete with, say, adjectives for prominence. Or second-syllable copulative or auxiliary verbs may compete with what may seem like more important words. In all such cases Attridge himself may not choose to stress the third syllable, but his position invites his students or others to perform the lurching movement that takes the beat on the third syllable, not the second. Consider how all of these lines from Shakespeare's *Sonnets* would sound with that lurch to the italicized syllables over the two previous ones:

35. And beauty making beautiful *old rhyme* (106:3)
36. The argument all bare is of *more worth* (103:3)
37. But do not so; I love thee in *such sort* (36:13, 96:13)
38. Say that thou didst forsake me for *some fault* (89:1)
39. Was it the proud full sail of his *great verse* (86:1)
40. Which eyes not yet created shall *o'er-read* (81:10)
41. In me thou seest the glowing of *such fire* (73:9)
42. Blessed are you whose worthiness *gives scope* (52:13)
43. Till I return, of posting is *no need* (51:4)

I venture to say that this is not Shakespeare's tune. It would be easy to adduce dozens more from Shakespeare's poems, and hundreds from the plays. Notice that in such lines a reader who jumps from the sixth to the ninth syllable over two intervening ones classed as minor, unstressed, and negligible, is likely to put more stress on the ninth syllable than on the tenth: *old* rhyme, *great* verse, *some* fault, *such* fire, and so on. What this kind of reading can do to the subtlety of Shakespeare's argument in these poems does not bear thinking of.

Or consider Milton. In "Lycidas," I make out about seventeen places where the Attridge lurch would be called into play, among them:

44. Together both, *ere the high lawns* appeared (25)
45. Batt'ning our flocks *with the fresh dews* of night (29)
46. Fanning their joyous leaves *to thy soft lays* (44)
47. *But the fair guer*don when we hope to find (73)
48. Set off to th' world, *nor in broad rum*or lies. (80)
49. But swoln with wind, *and the rank mist* they draw (126)
50. *But that two-hand*ed engine at the door* (130)
51. Ye valleys low *where the mild whis*pers use (136)
52. *On whose fresh lap* the swart star sparely looks (138)

And so on. It should be pointed out that if we lurch through 52 we lose entirely any sense we might have of the unusual combination in one line of what linguists call proclitic and enclitic phrases—the adjective and noun that in one case occupy a weak and then a strong position, and later a strong and then a weak position. You can hear that difference if you do not rush the line; if you lurch through the phrase, you may find yourself giving six beats to the line, failing to recognize that "star" occupies what Attridge calls an offbeat. Attridge's principles would probably oblige him to read the line as having six beats, because the adjective-noun phrases are the same grammatical construction and if we stress both members of one such pair—so he tells us (see below)—we *must* do the same with the other.

Lurching through some of the other lines (44, 45, 47, 49, 51) may also put a reader in jeopardy of speaking a four-beat line, "the unwanted triple effect" (*REP,* 261), something that Attridge worries about with lines of this structure and others (256–64), because his unwillingness to hear a beat on the second syllable of a pyrrhic before a spondee results in many more double offbeats than seem audible to a more traditional listener. In what seems to me a related argument, Attridge notes how rarely poets use what he calls stress-final pairing with linkage (265), the pattern shown in 54 of four successive syllables in which the first two are weakly stressed and the next two more strongly stressed, but in which the middle two form a single word:

* This is one of Attridge's examples.

53. And growing still in stat*ure the grim shape*
54. Remembering not, retains *an obscure sense.*

For Attridge, these two lines do not sound very different from each other (269), because in both he hears the beat on the ninth syllable, not the eighth. He notes that the second pattern, is much less frequent than the first, according to various statistical studies, that apparently both poets and metrists have more trouble with it. But he fails to draw the likely inference: that poets, as he says, feel more uncomfortable with the second pattern, because they find it goes against the grain to elevate the usually unstressed syllable of a disyllabic word to a beat position while the other, usually stressed, syllable does not receive a beat, but that *they do not find it so awkward to hear even a word like "the" taking a beat when the next syllable is a fairly important word like an adjective.* This suggests that, despite what he says about "lexically-determined" stress, poets and other critics must hear the eighth-syllable beat in pyrrhic-spondee combinations like (53) much more often than he does.

Attridge may respond that to let the beat fall on the minor syllable rather than the major one in such cases violates the phonological rules that govern normal English speech. But even in ordinary speech different structures may surprise our expectations. Natural speech has varying ways of observing the usual demands of English phonology. For one thing, *pace* Attridge, it may adjust to the tilting requirements of iambic verse; but even Attridge admits that there are many combinations where words of major grammatical categories may be less strongly stressed than so-called minor ones—in contrastive-stress situations, for example ("I was walking *from* town, not *toward* town"). (Compare Shakespeare's "On *this* side *my* hand, and on *that* side *yours*" [*Richard II*, 4.1.183]; or Auden's "The earth turns over; *our* side feels the cold"[13]—better than "our *side* feels the cold".) Phrasal verbs, too ("stand *up,*" to use Attridge's example), may seem to displace the stress patterns that our categorizing habits lead us to expect. When news anchors on our networks speak the phrase, "When we come back . . . ," as they do time after time, night after night, they never put significant stress on "come." They always stress "back," and they variously stress either "When" or (less often) "we." In the few similar phrases Attridge scans in these two books, he usually ignores the voice's option of reducing the expected stress on the verb:

x x *Ĺ Ĺ*
"We shall *grow old*" (*PR,* 257)

"Pleas'd, out of Heaven, shalt *look down*" (*REP,* 246)
  B   ŏ   B   ŏ   B ô B

"*glide o'er* the dusky green" (*REP,* 263)
  B   ŏ

"*bends toward* the east" (*REP,* 263)
  B   ŏ

preferring in the first two examples to perform the standard lurch, in the last two to read a standard but by no means obligatory trochee. Subtle as Attridge's analysis usually is, the language of verse seems to me still more subtle and capable of accepting in its stride even the unusual formations exemplified by 53 and 54.

One reason Attridge is almost obliged to rule out some of the alternative readings of the lines we have been reviewing is that, if he is somewhat suspicious of these, he is even more aggressively suspicious of the kind of line that would result from scanning lines 3, 8–9, 11–20, 25–26, 29–31, 44, 47, 49, and 51 as I suggest, because to do so would legitimize the dreaded trochee-spondee combination, and Attridge does everything he can to scotch this metrical figure, focusing at length (230–39) on lines like these by Pope and Shakespeare:

55. *Damn with faint praise,* assent with civil leer
56. For precious friends, *hid in death's date*less night

It disconcerts him that "faint" in 55, which ought to receive not only a stress but a beat, must be "subordinated" to "praise" in this formation. Later, in an article in *Eidos,* acknowledging that "Metrical subordination has remained a part of my published account of English verse with which I have never been very happy,"[14] he formulates for such combinations, which he finds disturbingly numerous, a rule he calls "double-offbeat demotion":

> *A stressed syllable, or an unstressed syllable and a stressed syllable (in either order), or two stressed syllables, may realize an offbeat between two stresses, or after a line-boundary and before a stress.* (5)

It is a measure of Attridge's willingness to reconsider some weak points in his theory that he can now accept some optional readings that use "metrical subordination" to achieve what traditional metrists would call a trochee and spondee, though he oddly attributes such metrical disturbances not to the pattern of stresses and beats involved but to the double offbeat. Such readings, he warns us in a phrase reminiscent of the worries of Halle

Hearing the Measures   175

and Keyser, "may push the line to the borders of metricality" (233). An interesting line in *Hamlet* "takes one to the limits of regular metrical form" (234). Earlier, another line, for another reason, "totters on the edge of unmetricality" (185). He admits that "the specific conditions of a particular line . . . can induce *any* monosyllable or dissyllable to lose some or all of its stress" (235). Yet, rather than tolerate lines that are like 55 and 56 but run a "spondee" over punctuation, he resorts to the fiction that expert writers like Browning, Milton, and Spenser preferred to hear lines of six beats where their verse form called for five (237). I give my scansion above the line, Attridge's below:

```
       /   ˇ   \   /   ˇ   /     ˇ   /  ˇ   /
57. Wretched man, wretched tree; whose nature weak
       B   o   B ô B    o   B    o   B o    B
       /   ˇ   \   /  ˇ   /   ˇ     /   ˇ   /
58. Weep no more, woeful shepherds, weep no more¹⁵
       B   o   B ô B o   B   o     B   o   B
```

For one line, his rigidities lead him into this unseemly passage:

59. The deep groves and white temples and wet caves (Browning, "Pauline")

One of the three adjectives would have to be metrically subordinated to achieve a five-beat line, but *as all are parallel they all demand the same degree of emphasis. To pick one out arbitrarily would be invidious,* and a momentary expansion of the metre to accept six beats is the only linguistically acceptable solution. (238; my emphasis)

Such language makes it sound as if we are talking about human rights and not metrical stress. To argue this way ignores the hardly disputable fact that poets like Browning did not momentarily expand a meter because they could not think of a way to say what they wanted to say within it. Attridge's argument postulates some wholly fictional rule about the English language's need to observe an egalitarian balance among adjectives, which ten minutes of listening to any native speaker should show is dubious. If you speak Browning's ten syllables quickly and "distinctly"—Attridge's word about other combinations (109)—but without much variation in stress, you can keep the sense of a more or less alternating rhythm and avoid worrying over whether you have violated any linguistic or metrical rule. In some puzzling lines Attridge allows for "rhythmic blurring" (238 and passim), his own version of what earlier metrists used to call "hovering accent" (182). But too often he seems bound by his frequently expressed insistence that the language has to follow some supposed rule of pronunciation. In discussing metrical subordination in the pattern discussed above (his "double-offbeat demotion"), he notes, to his surprise (232, and again in *Eidos* 4) that many poets use it; it "has therefore become one of the available alternatives enshrined by convention at the start of the iambic line, in spite of its potential disruptiveness" (233). The obvious inference is that poets and their readers have not usually found the pattern as disruptive as Attridge does, nor have they needed, in the lines cited above, to invent an extra beat. Clearly, he ought to recognize that his difficulty in hearing the tune is not a sufficient reason to excommunicate such lines or to regard them as marginally metrical. Rather, it is a reason to become suspicious of his own methods.

As for the democracy he posits as existing between parts of speech that look as if they had equal weight, I might note that at one time I collected instances in Tudor poetry, and in Sidney, Marlowe, and early Shakespeare, of lines that began with repeated monosyllables. They were very frequent, and yet this was a time when the poets, as almost everyone agrees, were writing a very regular verse, a verse that could be depended on to alternate the degree of stress from one syllable to the next. Gascoigne, the critic who stated most unambiguously that this alternating practice should guide poets and whose verse is still known for its regular alternating structure, uses "Pray, pray" several times in "The Steele Glas"; Surrey has "Flee, flee," in his translation of the *Aeneid;* Sackville writes "Cum, cum" in his "Induction" to *The Mirror for Magistrates;* Marlowe uses several phrases that way, most memorably Faustus's "See, see where Christ's blood streams in the firmament"; and my list of Shakespeare's similar phrases in metrical lines, merely from early plays, includes twenty-two different repeated words: among others, *Aye, Nay, Go, No, See, Down, Hark, Mount, Lord, Fool,* and even *Sans.* Attridge's belief that such repeated words must be spoken with exactly the same force (255), though the first might be subordinated metrically to the second, seems less persuasive than that the poet who wrote them probably expected the second to be said differently from the first—more weightily or emphatically or sharply, as we are likely to do in our own speech. Perhaps it should be noted in passing that, although Attridge's sensitive analysis of accentual poetry suggests that he is probably an excellent reader of verse, among his hundreds of cited lines in *REP* (and his practice is similar in *PR*) only eleven are of iambic pentameter in Shakespeare's plays, and there are no such citations from any other verse

Hearing the Measures   177

drama. Whatever students may learn from either text, it is evidently not intended as a guide for actors.

In the *Eidos* article referred to above (August 1987), Attridge makes a remark that almost gives the whole point away. He notes that "rhythmically, there is not a great deal of difference between 'You that poor Petrarch's long-deceased woes' [Sidney, *Astrophel and Stella*] and 'You that in Petrarch's . . .'" (4). Accordingly, Attridge now incorporates this variation into his rules (see the rule quoted above, p. 174) But if the *rhythm* is about the same, what does it matter if the word occupying the third syllable is a preposition or any of a group of adjectives, which Attridge lists in order of increasing importance and hence "of increasing rhythmic irregularity" (4) *sweete, great, fine, young, dumb, shrewd?* But Attridge's conversion is only partial: when the variation requires the reader to hear it straddling two phrases, as in 57–59 above, he still thinks the correct solution is to hear these as six-beat lines, no matter how strange it seems that Sidney or Spenser would ever toss such long lines into a steady stream of pentameters. Traditional metrics should have no difficulty with these lines, easily understanding that the second "foot" is a spondee,[16] unusual only in that it bridges two phrases, something that Donne's verse does habitually.

The root of the difficulty here is clearly Attridge's unwillingness to agree that in reciting verse the voice may even tilt the lines a little to augment the stress on syllables that in prose or speech would not attract it, or to diminish the stress on syllables that in prose or speech would receive it.

  a. He can accept ᴗᴗᴗ/ *(is as a death)* because the second syllable, having no competition for stress, is *perceived* as a beat, though the voice does nothing extra to attract it (*REP,* 168).
  b. He can accept ᴗ/\/ *(The long day wanes)* because this pattern often occurs in actual speech (168).
  c. He accepts most forms of /ᴗ\/ *(Damn with faint praise)* reluctantly because this variation occurs so often that he has to acknowledge it as a conventional form of metrical subordination.

But where the stress pattern is ᴗᴗ\/ he cannot accept the idea that it might sound very much like ᴗ/\/ *(On whose fresh lap)* or /ᴗ\/ *(Through the thick corn)*—that is, like milder versions of *(b)* and *(c),* where in both cases the beat in the first foot falls on an apparently weaker syllable. Yet these differences are often slight, and it would seem that a sure way out of the awkwardness he senses is to acknowledge that combinations like these can often, in effect, masquerade as *(b)* and *(c)* in traditional English verse.[17]

For free verse, Attridge, recognizing its fundamental difference from metrical verse, offers in *PR* what seems to me a useful but incomplete strategy of analysis. He is aware that the term covers many different varieties of verse and he is sensitive to the kinds of rhythmic movement that can be found in poets like Pound, Eliot, Williams, Rich, and Lawrence. But here, too, one may object that his insights—into the way phrases move us through a poem—tend to freeze into categories (movement *toward,* movement *away from,* a *static moment* [not a happy term], and *moment of arrival*), analytical terms (statement, extension, anticipation, arrival), and a graphic notation of capitalized abbreviations (ANT, ARR, STA, and EXT), to the point where he has students scanning for these phenomena as they scan lines for their metrical form. This procedure is interesting; some kind of phrasal or syntactic analysis helps us see why some phrases have special force. But this doesn't seem essential or crucially helpful, as metrical scansion is crucially helpful to our hearing of rhythm. Without it, we might go astray; without this sort of phrasal scansion, we still have no problem reading the lines and sentences. Metrical scansion needs to be graphic; this does not.

Analysis along these lines, conducted with Attridge's usual intelligence and lucidity, can illuminate the way different poets tend to construct their sentences, speeches, and verse paragraphs. So, one might add, would traditional ways of diagramming sentences or otherwise inspecting the grammar of poets. When we classify phrases according to this four-type system, we lose the possibly greater clarity and interest we might get from knowing just what sorts of grammatical phrases we are talking about—participial, adjectival, vocative, nounal, predicate, or whatever. It might help more to know whether a writer's sentences are periodic or cumulative, hypotactic or paratactic, whether they break with the line-breaks or against them, whether the poet uses sentence fragments, parallel constructions, rhetorical balances and contrasts, or unbalanced or inverted structures, and so on. Attridge may respond that we are still free to notice these things, too, but it remains unclear why the four elements of phrasing he highlights here deserve the centrality he gives them. In any case, it seems a cumbersome procedure to inflict on students, and it implies that the material being subjected to analysis—the movement toward and away from some kind of central assertion, has something like the same kind of audible patterning that metrical verse lines have. But it does not; its patterning is visible, and it bears the same relation to audible English metrical poetry as Attridge, in *Well-Weighed Syllables,* once pointed to as existing between that poetry and the visually apprehended quantitative verse of certain sixteenth-century writers, for whom "quantity" was something not perceived in the sound of words but "found in the minds of the Elizabethans, trained in the application of a complex set of rules to the graphic embodiment of lines of verse" (160).

III

Compared to other great poets in English, such as Spenser, Marlowe, Shakespeare, Donne, Milton, Pope, Tennyson, Hopkins, Whitman, Hardy, and Yeats, critics have often thought of Wordsworth's verse as relatively pedestrian, undistinguished, and undistinctive. Saintsbury's judgment, quoted by Brennan O'Donnell as typical, has been shared by many readers: "In no great poet does prosody play so small a part" (6). But O'Donnell argues persuasively, in *The Passion of Meter,* that Wordsworth, though certainly a metrical "conservative," studied closely the metrical craft of his great predecessors, thought intently and with considerable originality about the part meter plays in significant verse, and used meter in imaginative ways to amplify and reinforce his narrative and lyrical themes. The passion of meter interplays with the passion of syntax to form a strong verse language, which for Wordsworth either moderates the life-passions that form the subject of poetry or, in more contemplative modes, provides that passion. O'Donnell's scrutiny of the poet's many statements about meter makes clear how important Wordsworth thought it in the composition of verse and what varied uses he found for it. Any reader will find much wise and patient discussion of the art of prosody in this subtle and thorough examination of Wordsworth's metrical theory and practice.

In Wordsworth's poetry, O'Donnell argues, meter usually figures as an instrument of balance and counterweight to other elements in the poem, or else as a means of reinforcing or signaling certain tensions that are at work. In the first instance, it may operate to give dignity, through an elaborate verse form, to a narrative told in colloquial diction; "The Sailor's Mother," for example, "confronts the reader from the outset with a markedly incongruous relationship between humble subject and elaborate stanza form" (53). Similarly, in "The Thorn," Wordsworth's "principle of similitude in dissimilitude" develops a contrast "between slow speech and rapid meter" (66). O'Donnell also shows well the gradual process by which Wordsworth sloughed off the antithetical style of Pope's heroic couplets and learned to write couplets in a style of his own, considered "harsh" by early reviewers: lines that "tend to focus attention on the phrase, rather than the line, as the chief structural unit" (108). O'Donnell makes a case for the great metrical variety of Wordsworth's poems in *Lyrical Ballads* (115–178) and claims that in many poems Wordsworth's choice of meter and particular use of it are purposeful, subtle, and effective: as O'Donnell puts it in his rather scholastic language, "even the most ostensibly simple and predictable of Wordsworth's stanzas will reward careful attention to subtle tensions between the metrical frame and diverse realizations in actual sonic and rhythmic impulses" (154). In another long chapter, O'Donnell analyzes Wordsworth's increasingly skillful use of a Miltonic blank verse, especially in such different modes as "Tintern Abbey" and "Michael," on both of which his commentary is excellent.

This analysis is managed with considerable grace and eloquence, though, given Wordsworth's vast poetic production, O'Donnell does not attempt to examine all of it, or even a large sample. He deals mainly with some early poems, especially "An Evening Walk" and "Descriptive Sketches," with the stanzaic verse of *Lyrical Ballads,* and with the same volume's blank verse. That means that not much, if anything, is said about Wordsworth's later stanzaic poems, his odes, his hundreds of sonnets, or the vast production of blank verse poems that include *The Prelude* and *The Excursion.* Instead, he focuses on the early poems in which Wordsworth was establishing the principles that guided his metrical art for the rest of his career. This is a sensible decision, though one cannot help feeling disappointed at so little reference to most of the major poems on which his reputation rests.

O'Donnell likewise recognizes the importance of the poetry that most influenced Wordsworth: Pope for his early verse, then Cowper and other eighteenth-century poets, and Milton for the blank verse of his middle and later career. He notes, too, Wordsworth's interest in taking his place among the pantheon of English poets, including the Elizabethans and especially Shakespeare, but he says little about any specific debts he owes them. He frequently observes Wordsworth's use, for example, of line-ending polysyllables (like *piety* or *humanity*) that give the last beat of a pentameter line a rather weak stress, and he notes the incidence of this feature in Milton, but he never connects it to earlier poets like Marlowe and Shakespeare, in whose work it is habitual. Nor does he give credit to Shakespeare's late dramatic verse for having suggested to Wordsworth the advantages of closing one verse paragraph (or, in Shakespeare, one speech) in midline and beginning the next one there, a detail of verse architecture that Wordsworth was the first nondramatic poet after Shakespeare to use as an occasional resource in his major blank verse poetry.

O'Donnell's sympathy with Wordsworth's creative prosody is no doubt responsible for the clarity and understanding with which he sets forth its principles. But it also constitutes one major difficulty I found in the book— namely, that O'Donnell is insufficiently critical of Wordsworth's practice. He shows quite brilliantly how the poems reflect and embody—but also how they seem to justify—Wordsworth's theory of meter. His precise analysis is often concerned with what he admits are "minute effects" (224, 152, 206), and he occasionally writes a suggestive phrase like "insofar as it is effective" (89), or "this relatively wooden use of metrical contrast" (90), but usually he is content to explain Wordsworth's rationale for choosing a particular meter or for using some "disruptive" metrical variation, and the rationale is often so intelligent, and so intelligently explained, that we are invited to infer that the tactic is successful. But readers of Wordsworth's day and ever since have found that the combination of diction and prosody in "The Idiot Boy," for example, *does not work,* that is, does not produce that "pleasurable excitement" that Wordsworth was hoping for, and O'Donnell's expert presentation of Wordsworth's rationale for it (163–69) is no more convincing today than Wordsworth's was in 1800. The best one can say for a lot of O'Donnell's defenses of mediocre poems is that they are very eloquent, but they persuade us that Wordsworth did think this way about the poems, not that the poems have any notable merit. Useful as this book is and helpful as its author's studies are, they might have been even more valuable if O'Donnell had clarified for us where Wordsworth's theory works and where it does not, if with some critical acuteness along with his penetrating theoretical research he had shown us why, where, and to what extent the poems Wordsworth constructed so carefully fell short of his ambitious plans for them, and why others succeeded. O'Donnell does not really account for the great difference in merit between, for example, "The Idiot Boy" or "The Mad Mother" and, say, the Lucy poems.

As the book continues, in fact, the author is drawn more and more into graceful overstatements about the success of Wordsworth's metrical procedures. The last two lines of "A slumber did my spirit seal" can

> bring into sympathy the physical impulses of a reader in such a way that he may feel in the approximation and departure from the basic 4×4 rhythm both the power of a force extrinsic to individual expression and the human impulse to resist or escape such power. (154)

Ultimately, meter is conceded a power to register awarenesses that are fully cognitive, as when we are told that "Hart-Leap Well" incorporates the very impulses that it seeks eventually to rectify, forcing *a recognition at the level of minute and pleasurable rhythmic and sonic patterns* that human pleasure and pride is indeed . . . inextricably intertwined with "sorrow of the meanest thing" (and not only the meanest) "that feels." (163; my emphasis)

By the last page the grandiose claims take the following form, which can hardly be more than a pious hope, if we understand it to include all of Wordsworth's verse, the mediocre along with the truly impressive:

> In Wordsworth's metrical art, each sound, syllable, word, verse, stanza, or verse paragraph is represented as simultaneously an expression of spontaneous impulse and a fulfillment of a single controlling system of organization. (248)

And all his poems "may be understood as magnificently and diversely articulated expressions of a single system of 'tones and numbers'" (248). They are all, that is, "Wordsworth," as Allen Ginsberg used to think of all his lines as "Ginsberg." But this is undiscriminating praise, and many readers will long for a manner of criticism that will distinguish the really good poems from the clinkers.

But if O'Donnell's book, fine as it is in its clarification of Wordsworth's metrical principles and aims, suffers from this excessive deference to Wordsworth, it suffers equally from its excessive deference to his principal metrical mentor, Derek Attridge. He adopts Attridge's system absolutely, with all its elaborate terminology, from "initial inversion condition" (16) to "stress-final pairing with linkage" (233), and with those quaint schoolmasterish devices of "promotion" and "demotion" to explain the way Wordsworth places minor or major syllables in major or minor metrical positions. This wholehearted acceptance commits him to Attridge's insistence, modified in the theory of both writers but not in their practice by the flexible notion of "optionality" (33), that two minor syllables followed by two apparently more important ones must be treated as an occasion for lurching through the first two in order to get to the second pair, as in the numerous examples given earlier. Wordsworth's later feeling of unease at his own line

> 60. Impressed on the white road;—in the same line

is used (32–35) to substantiate the view that this poet must have spoken such lines as Attridge and O'Donnell evidently wish us to do, jumping over the minor syllables to stamp on the major ones.

>   Impressed on the white road;—in the same line
>   o   B   ŏ   B   B   ŏ   B   B

But whether Wordsworth did so remains in doubt. In a letter to John Thelwall, Wordsworth called this "the most dislocated line I know of in my writing" (quoted on 32), but we do not really know whether he thought it dislocated because he heard in it the lurching movement that Attridge and O'Donnell hear, or because in reciting it—in "chaunting" it, according to Hazlitt—he adhered to the metrical pattern and gave to each "the" a heavier stress than he would have done in saying such words in conversation, so that the meter "dislocated" the normal conversational rhythm. O'Donnell does not even consider this second possibility; it is evidently not an option. At the same time, following Attridge, he argues for a principle of "optionality" that allows us to be aware of alternative readings of many lines. In "My heart leaps up," for example, he suggests that we may read the verbal phrase iambically, stressing "up," or (in effect) spondaically, giving a stronger emphasis to "leaps" as well as to "up." This is perfectly sensible, but O'Donnell, in this case as in many others, exaggerates the difficulty of the line, claiming that "leaps" "dislocates the verse" because it is "in an offbeat position" (36). But such variations happen all the time in traditional iambic poetry, and their effect is not to dislocate a line but to vary the iambic pattern a little.

Despite the apparent generosity of their principle of optionality, Attridge and O'Donnell never concede that it is acceptable in a reading of iambic verse to give to a very minor word in stressed position enough weight to allow it to retain our sense that it occupies a metrical beat when it is competing with a word that belongs to a more privileged grammatical category. English phonology, they claim, insists that when we come across such lines we perform the metrical lurch. O'Donnell's book is full of such lines, and his procedure is usually to decide on the lurching scansion and then to explain its significance. But if the scansion is wrong or dubious, the explanation of its significance is bound to be, too. If Wordsworth and many of his readers did not hear the lurch that is second nature to Attridge and O'Donnell, then the elaborate inferences these critics draw from their analysis of it will not be valid. The "disruption" that O'Donnell hears in such lines will not be as disruptive as he claims, and the options that he offers a reader can be extended much further or in different directions than he appears willing to grant. Here is how he scans three lines of "Yew-Trees" (213–14):

There is a Yew-tree, pride of Lorton Vale,
o   B o   B   o   B   o   B o   B

Which to this day stands single, in the midst
 ŏ   Bô B   ŏ   B   o B̄   o   B

Of its own darkness, as it stood of yore
 ŏ   B   ôB   o   Bo   B   o   B

O'Donnell does not offer as an optional reading an "inversion" in the stress pattern of "There is," though my own voice finds that sound at least as natural as stressing "is." For the second line, he judges that its opening "stress-final formation" is especially "disruptive because of the relative weakness of 'this'" (214), but the simplest way of solving this problem either does not occur to him or is forbidden by some rule:

Which to this day stands single, in the midst
  B   ŏ   B   ó   B o B̄   o   B

Instead, he offers this option, then dismisses it for complex reasons:

Which to this day stands single, in the midst
  o   B̄ ó B   ŏ   B   o B̄   o   B

He prefers, then, to believe that Wordsworth started two successive lines with almost identical lurching rhythms and that he did so in the interest of preserving "rhythmic complexity." In this case, as in most others involving the lurch pattern, O'Donnell somehow manages to claim some kind of subtlety for what he argues are Wordsworth's metrical procedures and to ignore the banality or clumsiness of the rhythm he is trying to persuade us is Wordsworth's. All too often he makes large claims for metrically unexceptional verse, and Attridge's terminology can sometimes sound ludicrously clinical, as when "Stoops her sick head, and shuts her weary eyes" is said to illustrate a particular form of the "initial inversion condition" (94).

Occasionally, O'Donnell is willing, like Attridge, to believe that Wordsworth may have preferred to scan some lines as hexameters rather than subordinate one stressed syllable to another (94, 214). He persuades himself, too, that "[f]ive-beat" and "pentameter" "may be used . . . interchangeably" (16); so may "iambic" and "rising rhythm." These are seemingly harmless points, but what they imply is that lines may be classified as iambic by their deep structure, not by their surface rhythm. It means that no matter how many double or implied offbeats, say, they include (e.g., x / x x / x x / x x / x x / or x / / / / x /), they remain perfectly iambic, that Robert

Lowell's five-beat sonnets in *History* and *Notebook* are metrically of a piece with Sidney's and Shakespeare's.

Elsewhere, alert to the significance of midline punctuation, O'Donnell not so alertly identifies such punctuation as requiring pauses. This is a reasonable procedure when one wants to establish statistical norms for poets over great stretches of their poetry, as critics like Ants Oras and Marina Tarlinskaya do;[18] in such cases readers will understand that "pauses" does not necessarily mean pauses but may mean only syntactical breaks. But when one discusses individual lines, one ought to be on one's guard against assuming that every piece of punctuation requires a pause in delivery. In "Tintern Abbey," for example, it is hard to imagine a delivery of these lines,

> If this
> Be but a vain belief, yet, oh! how oft,

that would pause after "belief," after "yet," and after "oh!" and still keep any sense of pentameter rhythm. But O'Donnell does not shrink from aestheticizing the "triple pause" as helping "to create the impression of a mind engaged in a process of discovering—and making—the meanings it articulates" (192) As if one could not claim something similar not by counting the punctuation marks but by gauging the syntactical self-interruption and the surprising exclamatory way of resolving a sentence begun with an if-clause.[19]

In short, many of O'Donnell's readings of particular lines are questionable, and the claims that he makes for the significance of the minute variations that he discerns are thrown into doubt if he is not describing these minute variations accurately. His reliance on Attridge's system is almost a test case for that system, and, in the judgment of this reader at least, the system does not come out very well. Both O'Donnell and Attridge have many slighting things to say about traditional metrics and metrists; Saintsbury especially comes in for O'Donnell's scorn, and he often writes as if all later metrists who still think there is some validity in the traditional metrical analysis had never advanced an insight that might take us beyond Saintsbury's imprecise formulations and sweeping judgments. But it is still possible to read some lines as including pyrrhic-spondee combinations without behaving "as if each two-syllable unit were detachable and modifications within a 'foot' did not affect the structure of other parts of the line" (34). Detachable, indeed! Who ever believed that? Whatever their faults, many traditional metrists have written of meter's subtle but elusive effects with considerable insight, in the hope—it is O'Donnell's, too—of learning more about how poems and poets work.

IV

Alan Holder would disagree. His book *Rethinking Meter* brings charge after charge against traditional prosodists who hear in lines of most English verse before 1900 a distinct metrical structure. Making a show of reasonable inquiry, which cannot really survive the wisecracking and sarcasm that distinguish his polemical style, Holder assembles their more extreme statements, reports their disagreements with one another, and notes their inability to settle even elementary issues in the study of poetic meter. That the field is filled with casualties is beyond debate, and Holder has a good time picking at the wounds. He has read a great deal of prosodic criticism, and he writes clearly, though with a poisonous pen. His first three chapters survey the follies of traditional metrists as they go about their absurd and irrelevant enterprise. The fourth exposes their misguided attempts to analyze free verse as if it were still metrical. The last three show us Holder's idea of the kind of "phrasalist" and intonational analysis he thinks might be far more useful for our study of the sound of poems than metrical analysis can be—useful for free verse but also for traditional metrical poetry.

Holder is unsparing in his contempt for traditional metrical study and the academic critics who practice it. He is hard on their inconsistencies, their arrogance, their overreading, and often with good reason; but much of his irritation with them is for hearing more than Holder hears. Where they hear something metrical going on in poems, Holder claims to hear nothing but phrasing: words, words, words. The view he evidently takes is that those older poets who produced hundreds of thousands of ten-syllable lines heard them only as sequences of phrases; they never heard a meter at all. Or else he thinks that even if they did, the meter is not of much sonic importance compared with the rhythm of phrases. All those prosodists who have thought the great strength of much English poetry was its way of letting the phrasing somewhat alter the meter and letting the meter sometimes tilt the phrase are considered by Holder quaint enthusiasts or academic bullies, essentially wasting their time and the time of their students, when they might be focusing on phrasal arrangements to tell us something really useful about verse.

What is strange about this position is that it apparently never occurs to Holder that he might be mistaken, that all those fairly bright scholars and critics who say they have been hearing something metrical in poetry that he does not hear might really be pointing to something genuine. Almost alone among modern readers of older poetry, he hears none of its meter and he assumes, therefore, that it is not there—rather like a blind man telling us that *look*ing at a sculpture is of no interest; the only way to judge it is by touch.

Part of the problem is that Holder does not *want* to hear meter. Meter to him is a "tyranny" (134), a way of imposing uniformity on sentences and phrases, of reducing the interesting language of poetry to "a system" (65), to an "a priori model" (233), to an "arithmetic regularity" (116), to a "totalitarian 'scheme'" (65). He jeers at metrists' "hunger for a system" (64), at their "prosodic foot fetishism" (29, also 63), at the "Mystique of Meter" (22), at "that Napoleon of notions, the foot" (30): "the poem is treated, in effect, as a mechanism for grinding out clonelike lines" (48), as if it were the intention of metrists to take the fun and the life out of poetry. Doggedly skeptical about metrical pattern anywhere, he frequently refers to metrists' findings as "the alleged meter" (this or similar phrases on 38, 53, 57, 63, 85, 182, 199, etc.). In Holder's highly colored account, metrists are conducting a kind of war against lines of poetry, to "bring them to heel" (84), "to tamper with the stress values of a line's syllables" (84), or to make them "toe the mark" (85). Willfully dishonest and distortive (82), we persecute the poor line of verse, which "never had a chance of breaking out of the iambic mold" (88). Our aim, he charges, is to make feet all alike, to save the system from irregularities (47). Determined as we are to find feet even in the most unlikely phrases, we ignore performance and find what we are "disposed to find" (83). We bend speech "patterns into a presupposed shape" (266); we allow feet to "dismember words" (269 n. 35). Intent on "making the line safe for iambicity" (90), we "capture" lines "for the cause of iambicity through the intervention of . . . strategems," because "all is fair in love and prosody" (89).

On the other hand, our zeal for discovering patterns of metrical tension leads us to engage in "indiscriminate variation-fondling" (63) with the result that "iambic pentameter is awash in variations" (61). It is part of Holder's auditional disability, after all, that if he cannot hear metrical patterns he cannot hear metrical variations from the pattern. So he interprets our seeking both pattern and variation in verse lines as "yet another instance of a meter-minded prosodist wishing to have things both ways" (63). When we do venture to enjoy the "creative equilibrium" (94, a term of mine that he quotes) that a poet like Shakespeare in his late dramatic poetry sets up between the line and the phrase, Holder somehow takes this to mean that we see phrase and foot as *"inimical"* (93, his word, his italics), as "a simple, mutual enmity" (256, n. 31). This reading is understandable, because if he cannot hear beats he cannot hear the interplay between a verse line's metrical pattern and its phrasing. He thinks it peculiar that anyone should hear in the language of poetry a meter and a phrasing at once, as if musicians do not do something similar all the time, staying conscious of the beat and yet giving full attention to the melody coursing through the measures. But musical analogies make Holder extremely uncomfortable (53, 54, 96, 100–01), a natural enough response for a theorist who cannot hear a metrical beat.

For most traditional metrists, including Attridge, the disparity between the metrical pattern of a line and the speechlike way of saying it generates some degree of tension, but for Holder this is a fiction. "I would argue," he asserts pugnaciously," that in performing the poem, what we say is what we get, and *all* that we get" (52). He hears no tension from beats or meter; verse is like prose in its rhythms. This is a defensible position for a critic of much free verse, and the basis for many of Holder's judgments. His hostility to meter and metrists, though it may spring from his metrical deafness, owes something to his feeling that metrists and the very concept of meter are antagonistic to free verse, and to his wish to defend it from its prosodic enemies. He has a point, though he characteristically overstates it. He is right in noticing that many metrists try, often absurdly, to find the ghost of traditional meters in free verse poems, as if they could not bear to let free verse be free, and his chapter "The Haunting of Free Verse" is easily the best in his book. But he warms to the suggestion of one free-verse scholar that traditional verse, too, "ought to be read without the application of traditional scansion" (114), that is, without a sense of its meter.[20] And this overreaction to the follies of metrists in reading metrical pattern into free verse results in the equally flawed position that governs Holder's later chapters. If it is wrong to read free verse by the metrical standards of older verse, it is equally wrong to read older verse by the nonmetrical standards of free verse.[21]

Disbelieving in meter, Holder never uses the word "beat" except when he quotes metrists with whom he disagrees. One measure of his hostility to meter is that in summarizing Attridge's prosodic theory he misses its most striking feature, the analysis of virtually all English poetry except iambic pentameter as accentual, a view that leads Attridge to develop a notation based entirely on beats and offbeats. Holder mentions this notation but regards it as nothing more than "a terminological shift" (65), apparently not realizing the profound difference between a traditional scansion based on stressed and unstressed syllables (accentual-syllabic) and a scansion based

Hearing the Measures 189

on beats (accentual). Holder decides Attridge's system is just "essential traditionalism" (67). This misreporting is typical. Either through misunderstanding or deliberately, he rarely makes a good-faith effort to explain, without prejudice, the aim of a metrist's writing before he begins his work of demolition. Even when he occasionally comes close to acknowledging vaguely that there might be such a thing as meter at work in much poetry— after all, he says he wants to rethink it—it does not emerge as a rhythm that he hears. He wants only to redefine meter as phrasing, which of course is something else. It may be that, not hearing beats in verse of any kind, he cannot grasp what Attridge and other metrists are about and so cannot give a fair or judicious account of accentual or accentual-syllabic verse—indeed, cannot resist ridiculing anyone who professes to hear metrical patterns in poetry.

His only effort to deal with accentual verse comes when he accuses W. K. Wimsatt and Monroe Beardsley of wrecking the natural phrasing of Blake's line, "Ah, Sunflower weary of time."[22] It is revealing that Holder quotes only the first line of Blake's poem, so he does not give a reader a chance to hear how steadily Blake allows a fairly regular beat to be heard throughout the poem. Here is the first stanza:

> Ah Sun-flower! weary of time,
> Who countest the steps of the Sun,
> Seeking after that sweet golden clime
> Where the traveller's journey is done

Wimsatt and Beardsley point out what would seem elementary to most of us, that the beats in this highly accentual stanza can be heard on *"Sun-"*, *"wea-"*, and *"time"* (and later on *"count-"*, *"steps,"* and *"Sun,"* etc.). Holder accuses them of ignoring the secondary stress on *"-flow-"* as well as the expressive *"Ah,"* and of breaking into "word boundaries and syntactical groupings" (27) with their villainous foot divisions:

> Ah Sun | flower wea | ry of time,

Clearly, he does not grasp the elementary point that in accentual verse some otherwise stressable syllables do not occupy the beat. That does not mean the syllable disappears; it gets said pretty normally (in my saying), but you do not hear a beat on it. But Holder views what he calls, in discussing another poem, this "supression [sic] of normal stressing" (27) as taking us to "the heart of the morass that is meter country" (26–27).

The traditional notation that Wimsatt and Beardsley use is troublesome to many readers, and their tone at times is admittedly magisterial, but their markings constitute a graphic means of pointing to a pattern that is certainly audible to many readers. Even those who find it disturbing to suppress a portion of the possible speech accent in *"Ah," "-flow-," "Seek-,"* and *"gold-"* are likely to recognize the recurrent beat defined by the stresses on the other major words and their stressed syllables. Unless you don't *want* to hear it, you can't miss it. Holder misses it.

His missing it makes his intentions clear enough. It is not that he simply proposes we study additional dimensions of sound (those of phrasing and intonation) that metrists have traditionally ignored or undervalued. He wants us to "disestablish the standard notion of meter" (16) and to recognize what a tyrannical and wrongheaded enterprise metrical analysis has been from the beginning. "The concept of meter stands between us and our poetry" (16), he tells us, and all the evidence of this book, including its stumbling efforts to rethink or redefine meter, makes clear that he wants to scrap it. But his inability to hear any kind of recurring rhythm in poems, and his sense of outrage at the metrists who keep "imposing" it on innocent lines of verse, lead him apparently to take the unusual view that it is the metrists, not the poets, who have put the meter in poems. With a few exceptions here and there, the poets have not scanned their poems or placed foot dividers in their lines. They have simply presented phrases and lines to their readers, who should take them as they come and not invent metrical restraints to hem them in and make them "toe the mark" (85). But of course this is nonsense. Metrical scholars may disagree with one another, may propose unconvincing scansions and theories of scansion, may badly misread what poets have written (see the next section). But the evidence is clear that almost all older poets writing in English typically wrote lines that kept some sort of recurring beat, and a critic like Holder who blames the metrists for the poets' metrical patterns is trafficking in absurdities. (When he comes to offer his own pitch-scansions, however, he usually suggests that he is merely recognizing patterns in the line that the poet has put there.) Holder never quite says he does not think there is such a thing as meter, and he has one sentence that suggests he understands that it must exist ("There is, after all, a centuries-old tradition of distinguished metrical poetry" [127]), but his redefinition of Shakespeare's meter in Sonnet 116 (see below) is pretty conclusive evidence of his inability to hear anything like what most earlier listeners have heard.[23]

A metrical critic so scornful of others will surely see to it that his own work is free from errors and contradictions? Unfortunately, Holder's book not only frequently misrepresents other critics' views, but it is full of mistakes and riddled with misunderstandings. He thinks that a feminine ending constitutes a foot (27–28); on the other hand, he does not spot the feminine ending in the line "That looks on tempests and is never shaken," but thinks "shaken" scans as a trochee (180). He does not know that "spirit" was often pronounced as a monosyllable in the Renaissance (27–28). He misdefines Hopkins's term "outrides" as "extra syllables within a line" (80); he does not seem to know that Auden's poem "Streams" is syllabic (77). He does not understand that Attridge's demotions and promotions often do not, in Attridge's view, involve any change of stress, or that most of the adjustments that metrists make for metrical variations are slight. He cites Josephine Miles's interest in "phrasal poetry" in support of his own position (157–58), but he seems not to know that she is using the term in an entirely different sense.

As his almost obsessive comments on the subject make clear, he does not understand that graphic foot dividers are an analytical convenience and do not cut into the sound of phrases in some artificial way. Inconsistent as ever, in his own late-chapter effort to show how *he* would scan lines, he gives us this sort of thing (230). The poem is by Sylvia Plath; the levels are levels of pitch:

```
Then                         blue
              sub
         the       stanceless
```

For King Lear's line "Why should a dog, a horse, a rat have life," he proposes this arrangement of leaping pitches:

```
        dog,      horse,      rat
   a            a           a
```

One may pity the poor actor who, under Holder's direction, is not permitted to vary the pitch of the three words denoting animals, and is obliged to come back to the low pitch-level of "*a*" every time. Lear's line of *nevers* (214) is shown in the same obsessive two-tone:

```
    Ne      ne      ne      ne      ne
      ver     ver     ver     ver     ver!
```

Apparently, words " dismembered" (269 n. 35) this way please the same sensibility that is offended by foot divisions and frequently pleads for "respecting word integrity" (180). And these two-part inventions begin to look suspiciously like those "clonelike" lines and feet (48), those "countable clones" (116) he hated in other people's scansions.

Holder is not only prescriptive in such pitch-scansions; he is much more prescriptive than most metrical scansions are, which legitimize a range, even a class, of possible readings, whereas Holder's are so precise, so particular, that they seem to legitimize only one. Most scannings of most verse lines permit a reader to vary the pitch, the speed, the phrasing according to the reader's judgment, but Holder's precise delineation of pitch-levels seems, as he admits, to map a very personal way of speaking or hearing lines.

One cannot help noticing that Holder is guilty of many of the charges for which he indicts traditional metrists. As these pitch-scansions show, he uses a notation for free verse that breaks up the words of a line at least as much as traditional foot dividers do, indeed throws the words around the page. He is angry that metrists break up the line with foot dividers, but intonational patterning, he claims, gives us "a basis on which to break up a given utterance into parts . . . intonation units" (203). If prosodists are always "playing the old game of looking for foot-defined variations and trying to link them to an expressive effect" (99), Holder is doing the same with his fanciful pitch-scansions. He complains about Jonathan "Holden's animus against free verse" (121), but shows at least an equal animus against traditional metrical analysis. He indicts traditional prosodists again and again for "fuzziness" and sloppy thinking, but his own analysis is equally flawed. Noticing "a pattern of increasing concreteness in the sequence of nouns" in a line, he conveniently omits one of the four nouns in the sequence (89). He misquotes a line he is analyzing (224). He accuses Marjorie Perloff of using weak instances to condemn a whole field, but this is his own strategy throughout the book. He accuses Annie Finch of finding dubious patterns in Whitman's verse (117–19) but is equally fanciful in detecting in a Whitman line an effort "to dramatize the notion of a 'cluster' by clustering stresses" (119). His rhetoric is always loaded: "if ordinary pronunciation has to be deformed, so be it, say the system-mongers" (47); "Epstein and Hawkes have turned out to be metrical good old boys" (33); "her study keeps us stuck in the swamp of traditional scansion" (70). He is willfully distortive of the views of those he condemns, as when he pretends to think that Wimsatt and Beardley's strictures about syllables carrying greater or lesser degrees of stress in duple verse "mean the dissolution of the anapest" (25) in triple verse. Throughout his book he is just as assertive and absolute in his judgments of what is "sane" and sensible as any of the metrists he attacks.

He charges traditional scanners with a "passion for abstract pattern" (44); the work of one represents "the apogee of allegiance to abstraction" (45); but he has to admit that "the designated relative pitch levels" of his own "intonational schematizings" "represent something of an abstraction (but of a lesser degree of abstraction . . . than the schemes produced by foot scansion)" (229). But how so, one wonders? Holder does not explain. There is something in him of the child who thinks that his own transgressions are lovable. He despises metrists' tendency to prescribe readings, and then he prescribes his own: words set in lines must be spoken more slowly than "if they were set as prose" (140); and "I have to . . . insist that a pause be registered at the end of [every] line and that it be actual, however slight" (148). He decides that Lear's line of *never*s demands "four distinct pauses" (214). In fact, he boasts that his intonational "profiles" give us "a truer representation of Lear's words ['Thou'lt come no more'] than what traditional scansion would give us, namely, a pair of iambs" (216). But his raised profile,

	come no	
Thou'lt		more

besides being almost ludicrously unconvincing and unnuanced, with its mere two levels of pitch, deprives any rich-voiced actor of options that a more reticent traditional scansion leaves open. That is, despite all his reading of metrical theory, he does not understand that a scansion is not normally an analytical record of an individual reading but a quite generalized analysis of a class of readings within which a good actor or reader will find one that will be effective. It should *enable* performances, not script them.

Among the metrical critics whom Holder excoriates or mocks for their analytical absurdities are Saintsbury, Wimsatt and Beardsley, Shapiro and Beum, Turner and Pöppel, Halle and Keyser, Epstein and Hawkes, Attridge, Marina Tarlinskaya, John Thompson, Suzanne Woods, Dennis Taylor, Richard Cureton, Edward Weismiller, Paul Ramsey, Paul Kiparsky, Sandra Gilbert, Marjorie Perloff, Thomas Cable, Jonathan Holden, and myself. He has some good words to say about a few of these, but most of the time he does not try to give a fair and accurate account of what such critics are aiming to do. Instead, he usually prefers to discuss their most extravagant, wayward, or unwary pronouncements and to omit any explanation of the context in which they were made. So, in scoffing at a little article I once wrote on the meter of the poem, "Shall I die?"[24] which has been attributed to Shakespeare, he fails to cite any of the poem's lines that might have made my view of the poem's meter plausible; instead, he quotes that part of my article in which I deliberately cited some of the most bizarre lines. I did this to show that some lines of the poem were very hard to read as I was suggesting, and I was not applauding the poet for putting the reader in the position of having to wrench the lines' natural sound to keep them to the metrical pattern. I speculated that whoever wrote the poem may have been experimenting to see if he really could adhere to a cretic pattern for several stanzas, and if the result seemed odd in some places we are free to blame the poet. Holder gives his reader no sense of this context, and when he attacks other metrists I either know or suspect that he has sometimes taken their statements out of context and attributed to them views that they certainly do not hold in the form in which he presents them.

When Holder speaks of dead metrists, he does not usually moderate his scorn; living ones he tends to approach with more courtesy before he starts cutting them to pieces. He devotes many pages to the refutation of my own metrical studies, and I should acknowledge that he has some good things to say about my *Shakespeare's Metrical Art* ("a formidable work, a learned labor of love. . . . I do not think traditional prosody has anything better to offer us" [81]). Nevertheless, he deplores my "mind-set" (81) and calls me "a stresser pure and simple" (255 n. 27). His treatment of my work is distortive in almost every detail, full of willful misunderstanding and misreporting, and failing at every point to offer an accurate account of my claims and arguments. He attributes views, positions, and feelings to me that I do not hold (e.g., "The apparent trochee of the third food [*sic*] . . . appears to disturb Wright" [91]) and terms that I do not use (demote, promote [91], "demonstrated" [89]; and his wisecracking phrases ("meter-maintenance scanning" [91], "The Principle of Disinterested Meddling" [90], "he who has declared the limits of phrasalism" [172]) establish the tone of jeering and sneering that is almost constant in his discussions of traditional metrists.

In the course of disputing my readings of Shakespeare's dramatic verse lines in *Shakespeare's Metrical Art,* Holder offers this scansion of Sonnet 116, "with only stressed syllables marked (intralinear phrasal divisions have been indicated by the use of extra spaces)" (176):

Let me nót to the márriage of trúe mínds	1
Admít impédiments. Lóve is nót lóve	2
Which álters when ít alterátion fínds,	3
Or bénds with the remóver to remóve.	4
Óh nó! it is an éver fíxed márk	5

> That lóoks on témpests   and is néver sháken,   6
> It is the stár to évery wánd'ring bárk   7
> Whose wórth's unknówn,   although his héight be táken   8
> Lóve's nót Tíme's fóol,   though rósy líps and chéeks   9
> Withín his bénding síckle's cómpass cóme.   10
> Lóve álters nót   with his bríef hóurs and wéeks,   11
> But béars it oút   éven to the édge of dóom.   12
> If thís be érror,   and upón me próved,   13
> I néver wrít,   nor nó mán éver lóved.   14
> (176–77; line numbers added)

Holder argues at some length that the "forced pause" (178) he hears after "it" in line 3 results from the

> semantic hitch at the point where "it" meets up with "alteration," requiring a pause at an awkward place, after a pronoun functioning as a subject, which normally one would be inclined to join with its adjacent verb as soon as possible. (Here, it seems to me, is a real source of "tension," that is, between the way we would normally handle a pronoun-as-subject and the way we need to handle it here.) (178)

Later, among other bizarre suggestions for the "handling" of pitch in this sonnet (he almost always gives disyllabic words different pitches for each syllable [222–24],[25] he even proposes a "raised pitch" for "it" in line 3 (222). As my students have testified for decades, and as every recording I know of an actor reading the sonnet confirms (the ones I have heard lately are by Simon Callow and John Gielgud), line 3 offers no difficulty to any normal reader. It moves easily and smoothly through the series of somewhat greater and lesser stressed syllables. I have never known anyone to have trouble with the line until Holder appeared on the metrical scene and invented grotesque reasons for not taking the line simply as it comes. Instead, he "handles" the line in a fashion that I think most people will regard as preposterous, involving as it does an extremely unspeechlike stress on "it" and a rationale that is at least as wayward as any metrical misreading his book attributes to traditional prosodists. Indeed, Holder's way of scanning this line may serve as a measure of how seriously his rethinking of meter is to be taken.

I could be wrong, but I suspect that hardly anyone who has heard the alternating syllabic pattern familiar in English verse from hundreds of thousands (or millions) of poetic lines is likely to think Holder's an adequate substitute for some traditional reading of such lines. And it should be clear that he is proposing it as a substitute *scansion,* not as an arrangement of the poem's *phrasing* that is intended to supplement a metrical scansion. The stresses in his version combine with the unstressed syllables to form what he calls a looser version of a meter he prefers (no wonder!) to call decasyllabic: 9–11 syllables; 4–5 stresses in a line; normally beginning with an unstressed syllable and "using at least one such syllable to separate stressed syllables" (175). But of course this is no meter at all. It might imaginably be a meter if his scansion came close to adhering to his definition, but for Sonnet 116 he finds four lines (4, 9, 11, 14) that do not even qualify as having 4–5 stresses (one has 7!); and even if the notion of using "at least one [unstressed] syllable to separate stressed syllables" could really help the ear to identify a meter, he violates that prescription thirteen times by my count in fourteen lines. Some meter! It is not a meter because it has no audibly recurring pattern of beats, but such a pattern is what Holder's ear is apparently unable or unwilling to hear. His scansion of Sonnet 116 is his only effort in 240 pages to scan any English verse of the kind long recognized as iambic. What is more revealing, his only attempt to deal with accentual verse, that other great mode of English poetry, comes in the course of his criticism of Wimsatt and Beardsley's reading of Blake's "Ah Sunflower! weary of time," and even then, as I have said, he tries to "handle" only the first line of it. To repeat, because it may seem unbelievable: In a book called *Rethinking Meter,* this author scans *only one line of accentual English verse and fourteen lines of iambic pentameter!*

It is worth noting that, whereas most metrists are not troubled at finding eleven syllables in line 6 of Sonnet 116 because of the feminine ending, Holder rather congratulates himself on being able to reduce that number to ten. He argues that the word *never* "undergoes a standard contraction" (180) here (but apparently not in line 14). In fact, *never* appears sixteen times in the *Sonnets* and does not ever need to be reduced to a single syllable to make a line metrical. On the four occasions when the word is pronounced as a monosyllable, it is spelled *nere* by Shakespeare or whoever prepared the text for printing. In Shakespeare's plays the word is much more often given its two-syllable pronunciation than it is contracted—1,139 instances to 226, according to the *Harvard Concordance.* Holder here simply doesn't know what he's talking about. I often get the feeling that he has read much more traditional metrical criticism than traditional poetry, a charge that our next author will certainly not need to face.

V

If Holder's New Age scansions are embarrassingly bad, so is the sketchy book on meter cast forth by the prolific scholar, translator, and poet Burton

Raffel. His subtitle, *The Autobiography of English Prosody,* implies that the verse lines Raffel quotes, scans, and sometimes annotates will do the job of explaining how poets writing in English have used meter. Unfortunately, they cannot do this on their own, and Raffel's meager commentary (only about 80 pages out of 185) is superficial, cranky, and unreliable. He claims to be merely reporting "the facts" (xii, 111, 119, 123, and elsewhere), but his comments constantly take the form of praise and blame. The book is a slapdash production full of scansion errors, misunderstandings, eccentric judgments, plain blunders, and strangely chosen exhibits. Raffel ignores English dramatic verse altogether, chooses remarkably uncharacteristic poems to represent Donne and Auden (among others), declines to comment on Poe, gives us eight lines on Wordsworth and two on Yeats. He cannot recognize that the Dylan Thomas poem he scans is syllabic, the Masefield one dipodic. When he runs against a line he cannot scan, his typical response is to suggest that the poet has been incompetent, instead of suspecting that his own ear may be faulty. Unable to find likely readings of poems by Nashe and Jonson, he accuses them of "clumsiness" (58, 60). The Jonson line is especially revealing. Raffel scans it (using capitalized syllables to show stress, a method likely to encourage sing-song readings and mute the subtle effects of pyrrhics and spondees): FOR / whose SAKE, / hence-FORTH, / all his VOWES / be SUCH, instead of just letting the meter suggest a quite smooth reading: For WHOSE / sake, HENCE- / forth, ALL / his VOWES / be SUCH (59). "The awkwardly trisyllabic fourth foot" is used to establish "Jonson's frequent prosodic clumsiness" (60), and both can now be taken as "facts."

This kind of foolishness—misperceived lines leading to blanket judgments of poets' or even centuries' whole poetic production—is typical of the book and might lead even a patient reader to adopt the Holderian strategy of condemning metrical analysis wholesale for its "Disinterested Meddling." The heroic protagonist of this autobiography is what Raffel calls the "Chaucerian Compromise," that is, accentual-syllabic verse as practiced by the best poets from Chaucer through Pope. He praises Dryden and especially Pope for their "deft" (75) and "amazingly varied" (80) placement of caesuras, but he cannot even report accurately where they place them. The passage of Pope he quotes has a break in phrasing after the fifth syllable in five successive lines (amazingly varied?), but Raffel's list misreports three of them. What matter? Soon after Pope the prosodic roof falls in: the introduction of trisyllabic feet by nineteenth-century poets is treated by Raffel as a major metrical crime. He doesn't ask, as O'Donnell does, what the poets might have been trying to accomplish with their innovations; instead, he judges them to be "casual, even indifferent (i.e., uncaring)" (103), or lazy. Wordsworth gets off lightly ("consistently conservative" [96]) because Raffel has nothing to say about him; he judges Coleridge's prosody to be "remarkably like Wordsworth's . . . with an admixture of ballad- and folk-style poems in which bi- and trisyllabic feet are blended pretty much indiscriminately, with the folkish trisyllabic predominating" (97). But he is at his most peevish in writing about Shelley. Irritated at one line, he writes: "Scansion is an abstract, almost a meaningless game, when one employs it as Shelley does" (106). Somehow he seems unaware that it is Raffel who is employing scansion, not Shelley. He is similarly dismissive about the metrical practices of Keats, Tennyson, Browning, Hopkins, and every Edwardian he deigns to quote. Judging them all by his one rigid formula (how well they adhere to the principles of the Chaucerian Compromise), he hasn't a clue to what Browning was up to in "Soliloquy of the Spanish Cloister," he misunderstands Hopkins's aims and procedures, and even when he acknowledges that Whitman's verse "*should not* be scanned" (132, his emphasis), he goes on scanning it and all the other free verse he quotes. He cannot keep the beat in Blake's "The Shepherd" for two whole stanzas (89), and Holder may be pleased to know that Raffel cannot hear the beat in "Ah! Sun-Flower" and considers the poem "metrically . . . jumbled" (90)—evidence either of metrists' incorrigible disposition to disagree (Holder's point) or of Raffel's tin ear (my point). Unlike Holder, Raffel has apparently not read Wimsatt and Beardsley on this poem; their article does not appear in his "Works Cited and Recommended," which also omits standard works by John Thompson, Tarlinskaya, Attridge, Cable, Suhamy, myself, and others, or any of John Hollander's work except his brief and charming *Rhyme's Reason*. This is an author who thinks that his sensitive ear can make up for his lack of knowledge—a woefully misguided view.[26]

VI

One crucial issue in all these books is performance, a term that is understood differently by different schools of readers. Actors, poets, and most readers of verse, including Holder, are principally concerned with how to speak or hear the lines, with their performance on specific occasions. Even if they look for guidance in the form of general principles, they suppose that such principles will help them speak or hear lines with understanding of their rhythmic design.

Linguists, in contrast, have usually been concerned to study, at a higher level of abstraction, how structures of language interact with metrical, intonational, or other formal structures of poetry, to observe, for example, without commenting on a poem's aesthetic success or failure, the extent of the congruence between stress positions and the stressed syllables of major-category words. It is irrelevant to them how emphatically or lightly a line's stressed syllables are stressed, or whether minor syllables in stressed positions are given additional stress or major syllables in weak positions are "demoted" in sound as well as in status. How a line is sounded is often not of interest to them at all. They are especially wary of having their analyses thrown off by particular performances of lines. In theory, at least, and rightly, their studies maintain a comfortable distance between the abstract structure of a metrical line and actual performances of it.

In practice, however, they have to attend to performance in at least two senses. First, they must take into account the speech habits of native speakers of the language, modified perhaps by information they may have about the pronunciation of early performers (poets, actors, or others). They have to notice which syllables of polysyllabic words normally take the main stress, which syllables in short phrases of different sorts are most likely to attract stress, and so on. They are also inclined to generalize about the probability of major-category words being stressed more than minor-category words, and they eventually have to notice exceptions and alterations of such generalized features of the language under special conditions of phrasing. As they refine their account of the way a language is spoken, they have to be guided by speakers' performance in this sense, by the way native speakers normally speak and modify their speech according to the needs of particular situations.

But if they recognize and feel comfortable with this peculiarity of language—that it will change its rules or practices under the pressure of different *speaking* situations—linguists often feel distinctly uncomfortable with the notion that in *verse* situations another kind of pressure may be brought to bear on the stress patterns of English, the pressure that the meter may exert—in Wordsworth's phrase, "the passion of metre." But this pressure or passion is felt differently by different performers, poets, and metrists (to tilt or not to tilt?), and it is understandable that linguists are reluctant to make pronouncements about a matter that varies so much from one reader or performer to another. Understandable, too, that they should want to stipulate, therefore, that particular performances, no matter how brilliant (or perhaps especially if they are brilliant) should not be counted as relevant.

On one side, then, we have linguists, skeptical about performance, but having to acknowledge that the phrases and sentences we find in lines of verse usually are derived from a spoken language.

On the other side, at its extreme position, Holder, skeptical about meter, and refusing to grant that lines have beats, concerned with performance, but either a poor transcriber of its details or a poor performer himself.

Or are they both on the same side? Both not knowing how to handle the pressures (the passion?) of meter.

Attridge seems in some way caught in the middle, wanting the system and order that linguistic analysis might provide, but also concerned with effective reading. It is understandable, then, that, wanting to accept the insights of linguists about the relative importance of major words, he should devise a system designed to show the metrical poetry of English as built on the placement of stress on major syllables; but it also makes sense that, as a presumably effective reader of verse himself (everything in his books suggests that he must be a very good one), he should want some justification for adjusting his system to the little changes that seem called for if one is to read lines convincingly as being at once English and verse. For him, therefore, the crucial problem is "metrical subordination," and it is not surprising that he feels uncomfortable with it. There is the problem in a nutshell: whether and to what extent the meter can exert such pressure on our normal English habits of speech as to tilt a little the prose or speech pattern, just enough to make the verse pattern pleasurably audible. But as Holder refuses to hear beats, Attridge refuses to let the voice tilt, though he grants that the English iambic ear, so to speak, may sometimes *perceive* a tilt (*REP,* 164–68).

My own view is that much of the difficulty here could be resolved if linguists and actors, scholars and ordinary readers, would understand that the differences that matter for the performance of lines of iambic pentameter verse are usually very slight. One does not go lumbering (or lurching) through lines of verse, making huge variations between what count as stressed and unstressed syllables. Small increases or decreases of emphasis do not much change the basic pattern of alternating degrees of strength in a succession of English syllables. English is an accentual language, and there are some speakers (the late sports announcer Howard Cosell was a notable example) who habitually pounce on the major stressed syllables in word-groups. But as Attridge reluctantly admits, the difference between "You that poor Petrarch's" and "You that in Petrarch's" does not really amount to much. It should not be enough to make one change one's understanding of either phrase's metrical pattern in the line. Because good readers will often differ in the way they distribute stress, it makes sense to allow for such differences and to prescribe as little as possible, or at least not to think that one can resolve all the differences by a more and more precise accumulation of rules and conditions. As Aristotle said wisely a long time ago: "Our discussion will be adequate if it has as much precision as the subject matter admits of, for precision is not to be sought for alike in all discussions. . . . it is the mark of an educated man to look for precision in each class of things just so far as the nature of the subject admits."[27]

One of the problems of traditional metrics has been its inability to describe metrical patterns in language (and graphic notation) that would convey lucidly and interestingly the rhythmic patterns of English poetry. Readers irritated with the clumsiness of metrical description have justifiably complained that the formal study of meter often stands, as Holder tells us, between poems and their readers. Despite the continued overreading or misreading that Holder rightly disparages, I like to think that the situation is improving, that, at least in the hands of some sensitive readers, tactful modifications of the older formulas are making the system seem more flexible and are helping readers to hear with greater insight and pleasure our older poets' metrical designs. By the same token, linguists who analyze metrical structures in their own way, or literary scholars who ground their metrical theories in linguistic data and theory, need to be told when those theories seem to conflict with the evidence of ordinary phonological experience, with the testimony of poets, or with the practice of competent actors and professional readers of verse.

In line with this modest perspective, I recommend some words written in a useful and unpretentious book by Delbert Spain, *Shakespeare Sounded Soundly*.[28] This is essentially a "Handbook for Students, Actors, and Directors," and it contains very good advice, usually presented in plain English and a minimum of jargon. Spain has this to say as a general statement on the relation of dramatic poetry to ordinary speech:

> In the writing or the reading of poetry, there is always some imposition of the rhythmic form that is not quite inherent in the words. We make adjustments in the pulses and stresses when we read that may be so inconspicuous that we do not realize we are doing it. There are cases where we may need to notice such adjustments and make them arbitrarily. If we get heavy handed with them, we create an effect of sing-song that we do not want. Our goal is a happy compromise, enough delicate touch of stress applied in the line to make

it reveal its proper poetic rhythm without impairing the good sense and spirit of the words. (20)

Spain keeps steadily in mind the problems that face actors in the theater, especially their suspicion of declamatory verse and their all-too-frequent habit of trying to speak dramatic poetry as if it were prose. His book is designed to give them the knowledge they need—about Elizabethan pronunciation, about iambic pentameter and Shakespeare's patterned departures from it—to do justice to the poetry he describes as *"language on parade"* (1). In trying to help actors to solve the practical problems of verse-speaking, he summarizes only as much metrical theory as they will need, for he knows that if the actors do not give life to the verse, it will not be alive for the audience. The actors must sound it "soundly," must send it forth invisibly for everyone in that circumscribed globe to hear. In the theater there are no feet, no lines, no scansion marks or marks of punctuation. But we hear the words arriving in our ears; we hear a succession of syllables, some softer, some louder or sharper; we hear perhaps a pattern as they scurry or tumble by us; and if the language is verse and the actors speak it, we hear the poetry.

Pulse and Breath
An Exchange with X. J. Kennedy

Free verse is measured by the breath, traditional verse by the pulse. Pulse and breath are the two strong rhythms of human biology. At first they seem alike—both alternating, both incessant, both coterminous with life itself. But the differences between them are important.

Pulse may quicken or delay, but the beat is certain. The alterations of stress-slack, stress-slack, stress-slack form a structure within which everything is either one or the other. The rhythm may vary so that the slack splits into two halves; or, in ironic opposition to the arrangement of pulse, the language of poetry may run slack-stress, slack-stress, slack-stress, even as the single words counter the counterpulse: slack, stress-slack, stress-slack, stress *(O ever-changing beat!)*. But the burden of every syllable is to be found in its relation to an adjacent one. Constant repetition reminds us of time, of mortality, of the inescapable structures, the institutions, temporal and physical, supporting and oppressive, that bound our lives on every side. Nothing eludes the tension of the iambic pentameter line; every syllable is touched by its pressure. The system is closed and implacable, its patterns inevitable and implicit.

Breath is different, far more irregular, its rhythm subject to far greater deformations than pulse. It can be held, stretched, hurried, exploded. It issues in a stream, the stream on which language rides. But though it moves in and out, language rides only the outward motion, only downstream. Inhaling is almost silent: no speech, no slack or minor stress, only at most a pause, a moment of waiting before the next breathed phrase. The emphasis in free verse is therefore always on the pouring forth, the issuance of speech-lines. Not repetition (though there may be highly developed patterns of repetition in the sentence structure, imagery, or formal divisions of free verse) but assertion, creation, is the nature of free verse. The poet *speaks*—says, delivers, lets go lines of verse.

Both forms have sexual undertones. Traditional meter owes something of its power to the alternating pulse of sexual excitement, perhaps never in a metrical poem altogether released. Free verse implicitly celebrates the release—usually easy and free. Words coming out, rushing to conception, sometimes struggling for birth—this is what free verse is and celebrates. Its spirit is therefore that of constant discovery—not, as in traditional verse, of returning to familiar ground where old fixtures are seen in new light, but of new experiences now first known. The next pulse will surely be like the last; but the next breath may show us new scenes.

Still, breath wastes. It uses up, discards. Pulse expends nothing—nothing but time. So verse based on it is always about mortality. Breath consumes. Yet as it consumes, it produces. What it brings forth so easily, plants can use, must have. Pulse powers the life of man, but breath joins man to other life. So while regular verse seems monumental, of the museum, free verse seems just given, a conferring of life on others—not "responsibly" but following its own impulsive laws. Traditional verse plans and maneuvers; free verse winds and flows.

The patterns of meter are subtle and devious, but free verse is likely to seem sincere, unhurried, truer to the moment of speech and life. Language moves faster than pulse, and drives it on. But breath and language work in concert. They grow up together, their association is intimate and synchronous, they help each other. Community and harmony are stronger in them than tension, so perhaps free verse, which makes the most of this harmony, is especially expressive of peace and love. Traditional verse, after all, is a verse of conflict and tension—naturally so, for its elements, pulse and speech, are essentially hostile systems: pulse is regular, constant, metrical; speech variable, flexible, elusive. The conflict, the counterpoint, between them creates a poetry of immense power.

But perhaps we've had enough of immense power.

Formal Verse and Fascist Deviousness, by X. J. Kennedy

Despite the recent spate of new formal poetry and a critical patter of applause for it, surely free verse—or naked poetry, as Stephen Berg and Robert Mezey have called it—has thrived far more successfully than metrical verse in the past thirty-odd years. True, an occasional sonnet or rimed stanzaic poem turns up these days in our quarterlies, looking a bit uncomfortable and self-conscious, like an overdressed man who has wandered into a naturist colony. Yet a glance at any current little magazine that prints verse (except for bastions of tradition such as *The Formalist, Plains Poetry Review, Drastic Measures,* or *The Epigrammatist*) will show that free verse, by and large, still holds sway in America.

Hence it surprises me to find people still championing free verse as though it were an endangered species. Professor G. T. Wright in his "Pulse and Breath" (*The North Stone Review* 9 [1990]) seems one staunch champion, a thinker who brings to his subject impeccable credentials. I hate to differ with the author of *Shakespeare's Metrical Art,* himself a poet who has demonstrated high competence in both open and closed forms. Still, even the best of us are likely to settle comfortably into worn ideas as into an old pair of shoes, and it seems that in his essay Professor Wright kicks up two well-worn clodhoppers.

His main idea is familiar: free or open verse is like the breath—variable, issuing in a stream—while metrical verse is like the pulse, domineering and inexorable. Where have we heard this notion before? Certainly it recalls Charles Olson's 1950 manifesto "Projective Verse" with its tribute to the typewriter as a finely tuned instrument for measuring breath. Later scholars and critics have taken this theory more earnestly than did Olson himself, who was prone to admit (in conversation) that it was all a song-and-dance he had made up to justify the kind of poetry he and his friends liked to write.

Why Professor Wright favors breath over the pulse, I don't know; to try to get by without both would seem a mistake of the first order. But, admittedly, this physiological analogy becomes pretty rough and shaky when you inspect it. Does free verse faithfully embody the living breath? Let the reader try silently reading a few free verse poems, pacing his breath to the apparent pauses and alterations of the poet's diction and emphases. If such a reader is able to struggle through the poem in some fashion, catching a lungful wherever possible, he or she may well start gasping like a fish out of water.

Naturally, Professor Wright saves all his favorable connotations for free verse. The spirit of free verse is "that of constant discovery," the spirit of green and growing plants, while the spirit of metrical verse is associated with "old fixtures"—unwashed fluorescent lamps, I would imagine. Metrical verse is "monumental, of the museum"—funereal, paid-admission stuff. Here it seems that Professor Wright accurately senses what many poets have felt, especially those antitraditional poets of the early 1970s. To them, a stack of stanzas had a certain tombstone look, while a work of free verse, full of white space, appeared airy and vital.

It should be no news to any reader of poetry magazines that dead, oppressive verse can be written in traditional forms. A stanzaic poem that channels weak energy can be a monstrous thing: a pile of massive blocks raised to entomb a slug. Good metrical verse, like poetry of any sort, needs a certain amount of passion to bring it off. But, as a browse through current poetry will suggest, merely to write in nonmetrical forms will not guarantee a poem any vitality. A better question to ask a poem than "Is its form free or traditional?" might be "Is there any energy in it?"

Worst of all, Professor Wright hints, metrical verse is sly, machiavellian stuff: "The patterns of meter are subtle and devious, but free verse is likely to seem sincere, unhurried, truer to the moment of speech and life." This argument that metrical verse has to be calculated, while free verse can simply flow; that metrical verse is artificial and unnatural while free verse is somehow more faithful to spontaneous life, drops another old clodhopper. It seems to me that any good poem entails artifice, even one found readymade like Rosmarie Waldrop's arrangement as verse of a passage from *The Joy of Cooking.* Like opera, the ballet, or an animated cartoon, a metrical poem freely admits to such artifice—moreover, invites the reader to notice that artifice and even take pleasure in it.

A profound comment on this topic occurs in Jorge Luis Borges's story "The Secret Miracle," in which the Czech poet Hladik composes metrical verse at the very moment he faces a Nazi firing squad. God intervenes between the condemned poet and the Gestapo bullets, halts the passage of time that Hladik may complete in his head his masterpiece, a verse play in hexameters. Hladik, notes Borges, has chosen such a form because "it prevents the spectators from forgetting unreality, the condition necessary for art."

Borges touches here on deep truth. No poem can be actual, unretouched life, and if it pretends to be so, then it abdicates art's power over us. Indeed, by choosing not to be a ritual impossible to confuse with ordinary life (like a sonnet), a free verse poem unless informed by some passionate energy will often turn out to be something less than life, and nothing very special at all. I am left bemused by Professor Wright's suggestion that a work of art containing no conflict or tension is closer to life than a work (like a metrical poem) fraught with it. An art without conflict or tension would resemble no life I know.

Surely it is depressing to think that metrical verse cannot capture the spirit of the morning, nor reflect, without sly calculation, immediate and urgent life. This news might have come as a shock to John Keats, who so rapidly wrote "On First Looking into Chapman's Homer," dashed it off in a white heat with a single correction. It might have startled that Shakespeare "who never blotted line," or that Emily Dickinson who apparently kept impulsive, spur-of-the-moment observations in formal verse, as one might keep a journal of the day.

Indeed, Professor Wright's view of formal verse makes it sound unlike any formal verse I know. Free verse poets often charge formalists with calculated planning—with selecting a fixed form as though it were a hollow box, then coldly and methodically cramming it with words. But, like most formal poets I know, I find that to write in meter and rime you must blindly submit to a wild and surprising force. You allow a rhythm to take you over, let a rime-scheme suggest what you will say. Oh, you can resist some suggestions and encourage others, but when you rime you are definitely not your own boss. And it strikes me that the writer of free verse, unluckily, has no such barbaric force to cope with, and be nurtured by. Unaided and alone, he must hoist himself by his own bootstraps, inventing a poem by an effort of will and mind.

Students who aren't used to writing in meter often declare, "That's not for me—it's a straitjacket! I can't say what I want to say!" And that is exactly where meter, for the poet who can handle it, conveys a wonderful boon. Meter and rime inhibit the poet from writing smug displays of brilliant self-expression. They make it discouragingly hard to discourse on a subject that, he thinks, would be a smart idea to write a poem about. You may willfully open a poem with a remark or two on any subject you choose, but soon, when a rhythm grabs you and rimes start tempting you down odd bypaths, you will find yourself writing whatever it is that possibilities, suddenly revealed, prompt you to write. This experience can seem thwarting to a poet who thinks he knows what to write, knows better than the language does. But those who have been borne along on the river of meter well know that it makes for a carefree ride. Auden, in an epigram in "Shorts II," praises meter for just those limiting and restricting powers:

> Blessed be all metrical rules that forbid automatic responses,
> force us to have second thoughts, free from the fetters of Self.

To find metrical words, you have to plunge deeper than the surface of your mind. As W. D. Snodgrass argues in a recent essay, "Against Your Beliefs" (*Southern Review,* Summer 1990), you may find yourself obliged to say things that clash with what you had believed were your most cherished beliefs. You may even discover what you truly believe, as perhaps you didn't consciously know.

As a believer in the power of meter to knock poets out of their tight little smug cerebrality and cast them down into the foul rag and bone shop of the heart, I like Professor Wright's argument that formal verse, even more than free verse, has sexual undertones. "Traditional meter," he remarks, "owes something of its power to the alternating pulse of sexual excitement." Hear, hear. The same might be claimed for any steady drumbeat, for Ravel's *Bolero,* for a jazz dance. I wish Professor Wright had gone further into that fascinating supposition. Still, it seems a slur against the man- and womanhood of formal verse to charge that in metrical verse no sexual excitement is "altogether released." And it grieves me to think that readers of formal poetry must go around in a state of perpetual bowlegged frustration, like sailors whose ship has been too long on the high seas.

At this point in my argument, I can hear an alarm bell warning that it is dangerous to push these anatomical analogies. Still, I confess to a hunch that formal poems, more than free verse poems, tend to end in a satisfying bang, more or less like satisfying sex. This bang is, of course, not a literal shudder in the loins, but a kind of bang in the middle of the mind. The point can be made in verse:

> Meter
> Is the thrust rest thrust of loins and peter
> And rime,
> To come at the same time.

G. T. Wright is too temperate a critic to blast formal verse as fascistic, yet the implication is clearly there, and again, it is a familiar one. Free verse, he suggests, is "especially expressive of peace and love" because it doesn't cause words to struggle against a meter. By contrast, it would seem, traditional form must be warlike and hate-mongering. Yvor Winters, a liberal activist in politics though a traditionalist in aesthetics, once tackled what he called "the fallacy of expressive form" in an essay, "Before Disaster," and laid it to rest beautifully. Despite the principle (of architects) that form follows function, the form of a poem has only the most tenuous and unpredictable connection with what you can say in it. You can complain against hatred and violence in a sonnet, as Milton did, just as well as you can complain against it in free verse. As George Herbert, Emily Dickinson, Gerard Manley Hopkins, and Seamus Heaney have done, you can write of peace and love in strict stanzas, entirely convincingly. To write any poem, according to Pablo Neruda, who didn't divide one kind of poetry from another, is a peace-abiding act: "Peace goes into the making of a poem as flour goes into the making of bread."

Professor Wright's point that traditional verse harbors a certain conflict and tension seems undeniable. Richard Wilbur has characterized such a tension in his often quoted comparison of a closed poem to a bottled genie: "the strength of the genie comes of his being confined in a bottle." And I quite agree with Professor Wright that it is the conflict, the counterpoint, in a metrical poem "that creates a poetry of immense power." The immense power—lest anybody get the wrong impression—is, I would add, not a political or military power, not the power of a Saddam Hussein or a George Bush, but a quite different power indeed. It is the power to stir us to the core. I cannot buy Professor Wright's suggestion that we have had enough of such metrical poetry. Like the house of the Lord, as the saying goes, the house of poetry has many mansions. Good poetry, metrical or nonmetrical, is seldom in anywhere-near-adequate supply.

A Reply to X. J. Kennedy

If X. J. Kennedy understands something about the time and circumstances that produced "Pulse and Breath," he may be less indignant at the notions it toys with. I wrote it in the early 1970s, when free verse was flourishing and many of the formal poets of this century were either dying out (Auden and Berryman) or moving to freer verse modes (Lowell, Merwin, and Rich, among others). The little magazines of the time, except for heroic stalwarts like Kennedy's *Counter / Measures* (which I'm happy to say published a poem of mine about then), exuberantly abandoned formal structures, and it looked for a while as if we might really be coming close to the end of the great six-century tradition of formal English verse.

This was not, in my view, a happy development. I had cared about that tradition a great deal, so much so that it is ironic to find myself pictured in Kennedy's essay as one of its enemies and detractors. For several years before that time, and for almost twenty since, I regularly taught a course that explored the expressive devices of sound and form that English and American poets have used to give life to their work. Meter, stanza, and patterned rhetorical devices have been, to a large extent, my lifetime study. I have reveled in them. It is free verse, not metered verse, that I have had to learn to like. My preference for formally structured verse has to do, no doubt, with my sense that for our traditional culture it is this verse, the verse of meter almost always and frequently of rhyme as well, that has carried the culture's significant wisdom. Formal verse, not free, has kept alive the powerful rhetorical presence of ancient oral poetry, charged with the saying of whatever is important for the culture to keep in our collective cumulative memory.

To be sure, most readers, most intellectuals, most lovers even of literature, do not, these days, take this view of poetry. But there are many of us, Kennedy and myself included—for we are really on the same side—for whom (if I may quote from a recent article I wrote on this theme), "verse is itself a kind of magic-making theater," and I always enjoy reading even second-rate metrical poetry, whereas the undisciplined chatter of much free verse frequently bores me.

How, then, could I have written such a piece as "Pulse and Breath," which seems on its face to be sounding the knell of doom for formal verse? Well, as I say, I wrote it at a time when things looked particularly grim for formal verse. Things also looked bad for the country, and for the world. This was the time when Watergate and Vietnam had revealed, to my view, an appalling madness and/or corruption in the powerful men who ran the American government. We could cheer, perhaps, because at last these disgraceful episodes had ended, but they were surely enough to shake the faith of anyone who believed in the benevolent operation of traditional structures. Not that I ever gave up on these entirely—they were always the structures I preferred—but, along with many others, I saw that one had at least to give a hearing to ways of understanding the life of our time that were different, less rigid, more open. Rigidity and inflexibility had locked our leaders into terrible policies and practices, and a corresponding refusal to change traditional ways could be seen throughout our society in its attitudes toward women, minorities, the poor, outsiders of every kind.

"Pulse and Breath" emerged from this intellectual and political context. Kennedy is quite right to mark it as a political statement as much as a critical one, though "fascism" is his term, not mine. It seemed to me that one ought to be constant in one's suspicion of *any* authority, to regard all traditional structures fairly and critically, not to brand them as fascistic and tear them all down. Even "Pulse and Breath," though it made a case for the special appeal of free verse, tried to recognize—with a certain grimness of tone, I admit—the different strengths of metrical poetry. Its portrait of free verse was also not entirely laudatory: breath-poetry is shown to be rather innocent, naive, self-justifying, not "responsible," not subtle, without notable tension or power, a view that many free-verse poets would vigorously dispute. But what makes the essay sound odd is that it somehow didn't see print for fifteen years or more. I wrote it first as a kind of counterargument to be presented in the last week of the course in meter and form that I had been teaching. I had certainly long admired the free verse of Whitman, Williams, Eliot, and others, and, after a quarter in which I had, in effect, been inviting students to marvel at the expressive formal powers of traditional English poets, I wanted to make, as sharply and concisely as possible, the case for the *other* kind of poetry. That seemed only fair. I have never liked to impose my views on my students, to require them to see things my way. I was doing what the young Auden used to say he was doing whenever he wrote a poem: he was trying on a hat to see how it fitted, to see whether the form, the tone, and the attitude would work for him, would solve the technical and personal and ideological problems that were engaging him at the moment.

Something like that was behind my writing of this little piece. I gave it to James Naiden some years after I wrote it, but the next issue of *The North Stone Review* was suspended for more than another decade. By the time X. J. Kennedy saw it, he evidently thought it represented the view of some terribly behind-the-times professor in 1990. My book *Shakespeare's Metrical Art* would have helped him to realize how strongly I've championed the achievements of traditional metrical poetry. Maybe I should have withdrawn the piece in 1990, but by that time it seemed harmless enough.

But I don't mean to disown the essay entirely. I believe that what I said in "Pulse and Breath" has a lot of truth in it, that the contrasts between the two kinds of verse have some validity, even if their presentation is slanted too much in favor of free verse. There is a case to be made against formal poetry, though I would make it somewhat differently now, and I still feel ambivalently about it. I see formal verse as offering, at best, tentative, not final, coherences. That may be enough, for modest readers like ourselves: the making of shapely works of art is always a sufficient end. But, much as I cherish the old meters and patterns and the splendid and surprising designs that poets of talent and imagination have fashioned within them, I still have the sinking feeling that for a poet to use them without radically reinventing them is just as evasive as it is for a free-verse poet to blather on without the constraints of meter and stanza. The world isn't all loose and unimpeded, like free verse. But it isn't either, to my mind, intelligible, coherent, harmonious.

In the course of his genial rebuttal, Kennedy distorts some of my points—I don't at all subscribe to Charles Olson's foolish ideas about breath and the typewriter, and the paragraph describing my "view of formal verse" as "unlike any formal verse I know" gives the impression that I charge formalists with "coldly and methodically cramming [a fixed form] with words." I don't do this at all, and to suggest that I do quite misstates my position. On the whole, Kennedy makes an attractive argument against an exaggerated version of the view I was trying out some fifteen or seventeen years ago, but his response also seems to me to suffer from too great a willingness to believe what he wants to believe, to justify the forms he loves, and to suppress or ignore the clear evidence given by the poetic history of our time that metrical verse has undergone a major diminution of esteem and impact, not only in our culture generally, but among people who love poetry.

The key question, I suppose, is: what's going to happen now? I take heart from the recent resurgence of formalist poetry and from Timothy Steele's eloquent account (in *Missing Measures*) of the bad reasoning behind the modern free verse movement. But the reasons poets give for writing the way they do are often misguided, and pointing out the logical inadequacies of their arguments rarely changes anything. What Steele has done is to say, in effect, to young poets: "It's really O.K. to write in meter again." And that may help, may encourage some gifted poets to try their hand at metered verse. But something that goes beyond logical arguments has made the free verse poets feel justified in their choice of form, and their dominance through much of the twentieth century is not likely to abate until poets in large numbers come to sense a correspondence between the structure of the world they live in and the structural implications of metered verse.

I suspect that that won't happen, that the best we can hope for is some middle ground between the high order of strictly metrical verse—which speaks for a fundamental satisfaction with the orders that obtain in the world generally, or that latently underlie it—and a looser order that registers in its formal uncertainties not our poets' easy assurances but their insuppressible anxieties.

Another problem for metered verse in our country is that most American poets have sensed that the traditional force that it acquires through its interaction with passionate speech does not cross the ocean successfully. It's hard to say why not, but there it is. Something in American speech goes relatively flat in English iambic meters. Sure, Frost, Eliot, and Stevens did fine work in traditional meter; more recently, Lowell, Berryman, Wilbur, Merrill, Hollander, Hecht, and others have worked notably in this kind, but with what seem less spectacular results. The well-made metrical poem now has all the cultural impact of a well-turned pot. It pleases, even delights, but it leaves hardly any mark on the general culture, as once it certainly did. Not that free verse poems succeed much better. Neither kind carries much political or cultural clout, though both, as Kennedy suggests, can pack a more personal wallop. The problem for the poet, as Kennedy and I can agree, is still to do good work in any form.

Troubles of a Professional Meter Reader

In *Measure for Measure,* when Isabella first enters Angelo's presence her initial timidity is conveyed by the obliqueness of her approach, the politeness of her rhetoric, and the correctness with which her phrases sit down in the pews of her meter:

> There is a vice which most I do abhor,
> And most desire should meet the blow of justice;
> For which I would not plead, but that I must;
> For which I must not plead, but that I am
> At war 'twixt will and will not.
> (2.2.29–33)[1]

Despite the wordplay, which carries the promise of a more engaging mind than yet appears, the language has little spirit. Angelo is understandably impatient, and at his first sharp rebuff Isabella is ready to give up. Lucio, however, charging her with coldness, keeps her at her task, and gradually her language warms and reveals her intellectual power and subtlety:

> Why, all the souls that *were* were forfeit *once,*
> And He that might the vantage *best* have took
> Found out the *remedy.* How would *you* be

> If He, which is the *top* of judgment, should
> But judge you as you *are*? O, think on *that*,
> And mercy then will *breathe* within your *lips*,
> Like *man new made*.
> (73–79)

The meter here is not much less regular than before, but Isabella's speeches now pour emphasis on key words in her argument, the ones printed in italics. An actress might prefer to highlight other or additional words, but it seems clear that this speech moves more rapidly than the earlier one; the sentences unfold with greater freedom and suppleness; and the rhetoric, focusing on certain syllables dramatically placed at various points in the lines and in the clauses, conveys Isabella's growing engagement with the turns of her argument. By the time she is ready to indict the arrogance of "man, / Dress'd in a little brief authority" (2.2.116–17), her syntactical and metrical style has been transformed. One might argue that what succeeds in seducing Isabella (and Angelo) is her own sophisticated rhetoric, which signals her deep involvement in a worldly cause. But it is probably enough to claim only that in the course of the scene her manner has changed radically, and that the meter plays an important stylistic role in registering this change.

Shakespeare's prevailing method in the later plays is not to provide a deviant metrical style for his distinctive characters, but to write a standard verse speech for each play and let the characters' utterances vary from it according to their degree of distress, anger, or agitation. Furious as Leontes and his meter become, other characters in *The Winter's Tale* have recourse on occasion to a meter almost as disturbed as his, and when he recovers his sanity, his meter returns to what is normal for the play.

Excitement, too, may be of different sorts. It is not only anger or pleading that inspires metrical variation in a character. Wonder can bring out the trochees in a speechless king:[2]

> *Pericles.* Gíve mĕ | a gash, | pút mĕ | to present pain,
>   Lest this | grèat séa | of joys | rúshĭng | upon me
>   O'èr béar | the shores of my mortal | ĭtў,
>   And drown | mĕ wĭth | their sweetness. O, | còme híthĕr,
>   Thóu thăt | beget'st | hím thăt | did thee beget;
>   Thóu thăt | wast born at sea, | búriĕd | at Tharsus,
>   And found at sea again!
>   (*Pericles* 5.1.191–97)

Madness may break up the verse alarmingly:

> *Lear.* I pardon that man's life. What was thy cause?
> Adultery?
> Thou shalt not die. Die for adultery? No,
> The wren goes to't, and the small gilded fly
> Does lecher in my sight.
> Let copulation thrive; for Gloucester's bastard son
> Was kinder to his father than my daughters
> Got 'tween the lawful sheets.
> To't, luxury, pell-mell, for I lack soldiers.
> (*King Lear* 4.6.109–17)

    Characters take their metrical style from the play, but gusts of feeling blow through them, testing and tempering their measures. Of course, Machiavellian personages, early and late, such as Richard III or Iago or Lear's elder daughters, can change their tune according to who it is they want to manipulate. They can wear or doff their masks of friendliness or loyalty. Some earlier characters, too, speak at several levels of emotional intensity, which are reflected in their syntax and verse. But the middle plays go much further in permitting characters to alter their speaking styles radically under the stress of strong feeling or madness. Ophelia gives up pentameter verse altogether, but Hamlet, Lear, and Timon, in moments of distress and crisis, adopt a more turbulent verse style. The increasingly subtle language produces the illusion that the anger or anxiety characters feel is mirrored in their troubled meters, that altering measures are signs of altering feeling. All the main characters in *Hamlet* use different styles at different moments, in keeping with their emotional arousal or darker purposes. Hamlet's notably ambiguous character is the result, not the cause, of his speaking so differently on different occasions.

    This is one respect in which Shakespeare must have altered his verse in response to something he noticed going on in life—in this case, the surprisingly various ways of talking that any articulate person may develop under the pressure of circumstances. Other changes in his dramatic verse may have come about in response to other observations. Despite our sense of Shakespeare's language as typically elevated, despite the conviction of millions of undergraduates that it is hopelessly unlike normal speech, this is a playwright unusually alert to the way people talk. They use more or less the same English (in life or in a play); their social position may limit or fix their range of idiom, but within each class there is available to talented speakers a wide range of expressive options, to be exercised on a great variety of speaking occasions. As I have suggested elsewhere, the short scenes in *Antony and Cleopatra* that begin and end in midconversation imply a Shakespeare who has noticed how much we hear of the fragmentary conversation of others—as we move beside them in the streets, in pubs, or in the passages of great houses, as they pass in and out of our hearing.[3] We still have much to learn about other ways in which the verse reflects this playwright's alert observation of how people speak—and change their speech as circumstances, occasions, and settings keep changing.

But how marginal this subject is—in the double sense that most scholars, actors, readers, and critics pay little attention to it, and that it occupies a contested territory between various overlapping disputants: between linguistic and literary metrists, between literary analysis and theatrical performance, between those who read poetry mainly as measured speech and those who read it principally as spoken music, between the impulse to emphasize a poet's metrical debts to earlier texts and the impulse to read poems and their meters as largely autonomous achievements of proud, freestanding authors. In studying the motions of verse, is one studying language or art, text or voice, author or era? Is metrics a "human science" or a rhetorical and dramatic resource of the artist?

Such oppositions, seldom so cantankerously plotted, are still to be sniffed in the air that metrists breathe, but they do not exactly check off against those that are strongly present in the larger world of contemporary literary study. There is nothing that could be called feminist metrics; deconstructive metrical analysis is at best a mischievous offshoot of formalist poetics; and metrical theory that has a marxist tinge—that reads iambic pentameter as bourgeois capitalist in origin and recommends accentual poetry or free verse as ideologically preferable—seems hardly serious. Metrics is too technical a subject to respond with enthusiasm to political or otherwise fashionable critical creeds, though a metrist's choice of conceptual frameworks may indeed reflect a preference that is ultimately ideological and political. Or it may derive from training in a mixture of artistic or academic traditions that help to compose Western thought and art.

The personal backgrounds of metrists are probably as confusing and miscellaneous as their intellectual positions. Besides being British or American, Russian or French, they start from different pleasures and dispositions: from an interest in language or linguistics, from love of the theater, from knowledge of music, from writing or reading poetry (or even editing Shakespeare) and being puzzled or awed by a poet's skill in managing rhythms.

My own metrical interest has its source in many of these first affections: early singing and word games in a musical and verbal family, high school recitations and "oratorical" contests, boys' choirs and summer camp Gilbert and Sullivan productions, my verse writing, and Renaissance and Baroque religious music that I sang for years in Columbia University's St. Paul's Chapel choir.

In my time the choir at Columbia sang at services five weekdays at noon and on Sunday morning, a tour of duty that required three lengthy rehearsals each week. In addition, our intense enjoyment of the music we sang (Vittoria, Josquin Desprez, Palestrina, Byrd, Bach, and other expressive composers) led many of us not only to go caroling at Christmas but all through the year to sing a cappella on street corners up and down Broadway, on Riverside Drive, on subway platforms, and at parties in our homes, where we often essayed less familiar music from madrigals to oratorios. Such forays, in which feelings of love mixed uncertainly with diffuse religious (or antireligious) fervor helped train me in the double art of hearing and helping to charge with my own voice those musical works in which Renaissance artists registered the sensuous and evocative powers of words embedded in tones.

But our beginnings never know our ends. Years later, furnished with a literature Ph.D., I began to offer a course in English prosody. My "field" was modern poetry, and the puzzle most on my mind was free verse. But "free" from what? Where had it come from? Had it somehow grown out of earlier metrical verse? Why had our poets abandoned that rich old system of poetic sound for what seemed to me then (probably to the detriment of the poetry I was trying to write myself) an inferior, less emphatic, less enchanting verse? But what exactly *was* that older system? How had it worked? Why had it weakened? These questions, worried in and out of class, kept leading me back to Renaissance verse, to that decasyllabic line that had taken root so vigorously in the sixteenth century and shown such strength and resilience that poets for centuries continued to hear it (and fear it) as the great central meter of the language. What had transpired in that earlier English age between the language and the verse line (for in that interplay surely lay the secret) to produce such a wondrous technical instrument just in time for the powerful writers who came along then? And could even they have written so well without it?

Over time I worked out theories of my own and found few critics approaching the subject from a viewpoint much like mine. The metrical theory receiving most attention in the late 1960s was the dubious one (so it seemed to me from the beginning) of generative metrics, a system developed mainly by MIT linguists who showed little sensitivity to English verse but were trying to formulate sets of rules for writing it that they derived (by false analogical procedures, I suspected) from Noam Chomsky's ideas about the acquisition of language by children.[4] One book—John Thompson's *The Founding of English Metre*[5]—talked sensibly about how poets from Wyatt to Sidney had married verse and speech. But Thompson stopped short of the culminating achievements of Shakespeare, Donne, Jonson, and Herbert, and he also relied on linguistic theories that, in my view, were still saddling metrics with assumptions, terms, and emphases that impeded analysis more than they facilitated it.

From Thompson I roved back to earlier studies of English meter and saw what he was up against in venturing into this territory at all. Scholars had treated meter as language, as music, as theater, as poetry, and even as literary history. When systematic metrical study of Shakespeare's plays began more than a century ago, it was undertaken largely to assist in resolving questions of chronology and authorship. The appreciation of rhythmic effects in lines or speeches, by canny critics such as George Saintsbury, was more enthusiastic or impressionistic than analytical. New Critics who studied poetic technique challenged both impressionistic vagueness and aesthetically neutral scholarly exhaustiveness, but they usually concentrated on single lines or short passages, preferring to cite exemplary prosodic models rather than explore an author or a text with heroic thoroughness. Still, Yvor Winters produced some sensitive, if cranky, essays on metrical verse; Arnold Stein opened up some of Donne's accentual mysteries; Milton's rigidities and licenses were explored by Robert Bridges, S. Ernest Sprott, Edward Weismiller, and others; and W. K. Wimsatt Jr. wrote with unfailing intelligence about metrical principles.[6] But Shakespeare's work enjoyed no extended metrical analysis by modern scholars until recently, and the interest of strong researchers such as Marina Tarlinskaja and Henri Suhamy has been more linguistic than literary.[7]

From the beginning of the twentieth century, linguists have developed methods for analyzing the data, some of them very tellingly (see especially Otto Jespersen and Roman Jakobson),[8] but they have tended to break up into schools and to offer successive generations of critics incompatible or unpalatable paradigms for the analysis of speech and meter: structural linguistics, generative grammar, and intonational theory, among others. And with their narrowing focus on technical questions of stress placement, linguists have scanted the skill and artistry of poets. As a rule, they have seemed slow to understand that in some expressive poetic lines our metrical expectations often overbear to some extent the speech rhythms we might elect for the same words in a prose setting, and are overborne in turn by speech rhythms we cannot suppress. After Jespersen, even linguists sensitive to the rhythms of spoken English have rarely been attuned to verse rhythms. The New Critics' readings could be arbitrary, but the best of them listened to verse much better than linguists have.

My own aims have been practical and pedagogical, not philosophical or scientific. I want to entice students, readers, critics, and actors to follow and enjoy the technical artistry of poets. My purpose is not to study metrical patterning as a theoretical aspect of language but to understand how a poet uses his or her palette or keyboard for significant effects. My subject is aesthetic, formal, rhetorical, dramatic—"applied prosody," as the late O. B. Hardison reasonably called it,[9] and I can't disown the phrase, though it makes my precious discernments sound like a sort of prosodic engineering.

This distinction between what I try to do and what more linguistically oriented metrical scholars are about was not clear to me when I started, but little by little the terrain I had stumbled into became familiar ground. Here and there within its borders appeared a quaint and curious volume of forgotten lore—such as Ants Oras's admirable technical study, complete with fascinating graphs and charts, of "pause patterns" in Renaissance verse.[10] But the more I read, the clearer it became that I had been learning some things about the expressive uses of meter that weren't turning up in the literature on the subject, partly because New Critical perceptions of metrical artistry were usually not grounded in a thorough understanding of historical metrical practice, as I hoped mine would be. My original intention was to survey all English poetry and write a brief, technical, aesthetic history of its iambic pentameter; but this proved unworkable, and I narrowed my subject to Renaissance verse, interpreting "Renaissance" generously to include every major poet from Chaucer to Milton. The first version of my book tried to cover them all in some detail, but because what I chiefly had to say concerned Shakespeare most of all (a long essay on Wyatt having appeared separately[11]), I cut two hundred pages, including a lengthy essay on Donne's metrics, in order to focus on the poet whose intricate system of metrical variation and deviation, it seemed to me, had never been adequately set forth.

Among other things, I learned that the study of meter is laborious; it involves the reading of a whole library of theory and commentary as well as of masses of English poems and verse plays; and it changes one's views and one's life. In the course of writing on meter, my ideas about the proprieties of metrical analysis, my scruples about proper procedures, and my doubts about the methods of other critics (and even my own) have crystallized considerably. When I looked back recently at early notes for my book on Shakespeare's meter, I marveled at the naïveté that gleamed through early stages of this grandiose enterprise. I had started more or less as a formalist critic, but in time I learned to modulate into a newer sort, not quite a poststructuralist (though I have come to see meter as often undermining and unsettling the words it rides and drives), yet I still remained partly the dogged delver for data that older historical scholars had often been. Such delving is justified (to the worker) by two enormous rewards: the intense, partly musical pleasures of the journey, and the flashes of understanding that keep lighting up a crooked and troubled road.

The Trouble with Linguists

Most scholars understand the meter of a poem or passage to designate its basic—that is, its recurrent—accentual, syllabic, or quantitative pattern. That definition seems acceptable to me, so long as we understand that the pattern is either a sounded pattern or one that is silently "heard," not one that is merely represented graphically on a page, void of sound or virtual sound. Still, in practice I use the term to mean not only (1) the paradigmatic pattern but also (2) the set of variations from it that can be found in the poem or passage in question.[12] And implicit for me in this looser definition is (3) the range of expressive functions served by this complex of sounded pattern and variations. To study such a system—of paradigm, departures, and purposes—one has to have some feeling for (and technical understanding of) the style with which sentences and arguments unfold in English and rhetorical schemes and tropes (such as irony, metaphor, and all the figured arrangements of language that Renaissance poets and audiences exulted in) affect the intonation of lines and sentences. But because the subject is not just linguistic but aesthetic as well, a knowledge of linguistics and of rhetorical patterning is not sufficient.

One queerness of metrical study is that linguists who interest themselves in it care little, as a rule, about how poems sound. What they care about is the extent to which, in a given poet's work, the stress patterns of speech phrases correspond to the stress patterns of metrical lines. That sounds like sound, but it isn't—or it leaves out much that is. The interest is in *whether* the stresses in a phrase conform to the stresses in a line, not in *how* they do or don't, not in the style or force or flair with which they fit or fail to fit.

Many linguists find themselves at a loss to understand why literary metrists such as myself maintain that the metrical technique of poets consists less in the extent to which they put stressable syllables in stressed positions and minor ones in unstressed positions (the deviations from norms submitting to strenuous tabulation and empirical generalization) than in the artistry with which poets interweave the metrical pattern and the linear and syntactical schemes to provide another dimension of emphasis to the sheer prose sense of phrases and sentences. Typically, the pleasure of the metrical text resides in the perception of fluid shifts in the variation schemes forced on the meter by natural phrasing, usually over a passage of several lines.

> Thùs wás | Ĭ, sléep | ĭng, bў | ă Bró | thĕr's hánd,
> Ŏf Lífe, | ŏf Crówn, | ănd Quéen | ăt ónce | dĭspátch'd;
> Cùt óff | éven ìn | thĕ Blós | sŏms ŏf | mў Sín,
> Ùnhóus | 'lĕd, dìs | ăppóint | ĕd, ùn | ănél'd,
> Nò réck | 'ning máde, | bŭt sént | tŏ mý | ăccóunt
> Wĭth áll | mў ím | pĕrféc | tiŏns ŏn | mў héad;
> Ò hór | rĭblĕ, | Ò hór | rĭblĕ, | mòst hórrĭblĕ
> (*Hamlet* 1.5.74–80)[13]

Scansion marks recognize some of the accentual variety in feet and lines, but the phrasal segmentation, too—only partly registered by punctuation—is different in every line and often in the syntactical connection between one line and the next. Lines can also give pleasure by exhibiting an unexpected congruence between metrical pattern and authentically speechlike phrasing: "Methought I was enamor'd of an ass" (*A Midsummer Night's Dream* 4.1.77), or "I think it was to see my mother's wedding" (*Hamlet* 1.2.178) or by showing mildly or wildly unexpected disparities between them:

> (Ăs Ĭ | fòretóld | yŏu) wĕre | àll spí | rĭts ănd
> (*The Tempest* 4.1.149)

> Ríng thĕ | alarum-bell! | Múrthĕr | and treason!
> Bánquŏ | and Donalbain! | Málcŏlm, | awake!
> (*Macbeth* 2.3.74–75)

Sometimes we enjoy the meter's surprising but satisfying direction of emphasis toward what are usually minor syllables in English and away from major ones:

> Ŏn thís | sìde mý | hànd ànd | ŏn thát | sìde yóurs
> (*Richard II* 4.1.83)

There seem to be, in Renaissance verse, no limits to the ingenuity and inventiveness with which poets—Shakespeare is by no means alone in this—use the accentual patterns of speech and verse to modify each other and compose an authentic verse speech.

The Trouble with Timers

If meter's connection with language can be overstated, so can its connection with music. Though we speak of the musical qualities of verse, and though meter is a musical as well as a poetic term, it does not really function in poetry as it does in music. This is especially true of iambic pentameter, which scholars agree in calling an unusually speechlike meter. As with free verse, there may be moments when musical analogies can clarify effects, but neither of these verse modes, free or blank, is subject to the strict time-counting that is essential to most music. And if the time requirements are more relaxed, so are the pitch and duration—and even the accent—requirements. Actors or readers have far more discretion in producing and spacing the words than singers ever have. Furthermore, when words are set to music, they almost always forfeit their speech-rhythm, but much of the art of the skillful poet, especially in iambic pentameter, and most of all in the best Renaissance verse drama, consists in negotiating the interplay between natural speech rhythms and a minimal metrical observance of pattern. It is clear that different metrists may interest themselves in different sides of this complex subject, but for me its soul is this interplay: how the elements of metrical pattern display themselves in a poet or playwright's work, and how the strong rhythmic currents of spoken English submit to and strain that pattern.

The Trouble with Actors

If linguists tend not to listen to meter but to decide by abstract considerations which syllables in a sentence merit stress, people in the theater often distribute stress in obedience to their sense of prose sentences and let the meter shift for itself. In recent decades, however, some directors (notably, John Barton)[14] have begun to insist that one key to the sense of Shakespearean utterances can be found in the meter. But even well-intentioned actors can hardly follow the metrical clues without a better feel than most of them have for the variant and deviant lines that Shakespeare uses. My own work has been done partly in the hope of helping actors to master

Shakespeare's complex system of norm and variation and use their richly timbred voices to make the most of the dramatic opportunities offered by that system's abundant linear designs.

Some time ago, after a lecture, I was asked how a knowledge of Shakespeare's complex metrical system can help an actor find more effective ways to speak verse lines on the stage. I gave then a not very helpful answer, but was spurred to compose this practical advice: In preparing a speech, study the sentence and study the metrical line, and work out a way of speaking the words that is consistent with the stress requirements of both, that seems to spring from both, and that fits with your whole reading of the character and the dramatic situation. Then take advantage of your own voice and its special powers of timbre, volume, pitch, and pace to register nuance and expression.

But a professional meter reader has always to keep in mind that we can hear lines silently, too, though not all readers do. When I read poetry, I hear it in my head, the successive pulses tapping out the meter in my skull (or so it seems). I depart from this way of reading verse (and much prose) only when skimming, yet even then my insuppressible internal scanner may pick out lines here and there to "listen to." I read most lines metrically, without scanning or formulating their meter in prosodic terms, but I know instantly (and may look more closely to see why) when a line is odd or deviant.

If I "hear" poetry as I read it soundlessly, then the sound I hear from actors in the theater I "read" as falling into lines. Normally, this just happens: for Shakespeare's earlier plays, it happens without effort because of the frequent rhymes and the high incidence of endstopped verse; in later plays, where the verse is more often blank and enjambed and the lineation much more difficult to detect by ear, listening to the meter exacts a higher cost. One doesn't want to be distracted from the stage action by compulsive searching for the frequently submerging verse (although its problematical character mirrors the problematical later themes and plots). Still, even there I hear the surfacing verse whenever I can, again without analyzing but enjoying the flow of the syllables, the pulsing speechscape, sentences plunging forward on the currents of time and feeling that usually flow unobserved but are here marked and measured into paradoxically invisible lines by more or less equal sets of more or less periodic accents—and are thereby intensified, given additional weight and force, made more expressive.

Sometimes an actor's voice will bring out special rhythmic effects that silent readers may not have noticed. Yet all too often, in my experience, particularly of American performances, the rhythm of lines is abused, sense and emphasis are blurred, and the tune of a speech is distorted by an actor's or director's greater concern with making some visual or doctrinal point. No matter that the meter *might* serve a production's other purposes if the director and actor could take advantage of it. Their audiences rarely expect them to do so. On the British stage, actors are often uncomfortable with high-sounding verse rhetoric and work to flatten its tunes. In the American theater, metrical verse itself is suspect and may be concealed by those who speak it, as if it were a shameful relic of a distant age, like anti-Semitism, imperialism, melodrama, or patriarchal attitudes toward women. Indeed, some critics connect it with one or more of these ensigns of infamy.

The unhappy truth is that most American listeners to plays are deaf to metrical verse. It is poorly read to us by the parents or teachers or actors from whom we first hear it. We rarely find chances to practice reading it ourselves. Few American theater companies relish the verse; actors, like teachers, are more deeply stirred by other elements in Shakespeare's dramaturgy than by the movement, the sweep, the strength, the drama of the verse. Most of them have come late to the speaking of verse, and they have not really taken to it. They make adjustments and compromises; they deal with it as they can.[15] But they have not grown up with it, it is foreign to them, and this shows in their manner of evading or slurring the pulses, of fouling the metrical line.

In part the problem is that the blank or rhymed iambic pentameter that Shakespeare wrote most often is indeed a foreign verse, and most of the strongest American poets of our time have found it uncongenial—of our language but not of our speech. They have not heard in the old British line a suitable vehicle for the cadences of American talk. Some poets have successfully practiced a looser form of iambic verse, and a group of New Formalists have achieved some prominence, but for much of the century it has seemed that if you write iambs instead of the now canonical free verse, your work will be either derivative or comic.

Under these conditions, it isn't easy for an American reader or actor to form the habit of listening to Shakespeare's metrical verse as verse, of hearing how the meter makes or reinforces rhetorical emphases, deepens or shifts a mood or tone, powers an emotional sentence or period, and intensifies not only the speech but the action.[16] Not that British readers acquire these skills with ease, but they do have a better chance: the rhythms are native rhythms; their voices and intonational systems are closer in wavelength to those of Shakespeare's players and watchers; and they hear more often (not always, of course)—in the theater or on the BBC—actors and actresses who do indeed know how to hold a metrical current and clinch a metrical emphasis in a line, a passage, or a scene.

The Trouble with Readers

To some extent, I confess, this situation has driven me back to private and silent reading or to making a point of speaking the verse in the classroom, which I rarely do just for the sake of the verse but rather as an aid to analysis of motive or action. I try to give the speeches the animation, spirit, and semantic emphasis appropriate to the speaker's situation and emotion, avoiding two extremes: excessive excitement and lifeless mouthing of the words. But even when a line or a phrase of some length is repeated frequently in a class discussion, it should be cited, by student or teacher, in a voice that at least intimates its dramatic feeling. To be sure, there are instances—Lear's "Howl's" and "Never's"—that can hardly, in a classroom, be given their full force without absurdity. But nothing is deadlier to an understanding of metrical verse, more academic in the worst sense, than the pusillanimous speaking of a strong Shakespearean line. To treat an expressive line as mere idea, mere content, mere image, is to treat poetry not simply as if it were prose (because the principle applies as well to expressive prose), but as if it were fossilized speech, a piece of dead language that had broken off and crumbled on the tongue. For a teacher to do this encourages the student to do the same, to lose all sense of the distinction and of the special powers of poetry.

In our own speech we can say with genuine feeling, "I don't *want* you to do that" or "*Love!* his affections do not *that* way tend." But, faced with such words in print (and in class or on a public platform), readers regularly tone down the feeling and mitigate the italics, as poets often do nowadays in reading their poems, apparently as part of a half-century-long reaction against Victorian and modernist overstatement. It's as if they wouldn't be caught dead being eloquent—and they won't be. But one result is a serious weakening of the union between speech-feeling and metrical verse that is close to the heart of traditional English poetry. The New Critics themselves, by emphasizing poetry as a means of providing structures of cerebral experience (of tension, paradox, imagery, and textual decoding), may have helped to compromise the immediacy of expressive speech as a crucial element in poetry. And students have been further encouraged to think English poetry a meager and precious (and silent, if not absent) affair by the notorious, even ghostly, abstraction of contemporary theoretical criticism and its chronic remoteness from texts and performances.

Ultimately, in its fullest embodiment, the language of poetic drama is sounded and needs to be heard. For the verse, as for the dramatic action, the text is not the work of art. To see the text arranged in lines is, for modern readers as for Shakespeare's company of actors, a convenience only, although, to be sure, the silent text silently audited still offers an eloquent mute image of spoken words actually heard. It remains for the reader, the actor, the teacher, the scholar, over and over again—like Pygmalion on Cyprus—to bring that mute image to life.[17]

The Trouble with Theorists

> When I see verses bend from left to right,
> I have to think some bard's been swinging them.

Perhaps the severest problem for a metrist of my stripe is to resist claiming too much for the role of meter in constructing the meaning of texts. In my book on Shakespeare's meter I had occasion to glance at Antony Easthope's suggestion that iambic pentameter can be identified with "bourgeois liberal capitalism" and accentual meters with collective political economies.[18] This seems to me, on the face of it, preposterous—another moralistic attempt to see every feature of every past age as fatally implicated in its shame, to which it is the mission of the correcting critic to hold our guilty muzzle. But I see less difficulty in proposing that there is some structural similarity between the way even a loose meter like English iambic constrains natural English speech rhythms and the Renaissance view of how individual heroic aspiration must yield to temporal and divine authority and ultimately succumb to a universal mortality (*SMA,* 260). Such suggestions must be made very tentatively because they stretch the connections between verse speech and other social institutions and beliefs quite far; but, if proposed with tact, they can forge a link between my old aestheticism and some new historicism.

On a smaller scale, one has to be wary of attributing determinate meanings to specific metrical practices. It seems reasonable to draw inferences about which devices of sound or form Renaissance poets and attentive listeners found appropriate to certain subjects or dramatic behavior. But one never claims that pyrrhic variations (or trochaic or spondaic) always carry an identical content. Ironically enough, before my book was published, one critic took Easthope and me to task for allegedly having read specific meanings into literary devices: Easthope for that view of iambic pentameter I had already deplored, and myself for an earlier article on Shakespeare's use of the rhetorical figure hendiadys.[19] I had thought my analysis avoided the flaw this critic now found in it and suggested only that the evident meanings in a large number of passages described a range of meanings that after a while began to be recognizable as a range and could be used as a presumptive (and only a presumptive) instrument in the interpretation of others. That is, once you establish a range of effects in a good number of appearances of a literary or metrical device, you have the right to presume that further instances encountered in the same author's work will probably convey meanings within that range, but you recognize that such a range of meanings is not determined: there is always a chance that at the next occurrence of the device the meanings may fall outside the author's usual practice and either extend the theorized range or prompt a changed description.

On this view, I have felt justified in suggesting, for example, that Shakespeare's practice in writing variant lines of several sorts is not entirely mysterious, but that some kinds of aberrant lines—short or long or with missing or extra syllables—have effects that fall into perceptible patterns. You don't want to pursue such claims too far, or to imply that "often" means "always," but if patterns appear to be purposeful, you want to hear them.

Shakespeare's management of his resources results in departures from the norm (or realizations of it that seem notable in some way—for their energy or timidity, for their muted or commanding tone, for their grace under pressure) that fit with the meanings or feelings of the passage. But what is this "fit"? It certainly appears that the poets themselves understood some Elizabethan departures from metrical regularity as part of a code of metrical conventions that was never extensively formulated. Once we catch on to the system and are set to identify new designs within it, it begins to train us to accept some variations as intensifying, reinforcing, or qualifying semantic or dramatic meanings, just as musical dynamics does—getting louder or softer or faster for expressive purposes, alterations that listeners accept as they internalize the code. Shakespeare's metrical practice operated as a system of conventions, of understandings (by poets, actors, and initiates in the audience) about the relations of rhythmic sounds, stage action, and concepts that governed their perceptions of the world. Editors, I take it, try to adopt conventions of text presentation that will give alert readers every chance to read these conventions accurately.

The Trouble with Editors

The terms I use in metrical analysis are inevitably different from those employed by editors in explaining their editorial procedures and the impact metrical considerations have on their textual decisions. Editors usually want to make sure that the lines they provide for us are, on the whole, the lines that Shakespeare wrote for his actors, and they have to decide whether and where the lines of Folio and Quarto need emending. So long as a line meets the expected requirements, they are understandably not much concerned with expressive motions within lines or passages. It is important to me, on the other hand, that their commendable wish to present an authoritative text not lead them needlessly to "regularize" aberrant lines that fall within Shakespeare's acceptable range of variation. Not all of these will have clear expressive force, but some will, and the ideal text, from my point of view, is one that offers opportunities for forceful performance that are consistent both with our textual sources and with Shakespeare's common metrical practice.[20]

The Trouble with Meter Readers

When critics analyze meter, they have to adopt some system of graphic notation that makes clear to readers what goes on in Shakespeare's verse. One point at issue is whether analysis of a line's meter should use the old Latin measures, which represented what took place in a quantitative meter and were later adapted to describe an accentual-syllabic system like Shakespeare's. Analyzing metrical lines into feet is a curiously artificial custom, but it is no more so than the printing of plays or libretti. Neither the metrical foot nor the visible text has any audible reality. This circumstance has made many metrists uneasy about conventional foot-bound analysis. After all, a line is visible on the printed page, but a foot is not. Isn't it, therefore, a fiction? Yes, of course it is. But onstage, isn't the line a fiction, too? When I watch *Hamlet* being performed, I never see a single line of verse. We hear, in this play about a ghost, only the ghosts of lines. When I listen in the theater to a metrical "line," a string of syllables heard and measured by the ear, I may not hear the feet one by one (except in unusual lines such as "Will praise a hand, a foot, a face, an eye, / A gait, a state, a brow, a breast, a waist, / A leg, a limb—" [*Love's Labor's Lost* 4.3.182–84]), but as a passage continues (if the actors speak it well) I will normally have a sense of five somewhat similar stress-units recurring to my ear again and again—the tramping of ghostly feet, perhaps, and sometimes as difficult to detect as the position of galloping horses' feet before photography stilled them. When I look more closely at the words, I can see, in retrospect at least, that what I have heard is a kind of rippling current made up repeatedly, though with variations, of a relatively unstressed syllable followed by a stronger one. The foot, understood in this way, is no more a fiction than the bar in a musical score, which during a performance no one in the audience sees or hears or leans on. It is prudent, in a classroom, to make clear the provisional and heuristic nature of this "foot," but the term and what it stands for are still defensible.

Both foot and play text are comparable to a musical score. Although sophisticated musicians claim to be able to hear a musical work from the score alone, no blare from the page will ever pain their ears. Both the text we read and the foot we distinguish are guides to performance; and, as the score may give silent pleasure to the trained reader but cannot be fully heard until its music is carried by instruments, so neither the foot nor the dramatic text is fully realized until it is embodied in a voice or voices uttering speechlike English sentences that somehow describe metrical designs.

A difficulty with metrical analysis, with scansion in particular, is its seeming rigidity. When you scan a line, you seem to be saying, "Here is the way it must be read," when you usually mean only, "Here is one likely reading." In class you sometimes must add, "There are certain ways it cannot be read": for example, miscounting the number of syllables or not realizing which syllable of a disyllabic word conventionally receives stress in the scanner's own English—frequent beginners' mistakes, and they are mistakes, not just unpersuasive readings. What makes the subject more difficult to *write* about is that you cannot use your voice to exhibit a line. The delicate negotiation between stresses that goes on in Renaissance poetry can be conveyed in print only by, first, accurate notation (italics or scansion marks that offer at best a rough image of what we hear); and, second, lucid explanatory prose. What I try to do in the written metrical analysis of a passage is to make a reader or actor aware of the kinds of considerations that might guide our listening or speaking, not to close off options but to open up additional ones, to let the language move and engage as actively as—in our common personifying metaphor—it appears to have wanted to do.

The metier of the metrist (of *my* kind, at least) is to keep asking questions about poetry, in text or performance, that expose its stylish motions and the human issues they bring into play. I imagine all the elements of dramatic poetry (visible action, verse, characters) as held in a moving suspension before and within the enchanted reader or audience, "So that we look at it with pleasure, look / At it spinning its eccentric measure. . . ."[21] If we readily submit to the theatrical illusion that the persons onstage are deeply involved in the world the play presents, we can also assent to the parallel illusion that the verse has a life of its own. Along with the stage action, it constructs the characters and plot as it goes along, making its nuanced adjustments to suit (and keep inventing) the personages it speaks through. Even in a drama that has moved far from the highly stylized mask technique of the Greek theater or the Renaissance use of allegorical identities, Shakespearean dramatis personae are indeed masks through which the lines and speeches emerge.

So it is the verse that alters, not the character who selects a style or a meter (see *SMA,* 254–56). The text changes metrical modes (or shifts to prose) as a landscape changes, not whimsically but in response to pressures: the winds of feeling, volcanic violence, the warming and cooling of passion as weathers strike, confront, and dissolve. The play needs to shift as it does to present the tumult and harmony it is after, not to accommodate the personal styles of characters. Rather, the poetic drama *uses* Isabella or Hamlet or Leontes, as music—a Beethoven symphony, say—uses the voices of the orchestra. They are instrumental to their formal cause, which words like *work* and *play* conceptualize better than *text*. But poetry's medium is words, and what poetry of this strength and complexity provides is an aggrandized speech, the language we utter raised to a higher power, made to express more than we thought it could, to give form and heightened feeling to visions, images, revels that could not be realized, and ended, without it.

Is this bourgeois, regressive, patriarchal? Does it make too much of the words? Does it tempt us to forget the issues in favor of the audited design? Not really. But it does participate in that achievement of oral culture, or of traditional oral elements that survive in a literate culture, of making us feel that the words themselves sacralize something, keep for us some ghostly, culturally meaningful utterance that is sure to return to life if only our actors, our voices, can speak it.

ORAL OR LITERATE, SILENT OR SOUNDED

> . . . and strolled out to the theater,
> which is placed just at the headland, where the coast flinches,
> and you overlook both directions, as at a corner.
> —"Daedalus in Sicily"

Three essays published in the 1990s, starting with observations about metrical detail, raised questions about the cultural and experiential terms on which playgoers and readers encounter the dramatic and lyric poetry of Shakespeare's time. "Blank Verse in the Jacobean Theater" (1987)* noted the extent to which metrical variations in Jacobean dramatic verse, particularly at the end of the verse line, make that verse harder to hear in the theater *as* verse, and it borrowed insights from Fr. Walter Ong and Eric Havelock to question how and to what degree this stage verse might be called oral or literate. "An Almost Oral Art" (1991), risking some overlap, pursued these questions further in an effort to make more precise distinctions and assertions about the literate/oral character of dramatic poetry. "The Silent Speech of Shakespeare's *Sonnets*" (1996), focusing on Shakespeare's *lyric* poems, studies the relation between implicit and actual sound and silence in a poetry that does not require public performance. There is irony in the circumstance that the language's outstanding composer of a public oral-literate poetry should have led later English poets into a lyric poetry of mostly silent thought.

*Dates given here are not the dates of publication, but the dates by which these essays were substantially completed.

Blank Verse in the Jacobean Theater:
Language That Vanishes, Language That Keeps

My subject is the elusiveness of metrical verse in the Jacobean theater. I am not inquiring into the acoustical problems of the stage or the extent to which the actors' words were obscured by chatter or catcalls. Three connected questions do concern me here: how the increasingly problematical blank verse line could continue to be heard as a line of verse by audience members who had not read a written text; whether such verse is helpfully understood as oral or written; and what figurative or semiotic function such verse has in the theater of this period.

The End of the Jacobean Line

For Elizabethan iambic pentameter the crucial structural position was the midline pause or phrasal break; for Jacobean dramatic verse it was the end of the line. For decades poets had paused doggedly after the fourth syllable of almost every line, but by the 1590s most of them were learning to handle the midline break with greater flexibility and freedom. They perceived the attractiveness of a variously located midline phrasal break and of the occasional line that drives a trochaic countercurrent against the prevailing iambic rhythm—for example, from *Romeo and Juliet:* "And never trouble

Peter for the matter" (4.4.19),[1] or one with a masculine ending: "If Nature, sovereign mistress over wrack" (Sonnet 126:5).[2] But in practice, as the midline pause becomes more frequent toward the end of the line, the temptation of enjambment is more strongly felt, and the sense runs more often over the line-ending. For the Jacobeans the line-ending becomes the pivotal position, the site of a remarkable variety of metrical usages, which as a group compromise the mellifluous iambic line-structures of the 1590s.[3]

In retrospect, it may seem surprising that a few strong dramatic poets of the period should abandon a successful set of metrical procedures for some that are much more dubious. Many verse speeches in Shakespeare's late plays are difficult for a reader to scan and for an actor to memorize, and Webster, Tourneur, and Middleton follow Shakespeare's lead in writing lines whose metrical structure is puzzling, to say the least. For most of us the printed text does not raise sound problems with the same urgency as a theatrical performance: a reader troubled by the wayward meter can learn to ignore it and read the text "for its sense." All too many of our students will do so cheerfully. But in the theater the sound will not go away; neither will our instinctive readiness to hear whatever minimal metrical pattern the actors remain faithful to. Audiences may be only dimly aware of this patterning, but it cannot be entirely disregarded. It remains a presence in the theater: a beat, a wavelike acoustical design, that rises to different levels of awareness in different listeners. But in much Jacobean verse drama the beat is often disturbed and obscured, its coherence interrupted, and the disturbance and interruption appear to be part of the metrical strategy.

How much of the poets' metrical designs did contemporary audiences actually hear? Good evidence certainly suggests that Elizabethan playgoers were alive to the metrical patterning that characterized the usual language of the stage. The tumbling verse of earlier interludes kept the audience attuned to the beat; meter and rhyme combined to mark the length and shape of the lines unmistakably:

> So, sirrah, if I shóuld not with hím take this wáy,
> I shóuld not be ríd of him, I thínk, till doomsdáy.
> I will cáll forth my fólks, that, withóut any mócks,
> Íf he come agáin, we may gíve him raps and knócks.
> (Nicholas Udall, *Roister Doister,* 4.4.1–4)[4]

And it seems accurate to say that the gradual development of blank verse in the theater, from the stiff lines of *Gorboduc* through the more grandly constructed chains of endstopped lines that constitute Marlowe's mighty metric, to the skillfully modulated periods of Shakespeare's middle plays, trained the Elizabethan audience to hear (though not to analyze) iambic verse. By the end of the century playwrights could with confidence go far beyond the simple bifurcated line, with its all-but-obligatory break after the fourth syllable, that Gascoigne regularly wove out of one phrase of four syllables followed by another of six (the two phrases are separated here to emphasize my point):

> Behold, behold!   I see a swarm indeed
> Of holy saints,   which walk in comely wise,
> Not decked in robes,   nor garnishèd with gold,
> But some unshod,   yea, some full thinly clothed . . .
>   (Gascoigne, *The Steel Glas,* 1576)[5]

This rhythmic tune must have been familiar to readers of texts and to theatrical audiences. The pause after the fourth syllable makes it easier to keep one's sense of a ten-syllable line by dividing it into smaller units of four and six. Tumbling verse has more syllables but usually only four (strong) accents, and four beats are much easier to keep track of than five, especially when the five are not all equally strong. In Gascoigne usually, and in Marlowe often, the five *do* have a common strength; but in Spenser and Shakespeare and almost all later poets one or more of the main beats of the line is likely to fall on a syllable of minor semantic importance, and the midline pause will frequently come after the fifth, sixth, or some other syllable. This means that the theater audience's measuring of the line is going to be harder. The old four-and-six helped the audience to *hear* a line of ten syllables because it effectively divided it into a two-beat half-line followed by a three-beat finish. Now, as the audience accustoms itself to the variably located break, it learns new tunes besides the old four-and-six. It learns the five-and-five, the six-and-four, and other, more inventive combinations, often complicated by pyrrhic, spondaic, and trochaic variations:

> Her father lov'd me, oft invited me
>   (*Othello* 1.3.128)

> Who steals my purse steals trash; 'tis something, nothing
>   (*Othello* 3.3.157)

> I come to bury Caesar, not to praise him
>   (*Julius Caesar* 3.2.74)

> Sweet are the uses of adversity
>   (*As You Like It* 2.1.12)

If Shakespeare's audience was to continue to hear lines as lines, it had to get used to such relatively unfamiliar and demanding combinations and tunes.

The strong and graceful verse of this period—the nondramatic verse of Donne and Spenser as well as the dramatic verse of Shakespeare—emerges largely from a series of elementary technical perceptions: that the midline break may fall in different positions; that all the main stressed syllables do not have to be equally strongly stressed (and the unstressed ones equally weak); that pyrrhic, spondaic, and trochaic variations can make the language of metrical verse immensely more expressive; and that occasional enjambment of lines, along with these other devices, will help verse sound more speechlike by permitting phrasal waves to spill over the metrical borders. These procedures provide the poet's increasingly competent listeners with a verse that transcends the apparent limitations—principally, monotony and rigidity—of the single iambic foot, of the series of similar or apparently identical iambic feet, and of the pentameter line. Like bold experiments in any art, the variations in the line help it to sound both *less* like the norm and yet *still* like the norm.

But ultimately these procedures exact a price. The strong movement of sentences over the line-ending (and over increasingly problematical line-endings) makes it difficult even for practiced listeners to follow the meter line by line—either to keep track of the audible units or to imagine them as components of a linear text. It is hard enough for a textual editor to arrange the words in lines; for a listener in the theater to do so accurately or long is almost impossible.

In sum, as the flexible treatment of the midline pause makes possible the rich harmonies of Elizabethan verse, the flexible treatment of the end-line pause powerfully unsettles those harmonies. Even when the line is still endstopped, its forcefulness may be severely compromised if the ending is frequently pyrrhic, feminine, triple, or heavy; and run-on lines may dash, drift, or dawdle over weak, light, or feminine endings. These devices work in conjunction with the syllabic practices of compression and expansion, with short lines and long lines, and with other odd line-forms (headless, broken-backed, and epic-caesural) either to modify the iambic pentameter sound or to obscure the end of the line and our sense of the pentameter.

Four passages from the drama of this period can illustrate these oddities and uncertainties. The first exhibits Fletcher's habit of giving feminine endings to a high proportion of verse lines—in this passage, to all of them:

Blank Verse in the Jacobean Theater 239

> Quench me this mighty humor, and then tell me
> Whose whore you are; for you are one, I know it.
> Let all mine honors perish but I'll find him,
> Though he lie locked up in thy blood! Be sudden;
> There is no facing it; and be not flattered.
> The burnt air, when the Dog reigns, is not fouler
> Than thy contagious name, till thy repentance
> (If the gods grant thee any) purge thy sickness.
> (*The Maid's Tragedy* 4.1.50–57)

Such insistent feminine endings can contribute to a variety of expressive effects—here to a rather puffed-up anger but probably most often to a somewhat self-deflating pathos.

In Middleton we often hear another tune, whose chief motif is the heavy ending:

> You will do well, I warrant you, fear | ĭt nót sìr.
> Join but your own good will to't. He's not wise
> That loves his pain or sickness, or grows fond
> Of a disease whose property is to vex him
> And spitefully drink his blood up. Out | ŭpón't, sìr,
> Youth knows no greater loss. I pray | lèt's wálk, sìr.
> You never saw the beauty of | mỹ hóuse yèt,
> Nor how abundantly fortune has bless'd me
> In worldly treasure; trust me, I have | ĕnóugh, sìr,
> To make my friend a rich man in my life,
> A great man at my death; yourself | wĭll sáy sò.
> If you want anything, and spare to speak,
> Troth, I'll condemn you for a wil | fŭl mán, sìr.
> (*Women Beware Women* 3.2.355–67)[6]

Seven of the thirteen endings are heavy, and under their influence we are encouraged to lean heavily on two other feminine endings ("vex him" and "bless'd me"). The verse line so produced often drips with insinuation or self-indulgence, pathos or resentment. This effect is most striking in Middleton, but Fletcher's feminine endings often lean that way; Shakespeare never uses the heavy ending repeatedly in any speech.[7]

These two passages show the different sound given to complete and recognizably metrical lines by frequent feminine or heavy endings. With Webster and Shakespeare, on the other hand, (and with Middleton frequently) the problem for a listener in the theater is that we lose our sense of where the lines begin and end. Webster's lines puzzle, as a rule, because he has picked up from Shakespeare strange line-types and syllabic procedures that make the interior metrical design hard to grasp:

Cariola. Lét me but spéak with the dúke; | Í'll | discóver   265
        Tréason tó his pérson.
Bosola.   Deláys:—thróttle her.
1st Executioner. She bites and scratches.
Cariola.   If you kill me now,
        I͡ am damned; | I have | not been | at confess | ĭŏn
        These two years.
Bosola (to Executioners). When
Cariola.   I͡ am quick with child.
Bosola.   Why then,
        Your credit's saved. (*They stangle Cariola.*)   270
                      Bear her into th' next room;
        Let this lie still.
(*Exeunt the Executioners... Enter Ferdinand*)
Ferdinand.   Ís | shĕ déad?
Bosola. | She͡ is what
        You'd have her.ˬ But here begin your pity:
(*Shows the Children strangled.*)
        Alas, | how | have these offended?
Ferdinand.   The death
        Of young | wolves is | neve͡r to | be pi | tied.
Bosola.   Fix
        Your eye here.
Ferdinand.   Constantly.
Bosola.   Do you not weep?   275
. . . .
Ferdinand. Cover her face; mine eyes dazzle; she died young.
                (*The Duchess of Malfi* 4.2.265–75, 279)[8]

    Elision, syncope, multiple trochees, monosyllabic feet (265, 271, 273), one line with a missing stressed syllable (272), another with a late epic caesura (273), one line divided among four different speeches (269), one headless line with a fifth-foot dactyl (266)—these techniques, which all (except the last) occur in Shakespeare earlier than this, help make these lines sound either metrically unintelligible or close in character to the five-stress accentual prosody that has become fairly common only in the modern verse of Wallace Stevens, Robert Lowell, and others.⁹

In late Shakespeare, on the other hand, we become uncertain as to where the line begins and ends. It would be difficult, for example, to keep track of the lineation in the following passage from *Henry VIII*. As in much late Shakespeare, though the line-endings are hard to locate, the iambic rhythm remains very clear:

> And for me,
> I have no further gone in this, than by
> A single voice, and that not pass'd me, but   70
> By learned approbation of the judges: If I am
> Traduc'd by ignorant tongues, which neither know
> My faculties nor person, yet will be
> The chronicles of my doing: let me say,
> 'Tis but the fate of place, and the rough brake   75
> That virtue must go through.
>   (1.2.68–76; Folio punctuation)

(It is line 71's hypermetrical length, of course, that will throw off any listener in the theater.)

The Fletcher and Middleton passages are odd, but the difficulty the other two passages put in the way of the sympathetic listener is severe. The lines of Shakespeare and Webster (and often of Middleton and Tourneur as well) differ sharply from earlier and later English verse, dramatic or undramatic, in which the verse line revealed its shape through rhyme or, pruned of problematical deviations, offered its standard sound to its standard listener; and they differ, too, from traditional oral poetry, where the poet's perpetually new arrangement of familiar materials adheres to a metrical order his audience can appreciate and follow. The parallel with oral poetry is a natural one here, for in the theater the differences between oral and literate language and between different sorts of oral discourse become especially suggestive and revealing. The question naturally arises whether and to what extent language spoken in the theater is comparable, has remained comparable, to traditional oral poetry. In particular, a closer understanding of what "oral" means in this context may clarify the problems that cluster around dramatic verse. Is dramatic verse "oral," in Fr. Walter Ong's sense?[10] And did Shakespeare and other Jacobean playwrights really expect their audiences to follow their devious metrical designs? Or does meter make its presence felt subliminally in dramatic verse, as Eliot hoped it could do? In any event, what expressive or semiotic purposes does this elusive metric serve?

The Audible Line

"Oral literature," as Father Ong observes (11), is a contradiction in terms, but it refers to something genuine: a store or hoard or repertoire of oral works, capable of being summoned again into present being by performing artists. The opposite contradiction, "literate speech"—that is, utterances by members of a literate culture, whose spoken sentences may, from time to time, exhibit a syntactical and conceptual complexity learned from written documents (Ong, 56–57)—has a direct bearing on work composed for the stage by literate poets. It is relevant also for printed poetry and prose fiction, which always imitate at one or more removes the actual utterances of speakers,[11] but dramatic verse offers us a special case of the complex mixture of oral and literate.

In a literate culture, one in which people read or are presumed capable of literacy, what is oral and what is written continually interact with each other to form strange amalgams. They also interact freely with other levels of experience. Just as oral culture is often called, with prejudice, preliterate, much of our experience is pre- or nonverbal (semiotic, in Julia Kristeva's terminology: the realm of the felt but not formulated), and another region may lie at the other end of the spectrum: the postliterate, perhaps the electronic or televisionary. Still, the availability of the most advanced of these levels does not mean that the others are forsaken. Once people write, they do not stop talking. But the knowledge that what we say can be put in writing may change the way we choose to talk.

As Father Ong points out (12), the speech of people in a literate culture is always potentially tied to the literal elements that can be used to make it literally literate: letters, words, phrases, sentences, the visual components of a text. Sometimes conversation runs too fast for us to be aware, moment by moment, of sounds as having a textual dimension; especially when it is swift and emotional, speech partly escapes the hegemony of written culture; but its relation to writing can always be instantly retrieved. We need only detach a word from a stream of oral discourse and imagine it spelled, translated from a temporal to a spatial form. The more literate we are, probably the closer we come to unfolding every utterance we hear or speak as an imagined visual text on some threshold of awareness in our minds. An illiterate person, a person whose culture, personal or communal, is entirely oral, cannot have such an experience.

But we also know that, even in a literate culture, spoken language operates differently from written. Ordinary speech is normally both spontaneous and largely unremembered (Ong, 32). It appears out of nowhere and almost all of it vanishes, unlike writing, which, except for our own, is there before we read it and endures beyond our experience of it. But *some* oral language does *not* vanish, is designed to avoid vanishing, and the sign of this is that it exhibits a higher degree of patterning than the rest. Because patterned language is easier to retain, important language is deliberately patterned (Ong, 33–36). In effect, "oral" has two meanings, which are not always clearly distinguished, even by Father Ong. It always means spoken, but the phrase "oral tradition" calls attention to a kind of spoken language that is different from the rest by being marked for remembering. In effect, we have three modes of language: there is speaking that vanishes, speaking that keeps, and writing. Because the second kind of speaking relies for its effectiveness on human memory, it uses mnemonic devices. Speakers in a highly literate culture, if they want to remember something, write it down (or put a marker in a book) and resort less and less to mnemonic aids to train their verbal memories. But the mnemonic devices needed by the speaking that keeps have become, through human history, associated especially with poetry—that is, with the high literature of our culture, the verbal (and often quasi-musical) art that records especially significant action or wisdom. This feature of literate poetry, its privileging or foregrounding of recurrent phonic, lexical, and syntactic patterning, can be traced to preliterate poetry and poetic ritual. Such patterning then becomes a sign of the language that keeps, a signal that the words it touches, whether spoken or written, are special. They count more than most, they matter, they are marked.

Poetic traditions have always taken advantage of the patterning that is characteristic of this language that keeps. Writing, from this point of view, is another means of keeping speech and in some respects a less satisfactory means than speech itself—further removed, as Ong notes, "from the living human lifeworld" (81), sometimes inaccurately transcribed, and always less fully scored. But traditions of written poetry develop their systems of patterning in different ways, varying with culture, language, and genre. In time even written texts take for granted the literate reader's expectation that patterns of some conventional sort will be legible in the printed words, either as a visually perceptible pattern or as an imaginable auditory one. The text of a lyric poem not only provides a permanently available record of the poem's words; it also allows for the repeated conversion of the poem's visual text into a spoken one. The text of a play permits a company of actors to turn the written words into a sounded performance. In both cases the written record keeps the patterned language available for the speaking voice.[12]

And so does the line, which is really a microtext. Although for the poetry of literate cultures the line is central (analysis of meter focuses on the line's internal structures, analysis of stanzas on the relation of one line to others), "line" is clearly a visual term that means nothing for oral poets. If they were given to analysis, they might analyze a poem into successive temporal units, perhaps cola:[13] sentences or sentence-segments related in some way to breaths and pauses. But as soon as verse becomes visible, we find spatial terms to describe it. Words like "verse" and "boustrophedonic" suggest some analogy between the turning of the plow and the plowman at the end of a furrow and the movement from one line of verse to the next. The end of line or furrow is a natural pausing place, and it is worth noticing that "verse" literally describes the *end* of the line, where we *turn* and begin the next one. By Shakespeare's period, "line" meant something spatial to the playwrights and probably to many in the audience as well; "lines" were what the actors spoke, even though the words that came from the stage were strictly invisible, not arranged in visual rows but set in audible lines—another contradiction in terms.[14]

For centuries we have tended to think of plays as "literature," not as oral texts, because they are written down and preserved in books and libraries. But plays share many characteristics with oral literature. For just as the poems of an oral culture are always altered in performance, no two performances of plays, even in a literate society, are ever the same. The text of a play, like that of an oral poem, is constantly recomposed and may appear, as we are realizing more fully all the time, in significantly different versions that represent different hypostases of "the play." Actors "read" the lines differently from one production to another or even from one performance to the next. Modern productions, as a rule, still draw the line at adding new words or speeches to Shakespeare's text. But we cut at will, transpose scenes, eliminate characters, introduce mutes, music, video technology, exotic sets, and stage business of a kind Shakespeare never dreamt of; we play with gender designations, as Shakespeare did, and, in general, treat the "text" as a point of departure for our own creative work. Lyric poems, in contrast, we expect to have an authoritative form, and poets, like scholars, are likely to insist on absolute fidelity to line, letter, and point. When playwrights do so, they know, as we do, that the next performance will betray their efforts at strict definition. If there is life in the play, it will break out of those bonds. Insofar as a play is oral, it will resist being a text.

What Shakespeare's Language Keeps

Shakespeare would certainly not have used these terms, but he (or his text) evidently understood this situation, and the verse of his late plays offers a *frame that gives* for *language that keeps*. All the flexibilities, obscurities, and imbalances challenge the oral poet's audience to stay aware of the frame, to go on picking it up even when to do so is difficult. It is nevertheless worth doing, because the audience is used to having important knowledge signaled by patterned language. Whenever the language shifts unmistakably from prose to verse, the audience understands that, even though the prose material was not necessarily trivial, what the verse conveys will certainly be important. In the later plays the metrical patterning grows more elusive; it includes more rests, syncopations, grace notes; but it can still, if lost, be recovered, it will often be lost and recovered, like language itself, as we continually forget what people say but remember how to speak.

Thus, Shakespeare's middle and later plays reduce or make less prominent those mnemonic resources of rhyme, endstopping, and the composition of speeches in iambic pentameter blocks. The verse that results is harder to follow, to hear as verse. Paradoxically, one may get a better sense of the meter from a printed text (if we can trust the early compositor or the later editor) than from a performance. In the theater enjambed blank verse sounds much like actual, improvised (if elevated) talk, and though Shakespeare's later language is as figurative as ever, its figures run less and less in harness with the meter but cut across the lines and obscure their common accentual patterns. Though the grammar of the sentences and the meter of the lines constitute two orders that spoken words must follow, the tension between these rival orders in Shakespeare's Jacobean work appears to jeopardize the normal keeping functions of verse.

One set of devices within blank verse, then, aims at a natural verse speech, a speech that may be memorable but that retains some trace of the throwaway status of ordinary spoken language, of language that vanishes. At a certain point, that is, the conventions of Jacobean blank verse appear to run counter to the original purposes of metrical poetry: as the play becomes a text, it appears to preserve the evanescent, the trivial. In this respect, blank verse is not notably different from other literate technology: if in an oral culture some language that ought to be kept vanishes, in an age of writing much that deserves to vanish is preserved. Shadwell gets kept, along with Shakespeare.[15]

Blank verse, in fact, is doubly a technology: it preserves through its audible line, and it preserves through its printed form. But what, exactly, is it preserving? A dramatic action? natural speech? significant form? or a play of signifiers? The value-system of patriarchy or the class structures of bourgeois capitalism? However we negotiate these currents, much of the material framed in blank verse is of the disposable kind: casual talk, chatter, that class of eminently forgettable utterances that makes up most of our experience of speech. Yet interwoven with this material is the aphoristic summary, the fragment of wisdom that receives pithy phrasing: "While we look up to heaven, we confound / Knowledge with knowledge" (*The White Devil* 5.6.259–60)[16] or "We are such stuff / As dreams are made on, and our little life / Is rounded with a sleep" (*The Tempest* 4.1.156–58). But along with such obvious summations of wisdom important to an oral culture, the playtext preserves much language that acquires its significance largely from the fact that it accompanies, fixes, or forms the setting for crucial action.

To a large extent, the naturalistic techniques of Renaissance drama make the background and context of action and wisdom convincing. The aim is less realistic than instrumental (as Rosamond Tuve told us long ago). The relatively speechlike English, the recognizable tones of voice, the beginning and ending of scenes in midconversation (a notable feature of *Antony and Cleopatra* among other of Shakespeare's middle and later plays), the witty or angry exchanges, the expressive representation of individual emotion—are all instrumental to the action of comedy or tragedy. And the blank verse style that Shakespeare developed in his later plays contributes to the force of this drama. Gone is the well-behaved, strictly alternating iambic current that rested its weight amicably on the shoulders of every second syllable, paused deferentially at the end of the line, and was content with harmony and grace as its chief resources and means. Now the character's agony is conveyed in radically unbalanced, agitated lines—those of the jealous Leontes, for example, as he broods over his lack of sleep: lines in which certain focal words or syllables attract major stress and rise dramatically out of the once evenly alternating surface of the iambic pentameter line:

> Nor night, nor day, no rest: It is but *weak*ness
> To *bear* the matter thus: mere weakness, *if*
> The *cause* were not in being: *part* o' th' cause,

> *She*, th'Adultress: for the harlot-King
> Is quite beyond mine *Arm*, out of the blank
> And level of my brain: plot-*proof:* but *she*,
> I *can* hook to me: say that she were *gone*,
> Given to the *fire*, a *moi*ety of my rest
> Might come to me again.
>
> (*The Winter's Tale* 2.3.1–9; Folio punctuation, modern spelling, my emphasis)[17]

Performed by a scrupulous actor, such a speech can indeed convey to a trained audience a sense of its line-by-line structure, and of the unprecedented inner variety of lines that, one way or another, realize both the metrical pattern and the dementia of Leontes. To render the lines adequately, the actor must apprehend them as metrical units, in which the fixing of certain words in strong metrical positions underscores their rhetorical importance. Placed at different points in their respective lines, and in their respective grammatical cola, these kernels of sharp emphasis, italicized here, in effect construct a plot of passionate utterance that works with the grammatical plot and the metrical plot to form a complex polyphonic structure. The habit of metrical underlining—that is, of strategically placing words of great rhetorical significance in a few, and only a few, of the strong-stress positions—(a practice that Donne was developing in the 1590s and that Shakespeare may have learned from) both anchors the otherwise elusive meter and ties the agitated syntax to it.[18]

This is an art that goes far beyond merely varying the placement of midline breaks in syntax. If late Elizabethan verse modified the evenness of emphasis accorded to the stressed syllables, it did so by gentle adjustments in the interests of rhythmic variety. This new verse goes much further. Still plausibly iambic, it raises some syllables to an extraordinary prominence and abandons the metrically smooth pentameter in favor of a line with unprecedented gaps and chasms, long pauses, clamorous ascents to accent ("but *she* / I *can* . . ."), intense dwellings on two-syllable phrases like "no rest" and "plot-proof." The phrase-cuts help tell the metrically trained actor how to make the most of both rhythm and grammar to convey Leontes' deadly, demented jealousy. The meter inscribes on the ears of the playhouse audience the accents of passionate talk and thought, as later poets, lulled by the grace of the standard rhythmic line, would rarely even pretend to do.[19]

But even as the jagged meter presents Leontes' dangerous mood, it serves, here and elsewhere, as a powerful model of language vanishing, of speech almost ordered but eluding memory, safe (more or less) with the performers, as an oral culture's prized language would be, but imitating too the experience of the dissolving oral that is probably all the more pronounced in what we call a literate culture. The poetry here practices two distinct kinds of ancient art. It sometimes preserves wise speech, but it also mimes material that is essentially throwaway. It imitates the actual not to preserve central and essential speech, but to show how the casual serves as the ground of the significant. The oral tradition preserved sacred words, law, action; in a speech like that of Leontes, nothing is sacred, except the inscription of casualness on the air, on the ear. To fulfill its part in this work, enjambed blank verse uses the same means as its lineal descendant, enjambed free verse: it obscures the line-ending, traumatizes the line, and casts its own order in doubt. For a few Jacobean playwrights evidently sense that the significant matter that lies at the heart of their drama may keep better if the formal features of the verse are observed casually, even with apparent carelessness, a carelessness that may be taken to express, in almost equal measure, a character's distraction, an author's ambivalences, and an age's ethical distress.

For the audience in the theater to hear the new verse tunes, it must listen; the line is transcribable, but it has to be measured by ear. Taken as a whole, the new art that poises but may not pause on the problematical line-ending dramatizes the precariousness of order in a world where our sense of it is being constantly imperiled. It may be permanently there, like divine or ducal power, but our experience of it is unsteady. We sometimes have to take it on faith; sometimes (for prose passages) it vanishes altogether; then, after an interval, we once more make it out. The line comes back—shared, feminine, heavy, light, even long—to take its place again as the palpable, figured frame of all this showing.

This technique, still (I think) fundamentally oral, derives in part from a literate tradition of textual poetry, which understands verse to be written in visible lines, so that metrical units heard from the stage can be recovered in writing or imagined as print or script by anyone sufficiently well versed in such matters.[20] But the roughness of our early texts, their readiness to print some metrical units as prose or complementary half-lines as uncombined, and their general inattention to metrical niceties or "correctness" suggest that dramatic texts were thought of as scripts for oral performances rather than as books for a home reader's private library, though certainly the distinction between these two uses was at best hazy. That is, in the usual Renaissance poetic text meant for reading, the lines would normally be arranged to guide readers who wanted to hear or speak the lines: the visible text guides the reader's apprehension of its aural design. Probably at least the Quarto texts are mainly intended for the company of actors, who are presumed to be professionally competent at discerning the meter even where the compositor (or the author!) has not arranged the words as verse; the actors then present the rhythmically patterned words to an audience; the audience hears both the grammatically coherent sentence and the differently coherent metrical line as complementary elements in an aural experience that accompanies and merges with the visual experience of persons, gestures, movements, iconic pageantry, and symbolic action.[21]

"Sound," writes Father Ong, "exists only when it is going out of existence" (32, 91). Speech, of course, is a special kind of sound, a coded system of symbols that on the page is translated into another system of coded "marks on a surface" (75). To read the latter is to hear the former, but what distinguishes the former is that it is always disappearing. What print or memory secures is the capacity of important words to appear again and dissolve. By its very form, drama imitates speech (and action) vanishing. With a printed text we can always page back or forward, but the play does not play back. As it drives forward the words dissolve; only the image of a text remains. Each moment, each line, displaces the last, hurries it out of existence. "These words are not mine," says the King to Hamlet; "No, nor mine now" is Hamlet's sufficient reply (3.2.97–98). Not Shakespeare's, either, now. And ours only now and then, as, leaving the playhouse, we try to recover the form, the shape, the experience, the import of the whole and the parts that most matter, to freeze the significant images and gestures and retain the language that keeps.

Shakespeare appears to have given himself to this process, to have understood in effect that plays were oral texts and to have been content with that. Ben Jonson was not: he wanted to be sure that his scripts were kept as writing, as literature, as language of the study. For Shakespeare, the "little life" of the theater is "rounded with a sleep": it vanishes. But only until the next occasion when some troupe of rough magicians will require their potent art to wake their sleepers—not the audience, but actors and lines together—from the "graves" where they rest between performances.[22]

An Almost Oral Art:
Shakespeare's Language on Stage and Page

This essay continues an inquiry I have been making for several years into the difference it makes to Shakespeare's language (and that of other poets) whether we hear it from the stage or read it from the page (and whether, if we read it from the page, we read it silently or aloud—or a combination of both). My concern is not with how effective the stage performance is, how skillfully the actors "read the lines," how sensitive they are to the rhythms, and so on. What interests me is a theoretical question: assuming a high degree of competence in the reader or performer, what page/stage differences result? To a large extent, my interest in this topic has been an almost inevitable by-product of my scanning thousands of dramatic verse lines as they pose on the pages of editions of Shakespeare's plays and then hearing actors speak them in dramatic performances. I found eventually that I could not keep moving between the seen line and the sounded line without asking what authority either had to be thought of as *the* line or even to be thought of as a *line* at all.[1]

Let me begin with language as we hear it from the stage, focusing first on the technical differences between stage verse and stage "prose." On the stage, *verse* language must establish and confirm an aural pattern based on beats, though it may depart from the pattern in detail or briefly, for melodi-

An Almost Oral Art 251

ous variation or for expressive effect. The rhythm of its beats may be measured in two related but not necessarily consistent ways: either by the amount of time (isochrony) or by the number of syllables (isosyllaby?) between the beats. Its units may or may not be measured by rhyme. In iambic pentameter the force of the beats (the volume or sharpness with which they are voiced) need not be equal.

In contrast, stage "prose" must avoid definite metrical pattern or measure, though (as verse may occasionally depart from pattern) prose may approach or approximate pattern from time to time, but not for long: its stresses may seem isochronous (and even equal in strength) for a while, and they may come with a regular number of intervening syllables, but not for long. So in prose passages we may find such strings of words as the following:

> *Autolycus.* I knew him once a servant of the Prince.
> (*The Winter's Tale* 4.3.87–88)

> *Hamlet.* Thou wouldst not think how ill all's here about my heart.
> (*Hamlet* 5.2.212–13)

> *Lear.* . . . there I found 'em, there I smelt 'em out.
> (*King Lear* 4.6.103)[2]

Each of these is iambic. The first seems perfect iambic pentameter, the second an alexandrine, the third a headless line. After each of them, the text drops the iambic pattern and returns unambiguously to prose.

Verse embedded in prose, as in the above examples, raises curious questions about the language of the stage. A poet skilled in verse writing could easily lapse into meter even while writing passages that are mainly prose. But it is harder to account for the extended passages in Shakespeare's work whose classification as prose or verse seems indeterminate.[3] Clearly, the margins between these two realms are of great theoretical interest, and we can learn much by studying them closely. But my own observation of how prose and verse languages sound *in the theater,* while focused at times on the margins between them, has also tried to keep in view what is central and distinctive in each of these kinds of language. This habit of thinking has prompted me to wonder about the origins of both prose and verse, and to do so in terms that modern speculations about orality and literacy have made available to literary scholars.

For the question of prose and verse language in the theater or in the study is inseparable from questions having to do with the paradoxes, contradictions, and confusions that arise when we try to understand the status or nature, within a literate culture, of an oral art such as drama, and especially drama written largely in verse. Even when we have read or studied a play before we see it in the theater, its language comes to us there as sound—that is, more like the sounded language we constantly hear people speak than like words we see arranged in prose or verse on a page. In the theater the words are potentially visible; in the study the words are potentially audible. As readers of play-texts, we have no doubt about the thoroughgoing literacy of our activity, even though we recognize that the words and sentences we read have their source, in part at least, in the sounded language we or others speak or have spoken. But the language of the theater, though it is delivered orally, is variously and profoundly implicated in the literate culture we inhabit. Its logic, its rhetoric, its allusions, its style, the structure of its thought, are closely linked to the literacy we could not escape even if we were illiterate.[4]

Shakespeare's plays make an especially interesting test case not only because of their dramatic power and abundance but because they appear at a moment in Western culture when drama still has strong ties to oral traditions but has begun to establish its claims to reception as an art of letters. Shakespeare's apparently faint interest in publishing his plays suggests that his art worked mainly from the stage and that the language we find in the plays, though he *wrote* it and though some or many or most of his actors learned their lines largely from written scripts, had its primary reality for actors and audience as sounded words.

This is not to say that Shakespeare or his actors (like our own) did not think of their text as a sequence of "lines." That word is frequently used in the plays to designate the text of a poem or a letter that some character is reading. To cite two of many possible examples: "Lo, here in one line is his name twice writ," says Julia of Proteus in *The Two Gentlemen of Verona* (1.2.120); and in *Richard III* Richmond rejoices to have received "from our father Stanley / Lines of fair comfort and encouragement" (5.2.5–6). The culture of such speakers and writers is a literate culture, they are in the habit of seeing words in lines, and even illiterate speakers grasp how the literacy system works: namely, that the marks on the page stand for intelligible English words that both literate and illiterate people understand when they are spoken.

But, as scholars of orality have tried to show,[5] once a culture acquires the ability to store information in written texts, the condition of poetry changes, for poetry is, to begin with, the means an entirely oral culture uses to preserve the verbal knowledge that is important to it. Poetry keeps what

An Almost Oral Art 253

a culture regards as essential to its tradition; it keeps that which requires to be transmitted if the culture is to carry on. Oral cultures *do* carry on, and what they carry on, what they bear with them as they move through time and perhaps through space, is preserved in the poetic carry-all, the archive of numerous individual memories that must keep going over the material they repeat in perpetually varying form in order to preserve it, to keep it retrievable.

The particular devices of sound and structure that we associate with the earliest poetry (repetition of all kinds, but especially meter, figurative and formulaic language, recurrence of narrative and imagistic motifs, rhetorical strategies, and similar stylistic resources) have mnemonic value, and a poetry that is aided by such devices is further supported in oral cultures by other rhythmic modes, such as music and dance, that participate, along with spectacle, costume, and mask, in the common enterprise of socializing and preserving what the culture regards as essential knowledge.

If we try to understand the connection between Western literate poetry (from ancient Greece to our own time) and the poetry of oral cultures (ancient, recent, or contemporary), we may be able to gain a clearer view of exactly to what extent, and in what sense, the language of theater, of poetic theater especially, and of Shakespeare's theater in particular, shares the aims and the techniques that characterize oral performances in an unambiguously oral culture. For example, it has been traditional for critics and poets to claim that the language of poetry has a special value that less frequently attaches to prose; that it acquires this special value from its compression, its intensity, its capacity to "speak" with greater force and eloquence than prose; that these greater powers derive somehow from those formal features it shares with the very earliest poems; and that, in effect, verse *marks* language as worth preserving. Never mind that in a literate culture like ours, in which everything is preserved in print or on tape and not in memory (whereas the amount of material that an oral culture can preserve is limited by the capacity of individual memories), verse has turned out to mark also great quantities of language, from the Renaissance to our own time, that is surely not worth preserving. This makes extraordinarily difficult the job of reckoning which language, of all the language so marked, is *really* authentic, really important to the culture; no single authority can decide for the rest of us what criteria we can use to identify the works that centrally carry our cultural wisdom; and the current debate over the canon results from general loss of confidence in any certifying authority, and even in the process by which such certification goes on in a literate society.[6]

One consequence of these developments is the problematic role that traditional repetitive devices play in contemporary verse. Many of our poets have virtually abandoned them, along with any echo of the portentous tone, the high style, and the elaborate, often archaic, syntax that mark much traditional verse. Contemporary poetry typically conveys individual experience or insight in relatively undramatic language, and the poetic means on which earlier cultures, oral and literate alike, relied for their significant statements no longer seems appropriate to many poets' changed purposes. In this respect as in others, *The Waste Land* has served for several generations as the paradigm of a poem in which the process of cultural breakdown is both enacted and reflected upon: in the course of its five sections the verse crumbles, and the final lines recapitulate the demise of a literate civilization whose important knowledge, once embedded in significant texts, can be found now only in sequenced but disparate fragments whose meanings no one can any longer connect.

In short, a "primary" oral culture (Havelock's term) has no written language; what it inscribes as worth preserving is inscribed in the memory only. A literate culture inscribes in stored records whatever is worth preserving, but after a while it also inscribes almost anything at all. These kinds of cultures, then, have different means of inscription and habits of inscribing, and both must also have a vernacular speech, a language for everyday use, that bears some relation to the means of inscription. That is, the way people speak must affect the style of their inscriptions, but special features of the language they use to inscribe what is important probably enter into ordinary speech. Not only do people quote poetry, but forms and locutions that are peculiar to poetry make their way into spoken language, especially into utterances that spring from some rhetorical occasion. Indeed, rhetoric is, to a large extent, the residue of poetry in ordinary speech. Our daily talk cannot be carried on in meter, rhyme, and stanzas, but it can make occasional use of schemes and tropes, of figurative devices, of imagistic language, and of some degree of complex argumentative structure. Special occasions call for an appropriate linguistic behavior (i.e., rhetorical speech), and any particular occasion—the dedication of a cemetery at Gettysburg, for example, or even a more genuinely extemporaneous talk—may, in turn, be remembered for the particular rhetorical flourishes it inspired.

Shakespeare's drama, as I make it out, includes among all its varieties of language these two main strands: a verse language whose form marks it as significant or as carrying significant content; and a "prose" language that, for the most part, is the common currency of colloquial exchange. Clearly, this division is by no means "pure," and I would want to qualify the roughness of it with one observation about verse and another about prose. First, if some of what is said in verse appears pretty ordinary, it may be because Shakespeare found it inconvenient or deforming to make too many changes as the characters move into or out of The Significant. A kind of aura of significance surrounds the verse passages and, in a sense, mythologizes even the parts that are mere ordinary colloquial give-and-take. Though Shakespeare usually refrains from putting the most banal exchanges into verse (into iambic pentameter, that is; doggerel seems acceptable, as in *The Comedy of Errors* and *Love's Labor's Lost*), he often does not shift modes for much that is rather perfunctory and barren of the kind of authenticity I have been discussing. Or he takes care of necessary practical business by incorporating short iambic lines in the run of more normal ones:

> *Gloucester.* Shall we hear from you, Catesby, ere we sleep?
> *Catesby.* You shall, my lord.
> *Gloucester.* At Crosby House, there shall you find us both.
> (*Richard III* 3.1.188–90)

> *Brutus.* I trouble thee too much, but thou art willing.
> *Lucius.* It is my duty, sir.
> *Brutus.* I should not urge thy duty past thy might . . .
> (*Julius Caesar* 4.3.259–61)

The prose passages that "soar," on the other hand, remind us of the colloquial base from which even the language of poetry, the language of cultural inscription, derives. But we should be careful not to identify "prose" too neatly with the colloquial or speechlike. Havelock argues (110–16) that written prose is the "language" that in ancient Greece arises as the instrument of philosophical reflection, of thought about thought, language that discusses itself, as "primary" oral poetry never can do in the same way because its language is essentially narrative and sensory, not analytical and abstract. Prose in this tradition is the language of reason, verse of persuasion or affect. In Shakespeare's work, characters often use prose to make analytical distinctions, list parallel parts of a topic, and so on, a mode of speech perhaps most memorably illustrated by that quintessential reasoner, Dogberry: "Marry, sir, they have committed false report; moreover, they have spoken untruths; secondarily, they are slanders; sixt and lastly, they have belied a lady; thirdly, they have verified unjust things; and to conclude, they are lying knaves" (*Much Ado about Nothing* 5.1.215–19).

Insofar as theatrical prose imitates the colloquial, its source is speech; insofar as it imitates the language of Western philosophical reflection and analysis, it derives from the written prose of a literate culture. But then Shakespeare's *verse* often imitates prose reflection—that is, transports the material of philosophical reflection into a medium not designed to receive it, though centuries of verse composed by literate European poets had, of course, prepared poets like Shakespeare to write a kind of poetry in which the language of philosophical reflection or analysis can indeed play a significant role. Havelock notes (110) that the key to the development of a philosophical Greek prose was the development of the copula "to be," whereas oral poetry used active verbs and described actions that people "do." By Shakespeare's time, as we all know, it was possible not only to use the copulative verb frequently in poetry but to build a major verse speech of a major tragic hero on his reflection about the meaning of that very verb and its negation.

The complex picture might be drawn this way: Shakespeare's drama is oral in the sense that to some extent it uses the same formal means as oral poetry (mnemonic devices, such as verse) for the same purpose (to preserve important knowledge). But certain factors weaken or compromise this status: (1) it preserves prose as well as verse; and (2) its verse has been touched and changed by the two faces of prose, *(a)* the colloquial, which lowers its high-style, sacred character, and *(b)* the discursive or philosophical, which eternizes it so that what it presents is not just narrative of exemplary acts (as in stories of the Greek gods) but assertion of eternal relationships or powers (as in theories about the Christian God). Oral poetry narrates exemplary stories that show how love or courage behaves; literate poetry (or drama) may tell a tale, but it also discusses, or even frames into aphorisms, what love or courage *is,* and it claims something like sacred status for such assertions.

It is possible to regard the two languages or modes as exhibiting what is in Shakespeare's time a mixed situation, reflecting differences in status, occasion, function, style, and perspective. First, the *status* of dramatic poetry as a preserver of essential knowledge is no longer quite clear; poetry is felt to be important, to address topics intensely, portentously; but the topics it addresses are no longer just the central ones, an agreed-upon body of culture-binding tenets and customs, but a much wider range of materials, many of which are less easy to identify as the culture's basic beliefs and values. We get a far more various display of characters, actions, themes, and styles than would be necessary to affirm the culture's central concerns.[7]

Second, the *occasion* for this poetic display is no longer what it would have been in an oral culture. Despite the efforts of scholars to establish the origins of drama in religious ceremony, we know well enough that dramatic performance, even by Shakespeare's time, was effectively secularized. Drama may still use a highly charged verse, but no longer is it literally a ritual, because each performance no longer serves the function of fixing the culture's important knowledge more firmly in the cultural memory. What is cast in verse is not so much the official word-hoard of the culture as material that is being mythologized in our presence, material whose importance is not inherent but is asserted by the act of treating it in verse.[8]

But this suggests that verse is performing a far different *function* from that which it served in oral cultures. It is reaching out beyond the domain of the official and central to sacralize a great deal of material that could be available to treatment of this kind only in a literate culture. It seizes on historical materials from many generations or centuries ago; it records meetings of historical or nonhistorical personages and their subtle, angry, or amusing confrontations or debates; it preserves the progress of personal relationships and the nuances of family life, feelings of love, betrayal, triumph, irritation, bafflement. It holds the mirror up to nature, a mimetic aim that in an oral culture remains unambiguously secondary or merely instrumental to the didactic purposes of poetry.

Its *style* is different, too—indeed, it has many styles, developed to explore that wide range of human relationships that a literate culture no longer wishes to reduce to the primary elemental ones of man-to-God, husband-to-wife, father-to-child, and so on, along with a range of idioms, tones, and manners drawn from social and personal as well as from public life. Even the summations of truth we find in this verse proceed from a diversity of cultural experience that oral poetry cannot usually draw on. Oral poetry narrated myths that could guide conduct; only in a later, more literate stage does it fashion its wisdom into proverbs. Shakespeare frequently follows this proverblike form in sententiae like John of Gaunt's:

> For violent fires soon burn out themselves;
> Small show'rs last long, but sudden storms are short;
> He tires betimes that spurs too fast betimes;
> With eager feeding food doth choke the feeder. . . .
> (*Richard II* 2.1.34–37)

But Gaunt is being tedious here, and Shakespeare's more authentic way of presenting such material—in passages that begin, for example, "All the world's a stage" (*As You Like It* 2.7.139ff.) or "but man, proud man, / Dress'd in a little brief authority" (*Measure for Measure* 2.2.117ff.)—is to treat the proverbial form with an expansiveness of social reference that is usually foreign to oral poetry, with its more singleminded emphasis on the profound and the penetrating. In short, even the didactic element in this poetry is differently didactic.

Although many of its aphorisms or proverbs—those quoted above or "Sweet are the uses of adversity" (*As You Like It* 2.1.12) or "Uneasy lies the head that wears a crown" (*2 Henry IV* 3.1.31)—can be understood to express the wisdom of the culture, this literate poetry characteristically presents its wisdom not in the name of a culture for which it presumes to speak (despite claims to the contrary by marxists or new historicists or by older history-of-ideas critics) but from a *perspective* or *point of view* that is much more often eccentric, idiosyncratic, or personal. A new idea of the poet is perhaps beginning to form and to define its own multiple identities in the sixteenth century. Poets may see themselves as performing a significant cultural role, but, whatever interests they share, they have an unprecedented degree of autonomy in deciding exactly what beliefs they will speak for.

From the point of view I have been developing here, drama in Shakespeare's time is in the process of having its ritual function deconstructed (or dis-mantled); but until this process is completed, the verse of that drama continues to function as a secular instrument of sacralization. Prose, in contrast, often serves purposes of relief: the high pitch of sacred meaningfulness that verse implies and imposes is hard to sustain without a break—without, that is, an occasional descent into language charged less with metrical than with syntactical tension. But prose is also useful for its mimetic capabilities: it can imitate the speech of characters so "low" in social class or dignity that, unless they are privileged as Fools, they cannot serve as carriers of significant wisdom. The traditional aura of poetry survives strongly enough to exercise a prohibition—less than absolute, to be sure—against such characters speaking in the idiom reserved for bearers of culturally important language.

But two things keep happening in the course of Shakespeare's career as a playwright that modify and complicate this relatively clear-cut distinction between verse and prose (verse for sacralizing, prose for relief and imitation): prose keeps coming in for more and more important work, and verse gets harder to hear as verse—harder to hear in the theater, for that is where the differences most matter. Editors take great pains to make it easy for us to distinguish prose from verse in the texts they offer us, but in the theater

An Almost Oral Art 259

we have to do it with our ears. To be sure, the distinction between a literate and an oral culture does not translate neatly into the distinction between the written text of a play and its oral performance; a play written by a literate poet partakes of assumptions about language and thought that are available only to literate cultures. But for Shakespeare and many of his contemporaries, the theatrical performance was the primary way the play had of being; though the text came earlier in the sense that the playwright wrote out a version of it, it came later in the sense that most viewers of the play had not read its text beforehand and would not even have thought of the possibility of doing so. The world of Shakespeare's play production resembled the modern world of moviegoing; though there may be important exceptions to this rule, most moviegoers never think of reading the screenplay on which the performance is based.

If Shakespeare's plays, then, encountered their audiences mainly in the theater, not in the study, any inquiry into the differences between prose and verse has to consider the distinctive ways in which these modes reach a theater audience. (1) When the language is heard as verse, does that send some signal to the audience about the way it is supposed to hear the words, and is a different signal sent when the language is heard as prose? (2) To what extent does an audience recognize the difference in the theater? Does the audience sometimes become confused or doubtful about whether it is hearing verse or prose? (3) Does this uncertainty matter? That is, is it important for the audience to recognize the difference? If their consciousness of the difference is only marginal, does that have consequences, or will the poet's work be done just as well (as Eliot thought) if the audience is only subliminally aware that what it is hearing is verse?

What I have said so far suggests that Shakespeare's audience did understand a difference between the language they heard as verse and the language they heard as prose, that they recognized something of the sacralizing character of verse, at least of the more dignified iambic pentameter in contrast to the playful doggerel (which nevertheless serves carnivalesque functions that we should not undervalue). Rhymed verse in the theater is certainly recognizable as verse; and, even in Shakespearean comedy or farce, rhymed decasyllabic couplets have an elegance, a pointedness, that makes the language seem specially gifted and endowed without being officially sacred. But when, over the course of Shakespeare's career, the frequency of rhyme diminishes and the likelihood increases that extended speeches (or even short ones) will enjamb their line-endings and reach their clause or sentence endings at midline, it becomes harder for an audience to hear the verse as a procession of distinct metrical lines. The concomitant tendency of this verse to use deviant lines of various kinds—short, headless, brokenbacked, or epic caesural lines, or lines missing unstressed or even stressed syllables—and its increasing use of shared lines to bridge the speeches of different speakers combine to direct attention more and more to the advancing sentence and away from the discrete verse line.[9]

But this is to say that the verse is growing more proselike, and many critics have taken just that view of Shakespeare's late blank verse.[10] What they mean, I think, is that the language is becoming more speechlike, is moving away from song or chant, is coming to resemble the more loosely rhythmed language with which the people we know are accustomed to speak to each other in life outside the theater. That language—*pace* Molière's M. Jourdain, who is shown to discover the contrary—is not prose. Prose is written, not spoken, language. Prose may be quoted in speech, as speech may be quoted in prose, but the terms are not equivalent or interchangeable. For convenience, of course, we may call by the name of prose that other language that Shakespeare uses in his plays, but we are impelled to do so mainly by the form that language takes when it is reproduced on the page, not by the way it is sounded on the stage. There it is heard as talk—talk that, however rhythmical, is not obedient to the stricter metrical beat we have learned to recognize as iambic and as pentameter.

What is the significance of this difference we hear in the theater between the stricter metrical current and the language that has been released from that accounting? Does it correspond closely to the difference between the sacralized language of oral poetry (treating material so precious to the culture that it must be stored in individual memories and its continued existence periodically proved through the mechanism of ritual performances) and the ordinary, nonsacred talk that goes on in human cultures everywhere and that in literate cultures (and, within them, among the literate classes) includes a more speculative and reflective syntax? When we see the words on the page, they seem to echo that distinction, as we acknowledge when we say, for example, that the prose is to be spoken by the lower, not the courtly, characters (or by courtly characters only in certain moods or postures). But on the stage, all of it, as Emerson might have written (and have read from a platform), is "man talking." The "prose" passages are often highly figured, and hence bear some resemblance to actual verse; but the verse gets increasingly enjambed, dis-rhymed, and harder to distinguish from actual "prose." Still, by the end of Shakespeare's career the two forms have not yet melted into a common amorphous prose/verse or verse/prose; despite all the trouble editors and scholars have in assigning particular passages to one realm or the other, they are still usually distinguishable, not only on the page but even in the theater. Though iambic lines turn up in the "prose," and unscannable passages in the verse lead us to wonder about the authenticity of the text, we still can hear a difference. The difference is hard to describe in general terms, because it is differently heard in every play; each play has its unique mix of verse, prose, and song, its characteristic spread of tones and silences, cries and whispers, voices and verses. We may not be able to catch every change as it occurs in each passing moment, but we know when a character ceases to speak and begins to sing; and in some less definite way we also may recognize when the metered language resumes or leaves off, when the language grows tense once more with the presence of verse, even if we know this verse is finding its most eloquent form just when it has decided to abandon the stage.

For the form of Shakespeare's dramatic blank verse is moving in the same direction as its material. Even as this verse is attaining its highest point of power (i.e., its greatest ability to move audiences), its strength as a ritual poetry, as an almost oral art, is about to disintegrate. One might say that, insofar as this dramatic verse of Shakespeare's is oral, is received by its audience as a bearer of cultural wisdom, like Prospero's staff it achieves its apotheosis at the moment when it is breaking—as nowadays the book that has extended its speech is in danger of drowning. Soon after Shakespeare, dramatic verse in English forfeits virtually all of its original oral powers, and then, bit by bit, the formal vestiges of those powers; the stage soon turns to prose for its characteristic language; and verse in English becomes almost exclusively an affair of the printed page, with consequences for the survival of poetry that have grown steadily more ominous.

The Silent Speech of Shakespeare's *Sonnets*

> Then others for the breath of words respect,
> Me for my dumb thoughts, speaking in effect.
> —Shakespeare, Sonnet 85
>
> O learn to read what silent love hath writ.
> —Shakespeare, Sonnet 23

Absence, Silence

> O absent presence *Stella* is not here
> —Sidney, *Astrophel and Stella*
>
> He is not here
> —Tennyson, *In Memoriam*
>
> Non c'è.
> —*Madama Butterfly*

In his rich study of *The Portrait in the Renaissance,* John Pope-Hennessy observes that the painting of portraits, even collective ones, provided a record through which families and communities could "salvage the data of physical appearance on the threshold of the tomb."[1] The motive reminds one of Shakespeare's arguments in the first seventeen sonnets, urging the young man to marry "And your sweet semblance to some other give" (S. 13)[2] as a means of enabling his beautiful image to survive his own aging and death. Perhaps because we live in an era of photography some scholars find this argument and these sonnets trivial; we have ceased to feel anxiety over preserving pictures of those we admire or are close to, which are all too likely to clutter our closets and the closets of our own survivors. Yet *all* the sonnets written to the young man have a related motive. Some of them openly claim the power to keep his image alive "When all the breathers of this world are dead" (S. 81); many of the others are designed to imagine his presence during periods or hours of absence. Absence here is mourned as a kind of death, and the return to the friend's presence, or even to the thought of it, is celebrated as an achievement of "wealth" and "state" (S. 30, 29). What may also seem striking is that considerations of absence are usually mingled with considerations of silence, so that the art of the sonnet seems to be an art of "silent thought" (S. 30), in which the very act of conjuring up the young friend's vivid presence in the face of his palpable absence can only be managed through eloquent words that, at least to begin with, go unvoiced, unheard, that *we* read as silently as the unspeaking speaker speaks them.

Of course, we may choose to sound them. But they have their origin, and they often discourse on their origin, in a "time removed" (S. 97), when the young man's absence deprives the poet-speaker of his friend's highly valued presence and makes him suspicious about where the friend is and in what company. To be sure, this absence has its consolations, especially in providing "sweet leave / To entertain the time with thoughts of love" (S. 39). If it weren't for this separation, the sonnets would never have come to exist; in a sense, there would be no subject, for these sonnets, unlike many others by other writers, are more about absence than presence, more about the absence—experienced, feared, or forecast—of their radiant center than about the enjoyment of its presence, though there is enough testimony about its presence to make its absence seem all the more poignant.

Hardly any of the first 126 sonnets seems likely to have been written in the friend's presence, though we can imagine certain lines as having been generated there (e.g., "If I could write the beauty of your eyes" [S. 17]). The poet confesses, in fact, to being "tongue-tied" before his friend (S. 80, 85, and 23, and cf. 66, 140), as if his best "speech" required the injury of "distance" (S. 44) and the "torment" of absence (S. 39), as if, unlike much portrait and landscape painting, writing could be done only when its subject is not physically present. Some poems we can imagine the speaker writing and then reading or reciting to his friend at their next meeting, or presenting for his friend's own silent (or spoken) perusal. Sonnet 38 perhaps, yet its tone is very much like that of Sonnet 39, which speaks directly of—and *to*—absence. Many of them seem so ruminative in tone that we can easily take them to be not really spoken to anyone but as having been produced during those "sessions of sweet silent thought" (S. 30) that seem habitual with this speaker and familiar from our own experience. Indeed, we can imagine all of these poems (including the first seventeen) as unsounded, silent meditations, capable of being voiced by the poet or by the person addressed (or by any of us) but at least equally appropriately read without sound.

Speech without speech—is that what the *Sonnets* are: speech that comes not after but as long silence? This deeply reflective speaker—is he really a speaker at all? Isn't it more accurate to hear the *Sonnets,* and much other lyric poetry that shows the same reflective depths, as, primarily, language of silent thought, unvoiced, unsounded, unperformed, the words of a consciousness (his then, ours now) silently addressing itself sometimes and sometimes an absent other? It may even be claimed that this unsounded speech, perfectly familiar to all of us because we generate it constantly every day of our lives, is the basic "voice" of the *Sonnets,* at least of 1–126, and a great range of other lyric poetry, and that by scrutinizing this dimension of language we can understand better not only what sort of poems the *Sonnets* and later English lyric and meditative poems are but how thoughtful speech of a different kind—sounded and public—appears in Shakespeare's dramatic writing. Both modes use speech as their main verbal material, but they work it differently. To watch Shakespeare's mastery of both is, to say the least, instructive.

Of course, the speech of Shakespeare's plays may also be, and often is, read silently. But our usual view of it in this century is that its proper condition is as speech spoken and heard. We do not usually take that view of the language of the *Sonnets*.

Two Kinds of Speaking

Why do you never speak.
—T. S. Eliot, *The Waste Land*

My curiosity about this topic grows out of a long-standing fascination with how the verse of the plays sounded, especially with its metrical design, with how actors spoke the lines and with how audiences heard them, with whether and to what extent dramatic writing like Shakespeare's is "oral literature," and with corresponding questions for lyric poetry: how do poets think of their work (if they do) as being spoken and heard, and how do we actually hear it when we read it from the page? These seem to me pertinent questions to ask of all poetry, and trying to answer them may help us understand a little better these puzzling sonnets of Shakespeare.

The phrase "sweet silent thought" intrigued me when I used to teach a course in poetic meter, form, and sound and would try to persuade students to pronounce the syllables in a way I believed was consistent with Shakespeare's probable metrical practice—not emphasizing the first adjective more prominently than the second (swéet sílĕnt thóught), which would trip the meter of the line into a four-stress dactylic pattern that is rare in Shakespeare's iambic pentameter verse. Such a misreading also, to my ear, distorted the meaning of the phrase. No comma separates the two adjectives, whether we use Renaissance punctuation practice or our own, for "silent thought" is a compound substantive characterized here as "sweet." "I sometimes enjoy moments of delicious reflection," Shakespeare is saying, "sweet silent-thought." (Compare these examples from Shakespeare poems that are probably contemporary: "sweet bottom grass," "sweet coral mouth," "sweet friendship's oath" [*Venus and Adonis*, 236, 542; *The Rape of Lucrece*, 569]). Meter and meaning both ask us to recognize the first syllable of the compound phrase as requiring more stress than "sweet":

Whén tŏ | thĕ sés |sīons ŏf | swèet sí | lĕnt thóught

Shakespeare is identifying a mode of thinking, of reflecting, unusual enough in his time to merit being the subject of special notice here and elsewhere (S. 29, 85, 119, etc.)—almost an oxymoron, since for Renaissance people a stretch of words, to be recognized as such, would usually have to be spoken. But more of this later.

But the matter of silent thought is more important than that: it has come to seem to me crucial to the lyric poetry we and our predecessors have been reading almost since Shakespeare's time and still read today, though our custom of referring to a poet's "voice" or a poem's "tone" has obscured the fact that we usually read poetry in silence.[3] In pursuit of this idea, several years ago I wrote an essay that tried to explore this question as it was raised by the poetry of T. S. Eliot,[4] whose protagonists often ruminate as they amble about the evocative landscapes of a ruined or aging world. In *The Waste Land* many of the lines that purport to represent the "speaker's" thoughts are presented as silent words that pass through the brain of the ruminating Tiresias but are not meant to be taken by the reader as sounded. One clear indication of this intention appears in the poem's second section, "A Game of Chess," where dialogue of a sort takes place between the lady at the dressing table and a man, presumably her husband. Her lines appear in quotation marks, his do not, and this suggests that there must be a difference in the way we take in the two sets of words:

> "My nerves are bad to-night. Yes, bad. Stay with me.
> "Speak to me. Why do you never speak. Speak.
> "What are you thinking of? What thinking? What?
> "I never know what you are thinking. Think."
>
> I think we are in rats' alley
> Where the dead men lost their bones.
>   (*The Waste Land* 111–16)

Similar distinctions between voices we are meant to understand as speaking aloud (the hyacinth girl, the typist, Rhine maidens, and others), whether we read them silently or not, and a more muted or silent voice of the protagonist can be noted throughout the poem, and I suggested in that essay that much of Eliot's most impressive poetry is written in this "subvocal" register (the term is Susanne Langer's), one that we hear without sound within some internal chamber, a vocal mechanism that "hears" words without speaking them, a "voice of no speech," as Eliot called it in another poem. This is not, however, one of "The Three Voices of Poetry" he identified in an important essay, where he was more concerned with the possible audiences for different kinds of poems, and he never, to my knowledge, wrote in prose about the kind of distinction I have been pursuing here. It is worth noting, however, that when Eliot turned from lyric poetry to verse written for the stage, despite the frequent critical praise for the so-called dramatic qualities of his nondramatic verse, his use of this ruminative voice in his plays is rarely successful—mainly, I speculated, because that deep inner voice, so seductively solipsistic as it processes everyone else's speech in his poems, cannot convincingly overawe other voices when they meet as equals in the theater. The chronological pattern of Shakespeare's career, of course, was exactly opposite to Eliot's: before he wrote his sonnets he was already an experienced playwright and an actor accustomed to speaking lines from a stage. It is so much the more curious, then, that, as the only playwright among those Elizabethans who participated in the sonnet-writing vogue of the 1590s, he alone should have written sonnets in a style that stresses the solitude of the poet-speaker and the silence of his speech, probably because he had a sharper insight into the peculiar powers of speech and silent thought, and into the differences between them.[5]

On Poems as Messages

> To thee I send this written ambassage,
> To witness duty, not to show my wit.
> —Shakespeare, Sonnet 26

> Your letter comes, speaking as you,
> Speaking of much, but not to come.
> —W. H. Auden, "The Letter"

Sonnet 26 seems to say that the poet-speaker is sending this poem, this sonnet, to his friend, to be read by him. This implies what is true of most letters—that it has been written in the recipient's absence and will be read in the writer's absence. Letters may be intoned by writer or reader, but it was probably as true for Shakespeare as it was for W. B. Yeats when, "after long silence," he received a letter from a later Shakespear, that such letters are usually written and read in silence. (Like Auden, he sensed that the letter might be called "Speech" or "Speaking.") The typical assumption of the written message or lyric is that the writer will not be present when it is read but that the letter acts as his surrogate, sets up a supposed situation ("as if I were with you") that resembles the fiction of theater ("as if these persons were here before you, moving and speaking"). Suppose, the personal lyric says, that I am there with you, speaking to you, there where *you* are: then this is what I say. Many of Shakespeare's sonnets to the young man imagine this situation, for love messages, letters, or poems not only wish for the presence of an absent lover but (as the further side of a reciprocal design) request the recipient to imagine the absent writer as present. They arrive, as Auden puts it, "speaking as you." The lover's letter is not the lover's presence, but it is something; as one gentleman observes (insincerely) to another, "Thy letters may be here, though thou art hence" (*The Two Gentlemen of Verona*, 3.1.250). Each sonnet offers to both its intended and unintended audience—its immediate addressee and centuries of half-invited listeners-in—an occasion to hear the words spoken as the author might speak them if he were present. It offers, as it were, a play without a play.

But normally when we read the poem, we simplify the possibilities. We don't trouble to wonder whether the poet is to be supposed as speaking the poem directly to "you," or recites it to "you" the next day, or sends it or gives it to be read silently or aloud by "you." We just accept the words as supposed or virtual speech, as words addressed by "I" to "you," whether "you" is present or not. We don't inquire too curiously into the dramatic situation because we have no difficulty with it. We know from our own experience what it is to address someone who is absent. We know what it means to say what the speaker of these sonnets is constantly saying to the absent friend: Be yourself, be beautiful, be young, be here, love me. We know what silent thought is, and fruitless address; knowing they can't hear us, we have all addressed (quietly or loudly) stuck windows, headaches, yapping dogs, fools or hypocrites on television, and absent lovers. And when we read one of Shakespeare's sonnets to the absent friend, we know that mode of silent speech—its fluency, its readiness "To leap large lengths of miles when thou art gone" (S. 44), the "wealth" it "brings" (S. 29) on some occasions, how it breaks now and then into voice, and the ultimate pathos, poignancy, frustration, and grief of it.

This is so because what we find in lyrics or love poems is a sort of suspended speech—not the direct, actual speaking of genuine conversation, not even (except rarely) one-sided talk, but a measure of "speech" that is slowed down and prolonged and muted and indefinitely available for reference. It is inner talk turned to stone, as it were, speech that has never fully made it into sound but has been formed and preserved all the same, like those first sacred writings used by a newly literate people to transcribe and preserve the wisdom formerly kept in the songs, chants, and sayings of an oral culture.[6]

Imagining Voices

> Hearing you praised, I say, "'tis so," "'tis true,"
> And to the most of praise add something more;
> But that is in my thought
>   —Shakespeare, Sonnet 85

> Heard melodies are sweet, but those unheard
> Are sweeter
>   —Keats, "Ode on a Grecian Urn"

In our efforts to identify different speakers, selves, or tones, we sometimes lose sight of what we mean when we speak of voice in nondramatic poetry. We all use the term, and we know more or less what it signifies, but we seldom acknowledge that the voice we have in mind, the voice we suppose to be speaking from the page in any silent reading (which is our usual way of reading) is not really a voice; it does not speak, it makes no sound, it does not share with actual voices (or even whispers) the physical characteristics of pitch, volume, timbre, and accent. It is "unheard," like the music that hides in the shrubbery of "Burnt Norton" and echoes the unheard "melodies" played in "soft" silence by the pipers on Keats's Grecian urn. Such melodies, Keats tells us, are "sweeter" than the ones we actually hear, because it is "to the spirit" that they "Pipe . . . ditties of no tone." Keats's phrase gives a very high value to unsounded verse, even when the verse is as sensuous as Keats's own.[7]

We know the ruminant voice of *The Waste Land* not only through our experience of unsounded but formulated thought but also through our acquaintance with printed English poetry, which has trained us to read poems silently. We do not need to say the words aloud to capture their rhythms, or move our lips to savor the words. When we speak of them as sounded by a voice, we probably mean, among other things, that as we follow the phrases and clauses on the page, our own vocal apparatus is at some low level *set* to speak them, and/or that our hearing apparatus is set to hear a voice actually saying the lines—our own voice, Olivier's, Burton's, or Eliot's. Such imagined speaking may include the imagination of variations of stress between syllables, pauses, hesitations, natural pacing, effective strategies of emphasis, shrewd management of pitch, along with paralinguistic gestures, facial expressions, and body language. We are tempted to think that we hear (or see) all this in our heads, but we actually hear (and see) none of it. We are only *prepared,* set, to hear it if a voice materializes and speaks it. Silent reading, however muscularly persevered in, is silent reading. When engaged in it, we are *ready* to perform an action (in this case, to speak words) or to perceive a sense impression (in this case, to hear words) without actually doing it, though in reading poetry you may have the same experience I have of following the words silently for a time and then, occasionally, being so caught up in the eloquence of a passage that (at least if we are alone) we actually voice a phrase or a word without quite having realized that we were going to do so.

Rehearsing the Verse

> To write is not to be absent but to become absent; to be someone and then go away, leaving traces.
> —Michael Wood, *The Magician's Doubts*

> They but thrust their buried men
> Back in the human mind again.
> —W. B. Yeats, "Under Ben Bulben"

The two dimensions of speech that I have been trying to discriminate here—spoken, and unsounded—cross over so easily, our passages between them are so fluid, that we hardly notice them or pay attention to their differences.

Words form in our minds before we speak, as Montaigne observed even during Shakespeare's lifetime: "the sense of hearing . . . is related to that of speech . . . so that what we speak we must speak first to ourselves, and make it ring on our own ears inwardly, before we send it to other ears."[8] Later, as Eliot says (in "Burnt Norton"), "Words, after speech, reach / Into the silence," but they also have a way of following us: "My words echo / Thus, in your mind." This is the dimension of experience that is permanently lost when we forget it a moment or a day later—or, if we keep reverting to it, when we die, unless it is preserved in someone else's memory or in art, as Proust and Virginia Woolf steadily observed. So Time, with its "millioned accidents" (S. 115), ripples these waters, altering, reckoning, and rendering the changes that occur between what we plan to say, what we say, what we remember saying (the next moment, the next day, years later), what people report us as saying. Writing, of course, fixes what the poet "says." At least that is the case, by and large, with published lyric poetry, though even the most scrupulously edited text of an older poet (not to speak of an Auden or a Lowell) can fail to establish the authenticity of canonical versions of poems. The play-text, as students of Shakespeare know only too well, is even less reliable; if some of the quartos were, at least in part, the product of memorial reconstruction, that suggests a checkered history, indeed: from written play-text to spoken drama to partly remembered lines to printed version. But some such mixture of sources probably lies behind even the most hurriedly composed poem, as the poet writes down, in horizontal rows, the "lines" that have "popped into his head" or "just came to me out of the blue," speaks them aloud to test their sound, adds some more in silence perhaps, revises a phrase here and there, forgets them while he goes to lunch, falls asleep, or puts them in a drawer for years, and hears them chime together silently again as he gives them a more privileged textual life on the computer screen, the disk, the page, the book.

And there they stay, ready for posterity's inspection, just as he claimed, even if, after writing them down, he lifted not a finger to help them survive. What did the claim amount to, if, in the spirit of this inquiry, we interrogate it closely? In all of Shakespeare's sonnets that promise to preserve the young man's image and to make it "eternal" or "immortal" in the "monument" of his own verse (S. 15, 17, 18, 19, 60, 63, 65, 81, 101, 107), there is no claim that the lines that offer this hope will be spoken aloud again, only the claim that the young man's image presented in them will be preserved and wondered at. Only Sonnet 81 could be taken as pressing a stronger claim:

> Your monument shall be my gentle verse,
> Which eyes not yet created shall o'er-read,
> And tongues to be your being shall rehearse,
> When all the breathers of this world are dead,
>   You still shall live—such virtue hath my pen—
>   Where breath most breathes, ev'n in the mouths of men.

But as I read these lines, they may not suggest more than that later readers will be so astonished at the beauty of the young man as it is praised in the poet's sonnets that they will talk about it, as this poet refers to earlier poets' "descriptions of the fairest wights" in Sonnet 106. Even if we understand "rehearse" to mean "recite" and not just "recount" (see Booth on this line, 278), the recitation sounds very private, a mere whispered breathing of the words in which the young man, so resurrected, is sure to be buried and disinterred and buried again.[9]

Inner Voice on the Public Stage

> I see a voice! Now will I to the chink,
> To spy and I can hear my Thisby's face.
>   —Bottom, in *A Midsummer Night's Dream*

> Why couldn't a character carry on an external monologue that was in fact an internal monologue just coming out? And why couldn't it be off the wall or exploratory, the way the inner monologue really is?
>   —Sam Shepard

To sound a lyric phrase or line is to flesh it out, to bring it from what seems disembodied existence to physical embodiment—just the opposite of what the sonnet writer wishes could happen in Sonnet 44: "If the dull substance of my flesh were thought"—to turn the bodied substance into silent, unsounded but articulated thought and nullify "Injurious distance." Far from succeeding in this enterprise, all that the speaker of Sonnet 44 has to show for his exercise are his "moan" and "heavy tears," the voiced longing and the material "badges of . . . woe." That is, his thought has turned into just the physical and material stuff that he began by wishing he could bypass. The wish is not father to this thought. But that *is* what happens in poetry, which does succeed in turning absence into virtual presence, bringing the absent here, using metaphors, imagery, narrative to transport that "world elsewhere" to wherever we happen to be. If *Henry V* can do this for its audience in the theater, can count on their imaginations to

> deck our kings,
> Carry them here and there, jumping o'er times,
> Turning th'accomplishment of many years
> Into an hour-glass

and to do all this "within the girdle of these walls" (Prologue, 28–31, 19), poetry silently read does it all the time. Whether or not the reading is silent, it amounts to a granting of this wish: the substance of imagery—kings, lover, moan, and tears—becomes inwardly present, at least as shadow. Neither thought nor verse nor letter can bring the lover physically here, but all of these can bring his "shadow" or "shade" within the purview of our "unseeing . . . sightless eyes" (S. 43).

As some critics have pointed out (notably, Heather Dubrow, in *Captive Victors*[10]), the sonnets in many ways almost compel the reader to reenact the feelings of the poet-speaker: his confusion, his uncertainty, his ambivalence. They also make us experience an absence, a distance from the speaker, similar to that which the speaker experiences from his friend. He cannot hear or see his friend, or make him hear his own voice. If we must imagine the speaker (Shakespeare's persona, however we define it) as saying the poem (or as imagining his friend reading or hearing it), even if we grant that Shakespeare has done as he promised ("To make him seem long hence as he shows now" [S. 101]) and has kept the image of his friend alive for all these centuries, we understand (as he does) that the image is in most respects dim and blurred and that we can get no closer to him than that. Fortunately, perhaps: not naming his name blesses an ill report. Even if we speak the lines ourselves, or listen to a teacher or an actor read them (live or recorded), we shall never hear the voice of that speaker or the poet.

The theater offers us a different setting: there, as Bottom realizes, we see a voice, we hear a face. We have no text before us, no lines, no "black ink." All the words we are to hear have been written for human actors to con, to speak, and to forget, and those actors (or their modern counterparts) are present now physically. Some of them may pretend not to hear what is being said by others—in asides or soliloquies, or when they are supposed to be drunk or asleep or dead—but *we* hear everything spoken aloud. But we also hear—and have heard in plays for centuries, ever since Shakespeare returned to the theater, after his time out, during the plague, for writing his narrative poems and probably most of the sonnets—a kind of speech that is different from earlier dialogue. In speeches written after this time for some of his characters at certain dramatic moments, we hear what sounds in some ways like the voice that speaks the sonnets—a ruminative, private voice that deepens our sense of the dramatic character's inner self. We can hear it in Richard II's moving meditations or in Hamlet's or Claudius's; as I have suggested elsewhere, such characters "often take us into the psychic council chambers" where they reach their decisions.

> Their feelings take form on the stage or give signs of having been anxiously arrived at. The language in which they admit to divided feelings or disturbing passions is the language of "silent thought," now for the first time conveyed from the sonnet to the theater, in dialogue as well as in soliloquy. . . . The quiet voice of reminiscence or experience, the muted tones, the pyrrhic dips, the spondaic gravity, the metaphorical and figurative surface, all the stylistic regalia of troubled reflection familiar from the *Sonnets* make their presence deeply felt in the plays that follow.[11]

In short, an authentic inner voice becomes available after 1593 or so to many of Shakespeare's characters, who speak this private or intimate language from the stage as no one had ever done before. To convey what is going on inside a character, a playwright need no longer resort to flamboyant rhetorical gestures and postures, histrionic breast beating, or demonstrative actions; a person in emotional trouble can speak of his distress before an audience as if he were talking to himself. In the soliloquy, as Wolfgang Clemen observes, "monologue becomes dialogue"—in Arnold's phrase, "the dialogue of the mind with itself."[12] The inner discourse that at least some persons carry on is acknowledged by being represented convincingly on the stage, and it gives us the illusion that we are seeing deeply into their souls or selves. If the ruminative, private voice is more eloquent than our own or than we suspect our neighbor's is, it still is of a kind we recognize as coming from a realm we have visited, and the ease and force of its speech may seem at least genuine, at times uncanny—in Sam Shepard's words, "an internal monologue just coming out."

Within Be Fed

> [T]o possess a double mental personality has long ceased to be the sort of trick that only lunatics can bring off.
> —Robert Musil, *The Man without Qualities*

> Yond Cassius has a lean and hungry look,
> He thinks too much; such men are dangerous.
> —Shakespeare, *Julius Caesar*

But did Renaissance people read or think this way? Anne Ferry makes a compelling case for the view that they did not have the concept of an inner life in the sense of "a consciousness of leading a continuous internal existence."[13] If *inward* meant the opposite of those near homonyms *outward* or *uttered,* that which was unuttered, silent, usually appears to have been "inward states" (63–70) or "secrets" (55–59) or "hidden thoughts" (59), not a continuous wordstream; and when you looked into your heart, it was to find not what was personal and individual, your own private and particular version of reality, but the universal truth of man's fallen condition (40–43). But Shakespeare, following Sidney, moves toward the charging of an inner verbal current, with what sounds like authentic "autobiographical material" (29), a strain that we find first in the speaker of the *Sonnets* and later, most notably, in the character Hamlet, whose soliloquies and asides do suggest that the words he speaks issue from a personal consciousness continuously wording its thoughts, that many of these thoughts are not spoken, and that they compose a hardly interrupted inner discourse, which may appear to be independent of his outer behavior and ambiguously related to his uttered words.[14]

This is a reading of Hamlet worth considering, for it illuminates the difficulty other people in the play have in understanding Hamlet's behavior. It suggests that he has access to an inner mental life, which was thought to be characteristic of people who were notably devious or deviant. Gertrude and Ophelia think Hamlet mad; Polonius judges there is more to it than that: "Though this be madness, yet there is method in't" (2.2.205–6), and he suggests that if Hamlet is mad, it is the madness of love. Claudius, more astute and better informed, comes closer to the truth: "There's something in his soul / O'er which his melancholy sits on brood" (3.1.164–65). Like Cassius in Caesar's view, it appears to Claudius that Hamlet thinks too much, and too much to the purpose. For those who, unlike Claudius, cannot read the clues to Hamlet's behavior, he seems mad—which he is, in a sense: after all, he converses with a ghost.

In effect, anyone whose inner discourse gives signs of being intricate and continuous is likely to arouse suspicion in others: "such men are dangerous." The continuous inward and private consciousness that we now regard as common to the experience of almost everyone (or at least of the verbal people we are and know) could be taken by Renaissance observers as an indication of an aberrant personality, of someone who, whether mad or merely calculating, needed to be watched.[15] It suggested an uncanny, even inhuman, ability to carry on two lives, two discourses, simultaneously, one inner and private, the other outer and public, an accomplishment that seemed to them perhaps as difficult and burdensome as a chess champion's playing simultaneous games of chess seems to us: something, that is, that only specially gifted people (a Hamlet, for example) can do. Joyce's *Ulysses,* of course, shows us that ordinary modern people do it, too—not only intellectuals like Stephen Dedalus, but humdrum couples like the Blooms.

This idea may have some explanatory power for *Hamlet.* For the Sonnets, despite the speaker's occasional anxieties over madness (S. 119, 129, 140, 147, and elsewhere), the hypothesis of madness in the poet-speaker is hardly a promising one.[16] More to the point, perhaps, is the possibility that Shakespeare recognized the dangerousness of the *Sonnets'* "inward" language: that their speaker is to be suspected of being not so much a sexual as an epistemological deviant, of thinking too precisely on every event. Whether or not that recognition had anything to do with his failure to supervise or authorize their publication we cannot know. But Shakespeare may well have perceived that inwardness of speech, that continuous "silent thought," conducted not in fits and starts but in extended "sessions," as a new mode of discourse, which his plays would learn to exploit, in heroic and comic protagonists, by conveying their inward speech to the stage's public spectacle—in effect giving it a public audience that could hear it speaking to itself, sometimes in tones so intimate and appealing that we are drawn to sympathize even with the most appalling villains.

From this time on, any secretive person who follows a hidden agenda may use this private speech to review strategies and anxieties. To some extent, this quiet, confiding stance derives not only from the silent speech of the *Sonnets* but, more directly, from the dramatic voice of the medieval Vice, who traditionally informs the audience of his malevolent plans—in Shakespeare's early plays, most notably in the person of Richard III, and later in Iago, Edmund, and the Macbeths. But now the asides and soliloquies of these and other villains acquire a reflective tone that can hardly help suggesting that their evil plotting is an activity they carry on steadily all the time. That tone, that vocal bearing—befitting less an orderly program perhaps than a personal taking of stock—is audible as well in some speeches of other characters with restless minds, like Hamlet, Prince Hal, Henry IV, Cassius, and Brutus, and perhaps Jaques, Juliet, Viola, and Imogen; and in some of those, and in the language of other personages as well (e.g., Ulysses, Camillo, Prospero), that reflective voice seems to carry as well a wisdom that comes less from the mouthing of sententiae than from long experience and meditation, or, in the young, from genuine thoughtful insight. But it is evil or guilty characters especially who appear to be endowed with an almost uninterrupted conscious or nightmare life, those intrigue-ridden humans in whom mischief never sleeps and against whom average mortals like ourselves or their unsuspecting victims hardly stand a chance: Imogen against the unsleeping Iachimo; Duncan and his grooms sleeping and Macduff unwary against the insomniac and ruminative Macbeths; Hermione against Leontes, who complains, "Nor night, nor day, no rest" (*The Winter's Tale,* 2.3.1); and Hamlet's ghostly father, "Sleeping within my orchard" (*Hamlet,* 1.5.59), against "that incestuous, that adulterate beast" (1.5.42), who even while the Ghost speaks to Hamlet "doth wake to-night and takes his rouse" (1.4.8). Claudius's tormented argument in 3.3.36–72 ("O, my offense is rank") seems an excerpt from speech of the most private kind, thoughts he must be in the habit of revolving within his innermost self, like some of the frequently "rapt" (1.3.142) Macbeth's: "I have liv'd long enough" (5.3.22–28) as well as "To-morrow and to-morrow and to-morrow" (5.5.19–28). Even Lady Macbeth, her husband's trusty accomplice and instigator, though she shares with him "these terrible dreams / That shake us nightly" (3.2.18–19), cannot share his inner discourse with an invisible dagger, with accusing voices of drugged grooms, with Banquo's ghost, weird sisters, and prophetic visions, as he cannot see into her "mind diseas'd" (5.3.40) or her sleepwalking terrors. All too often it is these demonic characters whose private utterances sound most like the "silent thought" of the *Sonnets,* though their beleaguered victims also can sometimes adopt a reflective tone. But that only makes their position, and ours and the audience's, more treacherous. This new language, available especially to corrupt and wicked characters, allows the seventeenth-century Shakespeare to impress on us more powerfully than before the unexpected realization that such figures do not enter our world entirely as outsiders, from an unfamiliar cosmos of fallen and foreign angels, that they have motives and words and a habit of inner discourse like our own, only more fluent, more nuanced, and probably more dangerous. The gifted evil creature—Claudius, Iago, the Macbeths, and Milton's Satan—is all too fearfully like us, even *in* us, even *is* us.

To put it another way, that inner language, deeply ambivalent, becomes even more richly implicated, through its use in Shakespeare's plays, in guilt and sin—"subdued," as it were, "To what it works in, like the dyer's hand" (S. 111)—and this is a language, voiced in drama, silent in lyric, that much of later English poetry inherits. For many of us the figures of Shakespeare's mature plays have become defined very largely by those utterances of theirs that we think of as coming from these inner depths—the self-declarations, tainted by the "black and grained spots" (*Hamlet* 3.4.90) of an indelible guilt, of Richard II, of Henry IV and his son, of Hamlet, Claudius, and Gertrude, of both Macbeths, and of Othello and Lear at their moments of self-absorbed distraction. After the Jacobeans, English drama leaves that language behind in favor of couplets and prose, neither in this period capable of carrying the language of luminous meditation on the stage. But much of English poetry, in contrast, follows Shakespeare's dramatic verse into a speech that we usually experience as potentially sounded yet silent.

The silence of this speech probably makes it different from most earlier English verse—from Chaucer, Gower, and Lydgate, much of whose work was still presumably intended for recitation to a live court audience. The advance of printing would eventually make private reading more common. But Skelton invites expressive performance, much of Wyatt's verse was sung, and it seems likely that Tudor poems, like those we meet in the miscellanies, were often recited. Donne's love poems, too, seem grounded in speech; with their strong colloquial base, they appear to be meant for recitation and sometimes song, for lively entertainment, as do many poems by Herrick, Lovelace, and Suckling, and by some later writers, especially those who write frequently in other meters than iambic or pentameter, and in lively or racy stanzas.

But printing itself, by the sixteenth century, must have made it more and more impracticable for longer poems to be read or heard aloud by most readers. The very accessibility of poetic texts must soon have made silent reading (with all its concomitant options such as skipping, skimming, repeating, speeding and slowing, breaking off or looking back) more convenient, congenial, and solitary, and the physical situation of reading would presumably have led readers to find it more and more natural for the verse they encountered in their private sessions to sound like the same inner discourse they could recognize from their own silent experience.[17]

So in the prayerlike poems of Herbert they could hear the quiet, reflective tones of a lively but not necessarily sounded devotional verse. Milton makes the same kind of silent speech majestically audible in elegy and epic, and by the nineteenth century, after the more public narratives and essays of Dryden and Pope, a different rhythmic pattern of blank-verse lines, casting Augustan symmetries and balances aside, leads through a generalized eighteenth-century reflectiveness to the self-dramatizing and usually solitary wordstreams of Wordsworth, Coleridge, and Keats—poets whose "inward eye" is "the bliss of solitude" and whose "musèd rhyme," touching "the sad heart" amid "alien corn," finds its cadence in the silent bell of the word "forlorn." That later lyric poetry is often of this kind, that its readers feel comfortable reading it silently, even perhaps that they enjoy its apparently inherent character of guilty or anxious or ambivalent rumination and reverie, seems likely enough. It seems equally likely that Shakespeare's sonnets, though they lead to the classic dramatic expression in English of personal anguish, also provide the language for English poetry's chronic mourning of absence (or at least marshal it the way that it was going), through eloquent—one wants to say fallen—words that we mainly hear in a deeply charged silence.

In effect, the language of inner thought and feeling in English might be described as having this kind of history: first appearing with force perhaps in Sidney's *Astrophil and Stella,* it finds its most trenchant expression in Shakespeare's *Sonnets,* migrates from there to his plays, survives powerfully in Milton's poetry, and then, after being approached in verse for much of the eighteenth century, is redramatized (but silently) in Wordsworth and later nineteenth-century lyric poetry, however widely this poetry varies in tone: from the controlled rhapsodies of Tennyson to the jaunty but unspoken (often, unspeakable) monologues of Browning, the musical reveries of Swinburne, the suppressed outbursts of Hopkins, and the moody meditations of Yeats. In modernist poetry it sometimes takes to disjunctive forms in order to foreground neurosis, dream, and trauma, and at last reemerges, blocked and all but silenced, barely voiced, in the stylized drama of Beckett and Pinter.

The Poem as Book

> I am to wait, though waiting so be hell,
> Not blame your pleasure, be it ill or well.
> —Shakespeare, Sonnet 58

But surely poets for centuries—even those who appear in Shakespeare's plays—have been in the habit of reading their poems aloud to each other or to larger audiences, and lovers of the poems of Tennyson, Kipling, and Yeats, of Longfellow, Poe, and Frost, have been reciting them in public or private for generations. Even if we grant that this poetry of silence has taken the route I suggest and has come to dominate the poetic earscape for much of the last two centuries, there has surely always been a strong countermovement that has run through Dryden and Pope, those public poets who constantly engage us as immediate listeners to their full-voiced verse; through prosodic dissenters like Smart, Blake, and Whitman; and gathering momentum in poets still of the silent tradition perhaps but moving toward open talk, blues, jazz, or rock—Pound, Williams, Langston Hughes, Ginsberg, and a host of others. But, except for anomalies like Vachel Lindsay or Dylan Thomas, not in our century till the late 1950s do poems convincingly requiring to be *sounded* come to be composed, partly inspired by popular-music "poets" like the Beatles and Bob Dylan. The poetry of open or free forms, indebted to rap, reggae, or other contemporary musical forms, committed to performance, associating poetry with ritual occasions, celebrations, and even Dionysian joy in plenitude, and usually intensely hostile to the more silent Apollonian verse of tradition, serves in our time as its chief challenger.

But that tradition remains strong. I would guess that even today most American poetry is read silently and is written by poets with the understanding that it usually will be unsounded but, they hope, silently "heard," an eminently speakable verse that normally goes unspoken. Even if they think of their work as, ideally, read aloud by an excellent reader (themselves or another), they know that most of the time it will be read without sound from the page, that the poem, in effect, is a book.

We recognize that the language of Shakespeare's *Sonnets* is not entirely confessional, distressed, aggrieved. We should notice at least one other voice we "hear" in these poems, the voice in which, as in lyric poetry of all ages and many languages, the poet, like Hamlet or Iachimo, consigns or confides his thoughts, observations, and insights to writing, as a means of preserving them, delayed messages for himself or others. Sonnet 77 recommends this procedure to the friend, whose thoughts, committed to the pages of his writing tablet, can be retrieved at a later time "To take a new acquaintance of thy mind." In the *Sonnets,* however, as in much earlier and later lyric verse, material of this kind is likely to have a personal edge, as it typically does in the plays. Wisdom (or foolish generalization) is not to be detached from the person who speaks it, and from his or her personal predicament or character. The sententiae that precede and modulate into John of Gaunt's impressive description of England's greatness are those of an ill and foolish old man who wants the sense or self-control to save his eloquence for Richard's ear. Similarly, the expression of general truths in Sonnets 66, 94, 129, and others can hardly be detached from the situation of their implicated speaker, whose local experience often leads to general statements about life (e.g., in S. 25, 39, 54, 57, 59, 60, 70, 84, 116, 119, 121). Later English poetry, too, includes many poems that serve as delayed and indefinitely delayable messages of general reflection to whoever is disposed to hear them—the poet, an absent lover, or anyone at all. The resource of writing offers a poet the opportunity to transfer the silent, unspoken thoughts of his brain, however inflected with personal feeling, to the equally silent register of, say, a sonnet.

Unlike plays, which offer us a sequence of voices actually heard and normally irreversible and unrecoverable, poems provide a continuous silent speech, which is easily recoverable from the writing or printing in which it is coded. In a sense, the page is always speaking, though at any moment no one may be listening; the paper has kept, in effect, the property of silence it had in the forest as a tree. Or to put it in an opposite image: "All verbal expression, whether put into writing, print, or the computer, is bound to sound forever."[18] The page, the poem, the book is always carrying on its inner discourse, like one of the driven characters in Renaissance plays, or like the electrical current that keeps running through our houses though all the lights have been turned off. In a literate culture, the library preserves the common wisdom, even when the doors are locked for the night; the book itself is an emblem of this feature of the culture. But of all books, the poem best epitomizes this relation of books to a culture, partly because of all writings poems are most recently (and most anciently) oral, even to the extent that their acoustical features (such as rhythm, assonance, alliteration, and phonological contrasts and balances) are still prominent in this silent medium; and partly because its language is often, even usually, imitative of the language we use in speaking to ourselves or in imagining our speaking with others. The poem is a quintessential book, always ready to be silently (or even vocally) read, as the book is a quintessential library. The poem may not always explicitly mourn an absence, but it waits, like a letter, in its permanently tuned silence—or like the lover of Sonnets 57 and 58—not for its own but for its reader's presence:

> Being your slave, what should I do but tend
> Upon the hours and times of your desire?
> . . . .
> O let me suffer, being at your beck,
> Th' imprisoned absence of your liberty—
> . . . .
> Be where you list, your charter is so strong
> That you yourself may privilege your time
> To what you will

From this point of view, confined to the page, denied its voice, what is poetry but silent speech that aspires to the condition of sound? But therein lie both its limitation and its strength, as an image of perpetual desire, like those figures on Keats's Grecian urn, or like Yeats's image of Keats as "a schoolboy" who

> made-being poor, ailing and ignorant,
> Shut out from all the luxury of the world . . .
> . . . .
> Luxuriant song.[19]

The emphasis of many of the *Sonnets* on separation and absence, on silent and patient waiting, on the "ever-fixèd mark / That looks on tempests and is never shaken" (S. 116), even in the face of life events that exhibit clearly all the evils of alteration and inconstancy, should not surprise us. Art always depends on negations, on frames that mark it off from what it isn't. If Renaissance portraits provide images that mime the living force they lack, drama offers a voiced enactment of actions that must not be violated by the actual. That Shakespeare understood how art thrives on such conventions, and on their deliberate ruptures, appears in the silence of the *Sonnets* (which may always break into sound), in the imagery, the supposes, and the intricately coded mirrorings of plays from *A Midsummer Night's Dream* to *The Tempest* (which greatly amplify the apparent range of events represented on the stage), and is nowhere made more manifest than when, almost at the end of his career, he authorizes the statue of Hermione, a likeness without life, to shatter the barrier between nature and art and from her stony sixteen-year absence step once more into life.

NOTES
INDEX

Notes

Preface

1. W. H. Auden, *The Dyer's Hand* (New York: Random House, 1962), 50.

Hendiadys and *Hamlet*

Reprinted, with corrections and minor changes, from *PMLA* 96 (1981): 168–93.

1. See, e.g., Sr. Miriam Joseph, *Shakespeare's Use of the Arts of Language* (New York: Hafner, 1947), 61–62, 298–99; and Richard A. Lanham, *A Handlist of Rhetorical Terms: A Guide for Students of English Literature* (Berkeley: University of California Press, 1969), 53. Brian Vickers never mentions hendiadys in his otherwise admirable *Classical Rhetoric in English Poetry* (London: Macmillan, 1970) or in his essay "Shakespeare's Use of Rhetoric," in *A New Companion to Shakespeare Studies,* ed. Kenneth Muir and S. Schoenbaum (Cambridge: Cambridge University Press, 1971), 83–98. The linguist Geoffrey N. Leech, impatient with those scholars of rhetoric for whom "the identification, classification, and labelling of specimens of given stylistic devices becomes an end in itself," pounces on hendiadys as an egregiously ridiculous instance of this obsession. He scoffs at "the survival in modern textbooks of figures like *hendiadys,* which we can value only as curiosities. . . . It is so rare that I have found no certain instance of it in English literature" (*A Linguistic Guide to English Poetry* [London: Longmans, 1969], 4).

2. Throughout, emphasis has been added in quotations to stress examples of hendiadys.

3. See E. Adelaide Hahn, "Hendiadys: Is There Such a Thing?" *Classical Weekly,* 8 May 1922: 193–97; Charles Gordon Cooper, *Journey to Hesperia* (London: Macmillan, 1959), 128–32; and Kenneth Quinn, *Virgil's Aeneid: A Critical Description* (Ann Arbor: University of Michigan Press, 1969), 423–28. Both Hahn and Cooper call the term hendiadys a "misnomer." Quinn includes the figure among the many devices that show Virgil's preference for coordinating structures over subor-

dinating ones; the poet's conscious purpose is to enforce "the constant assertion" (424) of the narrative, the insistent forward movement of the living past. Wherever possible, therefore, Virgil places the elements of a situation in coordinate syntax and expects his readers to recognize "the differing flavour of his words in the two arms of the parataxis" (426).

4. Baldwin, *William Shakspere's Small Latine and Lesse Greeke* (Urbana: University of Illinois Press, 1944), 2, 43. I have relied also on Joseph Xavier Brennan's doctoral dissertation, "The Epitome Troporum ac Schematum of Joannes Susenbrotus: Text, Translation, and Commentary." Diss. University of Illinois, 1953.

Susenbrotus cited as sources of his work the earlier lists of tropes and figures compiled by Mancinellus (*Carmen de Floribus,* 1489) and by Mosellanus (*Tabulae de Schematibus et Tropis,* 1529), both of whom briefly mention hendiadys, but his account of hendiadys is fuller and clearer than theirs and indicates that he had evidently also looked closely at Servius. Richard Sherry, who relied largely on Mosellanus (see Baldwin, 2, 35–37), omits any mention of hendiadys in his *A Treatise of Schemes and Tropes* (London, 1550). It was Susenbrotus's treatment of hendiadys, available only from 1562 on, that was taught in the schools, that Puttenham and Day must have consulted, and that must have caught Shakespeare's eye.

5. In his single paragraph on the subject, Susenbrotus, evidently puzzled, defines his puzzling figure three times: "an adjective is turned into a noun . . . one idea [*unum*] is explained through two . . . for poetic effect one idea [*res una*] is divided into two by an intervening conjunction, whether the other of those words signifying that idea be an adjective or a noun" (Brennan's trans.). The first two brief phrases are adapted from earlier writers, beginning with Mancinellus in 1489; the last comes directly from Servius (*Servii Grammatici,* ed. Georgius Thilo [Leipzig: B. G. Terbneri, 1878], 1, 36), but its crucial concluding clause is original with Susenbrotus: "sive alterum è vocibus rem illam significantibus, adiectivum, sive utrumque substantivum fuerit" 'whether the second of the words signifying that (single) idea be an adjective or a noun.' This comment suggests that there are two patterns: in one a phrase consisting of a noun and adjective (say, *pateris aureis* 'golden cups') is split into two substantives (*pateris et auro* 'cups and gold'); in the other a phrase consisting of a noun and a dependent genitive noun (*molem altorum montium* 'a heap of high mountains') is split into two substantives (*molemque et montes . . . altos* 'a heap and high mountains'). (Servius and Susenbrotus cite both these examples from Virgil.) If Shakespeare worked from Susenbrotus, the playwright's normal procedure may well have been either to break open relatively bland adjectival phrases like *furious sound* or *horrible image* (both discussed below) into striking coordinate phrases *("sound and fury," "image and horror")* or to work from genitive constructions, from *law of heraldry* to *"law and heraldry" (Hamlet* 1.1.87). In English, the force is largely the

same whether the phrasing is "law of heraldry" or "heraldic law," and Shakespeare may have started from either phrase as a base from which to begin his hendiadic transformations. Shakespeare's hendiadys, however, often appears to originate in, and to be translatable by, more complex phrasing: for example, *morning freshness* (or *fresh morning*) seems to be first transformed, by metaphor, into *morning dew* (or *dewy morning*) and thence, by hendiadys (and amplification), into "*the morn and liquid dew* of youth" (*Hamlet* 1.3.41). By contrast, in Milton, who may also have learned hendiadys at school from Susenbrotus, the figure almost always seems to follow one of the two types described above. (I am grateful to my colleague Calvin B. Kendall for helping me to fix more precisely the perceptions described in this note.)

Almost all quotations and line numbers from Shakespeare are based on G. B. Harrison, ed., *Shakespeare: The Complete Works* (New York: Harcourt, Brace, and World, 1968), but numerous other editions have been consulted, including David Bevington, ed., *The Complete Works of Shakespeare,* 3d ed. (Glenview, Ill.: Scott, Foresman, 1980); Sylvan Barnet, gen. ed., *The Complete Signet Classic Shakespeare* (New York: Harcourt Brace Jovanovich, 1972); G. Blakemore Evans, ed., *The Riverside Shakespeare* (Boston: Houghton Mifflin, 1974); George Lyman Kittredge, ed. *The Tragedy of Hamlet, Prince of Denmark* (Boston: Ginn, 1939); George Rylands, ed., *Hamlet* (Oxford: Clarendon, 1947); R. C. Bald, ed., *Hamlet* (New York: Appleton-Century-Crofts, 1946); Hardin Craig, ed., *An Introduction to Shakespeare* (New York: Scott, Foresman, 1952); and Horace Howard Furness, ed., *A New Variorum Edition of Shakespeare* (1877; rpt. New York: American Scholar, 1965), esp. the two vols. devoted to *Hamlet.*

6. Eliot, "Philip Massinger," *Selected Essays* (New York: Harcourt, Brace, 1932), 185.

7. George Puttenham, *The Arte of English Poesie* (Menston, England: Scolar, 1968), 142.

8. Carroll, *The Hunting of the Snark and Other Poems and Verses* (New York: Harper, 1903), 21; Alexander Pope, *The Rape of the Lock* 3. 158, 8; *The English Auden: Poems, Essays, and Dramatic Writings, 1927–1939,* ed. Edward Mendelson (New York. Random House, 1977), 203, 235, 241, 258; and *Collected Poems,* ed. Edward Mendelson (New York: Random House, 1976), 224.

9. H. W. Fowler, *Modern English Usage* (Oxford: Clarendon, 1957), 607. Hendiadys is treated under "Technical terms of rhetoric. . . ."

10. Smith, *Words and Idioms: Studies in the English Language* (Boston: Houghton Mifflin, 1925), 173. Smith's lists of doublets are on 173–75.

11. One exception is the familiar construction in which we link a person with something that belongs to the person: "I wanted to talk with you about *Susie and*

her grades"—i.e., about Susie's grades. Or: "Do you have any comment on *your opponent and the charges* he has brought against you?"—i e., your opponent's charges. Not all such constructions are reducible to one noun phrase, but many are. The speech of Laertes that I analyze at length below begins in the same manner: "For *Hamlet, and the trifling of his favor,*" which means "As for the trifling of Hamlet's favor." Having recognized only very late that this construction is sometimes a form of hendiadys (thanks again to my colleague Calvin B. Kendall), I may have missed a few instances of this form in my count of hendiadys in Shakespeare's plays. But examples are often problematical. Cassius is using hendiadys when he says, "You know that I held *Epicurus* strong, / *And his opinion*" (*Julius Caesar* 5.1.76–77); but Joan La Pucelle, though she is echoing a phrase of Plutarch's (and possibly of Caesar's), has two distinct ideas in mind when she compares herself to "that proud insulting ship / Which *Caesar and his fortune* bare at once" (*Henry VI, Part1* 1.2.138–39).

12. *The Collected Poems of Dylan Thomas* (New York: New Directions, 1971), 142, 112.

13. From *Pseudodoxia Epidemica* (1646) and *Religio Medici* (1642), in *The Prose of Sir Thomas Browne,* ed Norman Endicott (New York. New York University Press, 1968), 97 and 47. I am grateful to my colleague Gordon W. O'Brien for calling my attention to Browne's use of hendiadys and for helping me read some Shakespearean phrases more accurately.

14. See *Paradise Lost* 1.233–34, 771, 786; 2.67, 69, 80, 346; 3.417; 4.562; 5.349, 10.345–46, 956; *Paradise Regained* 1.457; 2.29; 4.439; *Samson Agonistes* 2.34, 1654. These seem likely instances, 17 in 14,393 lines, or 1 in every 847 lines.

15. See, e.g., Maurice Charney, *Style in Hamlet* (Princeton, N.J.: Princeton University Press, 1969). In Renaissance lists of rhetorical schemes, hendiadys is treated as a figure, not as a trope, for its point lies in its peculiar syntax, not in the alteration of meaning that is usually felt to be the mark of a trope, whether the alteration occurs in a single word, as often in metaphor, metonymy, synecdoche, and so on, or proceeds from a governing design, as in allegory or a sustained ironic structure. But to find in the figure such extensive meanings as the present essay proposes is, in effect, to suggest that hendiadys has the force of a trope and helps in some measure to organize the meanings of the play.

16. Harley Granville-Barker, *Prefaces to Shakespeare* (Princeton, N.J.: Princeton University Press, 1946), 1, 169–70.

17. Editors frequently gloss this phrase in a way that confirms my reading of hendiadys. Harrison hears *indued* as "endowed; i.e., a creature whose natural home is the water *(element)."* Other editors offer such readings for *indued* as "adapted by nature" (Kittredge and Bevington), "in harmony with" (Signet), "belonging to" (Rylands), "habituated" (Evans), or "accustomed" (Bald). C. T. Onions's *A Shakespeare Glos-*

sary (Oxford: Clarendon, 1919) suggests "endowed with qualities fitting her for living in water." None of these has any warrant from the *OED,* but that work's fourth meaning for the word ("To lead on; to bring up, educate, instruct") is probably the one Shakespeare had mainly in mind. Ophelia seems a creature native to the water and brought up in it—two distinct ideas and hence not hendiadys, except that, since the historical confusion between *indued* (or *endued*) and *endowed* existed in the Renaissance, Shakespeare and his audience may well have heard not only the meaning just proposed but also, perhaps a little loosely, "natively endowed."

18. After this essay was published, in response to a helpful letter sent to *PMLA* by Prof. Katharine T. Loesch, I added a note on the medieval custom of using "two Old English words to render one Latin word" and on the practice, by Middle English and later writers, of joining "one native English word with a foreign derivative, a polysyllable with a monosyllable, or an abstract with a concrete term." Although "the peculiar elusive character of hendiadys does not enter into these early word pairs," Shakespeare, evidently "familiar with the rhetorical advantages of using asymmetrical word pairs but, unlike most of his predecessors, also aware . . . of the Virgilian pattern of hendiadys, learned to fuse the two techniques—to write phrases in which the two conjoined terms would not only mix styles (English with foreign, long word with short, abstract with concrete) but would also convey a sense of structural uncertainty and problematical meaning." Examples: *expectancy and rose, fantasy and trick, voice and precedent* ("Forum," *PMLA* 97 [1981]: 99–100).

19. Cf. Pyrrhus, in the heroic extract Hamlet begins and the First Player continues:

> So as a painted tyrant Pyrrhus stood
> And like a neutral to his will and matter,
> Did nothing.
> (2.2.502–4)

That "Did nothing" constitutes the whole of 1.504 emphasizes the blankness of Pyrrhus's stance and state of mind.

20. Cf. *"youth and liberty"* (2.1.24) and *"youth and havior"* or *"humour"* (2.2.12), which work the same way, and, in *All's Well That Ends Well, "youth and ignorance"* (2.3.171). Such phrases contrast sharply with those that join parallel terms—e.g., "youth and nobleness of birth" (*The Two Gentlemen of Verona* 1.3.33).

21. "In *form and moving* how *express and admirable!"* Hamlet has earlier exclaimed about man (2.2.316–17). Although the two nouns could be taken separately, they seem more effective in combination: "in his form, and in the movements of that form." It would seem more appropriate to describe the movements of the body as "express" than to speak so of the body at rest. The word *moving* sets the idea of *form* in motion.

Most editors have felt some anxiety about *express.* Several gloss it as "exact," one as "well-devised," another as "well-framed(?)." Rylands suggests "active, purposeful, *or* well-modelled (Lat. *exprimere,* to portray)." Kittredge offers "precisely adapted to its purpose—like a delicately adjusted piece of mechanism." (He does not say what mechanism—a Swiss watch? the 3:18 to Stratford?—Shakespeare may have had in mind) But most of the *OED*'s meanings for *express* emphasize the idea of distinctness: clearly outlined, sharp, definite, explicit. So "how express and admirable" probably means "how admirably distinct, how wonderfully clear and sharp in the articulation of its form."

22. Appendix 3 shows that the *OED* sometimes misreads words in Shakespeare because of misconceptions about his coordinate phrases.

23. The First Folio and First Quarto read "abstracts." Most editors prefer *abstract* and, in failing to gloss it, imply that it is an adjective, although Kittredge (after Clark and Wright) notes, "Always a noun in Shakespeare." The plural form fits better with *chronicles.* The singular form offers the modern reader a pleasing elusiveness—what is an abstract chronicle, exactly? But I take Shakespeare to have meant that the players (in concert, in what they perform together) are abstracts of the time, i.e., they summarize the time, extract its essence, in the form of brief chronicles.

24. The form of example 57 ("Poor Ophelia / Divided from herself and her fair judgment") is not analyzed in my list of deviations; it seems too anomalous. Still, Shakespeare frequently writes phrases that join a self with a part or a possession of the self or that join what seem to be two different kinds or parts of the self. *Antony and Cleopatra* has several such phrases: "I and my sword" (3.13.175), "Mine honesty and I" (3.13.41), "My resolution and my hands" (4.15.49). Cf. Lady Macbeth's "Your constancy / Hath left you unattended" (2.2.68–69); or "Virtue and she / Is her own dower" (*All's Well That Ends Well* 2.3.150–51). Such phrases show a kind of schizophrenic division in the self that is not unusual in Shakespeare. But if Laertes, in the speech discussed earlier in this essay, sees Ophelia as dual, this phrase of Claudius's seems to divide her into three. What part of her can be "Divided from herself," except another self? And both are to be understood as distinct from her judgment. But this strange situation forced on us by the syntax dissolves if we see that the last five words amount to hendiadys for "her own fair judgment."

The Lyric Tense

Reprinted, with minor corrections and a small title change, from *PMLA* 89 (1974): 563–79, where it appears as "The Lyric Present: Simple Present Verbs in English Poems."

1. Scholars wrestling explicitly with the uses of progressive and simple forms include Jacobus van der Laan, *An Enquiry on a Psychological Basis into the Use of the Progressive Form in Late Modern English* (Gorinchem: Duym, 1922); Fernand Mossé,

Histoire de la forme périphrastique, être+participe présent en germanique (Paris: Klincksieck, 1938); Thomas Satchell, "Expanded Tenses," *English Studies* 21 (1939): 214–17; Leah Dennis, "The Progressive Tense: Frequency of Its Use in English," *PMLA,* 55 (1940): 855–65; Edward Calver, "The Uses of the Present Tense Forms in English," *Language* 22 (1945): 317–25; Dwight L. Bolinger, "More on the Present Tense in English," *Language* 23 (1947): 434–36; A. S. Hornby, "Non-conclusive Verbs: Some Notes on the Progressive Tenses," *English Language Teaching* 3 (May 1949): 172–77; Anna Granville Hatcher, "The Use of the Progressive Form in English," *Language* 27 (1951): 254–80; Eric Buyssens, *Les Deux Aspectifs de la conjugaison anglaise au XXe siècle* (Bruxelles: Presses Universitaires de Bruxelles, 1968); F. G. A. M. Aarts, "On the Use of the Progressive and Non-progressive Present with Future Reference in Present-day English," *English Studies* 50 (1969): 565–79; and J. A. Van Ek, "The 'Progressive' Reconsidered," *English Studies* 50 (1969): 579–85.

Among more general studies of the English verb that try to throw light on the simple progressive problem are: Otto Jespersen, *The Philosophy of Grammar* (London: Allen and Unwin, 1924); H. Poutsma, *A Grammar of Late Modern English,* pt. 2, sec. 2: The Verb and the Particles (Groningen: P. Noordhoff, 1926); B. Trnka, *On the Syntax of the English Verb from Caxton to Dryden,* Travaux du Cercle Linguistique de Prague, No. 3 (Prague: Jednota c̆eskoslovenských matematiků a fysiků, 1930); George O. Curme, *Syntax,* vol. 3 of *A Grammar of the English Language* (Boston: Heath, 1931); A. S. Hornby, *A Guide to Patterns and Usage in English* (London: Oxford University Press, 1954); Archibald A. Hill, *Introduction to Linguistic Structures* (New York: Harcourt, 1958); Tauno F. Mustanoja, *A Middle English Syntax* (Helsinki: Société Néophilologique, 1960); Yngve Olsson, *On the Syntax of the English Verb,* Gothenburg Studies in English, No. 12 (Göteborg: Elander, 1961); Ralph B. Long, *The Sentence and Its Parts: A Grammar of Contemporary English* (Chicago: University of Chicago Press, 1961); F. R. Palmer, *A Linguistic Study of the English Verb* (London: Longmans, 1965); David Crystal, "Specification and English Tenses," *Journal of Linguistics* 2 (April 1966), 1–34; W. H. Hirtle, *The Simple and Progressive Forms: An Analytical Approach* (Québec: Presses de l'Université Laval, 1967); and what seem to me the most impressive works on the subject: William Diver, "The Chronological System of the English Verb," *Word* 19 (1963), 141–81; and Martin Joos, *The English Verb: Form and Meanings* (Madison: University of Wisconsin Press, 1964).

Study of the progressive, and of English verbs generally, has been complicated and probably obfuscated by the understandable efforts of linguists to explain what goes on in English by referring to only partly pertinent foreign models. In particular, they have been misled by the Latin participial adjective *(sum amans),* which for a long time gave uneasy justification to the English progressive, and more recently by the "aspect" of Slavonic verbs, a term that many of the above-mentioned writers use in trying to fix the respective functions of simple and progressive forms in English. English practice, however, so eludes formulation that virtually all scholars who distinguish aspects in English verbs do so differently from their colleagues. The result is Babel. Among the aspects proposed by various scholars are: point-action, momentaneous, ingressive, inchoate, inchoative, effective, imperfective, perfective, perfect, non-perfect, durative (including durative-progressive and durative-terminate, or indefinitely durative, ingressively durative, terminately durative and continuatively durative), continuative, continuous, terminate, terminative, egressive, iterative (including momentaneously iterative and duratively iterative), Iterativum, Frequentativum, Inchoativum, Intensivum, Kausativum, static, dynamic, common, progressive, temporary, and generic. For a fascinating history of the origins of the aspect hunt and an attack on the usefulness of the term, see R. W. Zandvoort, "Is 'Aspect' an English Verbal Category?" *Contributions to English Syntax and Philology,* Gothenburg Studies in English, No. 14 (Göteborg: Almkvist and Wiksell, 1962), 1–20.

2. E.g., J. Kerkhof, *Studies in the Language of Geoffrey Chaucer* (Leyden: Universitaire pers Leyden, 1966); Georg Fridén, *Studies on the Tenses of the English Verb from Chaucer to Shakespeare with Special Reference to the Late Sixteenth Century* (Uppsala: Almkvist and Wiksell, 1948); and the already cited works by Laan, Mossé, Dennis, and Buyssens.

3. This does not contradict the statement above that the lyric tense verb describes an action that takes place once and endures. For me at least it makes sense to say that the *poem* is repeatable; on each repetition the *action* of the poem resumes.

4. English is, of course, not one of the languages that use a special aorist form on such occasions; the simple present or simple past verb must do the job.

5. E.g.: "Here *let him tell* her a great long tale in her ear" *(Roister Doister); Exeat, Exeant* (many plays); "Here *must* Crapine *be coming in* with a basket and a stick in his hand" *(Supposes);* "*Pointing* behind to his torn breeches" *(Gammer Gurton's Needle);* "And *gave* him a good blow on the buttock" *(Gorboduc);* "*Fall* down and *quake*" *(Mucedorus);* "*Sit* down and *knock* your head" *(Friar Bacon and Friar Bungay);* "*Stab* him" *(The Spanish Tragedy);* "*Kiss, kiss, kiss*" *(Cambises, King of Persia).*

6. Other examples of introductory but unlocated pasts in familiar poems:

> I *struck* the board and *cried*
> (Herbert)
>
> I *made* my song a coat
> (Yeats)
>
> I *met* a traveler from an antique land
> (Shelley)

He *stood,* and *heard* the steeple
(Housman)

Burbank *crossed* a little bridge
(Eliot)

She *sang* beyond the genius of the sea.
(Stevens)

7. New York: Scribner's, 1953, pp. 267–68.

8. Louis Simpson, *Selected Poems* (New York: Harcourt, 1965), 138. The other lines, of course, are by Nashe, Gray, Keats, and Tennyson.

9. See Langer, "A Note on the Film," *Feeling and Form: A Theory of Art,* 411–15.

10. Poems quoted in this sentence are, in order: Shapiro, "Nostalgia"; Hughes, "Hawk Roosting"; Ginsberg, "Wichita Vortex Sutra"; Simpson, "American Preludes."

11. *Molloy* in *Molloy. Malone Dies. The Unnamable* (New York: Grove, 1959), 26.

12. That *I stand* or *I walk* should become paradigms for the assertion of reality in our time has abundant ironies: on the one hand, "I" is real, the source of thought, perception, and sensation, while "stand" or "walk" is unlocated and hence unreal; on the other hand, every "I" is mortal and tentative whereas the lyric tense action is eternal. The conjunction of the two serves almost as a figure for the contradictions and anxieties we feel in all our experience.

13. The lines surveyed were not, of course, all of the same length. Hence, for poets who use many short lines (Donne, Herbert, Herrick, Yeats, Pound, Roethke, and most recent poets), the ratios given should probably be lower than they are; for poets who use abnormally long lines (Whitman), they should be higher. On the whole, if such adjustments were made, the tendencies noted here would be even more pronounced than they are.

14. Or 164 years if we disregard Gray, two of whose three progressives are mere fooling around (e.g., "The Master of Maudlin / In the same dirt is dawdling").

15. Such highlighting frequently occurs in speech and prose. See Laan, 7, 13, 19.

Supposing a Measure for *Measure for Measure*

1. See George Gascoigne, *Supposes. Early Plays from the Italian,* ed. R. Warwick Bond (New York: Benjamin Blom, [1911], 3–73. I am indebted also to Donald Beecher's learned and helpful introduction to his and John Butler's recent edition of *Supposes* (Ottawa: Dovehouse Editions, 1999 [Carleton Renaissance Plays in Translation 33].

2. Shakespeare's plays are quoted from *The Riverside Shakespeare*, ed. G. Blakemore Evans, 2d ed. (Boston: Houghton Mifflin, 1997), his sonnets from *Shakespeare's Sonnets*, ed. Stephen Booth (New Haven, Conn.: Yale University Press, 1977).

3. "Sure, my mind giues me," says Lytio, "that we shall find a new *Erostrato* ere it be long" (4.6.26–27). Lytio is just talking loosely, but he turns out to be right. Another example occurs at 5.5.142–43.

4. See David P. Young, *Something of Great Constancy: The Art of "A Midsummer Night's Dream"* (New Haven, Conn.: Yale University Press, 1966 [Yale Studies in English, vol. 164] for some helpful analysis of the mistakes, misapprehensions, and mirrors in this play.

5. The casting of plays is another form of theatrical supposing *(What if Olivier were to play Hamlet or Richard III?)*, and the same could be said of every other aspect of production—sets, lighting, direction, etc.

6. In theorizing that Shakespeare's consistent technique in his comedies (and often in other plays) is to present discrepancies of awareness between different characters and between them and the audience, Bertrand Evans long ago developed an argument that bears some resemblance to the one proposed here (see his *Shakespeare's Comedies* (Oxford: Clarendon Press, 1960). Evans's detailed analyses of the "discrepant awarenesses" in the comedies, scene by scene and character by character, show clearly that whether limited awareness is brought about by active deception or by limited access to important information (both crucial to the action of *Measure for Measure*), the characters and the audience differ in their knowledge of what is going on.

Valuable as this analysis is, the idea of supposes requires a somewhat different perspective. The term implies a more active construction of a character's view than "awareness" does. For Evans, the characters, given or denied information, either know or do not know something. But *supposing* suggests that out of what they know and do not know they build their beliefs and base their actions. Shakespeare himself offers the best example in this very play, comparing "man, proud man," in his ignorance "of what he's most assured, / His glassy essence," to "an angry ape" playing "fantastic tricks before high heaven" (2.2.117–21). For supposing takes in not only the idea of limited awareness but also that of behaving foolishly on the strength of that mistaken belief—the basis, in fact, of much comedy and tragedy. The term *supposing* also brings into play, as we shall see, a wider range of contexts—grammatical, legal, rhetorical, ethical—which, along with more direct verbal and visual deceptions, contribute to our understanding of what is involved in "mystaking."

7. Even fewer scholars have found in Gascoigne's idea of supposes a key to *The Taming of the Shrew* or to Shakespeare's dramatic practice in general. A notable ex-

ception is Cecil C. Seronsky's excellent essay ("'Supposes' as the Unifying Theme in *The Taming of the Shrew,*" *Shakespeare Quarterly* 44 [1963], 15–32), which argues, among other points, that Shakespeare, with his usual penetration, made supposes the focus of the whole play—plot, subplot, and Induction. While other characters pretend to be tutors, Petruchio alone really succeeds as a teacher, and whereas Bianca turns out to be very different from what we and other characters supposed her to be, Katharina learns to be the admirable woman Petruchio has all along supposed her.

8. Alexander Leggatt's fine study ("Substitution in *Measure for Measure,*" *Shakespeare Quarterly* 39 [1989], 342–59) traces the manifold substitutions and parallels in the play and emphasizes how all of them hold good only up to a point. The play offers a long series of "representations that are vivid but not quite adequate, and substitutions that are revealing and fascinating but incomplete" (359). My emphasis here on "supposes" is meant to suggest that there is more to the play than even his seemingly exhaustive essay reveals.

9. See *A New Variorum Edition of Shakespeare: Measure for Measure,* ed. Mark Eccles (New York: The Modern Language Association of America, 1980), 301–87.

10. Evans, too, stresses the Duke's superior awareness to that of the other characters from the point in 3.1. when he overhears the intense exchange between Claudio and Isabella; and the audience from then on shares his superior awareness.

11. Directors and actors, of course, are free to produce a play that will have this look. Old plays can be put into new bottles; wine can be mixed with water or fizz. But what results is not wine, and a *Measure for Measure* that focuses on the Duke's personal and official meanness and corruption has traveled a fair distance away from Shakespeare's *Measure for Measure.* The quoted phrase appears on p. 375 of Harry Berger Jr.'s essay "What Does the Duke Know and When Does He Know It? Carrying the Torch in *Measure for Measure,*" in *Making Trifles of Terrors: Redistributing Complicities in Shakespeare* (Stanford, Calif.: Stanford University Press, 1997), 335–426.

12. For criticism hostile to the Duke and to Isabella, see Berger's essay cited in n. 11, and Graham Bradshaw, "Tempering Justice with Mercy: *Measure for Measure,*" in *Shakespeare's Scepticism* (Brighton: Harvester Press, 1987), 164–218. (These are both brillant critics whose other writing on Shakespeare I have usually much admired.) Bradshaw's indictment of Vincentio and Isabella is finely argued but fails to credit points that might be made in their favor, and, for all its impressive marshaling of authorities and analogues from Sir Thomas Elyot to *Billy Budd,* gives no reason to think that Shakespeare was guided more by Elyot on law than by Wilson on slander (see Appendix: On Slander and Self-Regard). Bradshaw is austere in following Elyot, permissive on slander; he scores Isabella's failure to express sympathy with

Julietta, but gives her no credit for kneeling, at Mariana's request, to beg mercy for an Angelo who she thinks has killed her brother.

Berger's equally eloquent assault on the Duke and Isabella is more tendentious and unrestrained. Accepting Jonathan Dollimore's doctrinaire view of the Duke "as an illustration or embodiment of the way patriarchal authoritarianism manifests and deals with the fears endemic to a social structure in which exploitation is mystified in hierarchy" (338), he is repelled by Isabella's "ferocity" (372) and by the Duke's "campaign against Angelo" (394), "his dirty work" (373), "The outlandishness of his discourse of self-exculpation" (416), vices perhaps to be found as well in the merciless intensity of Berger's own charges: "the traces of motivation given off by the Duke's language and behavior may be read as indices of something like a black hole that sucks in all exculpatory matter around it" (381). Lucio, in contrast, is "playfully fractious and irreverent" (375); Angelo at moments is "tormented and sympathetic" (373).

Berger's portrait of Vincentio as a vicious authority owes much to the political anti-authoritarianism of late-twentieth-century intellectuals, and at every point his indictment of the Duke, who is, ostensibly at least, trying to make his realm more just, might serve equally well as an indictment of the Christian God. Berger never makes this extension of his argument explicit, but, given that the parallel between God and earthly rulers was a Renaissance commonplace and has often been invoked in Christian readings of this play, it is difficult to believe it hasn't occurred to him. If Vincentio is "complicit" in the corruption of Vienna, as Berger repeatedly charges, then presumably God is equally complicit in the evil of the world that, according to Christian belief, He has created. But can Shakespeare have meant to indict the Christian God for trapping and scapegoating sinners (for setting up Adam and Eve, for example) as Berger claims the Duke traps Angelo? A reading of the Duke in psychological terms only, or in the context of twentieth-century politics, ignores Renaissance attitudes toward apparently earnest and well-intentioned rulers like Vincentio and Prospero. Even the title of Berger's essay ("What Does the Duke Know and When Does He Know It? . . .") suggests that he sees in the Duke an image, with all its shameful associations, of the Watergate Richard Nixon.

13. Critics have often commented on the sensuality of Isabella's imagery at this juncture, but more rarely on Angelo's infusion of this ostensibly abstract supposal with sensuous suggestion ("lay down the treasures of your body"—presumably looking them over as he speaks). The sexual suggestiveness of Ariosto's "suppositi" is also deftly realized in "To this supposed."

14. Here, too, Shakespeare has made the contrast more striking by presenting Angelo as hitherto an unusually righteous man; in earlier versions the equivalent character's good reputation makes a milder contrast with the story's exhibition of

his corruption. There is additional drama, then, in Angelo's falling-off from virtue, and additional point in the contrast with Isabella's refusal to compromise hers, even though in the course of the play she does learn to be more forgiving.

15. Even some middle-of-the-road critics (e.g., Darryl G. Gless, in *Measure for Measure, The Law, and the Convent* [Princeton, N.J.: Princeton University Press, 1979]) condemn Isabel for this anger, more than they fault Claudio for begging his sister to submit to seduction. What they seem to overlook is how human it is for both characters to see the case (as they suppose it to be) from their own deeply interested points of view.

16. Isabella's plea for Angelo's life is not the first favor she has done him. In consenting to the bed trick she is not, as some critics have claimed, behaving like a bawd herself; she is helping Angelo, bent on wrong, to commit a lesser sin, one that may be forgiven if he marries Mariana. (See Victoria Hayne, "Performing Social Practice: The Example of *Measure for Measure,*" *Shakespeare Quarterly* 44 [1993], 3–8.

17. Jane Williamson, "The Duke and Isabella on the Modern Stage," in *The Triple Bond: Plays, Mainly Shakespearean, in Performance,* ed. Joseph Price (University Park: Pennsylvania State University Press, 1975). See also Ralph Berry, *Changing Styles in Shakespeare* (London: Allen & Unwin, 1981); and Herbert S. Weil Jr., "'Your Sense Pursues Not Mine': Changing Images of Two Pairs of Antagonists," in *Images of Shakespeare,* ed. Werner Habicht et al. (Newark: University of Delaware Press, 1988), 149–69.

18. Alvin Kernan's admirable book *Shakespeare, the King's Playwright: Theater in the Stuart Court, 1603–1613* (New Haven, Conn.: Yale University Press, 1995) fills in the political background against which many of Shakespeare's Jacobean plays need to be read. On *Measure for Measure* Kernan writes: "Duke Vincentio of Vienna was not King James I of Great Britain, but everyone in the original audience would have noticed that they shared a number of personality traits, problems with the law, and ways of transcending the law to achieve justice" (63).

19. Biblical analogues to such special moments of celebration include the return of the prodigal son (Luke 15: 11–32), when the father's joy may seem unfair to the son who never strayed. The parable of the laborers in the vineyard (Matt.: 20:1–16) further suggests that a generous judge may, even in more ordinary circumstances, give equal rewards to workers who have toiled different numbers of hours. Although the Duke ostensibly commits his city to the measure-for-measure theory of justice, his practice follows more closely the discretionary model of Christ's parables and Isabella's "merciful heaven."

20. See esp. Philip C. McGuire, "The Final Silences of *Measure for Measure,*" in *Speechless Dialect: Shakespeare's Open Silences* (Berkeley: University of California Press, 1985), 63–96.

21. See Appendix: On Slander and Self-Regard, p. 000.

22. As Victoria Hayne astutely observes: "The typicality of the social practices the play performs suggests that most members of the audience would recognize that the Duke's orders complete what the couples themselves began; that, Lucio's protests notwithstanding, no one is forced to marry as punishment for crime; that the resolutions, however extraordinary the Duke's methods of achieving them, were the resolutions communities would have expected and the ecclesiastical courts did require of similar relationships in the world outside the play" (28).

Wyatt's Decasyllabic Line

This essay is reprinted from *Studies in Philology* 82 (1985):129–56. A much shorter and somewhat different version appeared in my *Shakespeare's Metrical Art*, 27–37.

1. Patricia Thomson, ed., *Wyatt: The Critical Heritage* (London: Routledge & Kegan Paul, 1974), 17.

2. The main recent text is *Collected Poems of Sir Thomas Wyatt*, ed. Kenneth Muir and Patricia Thomson (Liverpool: Liverpool University Press, 1969). But it has been sharply criticized by two other textual scholars: H. A. Mason, *Editing Wyatt: An Examination of Collected Poems of Sir Thomas Wyatt, together with suggestions for an improved edition* (Cambridge: Cambridge Quarterly Publications, 1972); and Richard Harrier, *The Canon of Sir Thomas Wyatt's Poetry* (Cambridge: Mass.: Harvard University Press, 1975). Poems cited here are quoted from Muir and Thomson, but some lines have been emended on the authority of Harrier. [See also *Sir Thomas Wyatt: The Complete Poems,* ed. R. A. Rebholz (New Haven, Conn.: Yale University Press, 1978).]

3. See H. A. Mason, *Humanism and Poetry in the Early Tudor Period* (London: Routledge & Kegan Paul, 1959); John Stevens, *Music and Poetry in the Early Tudor Court* (Cambridge: Cambridge University Press, 1961); Kenneth Muir, *Life and Letters of Sir Thomas Wyatt* (Liverpool: Liverpool University Press, 1963); Raymond Southall, *The Courtly Maker: An Essay on the Poetry of Wyatt and His Contemporaries* (Oxford: Basil Blackwell, 1964); and Patricia Thomson, *Sir Thomas Wyatt and His Background* (London: Routledge & Kegan Paul, 1964).

4. George Saintsbury, *A History of English Prosody from the Twelfth Century to the Present Day* (London: Macmillan, 1923), 1, 223.

5. Saintsbury, 1, 305.

6. Thomson, ed. *Wyatt,* 8–11.

7. "Extract from Unsigned Review of Tillyard's Edition of Wyatt's Poems," from *Times Literary Supplement,* 19 Sept. 1929, quoted from Thomson, ed., *Wyatt,*

170. Cf. C. S. Lewis's similar remarks in *English Literature in the Sixteenth Century, Excluding Drama* (Oxford: Clarendon Press, 1954), 225, also included in Thomson, 175–76.

8. Southall, 154.
9. Southall, 156.
10. "The Fifteenth-Century Heroic Line," in *Essays and Studies by Members of the English Association* 24 (Oxford: Clarendon Press, 1939), 28–41.
11. "The Rhythmical Intention in Wyatt's Poetry," *Scrutiny,* 14 (1946): 97.
12. Southall, 146–47.
13. Harding's phrasal theory, as developed by Southall, has been used by Andrew Welsh—unwarily, I think—for further speculation about poetic rhythm. See *Roots of Lyric: Primitive Poetry and Modern Poetics* (Princeton, N.J.: Princeton University Press, 1978), esp. 225–32. The quest for a phrasal metric in Chaucer has had two strong advocates in Ian Robinson and the late James G. Southworth. See Southworth, *Verses of Cadence: An Introduction to the Prosody of Chaucer and His Followers* (Oxford: Basil Blackwell, 1954) and *The Prosody of Chaucer and His Followers* (Oxford: Basil Blackwell, 1962); and Robinson, *Chaucer's Prosody: A Study of the Middle English Verse Tradition* (Cambridge: Cambridge University Press, 1971). But their quarrel is mainly with the antediluvian notions of a group of prosodists who clustered around James Wilson Bright of Johns Hopkins University at the turn of the nineteenth century. Bright claimed that English iambic poetry was best read by stressing every second, fourth, sixth, eighth, and tenth syllable, no matter how it distorted the "prose rhythm." (Some exceptions were made for initial and third-foot trochees.) When the ictus fell on syllables like *the* or *to* or on the minor syllables of major words *(pacíng, evér)*, those syllables were drawn out quantitatively and their pitch was raised. (One would like to have heard a reading based on this theory, which is a little hard to grasp without one.) What justified a verse that resulted in such distortions of normal speech (as in "Păcíng, păcíng away the aching night" or "Ĕvér the snare was set, ĕvér in vain" or "Ŏf thé mĭghtý prínce óf fămóus hŏnóur") was the "exaltation" of the poets, their wish to write a high "heroic line," which typically appears in stanzas we know by the lofty name *rime royal* and is appropriate to a "grand style." See Albert H. Licklider, *Chapters on the Metric of the Chaucerian Tradition* (Baltimore: J. H. Furst Company, 1910; Ph.D. diss., Johns Hopkins University). The examples given above are Licklider's own, scanned as he scans them (142, 151). See also Bright and Raymond Durbin Miller, *The Elements of English Versification* (Boston: Ginn and Company, 1910), esp. chap. 4.
14. *A Study of Sir Thomas Wyatt's Poems* (New York: Russell & Russell, Inc., 1964 [1911]). See esp. chap. 6.
15. "The Scansion of Wyatt's Early Sonnets," *SP* 20 (1923): 137–52.

16. *Lydgate's Temple of Glas,* ed. J. Schick, EETS (London: Kegan Paul, Trench, Trübner & Co., 1891), lvi–lx. Schick's classification derives from the more elaborate discussion of line-types in J. Schipper's three-volume *Englische Metrick* (Bonn: Verlag von Emil Strauss, 1888), available to English readers in Schipper's *A History of English Versification* (Oxford: Clarendon Press, 1910).

17. That the names for these lines—headless, broken-backed—sound remarkably violent for so sedentary a pursuit as prosody may suggest that there is more to this subject than meets the ear. I have been unable to learn who first used these terms, though "acephalous" (headless) goes back at least to the eighteenth century. Other terms, such as "waistless" and "double-waisted" for lines with too few or too many syllables at the caesura, were evidently coined by Eilert Ekwall, editor of Lydgate's *Siege of Thebes.* Some scholars prefer to call the "broken-backed" line the "breakback" line. Incidentally, Alan Swallow evidently misread C. S. Lewis's article cited in n. 6 and came away from it thinking that the broken-backed line is "four-beat doggerel," a "line of four marked accents divided in the middle by a heavy caesura" (4), a view that subsequently misled some abler critics. See his article "The Pentameter Lines in Skelton and Wyatt," *MP* 48 (1950): 1–11.

18. In Fitzroy Pyle's sample of two thousand lines by Lydgate, 97.55 percent of them break after the fourth or fifth syllable. See his excellent article "The Pedigree of Lydgate's Heroic Line, with a Note on His Use of the Line-types," *Hermathena,* 25 (1937), 26–59.

19. The final possibility—no caesura at all—may be only a theoretical one in this system, for where the caesura is so fixed a habit a poet cannot construct an English line that forbids that quasi-structural pause. Other variations from the types listed above, such as lines with monosyllabic or hypersyllabic patterns for other feet than the first or third, or lines of four or six stresses, are so eccentric that they seem to fall outside the system and, when they occur at all, to constitute deliberate violations of it. That is, they are in character closer to metrical variations than to line-types that serve as norms of the system.

20. See Sergio Baldi, *La poesia di Sir Thomas Wyatt* (Florence, Italy: Le Monnier, 1953), 123–24; and Robert Bridges, *Milton's Prosody* (Oxford: Oxford University Press, 1921), 9–37.

21. Pyle is especially convincing on this point (41–48). So is Eleanor Hammond in "The Nine-syllabled Line in Some Post-Chaucerian Manuscripts," *MP* 23 (1926): 129–52, and in the introduction (17–26) and extensive headnotes to various selections in her anthology *English Verse between Chaucer and Surrey* (New York: Octagon Books, 1965 [1927]).

22. Percy Simpson, among others, has wondered whether there was "in this period a much less marked difference between stressed and unstressed syllables." See

"The Rhyming of Stressed with Unstressed Syllables in Elizabethan Verse," *MLR* 38 (1943): 129.

23. For example:

    l. 2: Whĕre hé ĭs thát mÿn óft / móistĕth ănd wásshĕth   1af
    l. 4: Fŏr tŏ rést ĭn hís / wóroldlў párădíse   2b
    l. 6: Whăt wébbĕs hé hăth wróught / wĕll hé pĕrcévĕth   1af
    l. 9: Thŭs is it ĭn súche / éxtrémĭtĭe bróught   2
    l. 11: Twÿst mísĕrÿ ănd wélth, / twĭst érnest ănd gáme   1

Other readings may result from pronouncing final -*e* in *swete* or *rote*, but Wyatt seems not to pronounce a final -*e* when he doesn't need to.

24. All the lines of "They fle from me" are metrically intelligible by the system of line-types described in this essay. See *Shakespeare's Metrical Art*, where the first stanza is scanned (32–33).

25. See, for example, the lines quoted by Derek Pearsall in his *John Lydgate* (London: Routledge & Kegan Paul, 1970), 62–63.

26. Hammond, *English Verse between Chaucer and Surrey*, 22.

27. For all we know, many of the lines that give us difficulty may have been left in an unfinished state; Wyatt may have liked their phrasing but recognized their metrical problems and yet been unable to devise better alternatives before circulating them. To leave a poem—an unpublished poem, after all—slightly unfinished, or to abandon it with an awareness of its imperfections, would probably not have seemed a high crime to Wyatt. How could he know that 450 years later we would be weighing his syllables with such concern?

28. *The Siege of Thebes*, ed. Axel Erdmann (London: Kegan Paul, Trench, Trübner & Co., 1911), 168 (ll. 4088–94).

29. Pearsall, 62. Pearsall reserves his scorn for "aggressive variants which have no rhetorical point" (62). See also Pyle and Hammond (n. 21, above).

30. Hoccleve, too, is far more regular in his use of meter than has been generally recognized. As Jerome Mitchell has pointed out in his *Thomas Hoccleve: A Study in Early Fifteenth-Century English Poetic* (Urbana: University of Illinois Press, 1968), 97–109, the claim that Hoccleve constantly uses thwarted stress can be maintained only if one fails to see that he used the variant lines Schick found in Lydgate and that he engages in metrical variations rather freely and sometimes a little unconventionally. (That Mitchell goes on to accept James G. Southworth's rhythmic readings as plausible alternatives has the unfortunate effect of undercutting his own insights and of suggesting that with Hoccleve anything goes. The view that Hoccleve used thwarted stress cannot be effectively countered by the argument that his metric is too loose to have any stress-principles that might be thwarted.)

31. Even in these poems, and especially in the Psalms, Wyatt seems not always to remember to make use of these resources, which have the power to quicken his phrases. Here, too, as elsewhere in his decasyllabic poems, a modern reader will feel uneasy at his rhymes on unstressed syllables, especially of long words of Romance origins (díspleăsúre, ŭndíscŏvéred). Modern readers may also be disconcerted by what appear to be second-foot trochees in type-1 lines ("Thĭs sóng / éndĭd, / David did stint his voyce" [CVIII, 293]; "Mў hárt / pántўth, / my force I fele it quaile" [362]); or by fourth-foot trochees in type-4 or type-2 lines ("Of sword, of sekeness, / óff / fámĭne and fyre [332]; "He poyntes, he pawsith, / hé / wóndĕrs, / he praysith [520]). In most such lines, the key word is a disyllable *(endid, pantyth, famine, wonders)* that Wyatt almost certainly stressed on the first syllable, so he is either giving the word a highly artificial pronunciation or, more probably, using expressive variations, purposeful in every case, which jeopardize the reader's sense of the meter.

Donne's Sculptured Stanzas

The points made in this essay were suggested but not developed in my *Shakespeare's Metrical Art* (323 n. 6), and I have adapted much of that note's language for the first two paragraphs here. The rest of the essay offers examples intended to illustrate and support these opening general statements.

1. Helen Gardner observes that "a good many [of the early poems] . . . combine decasyllabics with octosyllabics, as if Donne were trying to achieve the soaring of song with the force of speech . . . [or] was trying to achieve a stanza that combined the weight of the decasyllabic with the lightness of the octosyllabic" (John Donne, *The Elegies and the Songs and Sonnets,* ed. Helen Gardner [Oxford: Clarendon Press, 1965], xxvi). But neither she nor anyone else demonstrates how this works in particular poems and stanzas, as this essay proposes to do. She does note that "all the poems that are addressed to the God of Love are in stanzas" that combine octosyllabic and decasyllabic lines (lxi).

2. See Martin Halpern, "On the Two Chief Metrical Modes in English," *PMLA* 77 (1962): 177–86.

3. All poems are quoted from *The Complete Poems of John Donne,* ed. John T. Shawcross (New York: New York University Press, 1968).

4. See Helen Vendler's remarkable studies of Shakespeare's "wonderful fertility in structural complexity" (22) in *The Art of Shakespeare's Sonnets* (Cambridge, Mass.: Harvard University Press, 1997), 21–25 and passim.

5. See my *Shakespeare's Metrical Art* (Berkeley: University of California Press, 1988), 265.

6. "Goe, and catch a falling star" reels back and forth between trochaic and iambic balances. The first six lines of each stanza establish the trochaic beat (with catalexis in the first four lines); then the short lines switch to iambic, and the last line returns to trochaic catalectic, though the final line of the poem begins trochaically but ends iambically.

But Donne hardly sets up this pattern before he lets the lines begin to question it.

> Goe, and catche a falling starre,
> Get with child a mandrake roote,
> Tell me, where all past yeares are,
> Or who cleft the Divels foot

The first line is perfectly regular; the second has a secondary stress on "-drake;" the third keeps the beat pretty well but has almost level stress in its last five syllables; and the first foot of the fourth, if it is to remain trochaic, requires us to lean more heavily on "Or" than the syntax would normally justify. The same is true of the second foot of the fifth line: to keep the trochaic rhythm, we can lean on "to" a little more, on "hear" a little less, than we normally would ("Téach mĕ | tò hèar | mérmàids | síngĭng"). The sixth line restores the regular trochaic pulse, only to switch in the following short lines to iambic monometer, then back to trochaic catalectic (with elision) in the last line.

The same reliance on our willingness to forgo the strong trochaic beat in some lines for a more level stress pronunciation that allows us to retain a beat on relatively weak syllables (the alternative is to lose the beat altogether) is found in lines 10, 13, 23, and 24. The hardest is 10: "Íf thŏu | béest bòrn | tò strànge | síghts," where the level-stress pattern must be maintained. Line 23 comes easily enough if we take the metrical hint and put stress on "were," followed by natural speech stresses on "when" and "met": "Thóugh shĕe | wére trùe, | whén yŏu | mét hĕr." In general, it can be said that the outrageousness of the poem's claim about women is matched by the outlandishness of the lively meter, which can only be maintained by a heroic commitment to level-stress reading when it is needed.

Yeats's Expressive Style

Reprinted with minor changes, and with the permission of the editor, from *Yeats Eliot Review* 7 (1982): 109–16.

1. See Marjorie Perloff, *Rhyme and Meaning in the Poetry of Yeats* (The Hague: Mouton, 1970).

2. See Richard Ellmann, *Yeats: The Man and the Masks* (New York: Norton, 1948); Ellmann, *The Identity of Yeats* (New York: Oxford University Press, 1964); Thomas Parkinson, *W. B. Yeats: The Later Poetry* (Berkeley: University of California Press, 1964); and Curtis Bradford, *Yeats at Work* (Carbondale: Southern Illinois University Press, 1965).

3. W. B. Yeats, *The Poems: A New Edition,* ed. Richard J. Finneran (New York: Macmillan), 258–59. Reprinted by permission of the Macmillan Publishing Company.

Lowell's Pentameter Line

1. Robert Lowell, "On Freedom in Poetry," *Naked Poetry: Recent American Poetry in Open Forms,* ed. Stephen Berg and Robert Mezey (Indianapolis: Bobbs-Merrill, 1969), 124.

2. See Marjorie Perloff's enlightening chapter on Lowell's syntactical habits in *The Poetic Art of Robert Lowell* (Ithaca, N.Y.: Cornell University Press, 1973), 100–30.

3. Quotations from Lowell's earlier poems will be cited from separate volumes abbreviated as follows:

Mills = *The Mills of the Kavanaghs* (New York: Harcourt, Brace, Jovanovich, 1951)
LWC = *Lord Weary's Castle* (New York: Harcourt, Brace, Jovanovich, 1946)
LS = *Life Studies* (New York: Farrar, Straus, & Giroux, 1959*)*
FTUD = *For the Union Dead* (New York: Farrar, Straus, & Giroux, 1964)

4. See his contribution to a discussion of "Skunk Hour" in *The Contemporary Poet as Artist and Critic,* ed. Anthony Ostroff (Boston: Little, Brown, 1964), 108–9.

5. *Notebook* (New York: Farrar, Straus & Giroux, 1970); *History* (New York: Farrar, Straus & Giroux, 1973); *For Lizzie and Harriet* (New York: Farrar, Straus & Giroux, 1973); *The Dolphin* (New York: Farrar, Straus & Giroux, 1973).

6. *Notebook,* 263. Subsequent parenthetical page numbers refer to this volume, except for the lines quoted from *Day by Day* near the end of the essay.

7. Even in Lowell's prose, iambic rhythms sometimes appear, as when he describes the best style for poetry in an alexandrine phrase, "something like the prose of Chekhov or Flaubert" (Ostroff, 108). Note Perloff's perceptive prosodic analysis of Lowell's prose reminiscence of Randall Jarrell (*The Poetic Art of Robert Lowell,* 109–15).

8. *Day by Day* (New York: Farrar, Straus & Giroux, 1977), 21.

9. W. H. Auden, "At the Grave of Henry James," in *Collected Poems,* ed. Edward Mendelson (New York: Random House, 1976), 243.

Hearing the Measures

Reprinted with minor changes from *Style* 31:1 (spring, 1997), 148–94.

1. *Tottel's Miscellany* (1557–87), ed. Hyder E. Rollins (Cambridge, Mass: Harvard University Press, 1928), 1.231.
2. Thomas Cable, *The English Alliterative Tradition* (Philadelphia: University of Pennsylvania Press, 1991), 114–31.
3. See James I. Wimsatt, "Rhyme/Reason, Chaucer/Pope, Icon/Symbol," *MLQ* 55 (1994): 17–46.
4. *Well-Weighed Syllables: Elizabethan Verse in Classical Metres* (Cambridge: Cambridge University Press, 1974).
5. O. B. Hardison Jr., *Prosody and Purpose in the English Renaissance* (Baltimore: Johns Hopkins University Press, 1989), 14.
6. If I understand him, I think what he means here is: *when the next or the previous offbeat is a non-final double one.* Offbeats are normally followed and preceded by beats, not by offbeats. But it seems to me a problem for Attridge's terminology that he often writes as though a verse line's character were defined by its offbeats rather than its beats.
7. John Barton, *Playing Shakespeare* (London: Methuen, 1984), 55–56 and passim.
8. W. K. Wimsatt Jr., "The Rule and the Norm: Halle and Keyser on Chaucer's Meter," *College English* 31 (1970): 774–88.
9. See Otto Jespersen, "Notes on Metre," in *The Structure of Verse: Modern Essays on Prosody,* ed. Harvey Gross (Greenwich, Conn.: Fawcett, 1966), 125; Yvor Winters, "The Audible Reading of Poetry," in *The Function of Criticism: Problems and Exercises* (Denver: Swallow, 1957), 94; W. K. Wimsatt, 775; and Cable, 123–27.
10. T. V. F. Brogan and Derek Attridge, "On the 'Crescendo Foot'," *Eidos* 4 (Dec. 1987): 11–12, 18.
11. Attridge specifically reads a virtual offbeat in this line but not in the others (248–49), apparently because the grammar is different in (8), though to my ear it sounds just like the others if I try to speak the line as I understand Attridge wants it spoken.
12. To be sure, Attridge does declare from the start in *REP* that "since my interest is primarily in the singleness of [the English accentual-syllabic] metrical tradition—in the capacity, that is, of the modern reader to engage directly with rhythmic forms produced over the past six hundred years—I have deliberately ignored its historical dimension" (vii). But if earlier poets did not hear lines as Attridge thinks contemporary poets and readers do, his account is bound to be flawed.

13. *The English Auden: Poems, Essays, and Dramatic Writings, 1927–1939,* ed. Edward Mendelson (New York: Random House, 1977), 144.

14. Derek Attridge, "'Damn with Faint Praise': Double Offbeat Demotion," *Eidos* 4 (Aug. 1987): 3.

15. John Crowe Ransom long ago suggested an at least equally plausible scansion for this line: Weep n*o* more, w*o*ful sh*e*pherds, w*ee*p no m*o*re ("The Strange Music of English Verse," in *Perspectives on Poetry,* ed. James L. Calderwood and Harold E. Toliver [New York: Oxford University Press, 1968], 190). This seems an appropriate way of recognizing that older poets enjoyed placing the same phrases in different metrical positions in a line and often did so with great expressive force, as Milton does here.

Attridge constantly faults "classical" metrics for being unable to do more than label a line's subtle effects with "trochee-spondee" or "pyrrhic-spondee," and so on (*PR,* 142; *REP,* 168, 232, 234, and elsewhere). But this is a bad rap. His own eloquence about rhythmic effects lies not in his elaborate notation but in his commentary, and that recourse is open to traditional metrists as well. He also makes traditional scansion seem more wooden than it is because when he tries his hand at it he usually declines to employ the secondary stresses that many traditional metrists now use to show an intermediate range of stress between stressed and unstressed.

16. Note that *spondee* throughout this review means spondaic iamb. We understand that in English it hardly ever happens that two adjacent stressed syllables will be stressed exactly the same. Similarly with pyrrhic.

17. Listening lately to John Gielgud's recording of most of Shakespeare's *Sonnets* (Caedmon, 1963, 1996), I noticed that he appears to have at least three different ways of treating the kind of double offbeat that I think of as a pyrrhic-spondee combination. I heard him definitely lurch twice, on the phrases "And the firm soil" (64:7), "And for that sorrow" (120:2), possibly also on one other, "that the world's eye" (69:1). His much more usual practice was to give either the first or second syllable of the four a substantial stress, either primary or secondary, enough to assure that it would be heard as a beat. Examples: *You should live twice* (17:14), *Nor shall death brag* (18:11), *To the wide world* (19:7), *That in black ink* (65:14), *From this vile world* (71:4), *as my poor name* (71:11), *Or as sweet seasoned* (75:2). What is perhaps most interesting is that Gielgud sometimes gives the first two syllables a distinct pronunciation that seems to my ear strong enough for the second one to retain the beat, but then raises the stress-level of the next two syllables, an elocutionary resource that I believe accounts for the effective speaking of many lines in the theater, but that metrists have paid little attention to. Is he doing this, as I believe, because the line seems to demand it, or because he is consciously treating the figure as comprising

two very different kinds of feet, both iambic? This is how he reads these phrases, among others: *But from thine eyes* (14:9), *It is my love* (61:10), *to thy fair flower* (69:12), *On your broad main* (80:8), *So thy great gift* (87:11), *is of more worth* (103:3). Gielgud's performance does not prove that the phrases must be spoken his way, but it ought to be harder to argue, in the face of such readings by an extraordinarily experienced actor, that the classification of minor syllables as belonging to an unstressed category resolves the question of where we can hear the beat in such lines.

18. See Ants Oras, *Pause Patterns in Elizabethan and Jacobean Drama: An Experiment in Prosody* (Gainesville: University of Florida Press, 1960); and Marina Tarlinskaja, *English Verse: Theory and History* (The Hague: Mouton, 1976); and her *Shakespeare's Verse: Iambic Pentameter and the Poet's Idiosyncrasies* (New York: Peter Lang, 1987).

19. Two other matters of detail are worth mentioning. (1) Despite O'Donnell's assertion (133), no part of "The Thorn" is dipodic. (2) O'Donnell has some elaborate charts that graphically map instances of assonance and "alliteration"; by the latter term he apparently means what many critics would call consonance, the repetition of consonant sounds anywhere in words, not especially at the beginning of stressed syllables.

20. If by this phrase he means simply that we should read traditional verse without laboriously assigning metrical values to every syllable, who would disagree?

21. Despite the justice of some of Holder's criticism of critics who apply traditional prosody to free verse, every claim that a free verse poem is "haunted" by older poetry should not be dismissed out of hand. It is obviously true of some of Eliot's major poems, and one of Attridge's best passages in *PR* analyzes the extent to which Adrienne Rich's "Night Watch" "derives its rhythmic quality from its existence on the borders of regular verse" (172).

22. See W. K. Wimsatt Jr. and Monroe Beardsley, "The Concept of Meter: An Exercise in Abstraction," *PMLA* 74 (1959): 585–98.

23. Holder's anger at a metrical "system" that bullies the phrases makes me wonder why he doesn't feel an equal outrage at grammarians. Isn't grammar as much of a system as meter? Doesn't it similarly break up phrases into fragmentary parts of speech? Shouldn't we regard the objects of verbs as oppressed by their transitive masters? Should we sympathize with adjectives and adverbs, which can only modify something? Or is it the case that poets can use both phrases and grammar at once, can hear the same words operating at once in a phrasal, a grammatical, and a metrical context, and with some kind of pitch-patterns, too?

24. "The Meter of 'Shall I Die?'" *Eidos* 3 (1986): 6, 11–12.

25. An example (222):

```
                        bends
                                 mov
                                         move
                 Or     with the re    er to re
```

Does that sound natural to anyone?

26. In a later article ("Metrical Dramaturgy in Shakespeare's Earlier Plays," *CEA Critic* 57:3 [1995]: 51–65), Raffel makes extravagant claims to hear "prosodic signals" in short or long lines. As we might expect, he has read no one else who has written on the subject; he mis-scans some lines badly; and he attributes remarkably explicit "messages" to mere metrical variations: "a signal of her unwilling but enforced acceptance of the nurse's inadequate pace of operation"; "It reveals Juliet's trust in the absolute reciprocity of her and Romeo's mutual affection" (56).

27. Aristotle, *Nicomachean Ethics,* tr. W. D. Ross, in *Introduction to Aristotle,* ed. Richard McKeon (New York: Modern Library, 1947), 1.3.1094b.

28. Delbert Spain, *Shakespeare Sounded Soundly: The Verse Structure and the Language* (Santa Barbara, Calif.: Garland-Clarke, 1988).

Pulse and Breath

The first brief essay in this group of three appeared in *The North Stone Review* 9 (1990). X. J. Kennedy, the well-known poet and critic, wrote a spirited response to it, which the editor, James Naiden, published in no. 11 of the same journal, along with the original essay and my reply to Kennedy. The three pieces are reprinted here from *The North Stone Review* 11. "Formal Verse and Fascist Deviousness" is copyright © 1993 by X. J. Kennedy and is reprinted by permission of the author. "Pulse and Breath" and "A Reply to X. J. Kennedy" are reprinted by permission of James Naiden.

Troubles of a Professional Meter Reader

From *Shakespeare Reread: The Texts in New Contexts,* ed. Russ McDonald (Ithaca, N.Y.: Cornell University Press, 1994), 56–76. Reprinted (with minor changes) by permission of Cornell University Press.

1. All Shakespeare quotations are from *The Riverside Shakespeare,* ed. G. Blakemore Evans (Boston: Houghton Mifflin, 1974).

2. In this passage and some others scanned below, only variant feet are marked, those that seem clearly pyrrhic, spondaic, or trochaic. Secondary stresses are marked \ .

3. *Shakespeare's Metrical Art* (Berkeley: University of California Press, 1988), 137–38. Hereinafter referred to as *SMA*.
4. See, for example, Morris Halle and Samuel J. Keyser, "Chaucer and the Study of Prosody," *College English* 28 (1966): 187–219; and Paul Kiparsky, "Stress, Syntax, and Meter," *Language* 51 (1975): 576–616.
5. John Thompson, *The Founding of English Metre* (New York: Columbia University Press, 1961).
6. See, e.g., Yvor Winters, "The Audible Reading of Poetry," in *The Function of Criticism: Problems and Exercises* (Denver: Alan Swallow, 1957), 79–100; Arnold Stein, "Donne's Prosody," *PMLA* 59 (1944): 373–97; Robert Bridges, *Milton's Prosody* (Oxford: Oxford University Press, 1921); S. Ernest Sprott, *Milton's Art of Prosody* (Oxford: Basil Blackwell, 1953); Edward R. Weismiller, "The 'Dry' and 'Rugged' Verse," in *The Lyric and Dramatic Milton,* ed. Joseph H. Summers (New York: Columbia University Press, 1965), 115–52; and W. K. Wimsatt Jr. and Monroe Beardsley, "The Concept of Meter: An Exercise in Abstraction," *PMLA* 74 (1959): 585–98. For other work by these writers, see the bibliography in *SMA*.
7. Marina Tarlinskaja, *Shakespeare's Verse: Iambic Pentameter and the Poet's Idiosyncrasies* (New York: Peter Lang, 1987); Henri Suhamy, *Le vers de Shakespeare* (Paris: Didier-Erudition, 1984).
8. Otto Jespersen, "Notes on Metre" in *Linguistica: Selected Papers* (Copenhagen: Levin and Munksgaard, 1933), 249–72; Roman Jakobson and Linda Waugh, *The Sound Shape of Language* (Bloomington: Indiana University Press, 1979).
9. O. B. Hardison Jr., *Prosody and Purpose in the English Renaissance* (Baltimore: Johns Hopkins University Press, 1989), xiv.
10. Ants Oras, *Pause Patterns in Elizabethan and Jacobean Drama: An Experiment in Prosody* (Gainesville: University of Florida Press, 1960).
11. See "Wyatt's Decasyllabic Line" above, 99–122.
12. Latin metrists, after all, do this, too. The difference is that in English the number of (stress) variations that lines may exhibit while still belonging to a given iambic meter is far larger. Because I include acceptable variations in my definition of a meter, I understand individual lines not as having started from the paradigmatic base and having then been changed (as all talk of substitution, promotion, and similar terms implies) but as realizing in their different ways the general form, as different members of a species all realize its paradigmatic form in their individual ways.
13. The wording and punctuation are from *The First Folio of Shakespeare,* prepared by Charlton Hinman (New York: Norton, 1968); the spelling is that of *The Riverside Shakespeare.*
14. See John Barton, *Playing Shakespeare* (London: Methuen, 1984).

15. As Marlon Brando did in the film *Julius Caesar,* trying to make up for a lifetime of metrical innocence by seeking the advice of an old hand (or voice), John Gielgud.

16. What we have lost is not merely the ability to hear verse as verse but the ability to hear it as rhetoric, just as we have lost our ear for the more recondite figures and schemes of the classical repertoire. The repetitions of meter are more closely connected to those of traditional figures than we usually recognize, even when we discuss differences between Renaissance prose and verse. I don't quite suggest that prose is a form of verse, but when we speak of Renaissance writing the idea is less crazy than we might think.

17. Cf. J. Hillis Miller's contention, in *Versions of Pygmalion* (Cambridge, Mass.: Harvard University Press, 1990), that Pygmalion can serve as a figure for the act of reading, in which we bring to life the suggestions of the printed page.

18. Antony Easthope, *Poetry as Discourse* (London: Methuen, 1983). See *SMA* 321 n. 8.

19. Ellen Spolsky, "The Limits of Literal Meaning," *New Literary History* 19 (1988): 419–40; and "Hendiadys and *Hamlet*," reprinted above, 3–43.

20. I have seen an unpublished early version of an essay by Gary Taylor, titled "Metrifying Shakespeare," which shows an admirable grasp both of Shakespeare's metrical options and of the principles that ought to guide an editor's treatment of the metrical evidence.

21.Wallace Stevens, "Notes toward a Supreme Fiction," *Collected Poetry and Prose* (New York: Library of America, 1997), 350.

Blank Verse in the Jacobean Theater

Reprinted with minor changes, from *The Elizabethan Theatre* 12, ed. A. L. Magnusson and C. E. McGee (Toronto: P. D. Meany, 1993), 1–18.

1. All quotations from Shakespeare's plays are from *The Riverside Shakespeare,* ed. G. Blakemore Evans (Boston: Houghton Mifflin, 1974).

2. *Shakespeare's Sonnets,* ed. Stephen Booth (New Haven, Conn.: Yale University Press, 1977).

3. For a fuller survey of Shakespeare's metrical practices and of technical terms used in this essay, see my "Hearing Shakespeare's Dramatic Verse," in *A Companion to Shakespeare,* ed. David Scott Kastan (Oxford: Blackwell, 1999), 256–76; or my *Shakespeare's Metrical Art* (Berkeley: University of California Press, 1988).

4. *Elizabethan and Stuart Plays,* ed. Charles Read Baskervill et al. (New York: Henry Holt, 1934). The later quotation in this essay from Fletcher *(The Maid's Tragedy)* is also from this collection.

5. *Poetry of the English Renaissance, 1509–1660,* ed. J. William Hebel and Hoyt H. Hudson (New York: Appleton Century Crofts, 1929), 91.

6. *The Selected Plays of Thomas Middleton,* ed. David L. Frost (Cambridge: Cambridge University Press, 1978).

7. On occasion Middleton goes even further and writes what may be called a heavy triple ending. Working from the model of Shakespeare's frequent triple endings (two unstressed syllables after the final stressed one, e.g.—

What's Hecuba to him, or he | tŏ Hécŭbă?
[*Hamlet,* 2.2.559])

he devises a line that has an additional unstressed syllable after the heavy ending:

Till supper-time; I'll take my leave | thĕn, nów, màdăm
(*Women Beware Women,* 2.2.179)

Everyone sees not; you can wit | nĕss thát, wìdŏw
(*Women Beware Women* 2.2.279)

Middleton may have recognized that the rhythm of such a line resembles that of the Latin meter known as limping iambics. See my discussion of this anomalous structure in *Shakespeare's Metrical Art,* 316–17.

8. *Four Great Elizabethan Plays,* ed. John Gassner (New York, Bantam, 1960), 108–9.

9. The last line of the Webster passage is also perplexing. Either "dazzle" is to be taken as monosyllabic or the line's second and third syllables may be syncopated:

Cóver her | fàce; míne | èyes dáz | zlĕ; shé | dìed yóung.

For Lowell's five-stress verse, see "Lowell's Pentameter Line," above, 144–53.

10. See esp. *Orality and Literacy: The Technologizing of the Word* (London and New York, Methuen, 1982). See also Eric Havelock, "The Oral Composition of Greek Drama," in *The Literate Revolution in Greece and Its Consequences* (Princeton, N.J.: Princeton University Press, 1982). Havelock is particularly illuminating on the mixture of oral and written elements in Greek drama: "It is to be inferred that Greek tragedy was composed in a state of continuous physiological tension between the modes of oral and written communication" (265).

11. See Barbara H. Smith, *On the Margins of Discourse: The Relation of Literature to Language* (Chicago: University of Chicago Press, 1978), 24.

12. Not that poets always remember to take advantage of that voice. In my experience, when contemporary poets read their own verse in public, they almost invari-

ably use far fewer tones and a much narrower selection of pitches than their own voices are capable of generating. To judge from early Elizabethan texts of nondramatic poetry, the natural voice of most sixteenth-century poets may well have been similarly limited to a few tones appropriate to doleful lament, fulsome praise, and narration. What Sidney inspired in the sonneteers who followed his lead in the early 1590s was a substantially wider range of speech-tones than earlier nondramatic poets had been in the habit of striking in their verse; and Shakespeare led the way in making accessible to dramatic characters an extraordinarily ample range of such tones.

13. Colon means "limb, member, clause of a sentence"—again, a visual term.

14. "Lines" in Shakespeare are usually military, ancestral, facial, fishing, or written, or they may serve as a short form of "outlines." In all these instances the emphasis is on something visual or derived from a written chart or map or drawing.

15. See Ong's section, "Writing Is a Technology," 81–83. For a fuller analysis of the kinds of language blank verse of this period is preserving, and on what terms, see the next essay in this book, "An Almost Oral Art."

16. *The Selected Plays of John Webster,* ed. Jonathan Dollimore and Alan Sinfield (Cambridge: Cambridge University Press, 1983).

17. Other readings are, of course, possible, but all readings are not equally good or even acceptable: the level shout, for example:

But she
Í căn hóok tŏ mé . . .

which makes hash of the meter. Cf. Nicol Williamson's reading, in the BBC *Macbeth,* of the formerly metrical line:

Bríng me nó móre repórts; lét them fly áll
(5.3.1)

Equally implausible is the reading that derives from the false understanding that because "hook" is an important word it must receive major stress:

Í căn hóok tŏ mé . . .

The passage is very logical. Leontes is concerned over his lack of sleep. His main source of misery is not that he has lost an old friend and a wife but that he hasn't dealt strongly enough with his injury. If he could deal strongly enough with it, his sleep would be restored to him. He *can't* deal strongly with Polixenes, who is (damn it!) out of his reach: Leontes can't get *at* him; he's plot-*proof.* The emphasis is on Polixenes' absolute safety, on his being immune to all attempts to reach him; hence the stress on "proof." Hermione, on the other hand, he *can* get at; and, the passage goes on to suggest, if he has her burnt, then he will get *half* his sleep back. The reasoning is precise, but the meter's powerful foregrounding of certain syllables at the expense of others suggests how unbalanced it is.

18. Of course, another and more familiar means of securing emphasis is the opposite one of placing an important syllable in an *un*stressed position (*"Given* to the fire"). Shakespeare's art of the trochee, however, is more complex than we usually think. See *Shakespeare's Metrical Art,* 185–206.

19. For an analysis of Leontes' speech from a somewhat different angle, see my "Hearing Shakespeare's Dramatic Verse," in *A Companion to Shakespeare,* 274–75.

20. Is there a connection between the strong incitement to visual imagery that Shakespeare's language offers and the incitement offered by his meter to visualize lines of verse? The two incitements grow more similar in the late plays as the problematical verse more and more resembles the complex, hard-to-visualize images. But Marion Trousdale has argued persuasively that Shakespeare's audiences were probably able to follow complex imagistic or syntactic patterns heard in the theater. See her "Shakespeare's Oral Text," *Renaissance Drama,* n.s.,12 (1981): 95–115.

21. Heminge and Condell claim to have published Shakespeare's "writings . . . absolute in their numbers, as he conceived the[m]." The tangle of literate and oral emerges for us also in this: "And what he thought, he uttered with that easinesse, that we have scarce received from him a blot in his papers." (In the Renaissance, to be sure, "utter" often means "offer for sale" or "publish"—in effect, bring to public view.)

22. The epilogues of Shakespeare's and his contemporaries' plays suggest again and again how evanescent they thought theatrical performances were. With the end of the play, the magician-playwright's "charms are all o'erthrown," and he is forced to cope with the world without the advantages of written script and assisting actors. Now he lives again with everyone else in a largely oral world.

An Almost Oral Art

Reprinted, with minor changes, from *Shakespeare Quarterly* 43 (1992): 159–69, by permission of *Shakespeare Quarterly.*

1. See my *Shakespeare's Metrical Art* (Berkeley: University of California Press, 1988); "Blank Verse in the Jacobean Theater . . ." (included above, 235–49); and "Voices That Figure in *Four Quartets,"* in *The Placing of T. S. Eliot,* ed. Jewel Spears Brooker (Columbia: University of Missouri Press, 1991), 152–62.

2. All Shakespeare quotations are taken from *The Riverside Shakespeare,* ed. G. Blakemore Evans (Boston: Houghton Mifflin, 1974).

3. See two essays by Jonas Barish: "Mixed Prose-Verse Scenes in Shakespearean Tragedy," in *Shakespeare and Dramatic Tradition: Essays in Honor of S. F. Johnson,* ed. W. R. Elton and William B. Long (Newark: University of Delaware Press, 1989), 32–46; and "Mixed Verse and Prose in Shakespearean Comedy," in *English Comedy,* ed. Michael Cordner et al. (Cambridge: Cambridge University Press, 1994), 55–67; and Brian Vickers, "Rites of Passage in Shakespeare's Prose," in *Returning to Shakespeare* (London: Routledge, 1989), 21–40.

4. Note Eric Havelock's point, in *The Muse Learns to Write: Reflections on Orality and Literacy from Antiquity to the Present* (New Haven, Conn.: Yale University Press, 1986), that being illiterate in a literate culture is very different from living in a preliterate culture.

5. Among a large literature that goes at the problems in quite various ways, see esp. Havelock, *The Muse Learns to Write,* and Walter J. Ong, *Orality and Literacy: The Technologizing of the Word* (London and New York: Methuen, 1982); both books have useful bibliographies.

6. There are still, nevertheless, a great many people for whom verse is itself a kind of magic-making theater, a setting that promises to be the scene of significant linguistic activity. Those of us in whom verse arouses this expectation know how often it is disappointed, but it survives, just as our comparable passion for drama survives bad plays and bad productions. How often one says, after a disappointing evening at the theater, "Well, at least I'm glad to have seen it!" I feel that way about almost all second-rate traditional verse—"Well, I'm glad to have read it"—though that pleasure doesn't extend, in my experience, to bad or mediocre free verse, to verse, that is, that lacks the formal elements I associate with significant verse.

7. Critics have sometimes noted the unusually wide range of Renaissance drama. To cite one example, see R. J. Dorius, "Tragedy," in *Princeton Encyclopedia of Poetry and Poetics* (Princeton, N.J.: Princeton University Press, 1974): "The large casts of characters in these plays, their complicated balancing of tragic and comic elements, plot and subplot, hero and fool, their vivid and violent action and frequent passages of philosophical reflection, and their richly metaphoric blank verse, interspersed with rhymed verse and songs, render these plays in many ways unique in the history of world theatre" (863).

8. Shakespearean proclamations are presented in prose not only because in this literate culture they were normally written in prose, but also because, by Shakespeare's time, most of what was merely official was recognized as unalterably secular, not sacred.

9. All these kinds of departures from what we are likely to think of as a metrical

norm I discuss in detail in *Shakespeare's Metrical Art* (cited in n. 1, above). On the advancing sentence as an alternative to the metrical line, see Northrop Frye's "Verse and Prose" in *Princeton Encyclopedia of Poetry and Poetics,* enlarged ed., 1974, 885–90, and *Shakespeare's Metrical Art,* esp. 222–28 and 262–63. Patricia Parker, in *Inescapable Romance* (Princeton, N.J.: Princeton University Press, 1979), points out the relevance for nineteenth-century poetry of St. Augustine's view of the sentence: "each syllable giving way in a successive, or syntagmatic, movement towards the 'rest' at its end" (225). It is tempting to read the audible segmented progress of successive stress-attracting phrases that little by little bring into "view" the form and import of the advancing sentence as ultimately undermining (or, in late Shakespeare and *Paradise Lost,* tensely engaging) the echoic nature of verse.

10. See Northrop Frye, *Princeton Encyclopedia of Poetry and Poetics* (1974): "The rhythm of Jacobean blank-verse drama has its center of gravity somewhere between verse and prose. . . . In *The Tempest,* especially the speeches of Caliban, and in some late plays of Webster and Tourneur, the barrier between verse and prose often comes near dissolving" (888); and F. E. Halliday, *The Poetry of Shakespeare's Plays* (London: Duckworth, 1954): "By concealing the linear structure, by infinite variations of the metrical pattern, and by the rejection of rhetorical artifice, Shakespeare has evolved a dramatic poetry with a rhythm that can be relaxed at will to approximate to that of prose, or tautened into the strictest formality of verse" (184).

The Silent Speech of Shakespeare's *Sonnets*

Reprinted with minor changes, from *Shakespeare and the Twentieth Century,* ed. Jonathan Bate, Jill L. Levenson, and Dieter Mehl (Newark: University of Delaware Press), 314–35.

1. John Pope-Hennessy, *The Portrait in the Renaissance* (Princeton: Princeton University Press, 1966), 9.

2. All quotations from the *Sonnets* are from *Shakespeare's Sonnets,* ed. Stephen Booth (New Haven: Yale University Press, 1977).

3. Later New Critical analysis made a point of stressing that "a poem is a dramatic fiction no less than a play" (Reuben Brower, *The Fields of Light,* quoted from *Perspectives on Poetry,* ed. James L. Calderwood and Harold E. Toliver [New York: Oxford University Press, 1968]) and "its speaker . . . no less a creation of the words on the printed page" (98). What Brower and others knew but didn't think necessary to say was that the "voice" and "tone" of a poem are also fictions. They are what we would hear if the poem on the page were to be read aloud, but in the usage of many critics this necessary qualification is not made, probably because the point is unim-

portant in the classroom, where the poem or the parts of it being discussed usually *are* read aloud. The contradiction becomes evident only on written examinations, when students are urged to write in virtual silence about such matters as voice, tone, and rhythm.

But as Barbara Herrnstein Smith insists in *Poetic Closure* (Chicago: University of Chicago Press, 1968), a poem is not an actual but "only a *possible* utterance" (16); "poetry is a *representational* art and . . . each poem is the representation of an act of speech" (17). Smith never forgets that any poem we read or hear may or may not be read aloud, and that what she claims for its form must be valid for both possibilities.

4. See "Voices That Figure in *Four Quartets*," in *The Placing of T. S. Eliot*, ed. Jewel Spears Brooker (Columbia: Univ. of Missouri Press, 1991), 152–62.

5. In *T. S. Eliot's Silent Voices* (New York: Oxford University Press, 1989), John T. Mayer studies the extent to which the "voices" composing the psychological dramas of Eliot's early verse represent internal, often fragmented, elements in his speakers' psychic consciousnesses, not their spoken words. Mayer shows how these silent voices differ from the voices of comparable nineteenth-century poems in, for example, their disjunctive syntax. But, relevant as his subject is to mine, he does not discuss whether we, the audience for this poetry, are to hear its words silently or aloud.

6. For more on this subject, see the two preceding essays in this collection: "Blank Verse in the Jacobean Theater . . ." and "An Almost Oral Art . . ."

7. This paragraph, and the one that follows, are based on passages in my "Voices That Figure in *Four Quartets*," 154, 157.

8. Michel de Montaigne, "Apology for Raymonde Sebond," in *The Complete Essays of Montaigne*, trans. Donald M. Frame (Stanford, Calif.: Stanford University Press, 1958), 336.

9. As Booth suggests, the parallelism between "o'er-read" and "rehearse" in lines 10–11 encourages us to understand "your being" and "my gentle verse" as equivalent. Still, line 11 "provides its own object for *rehearse—your being* (future tongues shall rehearse your being, i.e. recount your life, tell about you" (279).

10. Heather Dubrow, *Captive Victors: Shakespeare's Narrative Poems and Sonnets* (Ithaca, N.Y.: Cornell University Press, 1987), 254–56.

11. *Shakespeare's Metrical Art* (Berkeley: University of California Press, 1988), 89. Much of this passage originally appeared in "Shakespeare's Poetic Techniques" in *Shakespeare: His World, His Work, His Influence*, ed. John F. Andrews, 3 vols. (New York: Scribner's, 1985), 2.363–87.

12. Wolfgang Clemen, *Shakespeare's Soliloquies*, trans. Charity Scott Stokes (London: Methuen, 1987), 6. The Arnold quotation is on page 3.

13. *The "Inward" Language: Sonnets of Wyatt, Sidney, Shakespeare, Donne* (Chicago: University of Chicago Press, 1983), 61.

14. In Ferry's view, developed in persuasive detail in *The 'Inward' Language,* Sidney and Shakespeare "explode the boundaries of poetic convention" (28) as they "work through and beyond depiction of the lover's heart struck first by Cupid's dart, then by the lady's scorn, to an exploration of 'how hard true sorrow hits' [S. 120] when lovers injure one another's feelings" (28). Their sonnets' "more than usual intimacy of address, their elaboration of the lover's involvement in causing pain to himself and to his beloved, their dramatization of his imaginative entrance into another person's heart, make these poems radically different in kind from a representative sixteenth-century complaint" so that they become "intimate, private explorations of autobiographical material" (29). Sidney and Shakespeare are "the only two love poets to make central to their sonnet sequences the issue of showing in verse what is truly in the heart" (29), instead of seeking within for a reflection of the divine love or the conventional imagistic representation of human love.

15. Cf. Katharine Eisaman Maus's view that "in late sixteenth- and early seventeenth-century England the sense of discrepancy between 'inward disposition' and 'outward appearance' seems unusually urgent and consequential for a very large number of people" (*Inwardness and the Theater in the English Renaissance* [Chicago: University of Chicago Press, 1995], 13). Such a discrepancy is explored insistently and intensely in the *Sonnets* and with deepening subtlety in the plays that follow. Maus seems to me to argue very cogently against those critics who either "claim that a conception of personal inwardness hardly existed at all in Renaissance England" or "acknowledge that the rhetoric of inwardness is highly developed . . . but maintain that these terms inevitably refer to outward, public, or political factors" (2); and she notes that Ferry, in denying an inwardness in the love poetry of poets other than Sidney and Shakespeare, does so "without, apparently, sharing the philosophical agenda that motivates" these other critics of subjectivity (27 n.).

16. Still, the need of the speaker to defend himself against the *imputation* of a vileness that may amount to a kind of behavioral madness is evident in Sonnet 121 and seems parallel to Hamlet's defensive tactics against Rosencrantz and Guildenstern.

Carol Thomas Neely's study, "Documents in Madness: Reading Madness and Gender in Shakespeare's Tragedies and Early Modern Culture," *Shakespeare Quarterly* 42 (1991): 315–38, is helpful here: "Shakespeare . . . dramatizes madness primarily through a peculiar language more often than through physiological symptoms, stereotyped behaviors or iconographic conventions . . . Shakespeare's language of madness is characterized by fragmentation, obsession, and repetition, and . . . 'quotation.' . . . The mad are 'beside themselves'; their discourse is not their own" (323).

17. See David M. Bergeron, ed. *Reading and Writing in Shakespeare* (Newark: University of Delaware Press, 1996), and especially Bergeron's helpful introductory essay; and Gerd Baumann, ed. *The Written Word: Literacy in Transition* (Oxford:

Clarendon Press, 1986), a volume in which two essays are particularly pertinent: Walter J. Ong, "Writing Is a Technology That Restructures Thought," 23–50; and Keith Thomas, "Literacy in Early Modern England," 97–131.

18. Ong, "Writing Is a Technology That Restructures Thought," 31.

19. W. B. Yeats, "Ego Dominus Tuus," in *The Poems,* ed. Richard J. Finneran (New York: Macmillan, 1983), 161–62.

Index

Aarts, F. G. A. M., 291
Andrews, John F., 31
Antonioni, Michelangelo, 64
Arden of Feversham, 57
Ariosto, Lodovico, 73, 75, 296; *I Suppositi,* 73
Aristotle, 201, 308
Arnold, Matthew, 69, 167–69, 177, 273; "The Scholar-Gypsy," 167–69, 177
Attridge, Derek, 154, 158–79, 182–85, 188–89, 191, 193, 198, 200–201, 305–7; on beats and offbeats, 160–77, 305, 306; debate with Brogan, 166; on free verse, 161, 178, 307; and generative metrics, 159, 161–62; and metrical lurching, 166–74, 183, 200, 306–7; on metrical subordination, 166, 174–77, 200; and metrical tilting, 163–64, 167, 173, 177, 200; notation, 155–57, 161–63, 178, 306; on promotion and demotion, 162, 164–65, 168, 174, 182, 191, 306; on rules, 159–64, 168, 174, 175, 176, 179, 201
Auden, W. H., 6–7, 45, 48, 50, 54, 61, 69, 95, 119, 153, 169, 173, 191, 197, 207–8, 209, 211, 267, 270, 285
—Works: *The Age of Anxiety,* 119; "As I Walked Out One Evening," 61; "At the Grave of Henry James," 153; *The Dyer's Hand,* 285; "The earth turns over . . . ," 173; "In Memory of W. B. Yeats," 6–7; "In Time of War," 7; "Journey to Iceland," 6; "The Letter," 267; "Macao," 6; "The Quest," 7; "September 1, 1939," 45, 48, 50; "Shorts II," 207–8; "Streams," 191; "The Watchers," 54
Augustine, Saint, 315

Bach, Johann Sebastian, 218
Bald, R. C., 287
Baldi, Sergio, 300
Baldwin, T. W., 5, 286
Barclay, Alexander, 118
Barish, Jonas, 314
Barnet, Sylvan, 287
Barthelme, Donald, 64
Barton, John, 163, 223, 305, 309
Baskervill, Charles Read, 310
Bate, Jonathan, 315
Baumann, Gerd, 317–18
Beardsley, Monroe, 189, 192, 193, 196, 198, 307, 309
the Beatles, 279
Beckett, Samuel, 63, 278, 293; *Molloy,* 63, 293
Beecher, Donald, 293
Beethoven, Ludwig van, 231
Berg, Stephen, 205, 304
Berger, Harry, Jr., 94, 295–96
Bergeron, David M., 317
Berry, Ralph, 297
Berryman, John, 55, 209, 213; "Dream Song 76: 'Henry's Confession,'" 55
Beum, Robert, 193
Bevington, David, 38, 287, 288
Blake, William, 45, 46, 50, 54, 58, 189–90, 196, 198, 278; "Ah! Sun-Flower," 189–90, 196, 198; "London," 45, 50, 54, 58; "The Shepherd," 198
Bly, Robert, 62; "Driving toward the Lac Qui Parle River," 62
Bolinger, Dwight L., 291
Bond, R. Warwick, 293
Booth, Stephen, 271, 294, 310, 315, 316
Borges, Jorge Luis, 64, 206

319

Bradford, Curtis, 136, 304
Bradshaw, Graham, 95, 295–96
Brando, Marlon, 310
Brennan, Joseph Xavier, 286
Bridges, Robert, 219, 300, 309
Bright, James Wilson, 299
Brogan, T. V. F., 166, 305
Brooker, Jewel Spears, 313, 316
Brower, Reuben, 315
Browne, Sir Thomas, 10, 288; *Pseudodoxia Epidemica*, 288; *Religio Medici*, 288
Browning, Robert, 69, 164, 175, 198, 278; "Pauline," 175; *The Ring and the Book*, 164; "Soliloquy of the Spanish Cloister," 198
Burns, Robert, 68
Burton, Richard, 269
Bush, George H. W., 209
Butler, John, 293
Butler, Samuel, 68; *Hudibras,* 68
Buyssens, Eric, 291, 292
Byrd, William, 218

Cable, Thomas, 164, 165, 193, 198, 305
Calderwood, James L., 306, 315
Callow, Simon, 195
Calver, Edward, 52, 291
Carroll, Lewis, 6, 287
Cary, Joyce, 64
Charney, Maurice, 288
Chaucer, Geoffrey, 46, 65, 68, 69, 100–119 passim, 156, 157, 197, 198, 220, 277, 305, 309
Chekhov, Anton, 304
Chomsky, Noam, 154–55, 219
Cicero, Marcus Tullius, 4
Clark, W. G., 290
Clemen, Wolfgang, 273, 316
Coleridge, Samuel Taylor, 198, 277
Collins, William, 68
Condell, Henry, 313
Cooper, Charles Gordon, 5, 7, 8, 285
Cordner, Michael, 314
Cosell, Howard, 200
Cowper, William, 46, 56–57, 68, 180; "Conversation," 56–57
Crabbe, George, 168; *The Village,* 168
Craig, Hardin, 42, 287
Crane, Hart, 69, 72
Crystal, David, 291
Cummings, E. E., 65, 69

Cureton, Richard, 193
Curme, George O., 291

Daniel, Samuel, 68
Day, Angel, 5, 286
Dennis, Leah, 291, 292
Derrick, Thomas J., 94
Desprez, Josquin, 218
Dickinson, Emily, 207, 209
Diver, William, 291
Dollimore, Jonathan, 296, 312
Donne, John, 65, 68, 99, 115, 123–33, 157, 174, 177, 179, 219, 220, 238, 247, 293, 302–3, 309
—Works: *Songs and Sonets:* "The Anniversarie,"127, 129–30; "The Baite," 132–33; "Breake of Day," 127; "The Canonization," 131; "Communitie," 132; "The Curse," 125; "The Extasie," 133; "Farewell to Love," 131–32; "A Feaver," 133; "The Flea," 125; "Goe, and catche a falling star," 133, 303; "Good Friday," 1613; "The good-morrow," 130; "The Indifferent," 131; "The Legacie," 131; "Loves Alchymie," 131; "Loves exchange," 127; "Loves growth," 127–28, 131; "Loves infiniteness," 126–27; "Loves Usury," 128; "The Message," 132; "Negative Love," 132; "A nocturnall upon S. Lucies day," 129, 132; "The Relique," 130; "Riding Westward," 174; "Selfe Love," 132; "The Sunne Rising," 125, 131; "Sweetest love, I do not goe," 133; "The triple Foole," 124–25; "Twicknam Garden," 127; "The undertaking," 132; "A Valediction forbidding mourning," 133; "A Valediction of my name, in the window," 127; "Valediction of the booke," 127; "Witchcraft by a Picture," 127; "Womans constancy," 127
—Other poems: 128
Dorius, R. J., 314
Drayton, Michael, 68; "Since Ther's No Helpe," 68
Dryden, John, 10, 68, 169, 197, 277, 278
Dubrow, Heather, 272, 316
Dunbar, William, 104
Dylan, Bob, 279

Easthope, Antony, 227, 310
Eccles, Mark, 295

Index

Ekwall, Eilert, 300
Eliot, T. S., 5, 52, 69, 178, 211, 213, 259, 264, 265–66, 269, 270, 287, 293, 307, 313, 316
—Works: "Burbank with a Baedeker, Bleistein with a Cigar," 293; "Burnt Norton," 268–69, 270; *Four Quartets,* 313, 316; "The Three Voices of Poetry," 266; *The Waste Land,* 52, 254, 264, 265–66, 269
Ellmann, Richard, 135, 304
Elton, W. R., 314
Elyot, Sir Thomas, 295
Emerson, Ralph Waldo, 260
Endicott, Norman, 288
Englands Helicon, 67, 68
Epstein, Edmund L., 192, 193
Erasmus, Desiderius, 4
Erdmann, Axel, 301
Evans, Bertrand, 294, 295; theory of discrepant awarenesses, 294, 295
Evans, G. Blakemore, 287, 288, 294, 308, 310, 314

Fellini, Federico, 64
Ferry, Ann, 273–74, 317
Finch, Annie, 192
Finneran, Richard J., 137, 304, 318
Flaubert, Gustave, 304
Fletcher, John, 238–39, 241, 310; *The Maid's Tragedy,* 239
focal words, 214–15, 246–47, 312–13
Fowler, H. W., 7, 287
Foxwell, A. K., 102
Frame, Donald M., 316
Fridén, Georg, 292
Frost, David, 311
Frost, Robert, 61, 65, 69, 213, 278; "Mending Wall," 61
Frye, Northrop, 315
Furness, Horace Howard, 287

Gammer Gurton's Needle, 57, 292
Gardner, Helen, 302
Gascoigne, George, 73–75, 79, 90, 119, 170, 176, 237, 292, 293, 294; "Dulce Bellum Inexpertis," 170; "The Steele Glas," 176, 237; *Supposes,* 73–75, 79, 292, 293, 294
Gassner, John, 311
Gielgud, John, 195, 306–7, 310
Gilbert, Sandra, 193
Gilbert, W. S., 73, 218; *The Mikado,* 73, 80

Gilbert & Sullivan, 218
Ginsberg, Allen, 62, 182, 279, 293; "Wichita Vortex Sutra," 62, 293
Gless, Darryl G., 297
Gower, John, 27
Granville-Barker, Harley, 11–12, 288
Gray, Thomas, 50–51, 60, 293; "Elegy Written in a Country Churchyard," 50–51, 60; "Satire on the Heads of Houses," 293
Greene, Robert, 292; Friar Bacon and Friar Bungay, 292
Grimald, Nicholas, 170; "Marcus Tullius Cicero's Death," 170
Gross, Harvey, 305
Gunn, Thom, 63; "On the Move," 63

Habicht, Werner, 297
Hahn, E. Adelaide, 7, 285
Halle, Morris, 174, 193, 305, 309
Halliday, F. E., 315
Halpern, Martin, 302
Hammond, Eleanor, 300, 301
Harding, D. W., 102, 299
Hardison, O. B., Jr., 159, 220, 305, 309
Hardy, Thomas, 179
Harrier, Richard, 298
Harrison, G. B., 17, 32, 35, 38, 42, 287, 288
Hatcher, Anna Granville, 291
Havelock, Eric, 254, 255, 256, 311, 314
Hawes, Stephen, 108, 117, 118; "The Pastime of Pleasure," 108
Hawkes, Terence, 192, 193
Hawthorne, Nathaniel, 9; *The Scarlet Letter,* 9
Hayne, Victoria, 92, 297, 298
Hazlitt, Henry, 183
Heaney, Seamus, 209
Hebel, J. William, 311
Hecht, Anthony, 213
Heminge, John, 313
hendiadys, 3–43, 285–90; in Dylan Thomas, 9–10; in *Hamlet,* 17–20, 27–29, 31–36, 41–42, 288, 289, 290; in Hawthorne and Poe, 9; in *King Lear,* 12, 13, 14, 39–40; In *Macbeth,* 12, 14, 15; and medieval and Renaissance rhetoricians, 3–6, 286–87; in Milton, 10, 288; in *Othello,* 12, 14, 16, 40–41; in other Shakespeare plays, 12–16, 37–38, 288–90; in Sir Thomas Browne, 10; in Virgil, 4–10, 18, 285–86, 289

Henryson, Robert, 104
Herbert, George, 170, 209, 219, 277, 292, 293; "The Church-porch," 170; "The Collar," 292
Herrick, Robert, 47, 55, 65, 173, 277, 293; "The Argument of His Book," 55; "Corinna's going a Maying," 173; "Upon Julia's Clothes," 47
Hill, Archibald, 291
Hinman, Charlton, 309
Hirtle, W. H., 291
Hoccleve, Thomas, 108, 117, 118, 121, 301; "Dialogue with a Friend," 107; "Mâle Règle," 107, 108
Holden, Jonathan, 192, 193
Holder, Alan, 154–55, 158, 186–96, 198, 200, 201; hostility to traditional metrics, 154–55, 186–90, 192–95; intonational scanning, 191–92, 193, 195
Hollander, John, 198, 213
Hopkins, Gerard Manley, 50, 99, 145, 146, 179, 191, 209, 278; "I wake and feel the fell of dark, not day," 50
Hornby, A. S., 291
Housman, A. E., 68, 293; "Eight O' Clock," 293
Howarth, Herbert, 154
Hudson, Hoyt S., 311
Hughes, Langston, 279
Hughes, Ted, 62, 293; "Hawk Roosting," 62, 293
Hussein, Saddam, 209

inwardness, 150, 273–78, 317

Jacobean dramatic verse, 235–49, 250–61, 310–15; line endings, 235–41, 311; oral or literate, 235, 241–49, 250–61, 311–13; prose and verse, 250–61, 313–15
Jakobson, Roman, 135, 219, 309
James, Henry, 153, 304
James I (king of England), 81, 91, 297
Jarrell, Randall, 304
Jespersen, Otto, 165, 219, 220, 291, 305, 309
Johnson, Samuel, 28, 39, 169
Jonson, Ben, 40, 68, 69, 157, 170, 219, 249; "To the Memory of My Beloved, the Author Mr. William Shakespeare," 170
Joos, Martin, 291
Joseph, Sister Miriam, 285

Joyce, James, 55, 275; *A Portrait of the Artist as a Young Man,* 55; *Ulysses,* 275

Kafka, Franz, 64
Kastan, David Scott, 310
Keats, John, 45, 48, 50, 52, 58, 60–61, 167, 198, 207, 268, 269, 277, 281, 293
—Works: "The Eve of St. Agnes," 58; "Ode on a Grecian Urn," 167, 268, 281; "Ode to a Nightingale," 45, 48, 50, 60–61, 277; "On First Looking into Chapman's Homer," 207; "To Autumn," 52
Kendall, Calvin B., 287, 288
Kennedy, X. J., 205–9, 209–13, 308; "Formal Verse and Fascist Deviousness," 205–9
Kerkhof, J., 292
Kernan, Alvin, 297
Keyser, Samuel J., 175, 193, 305, 309
Kiparsky, Paul, 193, 309
Kittredge, George Lyman, 32, 42, 287, 288, 290
Kristeva, Julia, 242
Kyd, Thomas, 57, 292; *The Spanish Tragedy,* 57, 292

Laan, Jacobus van der, 290, 292, 293
Langer, Susanne K., 60, 266, 293
Lanham, Richard A., 285
Larkin, Philip, 63; "Church Going," 63
Lawrence, D. H., 95, 178
Leech, Geoffrey N., 285
Leggatt, Alexander, 295
Lessing, Doris, 64
letters and messages, 24, 70–71, 79, 126, 128, 252, 267–68, 272, 280
Levenson, Jill L., 315
Lewis, C. S., 101, 299, 300
Licklider, Albert H., 299
Lindsay, Vachel, 279
Loesch, Katharine T., 289
Long, Ralph B., 291
Long, William B., 314
Longfellow, Henry Wadsworth, 278
Lovelace, Richard, 277
Lowell, Robert, 144–53, 184–85, 213, 241, 270, 304, 311; blank verse, 148–52; free verse, 144, 147, 148, 151, 152, 153; mosaic verse, 150, 152–53
—Works: *Day by Day,* 144, 152–53, 304; *The Dolphin,* 144, 148, 304; *For Lizzie and*

Harriet, 144, 148, 304; *For the Union Dead,* 144, 147, 304; "Harvard," 150; *History,* 144, 148–52, 185, 304; *Life Studies,* 144, 147, 148, 190, 304; *Lord Weary's Castle,* 145, 146, 147, 304; *Luke,* 297; *The Mills of the Kavanaghs,* 145, 146, 147, 304; *Notebook,* 144, 148–52, 185, 304; "Skunk Hour," 147
Lydgate, John, 104–22 passim, 277, 300, 301
—Works: "Epithalamium for Gloucester," 108; "Letter to Gloucester," 107; "Prologue to *The Siege of Thebes,*" 108; *The Siege of Thebes,* 119; "The Temple of Glas,*"* 107

McDonald, Russ, 308
McGuire, Philip C., 297
Mackail, J. W., 4
McKeon, Richard, 308
madness, 15, 23, 25, 26, 42, 215, 274–75, 317
Mancinellus, 286
Marlowe, Christopher, 176, 179, 180, 236, 237; *Doctor Faustus,* 176
Marvell, Andrew, 49; "The Garden," 49
Masefield, John, 197
Mason, H. A., 298
Matthew, 297
Maus, Katharine Eisaman, 317
Mayer, John T., 316
Mehl, Dieter, 315
Melville, Herman, 295; *Billy Budd,* 295
Mendelson, Edward, 287, 304, 306
Merrill, James, 104, 213
Merwin, W. S., 209
metrical terms: dipodic verse, 158, 197, 307; enjambment, 107, 132, 146, 150, 152, 158, 224, 236, 238, 248, 259, 260; line-endings, double (feminine), 106, 107, 110, 111, 113, 191, 196, 238–39, 248; —, heavy, 238, 239, 248, 311; —, heavy triple, 311; —, triple, 238, 311; quantitative verse, 155, 158, 177–79; verse lines, deviant, brokenbacked, 109, 114, 238, 260, 300; —, headless, 109, 238, 240, 251, 260, 300; —, with epic caesura, 109, 111, 112, 121, 190, 238, 240, 260
Mezey, Robert, 205, 304
Middleton, Thomas, 236, 239, 241, 311; *Women Beware Women,* 239, 311
Miles, Josephine, 191

Miller, J. Hillis, 310
Miller, Raymond Durbin, 299
Milton, John, 9, 10, 55, 68, 69, 115, 122, 158, 172, 174, 175, 179, 180, 219, 276, 277, 278, 287, 288, 300, 306; "Lycidas," 55, 172, 175, 306; *Paradise Lost,* 174, 288, 315; *Paradise Regained,* 288; *Samson Agonistes,* 288
Mitchell, Jerome, 301
Molière, Jean Baptiste Poquelin, 260
Montaigne, Michel de, 270, 316
Moore, Marianne, 69
Mosellanus, P., 286
Mossé, Fernand, 290, 292
Mucedorus, 292
Muir, Kenneth, 285, 298
Musil, Robert, 273
Mustanoja, Tauno F., 291

Nabokov, Vladimir, 64
Naiden, James, 211, 308
Naked Poetry, 65, 69
Nashe, Thomas, 47, 52, 53, 60, 293; "A Litany in Time of Plague," 47, 52, 53, 60
Neely, Carol Thomas, 317
Neruda, Pablo, 209
New Criticism, 135, 155, 219, 220, 226, 315
New Formalists, 212, 225
New Historicism, 155, 227, 258
Nixon, Richard, 296
Norton, Thomas, 236, 292; *Gorboduc,* 236, 292

O'Donnell, Brendan, 154, 179–86, 197, 307; and metrical lurching, 182–84; reliance on Attridge, 182–85; on Wordsworth's metrical theory, 179–82
Olivier, Laurence, 269
Olson, Charles, 205, 212
Olsson, Yngve, 291
Ong, Father Walter J., 241–43, 249, 312, 314, 318
Onions, C. T., 33, 288
Oras, Ants, 220, 307, 309
Ostroff, Anthony, 304
Oxford English Dictionary, 30, 31, 39–43

Padelford, Frederick Morgan, 102
Palestrina, Giovanni Perluigi da, 218
Palmer, F. R., 291

Parker, Patricia, 315
Parkinson, Thomas, 136, 304
Pater, Walter, 64
Peacham, Henry, 4
Pearsall, Derek, 119, 301
Perloff, Marjorie, 192, 193, 304
Petrarch, Francesco, 110, 111–12, 120, 177, 200; "Orso; al vostro destrier si po ben porre," 111–12
Pinter, Harold, 278
Plath, Sylvia, 54, 65, 69, 191; "Ariel," 191; "Mary's Song," 65
Poe, Edgar Allan, 9, 197, 278; "The Fall of the House of Usher," 9
Pope, Alexander, 68, 166, 169, 174, 177, 179, 180, 197, 277, 278; "Autumn," 174; "Epistle to Dr. Arbuthnot," 174, 177; *Essay on Man,* 169
Pope-Hennessy, John, 262, 315
Pöppel, Ernst, 193
Pound, Ezra, 54, 61, 69, 72, 178, 279, 293; "Near Perigord," 61; "The Return," 54
Poutsma, H., 291
Preston, Thomas, 292; *Cambises, King of Persia,* 292
Price, Joseph, 297
Proust, Marcel, 270
Puccini, Giacomo, 262; *Madama Butterfly,* 262
Puttenham, George, 4, 5, 6, 286, 287
Pygmalion, 227, 281, 310
Pyle, Fitzroy, 300, 301

Quinn, Kenneth, 285–86
Quintilian, Marcus Fabius, 4

Raffel, Burton, 154, 196–98, 308; and the Chaucerian Compromise, 197–98
Ramsey, Paul, 193
Ransom, John Crowe, 306
Ravel Maurice, 208; *Bolero,* 208
Rebholz, R. A., 298
Rich, Adrienne, 153, 178, 209, 307; "Night Watch," 307
Richards, I. A., 134
Robbe-Grillet, Alain, 64
Robinson, Ian, 299
Roethke, Theodore, 293
Rollins, Hyder E., 305

Ross, W. D., 308
Rylands, George, 42, 287, 288, 290

Sackville, Thomas, 176, 236, 292; *Gorboduc,* 236, 292; *The Mirror for Magistrates,* 176
Saintsbury, George, 100, 101, 154, 162, 179, 185, 193, 219, 298
Satchell, Thomas, 291
Schick, J., 104, 106, 300, 301
Schipper, J., 300
Schoenbaum, S., 285
Schwartz, Delmore, 148
Seronsky, Cecil C., 295
Servius, Maurus, 4, 286
Sexton, Joyce H., 94
Shadwell, Thomas, 246
Shakespear, Olivia, 267
Shakespeare, William, 3–43, 68, 69, 73–95, 101, 105, 115, 122, 123, 128, 151, 157, 158, 163, 167, 170–72, 173, 174, 175, 176, 177, 179, 180, 185, 187, 190, 193, 194–96, 201–2, 207, 211, 214–17, 219, 220, 222–31, 235–42, 244–49, 250–61, 262–81, 285–90, 293–98, 301, 302, 305, 306, 307, 308–17
—Narrative Poems: *The Rape of Lucrece,* 70, 265; *Venus and Adonis,* 265
—Plays (or characters therein): *All's Well That Ends Well,* 12, 289, 290; *Antony and Cleopatra,* 6, 14, 95, 217, 246, 290; *As You Like It,* 12, 13, 84, 237, 257–58, 275; *The Comedy of Errors,* 75, 255; *Coriolanus,* 95; *Cymbeline,* 94, 95, 275, 276, 279; *Hamlet,* 3–38, 41–42, 55, 59, 74, 78, 81, 82, 95, 216, 222, 226, 229, 231, 249, 251, 274, 275, 276, 277, 279, 285–90, 294, 310, 311, 317; *1 Henry IV,* 95, 275, 277; *2 Henry IV,* 15–16, 95, 258, 275, 277; *Henry V,* 12, 13, 82, 271–72; *1 Henry VI,* 288; *2 Henry VI,* 12; *3 Henry VI,* 35; *Henry VIII,* 42, 95, 241; *Julius Caesar,* 7, 95, 237, 255, 273, 274, 275, 288, 310; *King Lear,* 12, 13, 14–15, 39–40, 75, 78, 92, 94, 95, 191, 193, 215, 216, 226, 251, 275, 277; *Love's Labors Lost,* 95, 229, 255; *Macbeth,* 12, 14, 15, 16, 79, 81, 101, 106, 109, 222, 275, 276, 277, 290, 312; *Measure for Measure,* 12, 14, 15, 73–95, 135, 214–15, 231, 258, 293–98; *The Merchant of Venice,* 95; *The Merry Wives of Windsor,* 12; *A Midsum-*

Index

mer Night's Dream, 73, 76–77, 222, 271, 272, 281, 294; *Much Ado about Nothing,* 78, 94, 95, 255; *Othello,* 12, 13, 14, 16, 39, 40–41, 47, 78, 79, 81, 94–95, 216, 237, 275, 276, 277; *Pericles,* 215; *Richard II,* 13, 41, 95, 173, 222, 257, 273, 276, 279; *Richard III,* 78, 81, 95, 216, 252, 255, 275, 294; *Romeo and Juliet,* 95, 235–36, 275, 308; *The Taming of the Shrew,* 3, 75, 79, 294–95; *The Tempest,* 76, 81, 82, 222, 246, 249, 261, 275, 281, 296, 313, 315; *Timon of Athens,* 216; *Troilus and Cressida,* 12, 41, 42, 43, 275; *Twelfth Night,* 12, 75, 79, 95, 275; *The Two Gentlemen of Verona,* 79, 95, 252, 267, 289; *The Winter's Tale,* 81, 95, 215, 231, 246–48, 251, 275, 276, 281, 312–13
—Sonnets: 159–60, 262–81, 302, 306–7, 315–18; sonnet *9,* 171; *12,* 109; *13,* 262; *14,* 306; *15,* 270; *17,* 263, 270, 305; *18,* 270, 305; *19,* 270, 305; *22,* 170; *23,* 262, 263; *25,* 170, 279; *26,* 267; *29,* 263, 265, 268; *30,* 167, 174, 263, 264, 265, 276; *31,* 171; *36,* 171; *38,* 263; *39,* 263, 279; *43,* 170, 272; *44,* 263, 268, 271; *51,* 171; *52,* 171; *54,* 279; *57,* 279, 280; *58,* 278, 280; *59,* 279; *60,* 270, 279; *61,* 306; *63,* 270; *64,* 177, 306; *65,* 270, 305; *66,* 263, 279; *70,* 279; *71,* 305; *73,* 171; *75,* 305; *77,* 279; *80,* 263, 306; *81,* 171, 263, 270–71, 316; *84,* 279; *85,* 262, 263, 265, 268; *86,* 171; *87,* 306; *89,* 171; *93,* 74; *94,* 279; *96,* 171; *97,* 263; *101,* 270, 272; *103,* 171, 306; *106,* 171, 271; *107,* 270; *111,* 276; *115,* 270; *116,* 190, 191, 194–96, 270, 279, 281; *119,* 265, 275, 279; *120,* 306; *121,* 94, 279, 317; *126,* 236; *129,* 275, 279; *140,* 263, 275; *147,* 275; *150,* 171
Shapiro, Karl, 62, 193, 293; "Nostalgia," 62, 293
Shawcross, John T., 302
Shelley, Percy Bysshe, 45, 49, 54, 60, 68–69, 198, 292; "The Fugitives," 69; "The Indian Girl's Song," 54; "Ode to the West Wind," 45, 49; "Ozymandias," 292
Shepard, Sam, 271, 273
Sherry, Richard, 4, 286
Sidney, Sir Philip, 68, 121, 122, 123, 157, 166, 176, 177, 185, 219, 262, 274, 278, 312, 317; *Astrophel and Stella,* 177, 262, 278

Simpson, Louis, 60, 62–63, 293
Simpson, Percy, 300
Sinfield, Alan, 312
Skelton, John, 107, 108, 110, 117, 118, 119, 277; "The Bouge of Court," 107, 108, 117
slander, 82, 93, 94–95, 295
Smart, Christopher, 278
Smith, Barbara Herrnstein, 311, 316
Smith, Henry Lee, Jr., 157
Smith, Logan Pearsall, 8, 287
Snodgrass, W. D., 69, 208
Southall, Raymond, 102, 110, 298, 299
Southworth, James G., 299, 301
Spain, Delbert, 201–2, 308
Spenser, Edmund, 70, 115, 157, 175, 177, 179; *The Faerie Queene,* 70, 175
Spolsky, Ellen, 310
Sprott, S. Ernest, 219, 309
stage directions, 57, 292
stanzaic design, 110–11, 116, 123–33, 136–43, 150–51
Steele, Timothy, 212
Stein, Arnold, 219, 309
Stevens, Wallace, 61, 69, 72, 149, 213, 230, 241, 293, 310; "Esthétique du Mal," 61; "The Idea of Order at Key West," 293; "Notes toward a Supreme Fiction," 310
sub-vocal register, 266
Suckling, Sir John, 277
Suhamy, Henri, 198, 219, 309
Summers, Joseph H., 309
supposing, 73–95, 267, 268, 281, 293–98; and characters' verbs, 84–89; in Gascoigne, 73–75; and the law, 83–89; in *Measure for Measure,* 73, 77–95, 294–97; in *A Midsummer Night's Dream,* 76–77, 95, 281, 294; in *The Taming of the Shrew,* 75, 294–95
Surrey, Henry Howard, Earl of, 99, 100, 115, 118, 170, 176, 300; Translation of *The Aeneid,* Book II, 170, 176
Susenbrotus, Joannes, 4, 5, 286–87
Swallow, Alan, 300
Swift, Jonathan, 155; *Gulliver's Travels,* 155
Swinburne, Algernon Charles, 47, 50, 69, 278; "A Vision of Spring in Winter," 47, 50

Tarlinskaja, Marina, 193, 198, 219, 307, 309
Taylor, Dennis, 193
Taylor, Gary, 310

Tennyson, Alfred, Lord, 61, 145, 169, 177, 179, 198, 262, 278
—Works: "Flower in the Crannied Wall," 61; "In Memoriam," 169, 262; "Morte d'Arthur," 169; "The Passing of Arthur," 169; "Ulysses," 177
Thelwall, John, 183
Thilo, Georgius, 286
Thomas, Dylan, 9–10, 69, 72, 145, 151, 197, 279, 288; "In my craft or sullen art," 9; "A Refusal to Mourn the Death, by Fire, of a Child in London," 9–10
Thomas, Keith, 318
Thompson, John, 193, 198, 219, 309
Thomson, James, 70–71; "Spring," 70–71
Thomson, Patricia, 298, 299
Toliver, Harold E., 306, 315
Tottel's *Miscellany,* 101, 156, 305
Tourneur, Cyril, 236, 241, 315
Trager, George L., 157
Trnka, B., 291
Trousdale, Marion, 313
Turner, Frederick, 193
Tuve, Rosamond, 246

Udall, Nicholas, 236, 292; *Roister Doister,* 236, 292
Unamuno, Miguel de, 64
Updike, John, 64

Van Ek, J. A., 291
Vendler, Helen, 302
verb forms: anomalous, 57, 84–88; aspect, 49, 291–92; conditional, 47, 84–88; historical present, 48, 49; imperative, 47, 57, 59, 292; past, 47, 48, 49, 51, 57, 58, 59, 140, 292; progressive present, 44–72, 290–93; simple present, 44–72, 290–93; subjunctive, 87–88
Vickers, Brian, 285, 314
Virgil (Publius Vergilius Maro), 4, 5, 7, 8, 9, 10, 18, 170, 176, 285–86, 289; *Aeneid,* 4, 170, 176; *Georgics,* 4, 9
Vittoria, Tomas Luis de, 218

Waldrop, Rosmarie, 206
Waugh, Linda, 309
Webster, John, 236, 239–41, 246, 311, 312, 315; *The Duchess of Malfi,* 240, 311; *The White Devil,* 246

Weil, Herbert, Jr., 297
Weismiller, Edward R., 193, 219, 309
Welsh, Andrew, 299
Whitman, Walt, 48, 50, 52, 54, 55, 179, 198, 211, 278; "Song of Myself," 48, 52, 55; "When Lilacs Last in the Dooryard Bloomed," 54
Wilbur, Richard, 209, 213
Williams, William Carlos, 63, 69, 178, 211, 279; "The Yachts," 63
Williamson, Jane, 297
Williamson, Nicol, 312
Wilson, Thomas, 94, 295
Wimsatt, James I., 305
Wimsatt, W. K., Jr., 164, 165, 189–90, 192, 193, 196, 198, 219, 305, 307, 309; and metrical tilting, 163–64, 173, 200
Winters, Yvor, 165, 208, 219, 305, 309
Wood, Michael, 269
Woods, Suzanne, 193
Woolf, Virginia, 270
Wordsworth, William, 58, 72, 106, 173, 179–86, 197, 198, 199, 277, 278, 307
—Works: "An Evening Walk," 180; "Descriptive Sketches," 180, 184; "Earth has not anything to show more fair," 72; *The Excursion,* 180; "Hart-Leap Well," 181; "The Idiot Boy," 181; "I wandered lonely as a cloud," 58; Lucy poems, 181; *Lyrical Ballads,* 180; "The Mad Mother," 181; "Michael," 180; "My heart leaps up," 183; "Ode on Intimations of Immortality," 106; "The Old Cumberland Beggar," 182–83; *The Prelude,* 173, 180; "The Sailor's Mother," 179; "A slumber did my spirit seal," 181; "The Thorn," 193, 307; "Tintern Abbey," 180, 185; "Yew Trees," 183–84
Wright, George T., 193–94, 205, 211, 231, 301, 302, 307, 309, 310, 311, 313, 315, 316
Wright, James, 55
Wright, W. A., 290
Wyatt, Sir Thomas, 68, 99–122, 123–24, 170, 219, 220, 277, 298–302; influence of Petrarch, 110–12, 120; and later English poetry, 105, 116, 118, 120–22; Lydgatian line-types, 104–10, 116–17, 300, 301; and rhythmical phrasalists, 101–3, 299
—Works: *VII,* 108; *VIII,* 108; *IX,* 107; *XXVI,* 105; *XXVII,* 111, 117; *XXVIII,* 117; *XXIX,* 112–15; *XXXIII,* 101, 108;

Index

XXXVII ("They fle from me"), 99, 106, 116, 130; *XLVII,* 120; *LXVI* ("My lute, awake"), 109–10; *LXXIX,* 107, 117–18; *CV* (Satire I), 108, 120, 170; *CVIII* (Penitential Psalms), 104, 105, 108, 121; *CCXI,* 120; *CCXVII,* 120; *CCXXIII,* 120; *CCXXXVI,* 120; *CCXXXVIII,* 120

Yeats, William Butler, 45, 48, 50, 51, 52, 55, 57, 60, 61, 62, 63, 69, 72, 134–43, 179, 267, 269, 278, 281, 292, 293, 303–4, 318
—Works: "Among School Children," 45, 48, 50, 51, 52, 55, 57; "The Coat," 292; "Crazy Jane on God," 136–43; "Ego Dominus Tuus," 281, 318; *The Green Helmet and Other Poems,* 72; *In the Seven Woods,* 72; *Michael Robartes and the Dancer,* 72; *Purgatory,* 141; "Sailing to Byzantium," 143; "The Second Coming," 62; "Speech after Long Silence," 267; "Under Ben Bulben," 269; "The Wild Swans at Coole," 61, 63

Young, David, 294

Zandvoort, R. W., 292
zeugma, 6–7, 9

Praise for *Reagan: A Life in Letters*

"Critics may be surprised to discover [Reagan] was dedicatedly dashing off thousands of letters to a wide assortment of pen pals, political allies, and even a few global enemies.... His hand-jotted observations on practically everything in life ... reflect an egalitarian curiosity, affability, and humility before fellow humans."

—The editors of *The New York Times*

"Reagan's letters tell the story of his family, his health, his Hollywood and political careers.... Taken together they provide remarkable and otherwise unobtainable insight into a singularly important and fascinating American life: "Dutch" up close and personal."

—*Publishers Weekly*

"[With] comprehensive selection and exemplary annotation... [the editors] have certainly done posterity a service in making [Reagan's] letters available in print."

—*The Washington Post*

"A treasure trove, chock full of rewarding glimpses into [Reagan's] mind and life.... [The letters] capture him; one can almost hear his warm, gentle voice, always unassuming, honest, and secure, by turns humorous, firm, and compassionate."

—*Richmond Times-Dispatch*

"The letters offer examples of a toughness, discipline, and canniness that his public geniality masked [and shed] new light on several key moments in Reagan's long political odyssey."

—*Claremont Review of Books*

"This definitive collection will astonish Reagan's allies and detractors alike."

—*Human Events*

*Other works by Kiron K. Skinner, Annelise Anderson,
and Martin Anderson*

REAGAN, IN HIS OWN HAND

STORIES IN HIS OWN HAND

REAGAN IN HIS OWN VOICE

REAGAN'S PATH TO VICTORY:
*THE SHAPING OF RONALD REAGAN'S
VISION: SELECTED WRITINGS*